THE

A Study of New York's West Side

AIRTIGHT CAGE

by Joseph P. Lyford

HARPER & ROW,
PUBLISHERS

NEW YORK, EVANSTON,
and LONDON

To families, past and present; to my father and mother, Philip and Ruth, in remembrance of our life together; to Jean, the wife I met on Ninety-second Street, and to Amy and Joseph, in whose lively midst I've found my place.

A publication of the Center for the Study of Democratic Institutions

CONTENTS

FOREWORD

More than fifteen years ago Ralph Ellison's novel *Invisible Man* recounted the plaintive odyssey of a Negro making his way from the pastoral South to New York by way of Tuskegee Institute. This was, and is, a journey in time as well as geography, and along the way Ellison's protagonist drops out of even the peripheral vision of white America, making his final appearance, prophetically enough, in the lurid light of a Harlem race riot.

In the current decade Negroes similarly situated have assumed, or had thrust upon them, the role of bellwether for all the American poor. In the process they have attracted much attention—some hostile, some sympathetic. Ellison, however, still doubts that his invisible man has taken on true lineaments. "Prefabricated Negroes are sketched on sheets of paper and superimposed on the Negro community," he wrote not long ago. "Then when someone thrusts his head through the page and yells, 'Watch out there, Jack, there's people living under here,' they are shocked and indignant."

Joseph Lyford has thrust his head through the page the other way, and his chronicle of the people living under there doubtless also will produce shock and indignation. If so, it will hardly match his own evolving response to the more than five years he spent as a resident of the Area—an enclave on New York's West Side running from Eighty-second to 106th Streets, from Central Park to the Hudson River. Despite a good deal of decaying commercial property it has become one of the most densely populated places on earth, with a highly variegated average of over a thousand persons per block.

Lyford did not come to the Area originally to do good, or even to satisfy his journalist's curiosity. In a fit of mild cupidity and temporary affluence he concluded that it might be sound business to buy an old house in one of Manhattan's depressed areas and thereby gain a convenient apartment for himself along with a source of rental income. For these pedestrian reasons he moved in from the Connecticut suburbs, a natural middle-class habitat where he had become settled enough to be nominated a Democratic candidate for Congress. In 1960 he became a New York landlord, technically at least, if not in spirit.

The next five years were a season of flux for everyone in the Area. Lyford's first house, in the southern reaches, went down before urban renewal bulldozers, and he moved to the northern edge, a transition that took him closer to the Harlem ghetto and reversed the proportion of Negroes to Puerto Ricans among his near neighbors. He changed his status from footloose bachelor to husband and father. Starting out as a detached and frequently amused observer of the exotic eccentricities of the slums, he wound up an embattled member of a district school board. After two years, too involved to move out and too outraged to look the other way, he asked the Center for the Study of Democratic Institutions, whose New York office he manned, to let him take on the Area as a case study. This book is the result.

Lyford's method is journalistic, with a heavy reliance on extended interviews. He does not, however, scorn the more precise, presumably objective, and often tedious findings of the social scientists; he has used a specially commissioned professional attitude survey as a check against his own impressionistic judgments. Moreover, he became a stubborn explorer in the municipal bureaus, skilled at getting behind the screen of statistics and summary reports that so often render unintelligible any important truths they may contain. It is a considerable virtue of *The Airtight Cage* that Lyford has managed unobtrusively to mortar these tangible measurements into meaningful background for the human actuality of the desperate poor, and of the usually dispirited bureaucrats who must deal with them.

There are only a few heroes in these pages: a tough Irish priest who won't admit he can't fight City Hall; an old-fashioned Jewish socialist who has somehow survived as a public school principal; an overworked visiting nurse; a compassionate cop or two; a badgered young teacher trying to help a bright child trapped by insensate regulations; a welfare worker risking his career by forging the endless signatures required to pry loose public funds in time to help a deteriorating family. These are presented in the round, without sentimentality, with aching feet as well as high purposes, and we see them as decent people from whom the human juices are slowly being drained by the antihuman system within which they must operate.

There are no villains at all in *The Airtight Cage,* unless one can count the system itself, which Lyford tends to treat in anthropomorphic terms. The system does, certainly, contain human beings responsible for infamous cruelties—dullards whose sloth and indifference clog the bureaucratic channels and keep food and medicine from needy children; self-serving neurotics seeking expiation, and in the process spreading their own sickness; and the overtly corrupt, grown callous enough for financial traffic in human misery. But Lyford finds these fewer than generally believed, and of little consequence since they also are the product of a process that would go on taking its grinding human toll even if they were rooted out.

The salient fact is that all the effective connections between the urban poor and society at large have been broken. On its high-rise fringes, along Central Park West and Riverside Drive, there are still remnants of the earlier groups that once gave the Area character and stability—the old-stock Protestants who gave way to the Irish, who gave way to the Jews, who are falling back now before a still rising tide of Puerto Ricans and Negroes. Unable to establish total immunity from the horrors to their rear, these middle-class citizens are sometimes moved to action by compassion or by fear. They turn to the patterns they or their parents knew on the way up and out, to the formation of neighborhood groups based on religion, national heritage, mutual interest, or in the best Abie's Irish Rose tradition, the simple accident of common location. This was the way the Area once rallied the people so they could speak in a collective voice and thereby translate their complaints into political action. But almost all such contemporary efforts have run a curve from hope through frustration to despair.

Lyford demonstrates in disheartening detail that these failures result from a fundamental misreading of the condition of the vast majority of the Area's residents. There can be no community because there are no neighborhoods to build on. And there are no neighborhoods because the dominant characteristic of the present-day poor is transience. Of overcrowded necessity, slum children are outdoor types, and to the residents of the Area the faces along the block soon become familiar; but Lyford found that when he went away for so short a span as the summer, he returned to find the usual, aimless pattern of childish behavior going on as before, only to realize with a start that almost all the faces were new and different. And there is the final dull horror of the corpse on the sidewalk, for whom the police can locate an address but no other trace of identity; the neighbors, with some effort, can recall seeing the deceased around, but no one ever bothered to ask him his name.

It has not made much difference whether the effort to take hold of this amorphous mass has been launched from the left, right, or middle. Radicals who go forth to preach revolution in the Area find that those who still have the energy to serve as a possible agency for social protest and action seem irrevocably committed to bourgeois goals. Poor Negroes are not interested in overthrowing the existing society, only in joining it. Despite inhibiting language and cultural differences, Puerto Ricans usually arrive already thinking of themselves as full-fledged members of the American middle class. The churches, preaching their several varieties of social gospel, have not been able to bridge the gap between the dwindling group of old-line parishioners and the deprived newcomers. Indeed, they usually have not even been able to hold their own against the Pentecostal storefront evangelists who peddle emotional opiates to dull the pain of slum existence. Catholics, to whom the Puerto Ricans are bound by custom if not commitment, and who also have the special leverage of their parochial schools, have done somewhat better than the others, but nowhere in the Area can the church be rated as a primary force. However, the most significant, and in many ways the most ludicrous, failure has to be charged to the liberal factions that have come to dominate New York city politics.

One who didn't know better might take as satire Lyford's straight-faced account of the singular career of the Franklin D. Roosevelt–Woodrow Wilson Democratic Club. This is the reform organization that took over an ancient stronghold of Tammany Hall in 1959, acquiring its hybrid title by splitting down the middle its very first time out. Ideological in-fighting of a bitter, intensely personal kind has enlivened its meetings, but it also has sapped the organization's effective strength by making its proceedings incomprehensible to those who are engaged in the day-to-day struggle for survival in the slums. The burning political issues that produce deep-seated traumas along Central Park West and Riverside Drive have nothing much to do with the Area, even when they seem to. Civil rights, for example, is still the great rallying cry that has brought down City Hall dynasties. But Lyford finds that his poor, black neighbors have no real concern with the Police Review Board, which has become the prime symbol of racial justice in New York and the albatross the new reform mayor, John V. Lindsay, had to hang around his neck in order to gain office. On the contrary, the harassed citizens of the Area want more policemen, preferably tough ones, to protect them against "the others"— the junkies, prostitutes, and assorted psychological and social cripples who are relentlessly hunted down in the city's middle-class preserves and driven back upon the respectable poor. The attitude surveys bear Lyford out; Negroes and Puerto Ricans, who are the usual victims of the police brutality that undoubtedly does exist, think much better of New York's Finest than do their middle-class neighbors.

Lyford has rigorously stuck to the limits he imposed upon himself, holding his account to a single section of a single American city. He deals with large issues of political and social policy only by inference, as they touch upon—or, more usually, effectively ignore—the 152,000 people who have found a temporary place in the Area's random urban assemblage. Yet, in its frequently painful concentration on detail *The Airtight Cage* raises essential questions that seem to have been lost in the very sweep of the attack upon poverty now being launched from Washington. For example, this inside view of a New York slum provides a full explanation for the spectacular failure, 3,000 miles away, of Los Angeles' effort to stage a grassroots election among its 400,000 certified adult poor. There the expenditure of $60,000 in federal funds, and much organized civic effort, resulted in a turn-out of less than one percent to vote for neighborhood representatives to the city-wide poverty council. This does not mean that Sargent Shriver has not been right in his insistence that the poor desperately need representation that is as knowledgeable as it is sympathetic. But to expect the poor themselves to somehow locate and recognize in their floating collectivity the rare individuals who possess such capacity is to ignore the rootlessness that afflicts them all, and for many reaches the point of acute disorientation.

It is simply romantic nonsense to expect rational, self-starting organization from people who no longer react rationally to the real causes of their distress. I found particularly poignant Lyford's description of his sidewalk combat with a Negro bearing a switchblade knife; in the moment of physical encounter between white man and black the Negro neighbors closed ranks and hurled at Lyford the standard Harlem epithet: "White Jew bastard!" It is a singular description, indeed, for one who speaks in the flat intonations of the Middle West, carries the imprint of the Ivy League in his dress, and wears a face that would not look out of place under a Coldstream Guardsman's helmet.

If adversity has shaken the poor's grip upon reality, affluence seems to have done the same for the rest of the community. Lyford diagnoses the prevailing American disease as a form of auto-anesthesia, a self-induced ability to ignore the sights, sounds and fetid smells of the human scrap heap every city seems to require—or at least to be unable to alleviate, even now when we have more wealth than we can count and have run out of all the traditional economic excuses for poverty. Looking at the Great Society from the vantage point of the Area, from the bottom up, one sees flaws not visible to those in higher places, and it is hard to gainsay Lyford's contention that these could be fatal: "The system I am talking about is turning more of our resources away from the nurture of human life and into the destruction of it." This book establishes the Areas as a primary target in the war on poverty, but its greatest value is as a reminder that, while the victims are here, the enemy is somewhere else.

HARRY ASHMORE

ACKNOWLEDGMENTS

MY GREATEST DEBT IS TO THE MANY HUNDREDS OF West Side people whose lives and ideas were the basis for this book. Only a few of those who gave their time so generously and who spoke so candidly to my tape recorder and notebook appear in the book by name, but the thoughts of all of them determined what was written.

My very deep appreciation goes to the Center for the Study of Democratic Institutions, the educational foundation which financed preparation of the book, and to its president, Robert M. Hutchins. My colleagues on the Center staff contributed valuable suggestions and criticism, particularly Edward Reed, director of Center publications, and John Cogley, who until recently directed the Center's Study of the American Character, of which this book is a product.

I owe special thanks to John Kraft, Inc., of New York City, for contributing to my project an extensive attitude study of residents of the Stryckers Bay area. In association with Mr. Kraft, Frances Farrell and Jeff Berryman directed the study and gave much time to evaluating its results.

The costs of coding the results of the Kraft survey were defrayed by a contribution from Harold Oram.

My everlasting gratitude goes to those people in the Center's New York City office who have given me their daily assistance. I was most fortunate in having Evelyn Glor as my research assistant. Sarah Weinberger, Virginia Lieberfreund, Mildred Agres, Kattie Cumbo, Kim Minor, and Marianne Brown transcribed endless tapes, typed innumerable drafts, and skillfully deciphered my cramped handwriting, all with a patience quite beyond the call of duty.

I am greatly in debt to Fred Johnson of the Police Athletic League for opening many doors I might have missed and for his perceptive comments on my manuscript.

To Richard McAdoo of Harper & Row, I owe a very special debt for tempering the severity of his criticism with steady encouragement and persistent good humor. I am also deeply grateful to Margaret Cheney for her thoughtful and careful copyediting.

Finally, there is my debt to my family, which endured without complaint the author's exasperating behavior during the three years the book was in preparation.

JOSEPH P. LYFORD

West 105th Street
New York City

INTRODUCTION

Purpose and Method

ONE PROBLEM IN TRYING TO LEARN SOMETHING about our society is that whenever a discussion gets started it is generally taken over by the experts. We hear and read a great deal about ourselves from people who make a profession out of analyzing us, and very little from the insignificant individual undergoing the ordeal of United States citizenship in a decade of political, biological, military, and technological explosions.

Some time ago I expressed this view to Robert M. Hutchins, president of the Center for the Study of Democratic Institutions, and added that I felt the Center, with all its splendid work in promoting the dialogue on democracy, had done its share to inundate us with experts. I suggested that one way of balancing the flow of expertise would be to undertake a series of reports on how the American citizen was behaving in his community, and how he described his own situation.

The series was approved by Mr. Hutchins and adopted as part of the Center's continuing Study of the American Character. The first completed study was *The Talk in Vandalia,* a report on life in a small town in central Illinois, published by the Center in 1962. *The Airtight Cage* is the second in the series.

When I began the book I had lived on the West Side of Manhattan for more than two years. My relationship to it had been that of many other middle-class people who had moved onto one of the wilder side streets. I had gathered impressions and formed opinions, but I had not consciously investigated what lay behind what I saw or experienced. I had moved to the Area to live in it, not to write about it. As an amateur landlord I had had to learn something about my tenants and about certain city agencies, but in other respects my connection with the Area during my first two years was more or less that of a passive spectator. This early experience was a help to me in my subsequent study. I found myself constantly comparing how I had once reacted to the Area as a resident and how I was seeing it as a reporter looking for information and hunting for reasons.

The book follows this evolution in my own viewpoint. The second chapter, "A Block," is a description of the surface of life as it struck me from day to day—a collection of impressions that embedded themselves so deeply that they still symbolize Ninety-second Street to me years later. The subsequent chapters, grouped under the heading "Of the People," mark the point at which I began to make a conscious investigation of my surroundings.

To what extent my close and changing relationship to the Area colored my reporting is a matter on which I cannot give an impartial judgment. I am sure my living in the community about which I was writing had its good and its bad points. On the one hand I wrote from intimate knowledge, but on the other hand was a participant with personal experiences, associations, sympathies, and institutional connections that determined to some extent what I emphasized, what I saw, and how I saw it. I hope the fact that I was a member of a local school board, a property owner, and a former Democratic politician did not greatly distort my view, but at the same time the reader should be on his guard against me.

The research for the book covers the years from 1962 to 1965, the period in which the Area "hit bottom" and began to undergo its greatest changes because of the demolition, relocation, and reconstruction accompanying urban renewal. While the West Side urban renewal site took up only 20 of the 125 blocks included in my study, its effects were felt everywhere. During preparation of the book the whole Area underwent continuous modification. Many new currents were set in motion. The war on poverty had not been invented at the time I arrived in 1960, but by 1966 its effects were beginning to be noticeable in many phases of local life—in the pre-kindergarten Operation Head Start classes for underprivileged children, in the rush of government money into ambitious social-work projects with such names as JANUS, PHOENIX, JOIN, VISTA, etc., and in the battle over whether the politicians, the established social agencies, or the poor should decide on how antipoverty money should be spent.

I gathered my information by (1) tape-recorded interviews, (2) a professional public opinion survey, and (3) observation and reading. The most important and time-consuming approach was the extended interviews with several hundred people who either lived in the area or who had connections with it, such as officials, volunteers, social workers, teachers, and heads of institutions. The interview sample includes people of different race, ethnic background, economic status, political viewpoint, religious affiliation, and age group; people from different types of blocks and living in different types of housing; and people with good jobs, illegal jobs and no jobs.

The interviews usually lasted more than an hour; frequently they took four or more hours. Transcribed for further study, they took up approximately four thousand typed pages. The tape recorder did not inhibit the conversations, so far as I could see, any more than my pencil and note pad. Most of the respondents seemed to forget about the recorder after a few minutes—in fact, I had to be on the alert to snatch the small microphone (slightly more than an inch square) off a lapel or breast pocket when a respondent got up to answer the telephone or doorbell. Exceptions to the rule were city officials, many of whom objected to being taped and who asked that I use my notebook instead.

The interviews were "unstructured" (to use a professional polling agency term). I had no standard sets of questions, there were no time limits on the interviews, and I was not looking for responses that I could count, in the sense that a Gallup or Roper poll tallies opinions "for" or "against" a policy or a candidate. I would try to start the conversation on some rather low-pressure matter—perhaps by asking the respondent something about his family history or children—and then let the discussion take the lines my respondent wanted it to take. At the same time, since we were having a conversation, I brought up various ideas and subjects and expressed opinions—mine or someone else's—always with the idea of getting people interested. I found that they talked more freely when they spent some of their time listening: they very quickly lost the feeling that they were being excavated. If education, housing, or welfare did not eventually bob up in the conversation, I encouraged my respondent to talk about them. However, such encouragement and suggestion often proved unnecessary; the people I interviewed had a rich supply of ideas and information to offer, and if they surprised me so much the better.

The conversational approach seemed the most natural to me as a journalist. I am not sure what a sociologist would say about it: the experience convinced me that there is not so much difference between one man's journalism and another man's sociology as the more rigid professionals on either side of the fence would have us suppose. At any rate, I did not rule out any subjects, threw out no testimony; I made estimates of the candor and reliability of my respondents; I was influenced by their personalities, looks, tones of voice, use of words, family histories; and I noted colors, smells, clothes, what was in the icebox—any data that might then or sometime later help me remember or understand more clearly. Such material would have been impossible to collect in structured interviews, which limit the area of comment and seek to bolt it down to simple affirmative and negative reactions. If objectivity means being uncontaminated by the local atmosphere, then I was not objective, because I sought to be affected and infected by whatever was flying about—and if I have not passed on a sense of involvement then I have failed in one of my purposes.

While I did not use the question-and-answer approach in my own interviews, an attitude survey based on this technique was of great use to me, in fact was one of my three most important sources of information. Staff members of John Kraft, Inc., New York City, one of the country's leading public-opinion survey organizations, collaborated with me in framing a questionnaire which became the basis of a depth survey of residents of the Stryckers Bay area—a forty-block section which included the West Side urban renewal site. This "structured" questionnaire contained both "closed-end" questions (which could be answered by a word or two) and "open-end" questions (which required some explanation). The Kraft interviewers spent more than fourteen hundred hours on the project.

In a sense the Kraft poll served as a control on my own interviews and supplemented my material. It gave me data on population, race, income, religion, family structure, and housing which were four years more recent than that provided by the 1960 census tracts. It also did something else I did not attempt, which was to count responses to specific questions and break them down in various economic, racial, and age groups. I did not particularly care whether the Kraft study

In and around Ninety-second and 105th streets were also many inoffensive people who were ordinarily invisible to the outsider because they were intimidated by their surroundings and were trying to isolate themselves for their own protection. Those who were making an effort to hang on to some semblance of an organized life—I am thinking especially of the Spanish families who had some success in resisting fragmentation—were constantly in fear of their children's defecting to the world of the pusher and the hoodlum. In such a world, fear and protectiveness were the signs of healthy resistance, like fever. If the fever subsided it meant that the family had broken apart, with the children spinning off in all directions.

The ordinary difficulty of maintaining one's sanity in the slum was considerably increased by the world outside the slum. Crime was not necessarily indigenous to any specific neighborhood, no matter how dilapidated it might be. There is a common idea that the slum manufactures its own criminals and spews them out on the rest of society. A Harlem or a West Ninety-third Street slum "breeds" crime and poverty, "breeds" violence, as the saying goes. The sayings are at least half false, and there is plenty of available evidence in the underdeveloped areas of the world, including our own, to show that traffic in criminals is a two-way street between the rich America and the poor America. A good percentage of Ninety-third Street's criminal population was transient, a collection raised from places all over the country which had, in effect, been dumped on the heads of the poor by a middle-class society which would not tolerate disruptive behavior in its own communities. The slum is only one of the many places where contemporary conditions of life are breaking down personality, as an examination of the family trees of West Side drug addicts quickly reveals.

When mental and physical illness reduces people to the point where they become inconvenient to their children or threaten the public safety, and where there is no effective program to prevent their breakdown or rehabilitate them, they must of course be deposited somewhere. Occasionally, for short periods, that "somewhere" is a jail cell. More often "somewhere" is what some social workers have called an "Area X." An Area X is always located in the heart of a slum because the people already living there cannot object to the dumping. They have not the economic power to make themselves heard, and their official political representatives have built their power on the ghetto and are committed to its perpetuation. In New

York City a vast, informal machinery funnels society's discipline and health problems into the West Ninety-third Streets, and just about every sector of the establishment participates in running the machinery or lubricating it: slumlords who rent to the dead as well as the living provided they get a good price for it and have immunity from fire, building, health, and rent regulations; the city employee who collaborates in the arrangement; the welfare and health departments that go along because they have no other alternative; judges who tap the slumlord on the wrist on the rare occasions when he is brought into court.* Approval of the system is given by business leaders who lead the fight against adequate welfare and housing, prosperous financial institutions that refuse to lend money for private investment in slum rehabilitation; foundations that avoid any significant commitment to abolition of the slum; labor unions that have abandoned the low-paid worker and practice racial discrimination; and white and black political organizations that have a vested interest in segregation and race politics. When the slum is used as a concentration camp for the criminal and disabled, the virulence of all the diseases endemic in slum life is intensified.

It is obvious, in view of the social utility of an Area X, that the poor do not get the same type of law enforcement as the affluent, any more than they receive equal treatment in the courts. The people with whom I talked—Negroes, white, and Spanish—do not blame these miseries on the racist attitudes or venality of some policemen. Their attitude contrasts with the preoccupation of many Northern civil rights leaders with police brutality and racial bias. Over and over my respondents asked for more police protection, not for civilian review boards. Their demands will not be answered because, if there are to be Area X's, the social problems shipped into the slums must be given certain immunities by the system that puts them there. The police tolerate a high level of crime in the slum for the same reason a building inspector tolerates massive violation of building codes in the slum. The system requires it.

It is often supposed that under such conditions the poor—especially the Negro, who has to contend with being black along with the other disabilities of poverty—are in a state of revolution against the middle-class white system that has underwritten the dumping process.

* In 1964 the average fine levied against a convicted slumlord was slightly over $18.

The supposition is wrong. Whatever attitudes slum life is creating, it is not developing revolutionary ideas, if revolution is defined as the overturning of a system in which competitive pressures and aggression are the means of survival. More often than not the Negro and Puerto Rican share most middle-class values and standards of achievement, and they unanimously accept the idea that the pressure group rather than a planned and cooperative state is the answer to their problems. Rather than disestablish the system or reform it in basic ways, they hope to come to terms with it. The means of coming to terms may be simply a matter of blind hope, or trusting to luck, the way the poor people of Madrid put their hopes on the lottery ticket. When I hear of the "white power structure" I get an uneasy feeling that it is the whiteness of the system that is objectionable, and that what is being demanded is not the abolition of injustice but an equal share in the political and economic process in which injustice is inevitable. Only Martin Luther King and Bayard Rustin seem to have raised fundamental questions about the system itself.

In view of the irrelevance and insufficiency of what currently passes for liberal ideology, there is no reason why the poor should be interested in it. They are conservative and pragmatic about their relationship to the system because they feel their immediate needs can be met without far-reaching political or economic reform. They want to make the present system serve them instead of exclude them, not to postpone matters until basic changes are made. The poor are interested in housing, education, health, and freedom *now,* and they view such things as education approximately the way middle-class society sees it—as a way to a job, to income, to status; they seek a personal, not a collective, escape.

If the white and Negro poor were truly "alienated" from what passes as the American way of life, it would seem as if they would pay more attention to such people as Rustin, one of the few Northern Negro leaders who expounds a revolutionary philosophy. Unfortunately for the prophets, the exclusion of the poor from the comforts and privileges of middle-class life has not made them skeptical of the system as much as it has guided their appetites. Whitney Young of the Urban League often calls attention to the conservatism of the Negro by complimenting him on his lack of interest in radical movements. As a tactical move to counter segregationist charges that the civil rights movement is infiltrated by Communists, this is probably necessary, but whether the Negro's distaste for radicalism is healthy is something else again. Perhaps his traditionalism is a measure of the extent to which his individuality and his expectations have disintegrated. Robert Hutchins is one who has some doubts about the Negro's ambitions for himself, once his freedom has been achieved. Hutchins has said the Negro shouldn't want everything the white man has even if he can get it. In another way Kenneth Clark expresses the same idea, when he remarks that equality will mean the Negro will inherit all the white man's neuroses and his suicide rate along with his freedom and his creature comforts. That the Negro should want what the white man has is inevitable, since he has accepted the system's success symbols, and is subjected to the same newspapers, television, movies, speeches, and advertising that are busy homogenizing our culture. Its social or political philosophy notwithstanding, the New York *Daily News* has far more influence on the taste buds of the poor, including the Negro, than James Baldwin. As far as the children are concerned, readings in Negro history will never get on the same list with the all-white heroes in such comic books as *Captain Fury and the Howling Commandos*.

If the poor feel excluded but not necessarily in revolt against the system, it raises questions about the widely circulated and persuasive theory that the striving of the poor is having a revolutionary effect on American institutions. A good argument for the opposite point of view can be made, that the cultural conservatism of the poor and their lack of an ideology may explain why they have been so easily suppressed and pacified in the past century, why their numbers have increased so steadily, and why the establishment has been able to digest their leaders as fast as they rise to the surface. Today the abandonment of the poor by organized labor and the destruction of semiskilled jobs by technology have further decreased the power of the poor to save themselves. It can be argued that social change comes only when the misery of the poor inconveniences the middle class to the point where it makes changes to re-establish its own comfort: we drain the marshes only when the mosquitoes bother the rich.

The sense that the poor feel themselves part of the very system that is victimizing them came through in many ways during my interviews. As they proceeded, I found myself categorizing people in very much the same way my respondents did. Subconsciously or consciously, there were always "the people" and "the others." One's affiliation depended mainly on what a person thought of himself. He was one of "the people" if he was making some sort of assertion in his own behalf, a demand on his society. Underlying the demand was an assumption that the system could deliver if it wanted to. Along with the assertiveness was the capacity for indignation, especially among the Spanish, with their sense of *dignidad*—they had never become used to taking the leavings of the system. The Spanish felt keenly that they were entitled to a place in the new urban renewal community on the West Side even though the economics of the system made it plain that most of them would be ruled out. "The people" laid requirements on their children as well as themselves—sometimes of a very low intensity, but they were demands. They were not content with something merely because it was a slight improvement over what they had had before. In the main, "the people" had an idea that there was a chance for them to get someplace in the system.

"The others" were the enemies of "the people." These enemies were usually unknown and close at hand, the ones who endangered life and property and destroyed the civic peace of mind. "The people" mentioned "the others" constantly. I saw "the others" in a slightly different light when I began to identify them as individuals. It was not their illegal or antisocial behavior that distinguished "the others"; in fact many bizarre and unconventional persons seemed to have retained a sense of place in the system. What marked "the others" was that they had no sense of belonging, even to themselves. And in fact they were not their own proprietors any more than a *bracero* or a prostitute is. If their way of life was illegal it was part of the game for them to be arrested any time the police took it into their heads to put them out of the way. They were what might be called "standing violations" of the system, living on a sort of informal parole with the understanding that they would stay out of respectable neighborhoods. If they were dependent on welfare or some other opiate they were indentured to the system and allowed to misbehave in limited doses, somewhat as was the Negro male on the slave plantation.

"The others," noticeable because of their eccentric behavior, have become the stereotype of the slum dweller. The stereotype is fortified by riots in the ghetto, which are mistakenly interpreted as community uprisings and by the type of non-journalism displayed by the ex-mayor of Philadelphia when, after walking through several blocks of one of his city's ghettoes, he emerged with the statement that he had not found a single sober man to talk to. Scores of such Dilworth reports, based on sightseeing trips and published in every city every year, leave the impression that the inhabitants of the slum are generally not fit to live anywhere else, and that most of them need expensive training programs to teach them not to urinate in the elevators of a public housing project.*

The inhabitants of the Area who appear in the following pages are quoted because they are especially pertinent to the discussion. In many cases they are identified by their real names; in some cases names have been changed to protect their privacy. All of them are real people. They spoke only for themselves, but they also spoke rather well for many others. Despite numerous differences, they had one thing in common. In one degree or another, they were experienced victims of the cities we have built for ourselves.

---

* Where a sensible screening procedure is followed, the prospective tenants for public housing make a satisfactory transition from the tenement to the project. The Greenleigh Study of the West Side urban renewal area found that slightly over a dozen families slated for public housing needed any "tenant education," although a large federal grant had been allocated for such an education project.

Part I: THE VIEW

I
XXXX

THE AREA

EXCEPT FOR THE GHETTO OF HARLEM, ITS SPANISH counterpart on the East Side of town called El Barrio, and the inner cities of Bombay, Calcutta, Shanghai, and Chicago, there are not many places on earth which before 1965 were afflicted with as dense a residential population as the upper West Side of Manhattan in New York City. Take for example, the Area, a 125-block sector running from Eighty-second to 106th streets and bounded by Central Park on the east and the Hudson River on the west. Before urban renewal began to rip out the heart of the Area, it was inhabited by 152,000 people, or more than 1,000 people per block. The population included 105,000 people with white skins, the largest single segment of which (40,000) was Jews of West European or Slavic origin; 26,000 Latin Americans, mostly Puerto Ricans; 18,000 American Negroes; and 2,500 others, mainly of Japanese or Chinese origin. Only in Honolulu is there a greater confusion of blood, ancestry, language, and culture in as small a space.

The people who live in this part of town have been calling it "the Area" long before it was hit by a vast urban renewal program. The Area is a conglomeration of people and real estate, mainly extremely good and extremely bad, rather than a community or a neighborhood. Land here is valuable no matter what is on top of it. An 18-by-100-

1

foot plot on a rundown side street will sell for as much as a 100-acre farm in central Iowa. One rarely hears the word "community" applied to the Area except at political meetings, but the Area does have a certain distinctiveness. It is different from other sections of the West Side. To the South, below the Eighties, the people are more prosperous, housing is better, and there is less turbulence. Directly to the north of the Area, Morningside Heights takes its flavor from Columbia University, which is expanding in all directions, and a whole universe of other enormous institutions, such as St. Luke's Hospital, the Cathedral of St. John the Divine, and Riverside Church. Then, to the northeast, spread out flat, is Harlem. The Area is where all of these other places meet and begin fighting with each other.

The Area has no taxpayers' association or watch-and-ward societies guarding it. It is vulnerable to anybody from speculators in real estate to heroin peddlers. Other than its rectangular grid of east-west streets and north-south avenues, the Area has no particular pattern or weave or grain and the inhabitants are all members of minority groups that grind and cut against each other. Despite what has been written about melting pots, the frequency with which people move around inside the Area, and in and out of it, helps keep the grinding process going, as does a general mistrust and competitiveness that discourages sociability. The Area has a good representation of every nationality to be found in New York City, but the newcomers scatter about like dried particles.

It is easier to keep track of the white inhabitants because they do not move as often and they tend to settle in more sharply defined sections of the Area. Also, they have a regard for addresses. When Jonathan Ruggles, a nine-year-old, drops out of P.S. 166, his family will leave an explanation with the principal and a card at the post office directing the family's future mail to Westfield, New Jersey. Many of the other departures from the Area take place without any such notification, because the people concerned are not used to having a personal mailbox, or anything else permanent that might anchor them or identify them, including wives, husbands, children, jobs, or religion. They do not have a clear connection with organized society.

The population's heterogeneous racial, ethnic, and economic composition may leave the impression that the people of the area are not especially concerned about skin color or the economic status of their neighbors. People of all races and ethnic groups are found in close proximity to each other, in apartment buildings, schoolrooms, super-markets and churches. In some cases the rich and the poor also seem to be amalgamated geographically, with luxury housing complexes and federal housing projects facing each other on opposite sides of the street. However, in their conversations the people betray a singular and anxious preoccupation with race, economic status, color, and creed.

Middle-class discussions about education often center around whether an individual school is racially "balanced" or "imbalanced," and whether or not Puerto Ricans should be classified as "nonwhite" or "white" in calculating such balances. One hears much to the effect that such and such a school needs more or fewer white, Negro, or Puerto Rican teachers, and parents debate the values of "homogene-ous" versus "heterogeneous" groupings in the classroom. Real estate and race are also inseparable. Clergymen and legislators oppose or support racial "quotas" in public housing. Landlords qualify or disqualify prospective tenants on the basis of race. Property values are said to depend on whether a particular locality is "black," "Spanish," "mixed," or "white," and New York City banks draw a line around the dark areas of the West Side and refuse mortgages to homeowners in these places. Apartments are not only categorized by their rent levels; they are also given a tacit color tag. For example, "luxury housing" is a generic term for "white housing"; middle-income housing can be "mixed" but is still predominantly "white"; and public housing is synonymous with "black" or "Puerto Rican." Other color-linked words are "underprivileged," "disadvantaged," "culturally deprived" (mainly black), and "homeowner," "business-man," "housewife" (usually white). Almost every adjective one can apply to a group has a place on the color palette. The psychotic's gift to the public furor over ancestry is the underground gallery of *graffiti* at the subway stops, where "spick," "nigger," and "jew" can always be found in association with various symbols of hate and fornication.

The attitudes of people in the Area are difficult to assess. Those who are most articulate advertise their tolerances and conceal their prejudices—exactly the opposite of the Mississippian who makes a point of publicly asserting his bigotries and of hiding whatever instincts he may have toward moderation. For every statement that can be made about the Area that is partly true, a contradictory one can be made which is not entirely false. The Harlem Negro considers the Area an escape to something better: no matter how bad his living conditions, he seems to prefer it to the ghetto or the South. The Puerto Rican, on the other hand, who took his rights as a citizen for granted on the island, discovers on his arrival in the city that these rights have been devaluated because of his skin and his language. In different degrees the lives of everyone—white and black, rich and poor—are tinged with anxiety and frustration, and subject to the intrusions of violence. On a wild side street privacy is hard to come by, yet people can wall themselves off and achieve almost total isolation.

On the surface, the Area appears to be highly "organized," with its scores of block associations, political clubs, fraternal and church groups, parents associations, etc. Actually the active membership of most of these organizations is infinitesimal and unrepresentative, and their meetings are almost always badly attended. Civil rights is a popular cause with many of the Area's most vocal middle-class whites. Money can always be raised for freedom marches in Alabama and Mississippi, but the Negro or Puerto Rican around the corner, victimized by slumlords, ill health, and joblessness, rarely gets any tangible help from those middle-class neighbors who champion the poor in theory. Even where there is a capacity and desire for service to others, there is a division of the spirit. Some militant friends of the poor go about their work with the arrogance of a fundamentalist missionary while others silently develop styles of cooperation unsurpassed anywhere in America. The greatest anomaly in the Area is the fact that, on certain levels, revolutions are taking place, and, on other levels, the status quo is impregnable.

The Area has a history somewhat like that of the human body, with new cells constantly replacing the old. After the Civil War the West Side was populated mainly by Protestants, a minority group now known as the WASPs (White Anglo-Saxon Protestants). During the latter part of the nineteenth century the WASPs built the brownstones and mansions, some of which became the rooming houses and slums of the 1950's and which are now disappearing by the scores in the face of urban renewal. The WASPs set the style of architecture, fashioned the social procedures of the upper crust, and gave their churches prestige and financial security.

In the 1870's the Irish began moving into the Area in large numbers. They were people of modest means and attainments—workmen, tradespeople, women who "lived in" as domestics for WASP families. They settled, for the most part, in long rows of pleasant, well-kept tenements along Columbus and Amsterdam avenues. As time went on and they prospered, some of them bought brownstones and rented out rooms if there were rooms to spare. The Irish controlled the Area's Democratic organization on Tammany's behalf and sustained the large Holy Name, St. Gregory's and Ascension parishes. A symbol of their upward movement was the fact that in the latter part of the nineteenth century Irish common laborers built the elevated railways along Amsterdam Avenue, while in 1902 the Italians dug the subways and the Irish supervised.

The Jews arrived in force shortly after World War I, many of them moving down from the then highly desirable residential sections of Harlem along Lenox Avenue and its side streets. Others, "cloak-and-suiters," as the Irish called them, with the beginnings of their fortunes made, came from the lower East Side and Chelsea. Like the Irish, the Jews did not take to the brownstones at first, preferring the spacious apartment houses along Riverside Drive and West End Avenue, where, it was thought, an elegant address would make it easier to marry off a daughter to someone who was a success, or who had prospects of becoming one.

The rise of Hitler in Germany during the thirties accelerated the influx of Jews to New York City and to the West Side in particular, to the point where they far outnumbered the Irish minority. The politician Dennis Mahon, then thirty-five years old, recalled looking down the street from his home on Eighty-ninth Street and watching the flat-bed trucks roll up to the warehouse loaded with huge crates marked "Essen," "Hamburg," "Wiesbaden," "Düsseldorf." Their contents were "marvelous to behold," he said, the most magnificent, finely wrought furniture he had ever seen, and Oriental rugs, vases, chandeliers, screens, and tapestries.

Although they overwhelmed the Irish, Germans, and Italians and quite changed the Protestant flavor of the Area, the Jews were politically assimilated very quickly. For the next two decades they became the backbone of Mahon's Tammany organization, and Mahon responded by helping select Sol Bloom as the district's first Democratic congressman that anyone could remember. Even at the moment Mahon was defeated by a reform movement led by former Governor Herbert Lehman, 60 percent of the Tammany club rank and file were Jews.

Today the Jews, the oldest of the Area's "refugees," have been outnumbered in turn by other groups that have arrived to get away from some sort of political, social, or economic oppression. Since World War II, particularly in the past decade, American Negroes, Latin Americans, and West Indians have diversified and increased the population. The Negro, moving vainly to get out from under a cloud that follows him wherever he goes, usually comes to the Area from somewhere else in the city, mainly Harlem or its Brooklyn version, Bedford-Stuyvesant—less than 15 percent of the Negroes in a forty-block section of the area between Eighty-sixth and Ninety-sixth Streets have arrived directly from the South. The Puerto Rican migration was the first and biggest of the postwar period, but, since Castro, Cubans have trickled in from Havana, or from earlier stopoffs in Miami or in the Chelsea district of the lower West Side. Growing numbers of Spanish-speaking Dominicans and French-speaking Haitians have been registering their children in West Side public and parochial schools.

The size and suddenness of the Puerto Rican immigration over-whelmed churches, schools, social service organizations, and munici-pal institutions, which were quite unprepared to deal with a new language, and new habits, necessities, and expectations. Like the Negro, the Puerto Rican usually comes to the Area from another part of the city, probably El Barrio—Spanish Harlem—or the lower East Side. Once located on the West Side, the Puerto Rican frequently decides he likes it well enough to stay in spite of the decrepit housing.

The essential nature of the housing into which dark-skinned new-comers are funneled can be described very simply. The larger and poorer the family unit, the less living space it has, and the more dilapidated the housing. In one typically overcrowded sector of the West Side, for instance, 62 percent of the Negroes and 42 percent of the Spanish lived in one or two rooms. Even this does not tell the whole story: of those Spanish families in one- or two-room apart-ments, 68 percent had one or more children.*

* *Survey of Attitudes and Population Characteristics: Stryckers Bay* (Novem-ber, 1963–February, 1964), by John Kraft, Inc., 527 Madison Avenue, New York City, and sponsored by the Center for the Study of Democratic Insti-tutions, Santa Barbara, California.

The relatively small percentage of Negro families with more than two persons in the family unit (38 percent) is partly accounted for by the fact that a very high percentage of the Negro respondents were single persons. The Kraft study found that 67 percent of the Negroes responding were male, while there was a fairly even distribution of male and female in both the Puerto Rican and white groups interviewed.

Employment and income statistics of the main ethnic and racial groups in the Area give the bare outlines of the economic plight of the area's Negroes and Puerto Ricans. The 1960 census reveals that 11 percent of Negro males and 13.7 percent of Negro females living in the 125 blocks were unemployed, more than twice the national average for all racial and ethnic categories. In one census tract for the area, the unemployment rate for Negro men exceeded 23 percent. Since official unemployment figures are based only on those people who were once employed and who are still looking for work, they do not include those drifting adults and teen-agers—many of them Negroes—who have never had a job and who are considered in some cases as being unemployable or not part of the labor force. Unemployment figures do not reflect the total extent of economic privation for another reason as well: they include none of that group of people, larger than the unemployed, who work at jobs that cannot support a minimal standard of living. The area is filled with these underemployed, earning $40 or $50 irregularly as dishwashers, handymen, helpers, messengers, chambermaids, window cleaners, building superintendents, etc.

The Puerto Rican of the Area has fared a little better in a social sense than the Negro, but usually worse from an economic point of view. His unemployment rate in some parts of the Area is 20 percent, and it averages 14.6 percent higher than the Negro's. In 1960 his average annual family income was $3,042 as compared to $3,275 for the Negro and a median figure of $6,044 for all families. Handicapped by an inferior grade-school education, without useful skills, many of the Negroes and Puerto Ricans have few prospects for employment now or later. As automation destroys the unskilled jobs for which they could qualify in the past, these prospects grow even dimmer.

Educationally the Puerto Rican has been worse off than the Negro, a fact which has, of course, materially affected his chance of employment. Census figures covering the 125 blocks show that the Puerto

Ricans completed a median of only 7.6 years in school, compared to 10.7 years for Negroes, and 11.9 years for all residents of the area. There has been some evidence that the Puerto Rican's situation educationally and economically has improved since the census to the point where his language difficulties are decreasing, and a small number of Puerto Ricans are achieving something analogous to middle-income status. However, the great majority of Puerto Ricans still suffer from severe unemployment, underemployment, or, at best, employment in jobs not resistant to automation.

One part of the Area with a destiny of its own is the twenty-block site of a multi-million-dollar urban renewal program lying between Eighty-seventh and Ninety-seventh streets and bounded by Central Park on the west and Amsterdam Avenue on the east. Financed by a combination of federal, state and city, and private developers, a new "community" is being built which will be composed of "fully tax-paying" (luxury) apartments, middle-income cooperatives, rehabili-tated brownstones (for middle-income families), and public housing. In order to accomplish this transformation, the city had to displace 6,344 tenant households, most of them low-income Irish, Puerto Ricans, and Negroes, who inhabited condemned buildings. The city took title to these properties in February, 1963, and relocation began slowly in the northern, or "first phase" of the urban renewal site. Wrecking on a small scale began to take place a few months later, but even two years later there were far more of the old buildings standing than there were gaps between them. Broken façades of tenements hovered threateningly over passersby for months, and huge piles of bricks provided throwing ammunition for the schoolchildren.

In contrast to the new spires of public housing, the rest of the urban renewal area appeared to be in a state of mummification. Row on row of depopulated rooming houses lined the side streets, their windows and doors sealed with green tin. The air had the ripe odor of mold mixed with plaster and brick dust. The spaces left by the demolition of a building filled up with metal brick, wood, garbage, and the excavations in the streets laid bare a network of rusted sewers and pipe lines.

The urban renewal area undergoes a nervous as well as a physical breakdown, a characteristic of which is the inability of the average inhabitant to comprehend what is happening to him. Sometimes he becomes so paralyzed that at the end the city has to almost carry him out of his home. In the midst of the collapse the Puerto Ricans and Negroes of the side streets and the Irish in the tenements on Columbus and Amsterdam avenues drop into an invisible stream of immigrants to some other place inside or outside the city. Although nearly three-quarters of the people in the Area questioned about their plans indicated they wanted to remain on the West Side, most of the Negroes and Puerto Ricans will not be able to afford to live in the new community or qualify for the limited public housing. The ineligibles will be moved again and again, the records on them will be lost, and they will become mired in a gray, deteriorating area in another borough with neither the will nor the energy to retrace their steps. The unemployed Negroes and Puerto Ricans leaving the area are the people always found in neighborhoods being torn down, rehabilitated, or renewed for someone else.

In addition to housing the poor, some of the side-street slums in the renewal area attract the criminal, the disorderly, and the sick. During the summer the Area is always in turbulence. There is a general conviction that the police are powerless to control matters, that they are indifferent to the situation, or that they are taking "payoffs." Most of the slum buildings are unprotected. Front doors have been broken or removed. Hallways and bathrooms are collection points for trespassers. The masses of TV aerials on the rooftops are deceptive—many of the tenants have had their television sets stolen and have never bought others.

The children who live on these blocks or walk to school through them begin their education before they get to class in the morning and continue it after school. Unless he is a Puerto Rican or Negro with a very protective mother, or he lives on Central Park West comparatively isolated from the side streets, a child will have learned how to identify an alcoholic before he hears him speak and spot any one of a variety of homosexuals. He has seen at close range the transactions that take place between men and women in hallways or on corners between Broadway and Amsterdam Avenue. He may know that a certain grocery store is the local "drop" for a policy game, and he will have seen policemen accepting money from street peddlers, storekeepers, and contractors. He knows that a red welt on the inside of the forearm is the entry point of a hypodermic needle and he understands at least a few of the words of the language of the junkie and the hustler.

The twin pressures of incoming Puerto Ricans and urban renewal have been a deathly experience for the Irish. For those who did not vacate when the newcomers started arriving en masse, there was the infamous Manhattantown slum clearance years ago, between Ninety-seventh and 100th Streets. Although they protested vehemently, many of the Irish on the site of the clearance were forced out of the area in an exodus that cost Holy Name School four hundred children. What added to the irritation of the parish was that after the tenants had been displaced and the land cleared it was neglected for several years and used for part of the period as a parking lot—a clear violation of the agreement the private sponsors of the project had made with the city. Today on the site of Manhattantown is a huge middle-income apartment building complex, Park West Village, which the Irish see as a tombstone commemorating a host of Murphys and Dohertys sent packing by the real-estate conspiracy.

Then there was the West Side urban renewal. The few remaining blocs of Irish holdouts who lived in the old-law tenements found themselves right in the path of the bulldozers. Again they protested, pointing out that no new construction could be as roomy or inexpensive as what they already had. However, they could not overcome the argument that the buildings were old, and since they lived in a city where age automatically is equated with obsolescence, they lost the argument. The Columbus and Amsterdam Avenue Irish, along with a few Germans, Italians, and Jews, were not the only ones to lose out. The ground floors of the old-law tenements housed many small businesses that were also forced to close. Some had been in the area for twenty years or more, others were thriving Spanish *bodegas* that had sprung up in the past five or ten years. It became a depressing experience to walk down past the rows of dead groceries, lunch counters, glaziers' and plumbers' shops, credit jewelers, and laundries. Somehow the local feeling was that the shutdown was not so much a prelude to great civic improvements as it was a repudiation of the past. At any rate, the closings were a disaster for the people who had operated businesses until urban renewal bled them of their customers and then evicted them with vague promises about relocation someday, somewhere.

The Irish pub that held out the longest was Pete McGlade's, the last respectable bar on Columbus Avenue. At McGlade's, long after all other business had been silenced, one could listen to the same meandering arguments that had gone on for a quarter of a century. The customers were loyal to the end. But McGlade's was an exception. The other Irish pubs died meekly—in their sleep, so to speak—like the Shamrock, which was found to be locked up one morning and which for several weeks thereafter was stripped of its fixtures like an old man having his insides removed on an operating table.

No such tragedies and dislocations have disturbed the bulk of the middle- and upper-income (white) population, which is concentrated along the eastern (Central Park West) and western (Riverside Drive and West End Avenue) boundaries of the area. Central Park West is an impressive parade of high-rise elevator-equipped apartment buildings with rococo, baroque, or RKO-Keith lobbies of mottled marble, gilt, mirrors, and pilasters. White-and-gold canopies over the front entrances keep the apartment dwellers dry on rainy mornings when the doorman whistles up a taxi. Between 8 and 8:30 A.M. station wagons stop at many of these buildings to pick up children and take them to private schools on the East Side.

Riverside Drive, facing Riverside Park, on the western border of the area, is also lined with spacious apartment houses. The buildings are not quite so tall, the rents not so high and the doormen (if the building has one) are not so elegant as on Central Park West. A block to the east, and parallel to Riverside Drive, West End Avenue has the same middle-class, white, predominantly Jewish population, but a different aspect. Whereas the drive is a narrow, one-way street that jogs sideways and goes up and down hill in a rather informal manner, West End Avenue is a broad, two-way street prohibiting heavy commercial traffic. The massive apartment buildings on either side of it are solid, all about the same height (ten to fifteen stories), with less exterior ornamentation than the Riverside Drive apartment houses. There seem to be less sky and sunlight over the avenue, less informality in the street. The height of the buildings gives it more the atmosphere of a canyon. On weekends, the many children who live on the avenue get themselves over to Riverside Park as quickly as possible.

Central Park West, West End Avenue, Riverside Drive, and Eighty-sixth Street, plus some apartments and brownstones scattered around the side streets, supply most of the people who organize and run a vast number of voluntary organizations, which range from parents' associations, political clubs, churches, and synagogues to peace groups, music societies, and block associations. The grand profusion of these clubs and institutions has given the area the reputation of being overorganized. Despite the political liberalism of most of these organizations, they do not attract many low-income people.

The main thoroughfare—in Spain it would be the *paseo*—is Broadway, a place to walk up and down and be stared at. There are some old-timers around who remember when it had horse traffic, was paved with gravel and was called "the Boulevard." Upper West Side Broadway has little resemblance to the big white way that cuts diagonally through Times Square downtown. The customers and the layout are different. For instance, a good percentage of the daytime street population is old people who sit on the benches at the crosstown traffic islands when the weather is good. Uptown Broadway straightens out and splits into two broad lanes, one for south and one for northbound traffic, separated by a band of dirt and bushes. It runs through a collection of supermarkets and other neighborhood-type commercial establishments including half a dozen movie houses. One of these, an old standby named the Olympia, has "gone Spanish," while two others, the Thalia and the New Yorker, specialize in foreign and old American films.

Upper Broadway is "convenient," in that it has just about everything necessary in the way of stores, entertainment, and places to eat. Among the latter are an Israeli coffeehouse with a minimum charge and a floor show, a Russian samovar, several kosher restaurants, steak houses, pastrami-on-rye delicatessens, an expensive Indian restaurant, and several inexpensive Chinese places whose quality can be attested to by the fact that at any given time a third or so of their customers are Chinese. Just off Broadway a Japanese restaurant coexists in the same building with an Irish tavern, next door to a gypsy palmist. Several blocks further downtown is a night club which appears to have become a relocation center for Havana prostitutes.

Besides the usual assortment of drugstores, luncheonettes, cafeterias, liquor stores, and bars, there are bookstores, a ping-pong academy, Japanese gift shops, a pet store, pizza parlors, frozen custard and Italian ice counters, hot dog wagons with striped umbrellas, French bakeries, a driving school, a tobacco shop whose proprietor sings arias about his cigars, several greengrocers, beauty parlors, bric-a-brac and antique shops, dress boxes, a Woolworth's and a Kresge's, and, on the corner at Ninety-sixth Street, a colossal newsstand where a gang of newsboys assemble several thousand copies of the *New York Times* and the other Sunday papers every Saturday night, snow or rain notwithstanding.

The largest buildings on Broadway, and just off it, are the transient and apartment hotels. Some of these (the Sans Souci, the Bretton Hall, etc.) seem to have been named after Pullman cars. The hotels have no uniform character. Since the war they have traveled two different directions, either keeping their gentility, like the Marcy and the Paris (families all over the Area buy season tickets to its swimming pool), or decomposing to the point where they have become a gathering point for all sorts of rudderless human beings who are generally considered a threat to the peace. The Area has several of these latter establishments, any one of which in a more pretentious neighborhood would cause a general public outcry.

On late spring and summer nights almost everyone at some time or another is out on the Broadway sidewalk. Colors and faces are very bright and sharp under the neon, and although the scenery is not as self-consciously grotesque as that on Macdougal Street in Greenwich Village, there is a bigger world to look at and listen to: a world of stretch pants and baby carriages, stage makeup, a half-dozen foreign languages at a time, including junkies' English, which is the most incomprehensible of all. Everyone is in the parade, the belongers and non-belongers: bongo drummers performing on someone else's automobile top, folk singers, students, prostitutes, roommates, homosexuals, hangers-on, families out for dinner, readers of newspapers, blind people, restless children, readers of faces, a body under a blanket on the street with a policeman standing by.

If there is any place in the area where a man can have a little of the illusion of freedom, even privacy, it is Central Park. In the daytime, at least, everyone can disperse or disappear in it and shout as loudly as he wants to as long as he does not sound as if he is calling for a policeman. People can press the bottoms of their shoes against the grass and very easily imagine, if they are deep in the park, that they are somewhere out in the countryside smelling New England leaves and bark and musty lakes. The children fish in the smaller ponds for nonexistent fish and whatever happens to be lying on the bottom. The park seems to bring out the prospector in them. In the hillier sections north of Ninety-sixth Street they dart in and out of the woods and peer out at people from behind stone walls or from under footbridges. Although I have never actually seen any children climbing trees—for all I know this may be against some park regulation—it is obvious from the calluses on some of the big, comfortable branches that there are quite a few tree climbers around.

The park, which is 840 acres, is not usually as crowded as one might expect, considering that it lies in the heart of Manhattan. From nine to five, most of the park users are busy somewhere else, and at night very few people dare go into the park for fear of being robbed or beaten, so it gets a good twenty hours' rest on weekdays from everybody except babies in carriages, bench sitters, and men who take naps under newspapers. Also, though the playing fields are always used during the good weather, thousands of the smaller children prefer to play in the streets and many adults who live near the park and love it rarely go into it. They will gaze out their windows several times a day and congratulate themselves on the park's just being there. On a weekday morning in the fall, with the leaves turning and a light blue haze in the air, the park might as well be a patch of the Berkshires, for all the people who can be seen.

Nobody objects to this situation. If everybody used the park, there would be no grass for anybody to put his feet against, no places to read or have a family game of catch. It has also been a blessing that the type of people who knock down telephone booths have not gone to work on the trees. I do not mean that the park is treated gently; tree trunks have the usual quota of initials cut in them, and the fact that the ponds are used as junkyards becomes apparent in the dry seasons when the pond surface drops down and bedsprings, baby carriages and all other sorts of trash push through the lily pads. The Sunday-afternoon baseball fans also dirty up the park and by evening the grass around the stands is covered with a layer of beer cans which the children like to bat around with sticks. It is illegal to peddle beer in the park, but wherever there is a crowd there is also a man with a zipper bag muttering, *"Cerveza, cerveza"* under his breath, or "Hey, beer." Some of the peddlers wear baseball uniforms, but disguises are superfluous since the police are more interested in quieting disturbances and pay little attention to bootlegging or the dice games which go on all over the northern end of the park. The dice player brings along a board marked with half a dozen squares and puts it on top of a trash basket, and when enough players gather around the game is on. Since dice boards take a number of trash baskets out of circulation, this adds to the debris which the city has to clean up. However, the park employees do an efficient job and by Tuesday one can see the grass again.

Everyone has his own sport, and most of the athletic activity seems to be segregated in some way or another. Generally, there is not much intermingling of white, Negro, and Spanish children. They all have their own football games, for instance, although they may play against each other once in a while. On weekdays, baseball teams are mainly white youngsters from East and West Side private schools. The Puerto Ricans and Negroes take over the diamonds on Saturdays and Sundays. Tennis, played on thirty public courts near the Ninety-third Street entrance to the park, is mainly a white man's game, as is handball. The soccer leagues come from various enclaves all over the city: Scots, Armenians, French, Irish, Ukrainians, Turks, Colombians, Argentinians, Yugoslavs, Jamaicans. Most of the men on Stade Breton, the French team, come from Morbihan in Brittany and work as waiters, busboys, or chefs in convincingly French Manhattan restaurants. They take the game very seriously, and bring along their wives, children, lunch, and wine.

The park playgrounds have crossbars and swings, benches for the mothers and pretzel vendors. In the summer there are picnics and family outings. For free performances of Shakespeare every evening, people line up with sandwiches and thermos bottles as early as noon to be sure of seats. Occasionally someone will set up a marionette stage in a clearing and put on Punch and Judy and Rumpelstiltskin. Undercover political meetings have also taken place. For a while a group of Puerto Rican mothers met in a secret patch just after sunrise to talk about Puerto Rican independence, under the impression that if they were discovered they might be put in jail or have their rents increased.

The children seem to get the most excitement out of the park in winter after a real snowstorm. They line up their sleds at the top of the slopes inside the park wall along the Nineties. When someone gives the signal, they push off downhill. Halfway to the bottom the line breaks apart like a string of beads and they roll off all over the landscape. If there is rain followed by a sharp drop in temperature the sun shoots red, yellow, blue, and white fire through the trees. The ice on the ponds breaks up in late February or early March. The wind patterns move across the water, the trees hum, and the horseback riders come into the park at Ninetieth Street. Then, in April, a green vapor rises in the woods.

A BLOCK

My connection with the Area began in April, 1960, with a transaction. By assuming two mortgages and making a down payment, I became the owner and an occupant of a four-story brownstone house with tall windows, a new furnace, and six milk-colored marble fireplaces. The original owner had disappeared into a nursing home two years earlier, and a builder had renovated the house, dividing it into six apartments. Over the next few months I acquired a family of tenants that included two schoolteachers, a dancer, an actress, the night watchman of a bread factory, and a newlywed couple from Colorado.

At the time I moved onto the block it was one of the most crowded in the neighborhood, with anywhere from four hundred to eight hundred people living on a residential acre. Like many of the other side streets, ours had all sorts of housing, some very good but most of it extremely bad. The people who lived in the high-rise elevator buildings on the corners at Central Park West paid anywhere from $250 to $400 a month rent and got their money's worth, but as one moved in along Ninety-second Street the quality of the housing took a steep dive. The worst of it was a long line of earth-colored rooming houses on the south side of the street. At one time these buildings may have had some characteristics that distinguished them from one another, but the blight had worn away their faces. The fact that the buildings were all about the same height increased the monotony, except for the children, who used to race along the cornices and jump over the spaces between rooftops.

Most of the rooming-house tenants were Puerto Ricans. They paid their rents to the City of New York, which had condemned the buildings to make way for a new school. I do not know what the rents were, but I suspect they were too much. The private owners who had run these places into the ground had obviously enjoyed a friendly relationship with the city's building inspectors, and now the official landlord, the Department of Real Estate, made no pretense of maintaining the properties or of providing janitor service. The south side of Ninety-second Street was the first municipally operated slum I had ever seen, and although I was to come across many more of these civic monuments, I do not remember any of them having been in such a state of total decomposition.

The north side of the street, where my house was located, had a great deal more variety to its architecture and population. In a few spots there were even touches of elegance—a red door, a polished brass knocker, a few private homes with wooden blinds, and three attractive apartment houses with doormen, one of whom wore a uniform. The apartment houses took care of most of the middle-income population of the Block, and one of them rented to Negroes as well as whites if they could afford the rent. Several grades down the housing scale was a bay-windowed ark mainly filled with old people. Then, at the very bottom, near Columbus Avenue, was a string of rooming houses and tenements very much like the ones on the south side of the street.

The block was usually quiet in the winter, and after a heavy snowfall the rooming houses looked rather quaint. In the summer, however, they came to a slow boil and hundreds of people would spill out into the streets. On the hot days the grownups drank beer and cheap wine out of bottles and cans wrapped in brown paper bags. The Puerto Ricans played cards and dominoes in the open concrete areas below street level in front of the basement apartments, and onlookers could kibitz up above on the sidewalk. By the Fourth of July a Mr. Softee truck would come around afternoons and evenings, parking in the middle of the block. When the truck announced itself by playing "Mary Had a Little Lamb" on some sort of tinkling instrument, children would come running from a block away. The children eddied about, harassing each other or playing stickball or hopscotch, jumping rope and spinning tops. As the summer wore on the noise level of the street rose higher until, by late August, the block was overflowing with yells, horns, cheers, night baseball broadcasts, rock and roll,

Spanish music, baby cries, singing, curses, and the sound of the sirens on Central Park West and Columbus Avenue.

Having lived in Hell's Kitchen and on the lower East Side at various times, I was used to ordinary scuffles and street noises, but there were certain noises on Ninety-second Street that were difficult to block out because they were threatening and full of fear and hysteria. They used to rise intermittently to the surface early in the morning, after the general racket had died down and people had gone indoors or wandered off somewhere else. Several men would try to curse each other to death, a woman would scream incessantly, or a fist fight would break out so close to my window that I could hear the blows being struck and the soles of shoes scraping on the pavement.

I remember one of these night commotions very well because it more or less set the tone for the block. It was the first of many violent tragedies I watched take place, or the results of which I witnessed. Early one morning I woke up thinking I had heard the telephone. From my window I could see the woman who had sounded like the bell. The upper part of her body was hanging out of a fourth-floor window across the street. She would jerk her head up and collapse at the waist like a jackknife, then I would hear the sound again. A man in the room was holding her around the knees and shouting something in Spanish. By the time I had run out onto the sidewalk, he had pulled her back into the room, where she moaned until daylight. The sequel began a few nights later with a man in the same fourth-floor window screaming down at a man in the street. After shouting back exchanges, the man in the street walked off down the block and returned carrying a long piece of iron pipe. As he walked along he bashed several parked cars with it, giving off sounds like pistol shots. By this time a crowd had gathered outside the house and on the stoop next door a Negro woman was wringing her hands and moaning. The man with the iron pipe went into the house and came out about five minutes later, this time with a broken baseball bat. Swinging the bat in great circles and cursing, he broke the windshields of several cars, including mine. At this point, half an hour after the disturbance had begun, a police car swung around the corner. I flagged down the car and pointed out the man with the bat. Two policemen forced the man against the wall with his back to them, searched him, then turned the man around and shoved a flashlight into his face. It had been slashed to ribbons.

Two other police cars arrived and took me to the 24th Precinct police station. In the station house three policemen were looking down silently at the "pipe man," writhing on the floor and grinding his face into a pool of blood. Upstairs, the duty officer told me the police had just phoned to say the man on the fourth floor had been stabbed several times. The officer took my name, told me to go home, and said they would call me if they needed me. I never heard from the police again, nor did I ever find out what happened to the "pipe man," the man he had cut open or the woman who had once tried to jump out the window and who seemed to have caused the whole disturbance.

Another fight took place across the street the following day, between a Puerto Rican and a Negro, both about fifteen or sixteen years old. They were slender and lively, and had on boxing gloves. The usual audience watched from stoops and windows. The boys' gloves made their skinny arms look like erratic clock pendulums, but their footwork was very fancy and impressive. Each boy would venture into the enemy's radius for a split second and then shoot up and out of the danger area like a rocket. There were one or two glancing blows; the rest was brilliant evasion. Finally the two boys leaned on each other, exhausted and laughing.

Many of the fist fights on Columbus Avenue take the place of minor court proceedings—the ordinary processes of the law are not available to the poor or the mentally disabled—and bystanders are advised to stand clear. I nearly violated this custom when I once saw a man prop a woman against a car and pound her for two or three minutes as if he were driving a railroad spike. When I made a move to stop the man several bystanders advanced on me and I moved further up the block. After the man had finished with the woman, she tottered about, wiping her face with her sleeve, and then walked off.

On other occasions, women battle men and give a good account of themselves. In a single week I saw a woman knock a man flat on his back with one punch, and two prostitutes bombard a man with bricks until a friend dragged him away. Female assaults on males were not limited to Ninety-second Street. On a summer afternoon in 1961 at Broadway and Ninety-fourth Street, several hundred people watched a woman knock an old man to the pavement and then, with his body half on the sidewalk and half in the street, kick him in the groin and pound him on the head with a large pocketbook until compact, money, papers, lipstick, beads, and other objects flew all over the pavement. By the time a police car arrived, twenty minutes later, the lady had collected her possessions and departed.

A number of these violent people lived in the tenements near the corner of Columbus Avenue. Their main personal identification was a bruised face or a leg lesion or the dazed expression of an alcoholic. They were nameless because the other people in the block were determined not to notice them even if they could not avoid seeing them. When young secretaries in Bermuda shorts walked by on their way to the supermarket they looked straight ahead and held their breath.

The one encounter which would upset everybody on the street was any altercation between a white man and a Puerto Rican or a Negro, or between a Negro and Puerto Rican. It was assumed that such a fight would automatically become a racial incident. The Ninety-fourth Street local people had had a sample of what might happen when a Puerto Rican had criticized a Negro woman for punishing her child too severely. Within fifteen minutes the block was jammed with people, shots were fired and the police put a special guard on the block for several days. Although nobody was seriously injured, the incident sent a wave of apprehension over the area, and there was a flurry of brick throwing the next night.

One incident pointedly taught me to disguise my temper. On mid-morning one summer day I asked a Negro to move his truck so that a woman could unpark her car. There was an argument; the man struck me, and foolishly I struck back. After the fight had gone on for two or three minutes, I knocked the man down, at which point someone seized me from behind, apparently trying to stop the fight. My adversary got up, took a switchblade knife out of his pocket and lunged at me. I twisted clear of the man holding my arm, backed down the street to the front door of my house and kicked the gate shut with my foot. The man with the knife stood facing me on the other side of the gate for a minute, then walked across the street and got into his truck. I went inside, called the police, then came back to the sidewalk. The man returned and threatened me again, this time with his fist bunched in one of his trouser pockets to let me know he still had the knife. When the policemen—a Negro and an Italian—arrived, I told them the man had attacked me with a knife and that I wanted to bring charges against him. The Italian faded into the background and the Negro officer took over. First he said in hostile tones that if I brought charges he would advise the other man to bring countercharges against me. Furthermore, he had searched the man and found no knife. I explained that the man must have thrown the knife away while I was calling the police station, and said there had been witnesses. "Find them," the policeman said.

I went to a group of eight Negroes standing on the curb and asked them one by one to testify that the man had attempted to use a knife. All refused. One woman said I had made up the story to cover the fact that the man had beaten me fairly. The eight people looked at me with the same hatred as the man who had tried to kill me. "White Jew bastard," the woman said.

Most of the adults on the block always struck me as rather tight-lipped and defensive, especially the middle-class whites. The children, on the other hand, seemed to be curious and friendly, which was somewhat surprising in view of the nature of the block and the warnings they got from their parents. The Puerto Rican children were especially interested in how people lived. When Mrs. Jill Beecher in the apartment house next door to me asked a small Spanish boy to come up for a drink of orange juice, he said, "Just water." When he left he blurted out suddenly, "You have your own rooms!" Since my apartment had a ground-floor door, children were always ringing the bell for a drink of water, which I discovered was a dodge to get into the house and find out how I lived. The child would drink the water very slowly, his eyes looking around the kitchen, then there would be such questions as, "Do you live here all alone?," "What's upstairs?," "Are you the super?" Another child might gulp his drink, hand the glass back straight-armed and back out of the house without a word.

The small children on Ninety-second Street lived on the edges of everyone else's activities. They had no need to invent their own disturbances, and the violence of the adults seemed to overawe them. Whatever minor nuisances they committed almost always struck me as the result of absent-mindedness or nervousness, or of getting in the way of grownups, whom they almost always seemed to irritate. It was difficult to know how a Negro or Puerto Rican child from one of the rooming houses would react. If a strange adult spoke kindly to him, he might start up in surprise, or begin to cry. Or, behind a smile, there might be the sort of resentment that would take him up on a rooftop where he could throw pieces of concrete into the bedroom of an apartment house where he could see a white child playing with his toys.

Most of the children from across the street never went to Central Park, which was only a few hundred feet away. Six or more of them preferred to ride my gate, opening and slamming it shut a hundred times a day. I often saw a curly-headed Puerto Rican boy of about four or five, with a dusky, tired face and red-rimmed eyes, twisting his hands around the top of a hydrant in front of the house. It was something he did several times a day. After he stopped this he took to ringing the apartment bells in the vestibule of my house. If I caught him in the act and spoke to him about it, he would look at me impassively as if he didn't hear me. He might even go back and ring the bells again while I stood there. He was one of many dozens of children I met who seemed to have made themselves deaf by an act of will. He had the indomitable persistence of a ten-month-old infant reaching over and over for something that was always being taken away from him. I knew that he could speak English so this was not the problem. Finally I tried slapping him hard across the legs, but he would go right back to the bells even while the tears were still running down his cheeks. Then he lost interest in the bells too and went off to something else. In all the time he was on the block I never saw him smile or an adult speak to him except to tell him to stop doing something. About a year after the doorbell war, a moving van almost ran over him. When I got out on the street he was running around the corner, and that was the last time I saw him.

I thought of the boy some months later when a local teacher told me about passing by a window every day on her way to school and seeing a Spanish boy about five looking out. After many weeks, the child suddenly smiled at her and said, *"Mi amiga."*

"Then the next day, when I came by looking for him, he was gone. The family had moved away." It was the same way in school too, she said. As soon as you began to know a child he would be taken off somewhere else.

Alarums and "Airmail"

People on the block who had a rear-view apartment actually lived on two streets, the second street in our case being Ninety-third.

Through my living-room windows I could look out at the backside of two hivelike buildings located at 36 and 38 West Ninety-third. Over the years I came to know some of the inhabitants of these places very well, although none of us was ever formally introduced to each other. The open area out back acted as an amplifier and echo chamber, so that in the summer when everyone's windows were open we were all bombarded with other people's radio programs and the great American every-other word of the underbelly society, "fuck." The owner of 36–38, who lived in New Rochelle, had leased his buildings to a corporation, which in turn hired an agent with instructions to keep them filled up. The tenants, most of whom seemed to move in and out rather frequently, appeared to be trying to tear the place down, yet, with all the breaking of furniture and windows, explosions, and obscenities, I rarely heard anyone object to the noise. Later I discovered that many of the people in the rear apartments along Ninety-second simply went to bed with plugs in their ears. "What would be the use of complaining?" the doorman of one apartment house asked me. "You'd be calling the cops every five minutes, and after a while you would get the reputation of being a nut."

I suppose everyone has his own way of adjusting. For a while I used to start up out of bed and listen anxiously to the sounds of torture and murder, then I would check the *Journal-American* the next day for details. However, when nothing ever appeared in print about 36–38, I decided that I had been hearing a type of low-level conversation—what a psychologist might call a "social interaction." I felt guilty about being upset by situations which never seemed to bother anyone else and resolved from then on I was not going to be an alarmist.

I did not become adjusted to "airmail," probably because it was a tangible and perpetual inconvenience which could not be blamed on my imagination. My first introduction to airmail was a bag of rotten food that landed in my back yard a week after I bought the house. Since this airborne refuse was also a major irritation to everyone else on the block, some details about it are warranted. I could not get the police or the sanitation department to stop the airmail so I collected it. Twice a week I would go out back (after a few beer bottles whizzed past my head I wore my tin hat from World War II) and shovel up three or four days' accumulation of chicken bones, pieces of rancid fowl, chop bones, half-empty cans of beans and other vegetables, eggshells, bags full of fat, nylon stockings, underwear, fruit rinds, condoms, and bloody bandages, which I at first mistakenly thought were battle dressings for the victims of fights I had been hearing. I finally made the right connection when I discovered several glass ampules and hypodermic needles.

After I had filled a trash can, I would tip it over my back fence and the stuff would go crashing down on the concrete apron behind 36–38, several feet below the level of my back yard. The handyman for 36–38 would come out every morning and shovel up everything that had been dumped on the apron the night before. He told me he enjoyed scraping his shovel on the concrete. He had proof that it irritated the garbage throwers, who would be trying to sleep at that time of day, because sometimes they would retaliate by bombing him with cans and bottles. The man never objected to my dumping garbage back onto his premises; we got to be back-fence acquaintances and often discussed the airmail throwers. The handyman said that four-fifths of the people in his building were "taking pot or worse" and that the place was full of "hustlers and homos."

The police technique for discouraging complaints about airmail would be to tell the complainer to be his own detective. "I'll make an arrest, mister," the sergeant would say, "but you have to identify the man. That means you have to catch him in the act and see his face clearly enough to pick him out when we go to his apartment."

"I don't suppose you could come around sometime when the garbage is coming down and make the identification," I would say hopefully.

"Oh no, we can't assign personnel for that, mister. You have to make the identification and report it to us, and then we give the man a summons. Why we might have someone up here all day looking around and never see anything."

I reasoned that if I could catch one person posting the airmail, making an example of him would discourage the rest, but I was up against an unbeatable system. I had no trouble spotting the apartments where the airmail came from, but the people who threw it in the daytime would pull their shades down first. Shortly thereafter a whole cloud of chicken legs and beer cans would shoot out the window and descend in a lazy arc to the concrete or my yard. The stuff must have been hurled with considerable force from a point inside at least two or three feet away from the window. At night the odds in favor of the thrower were even better. He could get rid of much more at a time because he did not have to hurl the stuff halfway across the room. He simply turned out the light, pulled up the shade and dropped two or three days' supply of basic junk onto the fire escape and concrete below.

The airmail I disliked most was the bottles; they went off like mortar shells when they hit the concrete and a batch of fifty going off like a string of huge firecrackers would be enough to wake everyone on the block. Although people may have had a practical reason for throwing out garbage, since it saved them a trip four flights downstairs to the trash pails, the bottle throwing was obviously for amusement; people who enjoyed inflicting hell on society in general could toss out a bottle every half minute for an hour, as often happened.

The Department of Health and the Department of Sanitation never bothered about airmail, and the rats that prospered in it. The refuse that dropped out windows did not seem to fall into anybody's jurisdiction. Garbage in cans, out front where garbage was supposed to be, or in the street, was something else and the sanitation workers and trucks swept and toted this all away every day except Sunday.

In order to identify the airmail throwers in accordance with police requirements, I began to observe my neighbors more closely. I was never able to identify any airmailer's face, but I discovered other activities in 36–38 that took my mind off that subject. An interesting apartment was one on the second floor rear of 36 West Ninety-third. There were always two or three people in the room but the only regular tenant was a man who wore dark glasses even while he was eating his supper at night. The greenish-blue room was lit by the usual doughnut-shaped fluorescent bulb in the center of the ceiling. In the back was an old refrigerator, to the right of the window a bed and in front of the window a small table and chair. The same ritual took place at the window almost every night. The man with the dark glasses would sit down and, while he was talking to somebody else, light a match or candle, then hold some sort of metal instrument over the flame. After the flame had gone out, he would rest his left arm on the window and tighten a piece of cloth around it just below the elbow and slip a hypodermic needle into the arm as he clenched his fist. At other times he would hold his bandaged arm out and another person I could not see to the left of the window would administer the needle. After the injection, the man in the dark glasses would turn around and sit with his back to the window. Soon his head would move from side to side and his body would sway as if he were falling asleep.

It turned out that one of my tenants, a husky Negro named Charles Arnwine, who had been a football star at the University of Kansas, had also been observing 36–38. After asking me if I knew what was going on out back, he said he had seen addicts cooking heroin before when he was in the service. We had both been watching the same apartment. Arnwine thought the people kept their dope near a window at the end of an adjacent hallway. He had also spotted addicts in three or four other apartments higher up in the building.

Since there were two of us as witnesses, I thought we ought to let the police know, so in the summer and fall of 1961 I made several calls to the narcotics division, offering my living room as an observation point. The first time I phoned I was told a detective would come. When nobody appeared, I tried again and this time an officer promised he would call me the following evening at 6 P.M. for an appointment. He didn't call, so I phoned a third time and was told "someone would get in touch with me." I said I needed to know an exact time when I could expect the officer because I lived alone and worked during the day, which meant that I would have to make special plans to be in. When the officer said he couldn't tell me an exact time, I told him to forget about the whole matter. It was obvious the police were not interested.

The prostitutes and homosexuals at 36–38 were as open in their activities as the addicts. Together they occupied most of the building. There were also a few families with children. One small Negro girl used to hang her doll's clothes out to dry over a fire escape, and two others would plant themselves in a third-story window and look down at the Siamese cats in my yard. When the children crept out on their fire escape an arm would snatch them back into the room. If there were other children in the buildings they were kept out of sight. A gang of boys who played on the roof of 36–38 used to throw hunks of concrete and brick, and fire air rifles. The night watchman who had an apartment on the top floor rear of my house was a favorite target apparently, judging from the round holes in his window panes. The boys came from another part of town and could get to the rooftops of

36–38 because the entrances to the buildings were always open and there was never anyone in the hallways who cared what they were doing.

My tenants endured the commotion on the block pretty well, but I would lose one now and then. The first to leave was Jean McKee, a teacher at the Dalton School, who had rented the garden apartment on the first floor. After she moved she gave me the following account of her experiences on the block:

"The first night I spent on this street I was really afraid for the first time since I lived in New York because the noises were different from anything I had ever heard before. On Ninety-fifth and Ninety-fourth Streets, where I used to live, there were noises of people living, having fun, fighting—yes—but the way everyone fights with a wife or husband or children. Here they were really like animal noises. I was afraid to go out front, afraid to go out back. Once it got dark, I stayed inside. I got used to being by myself more. I never had the feeling before that my neighbors hated me, either. It was as though you were a toilet and they were dumping everything on you. It was very antisocial, not just careless or thoughtless. I had some hope for a while the second spring when my daffodils came out, because there was a time when people didn't throw things. I thought perhaps it was deliberate, that they tried to kind of miss the flowers and the grass. Several times when I was out back and someone threw something that went in the yard, they apologized and said, 'I'm sorry—I aimed for next door.' But the garbage began coming down again after a while and I realized I was an enemy.

"And I remember a light brown girl on the fourth floor of 38. She would sit in the window on Sunday mornings with her back against one side of the window and her knees bent up and toes against the other side smoking a cigarette, naked. She would gaze up at the sky, feeling the breeze. Nobody ever whistled because nobody wanted her to go away. That was her summer place. Then one Sunday she wasn't there, or on Sundays after that either. I looked into her window one night and there was a huge dresser against the wall where a small mirror had been, so I guessed she had moved out.

"I was robbed three times, once when they came in through the front door. That was typical. It's easy enough to break locks when no one is around during the day. But the second robbery was frightening. After being home all evening, I went out shopping. It was right before

Thanksgiving and I was going away. I had to go out and buy cat food. I was only gone an hour and I'd left the lights on. Obviously, whoever came in knew I had left and the only way they could know was because they had been watching me. This was what frightened me terribly. I had a collapsible iron gate on the door leading into the garden. It was locked. The draperies didn't quite meet in the middle of the door, so there was a slight crack you could see through into the room. They were probably standing right on the step looking in. The robbery was the beginning of my feeling hopeless about the whole business. Then there was a time in the summer when I was sleeping and someone touched me. I woke up very scared. It was pitch black but I could see a man standing over me. I said, 'What are you doing here?' This man sort of mumbled. I could smell alcohol on his breath. I thought, my God, I'm really at his mercy—I can't go out front. In those days Ninety-second Street in front was even worse than the back. It passed through my mind, be careful. So in my most school-marmish voice I said, very sincerely, 'Get out.' The guy responded almost as though he were a child and said, 'How do I get out?' I said, 'The same way you got in.' So he started walking toward the back door, and he turned around and said, 'Wait a minute'—as though it had hit him that he was minding me without thinking. He said, 'There's something I want to try,' and he started approaching me. Well, at that point all control left me and I just screamed and screamed and he ran out the door.

"I remembered the man's voice. I heard it again a few nights later and this time it frightened me even more. I was by myself, completely dressed, sitting and reading, and I heard this voice call down and I recognized it as the same man who had come in that night. I could never forget it. He said, 'Ah, now you have a gate on your door. How are the cats; how are you?' I understood the horrors of someone who's a paranoid at that point, that the whole world's hostile and you are just trying to find some little island where you'll be safe—because that's exactly the way I felt. I turned out all the lights, I closed the blinds, locked the outside door even though it was hot, and I just sat up and watched the *Late Show,* and finally went to sleep after it got light. I learned what it was like to have somebody watching me and not from idle curiosity but because he wanted to harm me. The police came after this and also after the robberies. Their attitude was: you'd better move—there's not much you can do. They were pleasant and nice about it. They said about the second robbery: 'Well, it's a job, these people just rob, they're professionals.' One of the policemen said: 'You know, what you ought to have is a shotgun because it's not a concealed weapon.' I said if I had a shotgun I might shoot someone with it. He said: 'Well, that's the idea.' I said what would really happen was, if I had a shotgun, somebody would come in and take it away from me and shoot me with it. He said: 'You're right, you'd better not get a shotgun—just move.'

"Every time something terrible happened I made up my mind to leave. Then a few days would go by and I'd say: Well, maybe that's the end of it. But it never ended. One day I looked out at the yard, at all the broken bushes and my plants covered up with garbage and I just went to my closet and started packing."

The summer after Mrs. McKee left was memorably hot and dirty. It seemed as if the whole block were going to blow up like Vesuvius and bury us all in soot and ashes. The one cool noise was the river that rushed down the street when the children would turn on the hydrants. It was quite a sight to see a hundred or so of them standing in the gutters under the blue street lights with the water up to their ankles. The other relief was the music. Four or five times in the early morning a black girl would perch on a fire escape at 36–38 and sing the blues while people would hand her beers and chant in the background. People all over the canyon would come to the windows. She had a voice very much like Bessie Smith's, and the acoustics were just right for her. We also had two trumpet players that summer, one on our side and one on the Ninety-third Street side. They would talk back and forth on the horns. The first man would start off with something slow and sad, the second man would pick up the tune and warm it up gradually until it was right on the outskirts of Kansas City. Finally the first man would take it back and calm it down almost to a lullaby.

Occasionally modern jazz would come up the radiator pipes from Mrs. McKee's old apartment on the first floor. A young ad-agency art director named Mike Latta had moved in there with a stack of records and a hi-fi set. Latta was something of an inspiration. He put dark red shades over all the lights and polished the floor until it looked as if it were coated with ice. He did a great deal for the block by parking his Vespa and sports car out front. The only other pieces of furniture he had were a couple of Danish chairs, a teak bed, and a bar on which he piled a pyramid of beer cans, and I doubt whether he ever used the stove because when he had guests he ordered his dinner from an East Side caterer. To give him some peace of mind, I put in a burglar alarm and installed an outside floodlight that lit up the back yard like a skating rink. Then, in a joint fit of genius we solved the airmail problem by building something that looked like a backstop in a ball park, made of chicken wire and two-by fours. It slanted toward the back yard of 36–38 so that when the garbage hit the chicken wire it slid right back down onto the concrete on the other side of my fence.

Since Latta had no interest in trying to bring Mrs. McKee's garden back to life, when we finished our engineering miracle he just nailed his rear door and windows shut, hung some black curtains over them, and the buildings out back disappeared. Otherwise, life went on pretty much as usual. By the end of the year the house had been robbed eight times, the burglar alarm system smashed and several windows broken.

Demolition and Displacement

I watched a whole block vanish. One day the Department of Real Estate put up yellow signs near the doorways of all the rooming houses on the south side of Ninety-second and the north side of Ninety-first, quarantining them against newcomers. The families in these places would have to move or be moved and the site cleared for the new elementary school P.S. 84. Once a tenant departed, his apartment was padlocked and, theoretically, was not to be rerented. The execution of the plan strayed from the blueprint. Children ripped off the metal sheets that had been nailed over the doorways and windows of the vacant spaces and meandered through empty rooms choked with dirt and broken furniture. At night the prostitutes and derelicts moved in. Whole communities of males took over some of the apartments, for what purposes I don't know; certainly there were too many to live in them. One morning I counted thirteen men trailing out of one basement, all of them carrying suitcases.

After all the legal tenants had been moved out of a house and the water and electricity had been turned off, the hallways and stairways became public toilets. Weeks went by without sanitation, health, fire, or building inspectors coming near these places, and for some reason there was a long delay before demolition started. During the period of abandonment, the rats came to the surface, some of them as large as cats, and like other brownstone owners on our side of Ninety-second I sealed my ground-floor windows and took extra precautions to keep the vestibule door locked. I saw several of the shiny and well-fed rats crossing the street in broad daylight with an odd jiggling motion as if they were being pulled along on small, uneven wheels.

As the displacement of the population went on, the air grew heavy and moist with decay. The city's Department of Relocation gave bonuses and moving expenses to families that found other places to live. Those who made no effort to get out became wards of the department, which was supposed to find them a "standard dwelling" in some other part of the city. The single people got no money from the city. They dropped out of sight and reappeared in rooms elsewhere like the ones they had just left. When the city had announced it was taking over the rooming houses, there had been a brief flash of hope—when the city became the landlord things were bound to improve. The hope died quickly. Under the management of the Department of Real Estate, the rot accelerated and even the most elementary maintenance was abandoned.

Meanwhile written and verbal announcements by city agencies warning people not to panic created several waves of anxiety. Vague details about the future changed from month to month. Tenants tried to talk with anybody who came around wearing a necktie or who seemed to have any other badge of association with the "city," pestering building superintendents, rent collectors, appraisers, even plumbers who appeared once in a great while to repair a broken toilet. Since most of these functionaries had no information and could not resist answering the tenants' questions, every day another trunkful of rumors was broken open and the contents scattered around the block.

The rooming houses reached the stage where it seemed as if they might collapse of themselves. They did catch fire repeatedly, and two families still left in one building narrowly escaped a broiling. On a Friday, after three separate fires had broken out in the same house on a single day, a fire captain asked me if I had seen a couple of old women running around the rooftops. Somebody—there is always a "somebody"—had seen them and was sure they were pyromaniacs. I had not seen the old women, but everybody except the fire department knew that gangs of youngsters had been building bonfires out of debris in and around the rooming houses. Later, when demolition had started, the children would put up pyramids of wood and debris almost fifteen feet high and we would have several minor holocausts a week, mainly in open areas where, so far as I know, nobody was injured.

The fire department did its best, but it seemed resigned to the fact that where another city department was involved violations of regulations were inevitable. However, the department did crack down on private landlords on the north side of the street. A fire inspector who descended on me and made floor-to-ceiling inspections gave me a stern warning to solder a broken wire which was supposed to lock the main valve of my protective sprinkler system. A few days later he came around to see that the job had been done. The superintendent of a building near me told me I was obviously new at the game: when a fire inspector comes onto the block, supers and landlords are supposed to disappear or not answer the doorbell.

I was one of the curiosity seekers who used to take field trips through the deserted rooming houses. My purposes were mainly historical, although I made a sideline of collecting the wooden knobs off the tops of banister posts. Coming out of a black hallway into the brilliant sunlight of a back yard was always the prelude to some sort of archaeological discovery. I spent many hours poking around in what had been gardens forty or fifty years ago, but which by this time were layers of stratified junk.

The houses were architectural curiosities that had gone through exactly the same life cycle described by Jacob Riis in 1890 in *How the Other Half Lives*. No landlords had ever cultivated land more intensively for rent purposes. I could see the grooves and marks of old partitions taken out and replaced by even more constricting ones, walls that bisected closets and even fireplaces, and foyers turned into kitchenettes. In the beginning there was a spacious one-family home, then the floor-through apartments broke this unity. The single rooms came next and, finally, even these solitary cells were subdivided. The fissioning process took place within a fixed space, and the result was the modern rent explosion, in which one rent became two, two became four, and four became eight. The human victims of this explosion apparently offered little resistance: at least this seems a reasonable assumption from looking at the frail gypsum board partitions which were used to compress more and more people into smaller spaces.

The rent explosion had, of course, obliterated art and taste as well as air. Where once had been a parquet floor with diagonal stripes of polished hardwood inlaid with mahogany was now a piece of soggy linoleum. The marble fireplaces, sealed up to prevent the escape of heat, had been painted over as had the cherry and oak woodwork. Closets had sprouted toilet bowls and sinks. A lady's powder room in 1925 had been transformed into a combination bedroom, living room, and kitchen with cardboard closets. Coal cellars had been converted into apartments. There must have been many infants for whom such places were the first and sometimes the last shelter outside the womb. No single person or corporation deserves the whole credit for the imaginative engineering that transformed these houses. The conversion could never have been possible without the approval of municipal authorities. The rooming house is one of those rare examples of successful cooperation between government and free, private enterprise. It was unfortunate that no university ever made a serious attempt to study one of these Ninety-second Street specimens before they finally went down.

When the city began to get rid of them, vaporized plaster drifted through everyone's windows and doorways. The wreckers would put up a one-story scaffold in front of the building to protect automobiles and pedestrians, then begin at the top, working down story by story, gutting the rooms, ripping out woodwork, electrical wiring, plumbing, and fixtures. Once this was done, the men would hammer the shell of the house with sledges. Sections of brick wall would shudder, undulate for a second and dissolve into fragments that fell in slow motion. When the fragments hit the ground, the dust rocketed several feet into the air. The heaps of brick and plaster, coils and stems of rusty pipe attracted children from all over the area. On weekends and after 4 P.M. on weekdays, they would scamper from building to building, dancing in second-, third-, and fourth-story rooms where fronts and backs had been knocked out, bombing each other with bricks and bits of concrete. Sometimes when they were dashing in and out of clouds of smoke and dust, with ruined buildings in the background, the children looked as if they were taking a town over under heavy artillery fire. The city eventually assigned a guard to stop the children but apparently there were too many of them to handle and the pandemonium continued.

Since I needed bricks to build a planter in front of my house, I made an occasional trip to the rubble piles with a shopping cart. I would search for a whole brick, then rap it with a hammer to remove bits of mortar. I had volunteer child labor to spirit off a ton of bricks if I had wanted them, but the trip to the rubble piles ended when a man in a green uniform told me it was against the law to take city property. However, I had enough to make the planter, which is standing as a secret monument to the old rooming houses.

By the time the last of them had been torn down, the sunshine lay all day long on Ninety-second Street. There were flashes of color the street had never had before. The side of a tenement still standing on the south corner of Columbus Avenue was a mosaic of green, pink, gray, and white painted squares which had once been the walls of other people's bedrooms and living rooms. The street was quiet and there were no questions asked about what had happened to the 750 families who had once lived in the block across the way.

Part II: OF THE PEOPLE

3

>XXX<

A CHANCE FOR SOME

Spanish

THE SIGNS ARE BETTER FOR THE PUERTO RICANS
in the Area than for the Negroes for many reasons, one of which is
that the Spanish identify with each other. Their family relationships
have taken a battering but they are in better condition than those of
the low-income Negro. The Kraft survey of Stryckers Bay found
many indications of this. Puerto Rican males and females just about
balanced each other and there were more "nuclear families," whereas
two-thirds of the Negroes in the same area were single, usually
transient males. The Puerto Ricans came to the mainland from an
island where they had been accustomed to equal rights and they had
not given up that status in their own minds in the face of discrimination, no matter how severe. In contrast, the Negroes' past was a
crippling handicap in every phase of their lives.

The Spanish, by and large, impressed the Kraft interviewers* as they
impressed me, as voluble, protesting, and specific in their demands
for better housing, education, law enforcement, playground space,
etc. They behaved as people new to injustice would be expected to
behave, as if they were saying, "They can't do this to us." The Negro,

* See footnote p. 6.

37

accustomed to defeat and displacement and to seeing other minority groups pass him by on the way up the ladder, had more the attitude of "This is what they are doing to us," and he was more or less inclined to silence.

To say that the Spanish are beginning to "make it" is considered an unfriendly remark by Puerto Rican politicians, who feel that in order to get more attention for their constituents they have to prove that the Spanish are worse off than the Negroes, and they tend to try to place the demands of the Spanish in competition with those of the Negroes. The theme is stressed, for instance, at antipoverty meetings and in such documents as the Puerto Rican Forum's request for federal antipoverty money: 1960 census data showing the Negro's slightly higher income and education level is used to make the point. But it is difficult for an observer to avoid the impression that the census figures may very well no longer reflect the actual situation of the two groups. Immigration of Puerto Ricans has slowed down considerably, which means that the Puerto Rican averages are not pulled down each year by new arrivals who are among the poorest group. There are also the small but lively successes of the Spanish storekeepers (there are around 6,500 Spanish-owned businesses in the city), the competitive spark, the idea of "I can do it," an improving mobility resulting in the trickle of Spanish to better communities, and their sense of "belonging."

The Spanish are not activists in the usual political sense—their dozens of organizations are primarily social, and have little coordination; it is hard to drag them to meetings (which may be a sign of their good sense), but they have a cooperative spirit and a responsiveness to a teacher, priest, or neighbor whom they trust. They seem to have made more out of the meager resources offered by the area's churches than the Negroes, who see very little hope in that direction. Many of the Spanish have high expectations if these have not been siphoned out of them by illness and the shock of unemployment. In looking at the Spanish, we should not note so much what they have accomplished so far as we should note the resources they have to fall back on, especially their state of mind.*

* An encouraging development among the Puerto Ricans is often balanced by a depressing one. For instance:

"The occupational distribution of second generation Puerto Ricans is basically different from that of the Puerto Rican born group, reflecting the educational advantages and the greater degree of acculturation of those born in

Families like the Serranos, Acostas, Garcías, Pérezes, and Tomáses illustrate the point, even if, like the Acostas, they are keeping just clear of the brink of disaster. The Acostas and Serranos had to move because their buildings were condemned to make way for urban renewal. Before they were moved to another gray area in the Bronx, the Acostas lived on the ground floor of a malodorous place on Ninety-fourth Street, and the Serranos had a fourth-floor apartment in a building on Ninety-third that was also old but had a superintendent who kept it clean and listened to the tenants.

The Serranos had an added advantage in that they were lucky enough to find one of those exceptional apartment houses which were rent-controlled in fact as well as in theory. They paid $54.27 a month for seven rooms. The Acostas' building was also supposed to be rent-controlled, but by various tricks and dodges the landlord was able to boost the rent to $120 for two rooms, one of which was about the size of a wardrobe closet. The differences in the situations of the two families was symbolized by the fact that the Serranos lived on a high, airy, safe floor while the Acostas lived on a damp first floor vulnerable to intrusion from front and back.

Frank Serrano was one of the older children in a large family that came to the United States from Puerto Rico ten years ago. He studied at night school with the idea of becoming a social worker, served a hitch in the service, and returned to take up his career. His father owned some houses in Puerto Rico, and it was the parents' hope that when their children had grown up they could return to the island so they could die there. They will die without their children about them because the children intend to stay in the States. Frank said that in New York you have a chance to get someplace, somewhere better than Ninety-third Street. Frank considered the block a "bad" one.

---

the states; most significant is their movement out of the blue collar occupations, especially that of operatives. Fifty-seven per cent of the women and 31 per cent of the men in the second generation group were white collar workers. Again, New York City large scale employment of clerical workers accounts for this development." *Puerto Rican Profiles,* p. 52, Board of Education, New York City, Curriculum Bulletin No. 5, 1964–65 series.

On the other hand, in 1964, 20 percent of the city's Puerto Rican population was on public assistance as compared to 15 percent in 1957, an increase of 63 percent. (In comparison, 17 percent of the Negro population was on relief in 1964 but the rate of increase of Negroes on relief had been 73 percent since 1957.) *Many Gains Noted by Puerto Ricans,* by Peter Kihss, *New York Times,* March 2, 1964, pp. 47–48.

His sisters did not talk to anyone in the hallways or on the stoop, minded their own business, came straight home from work, went upstairs, and didn't go out again until morning, when they went to work. The Serranos wanted to stay in the neighborhood because it was "convenient" to the subway and Central Park, and they felt that urban renewal would clean things up.

All the Serranos had jobs. Mr. Serrano had been a paint sprayer at the Copeland Window Display plant for seven years and earned $75 a week. Mrs. Serrano earned $70 a week, sometimes more on piecework, as a sewing-machine operator in a factory that makes baby clothes. She belonged to the International Ladies Garment Workers Union. Frank's brother was also a paint sprayer, in the same plant as his father, and his wife also worked. A sister was a secretary. Frank spoke excellent English, which he began learning in a city school in Puerto Rico. He said many Puerto Ricans who appear not to know English actually do understand and speak it, but they are afraid to use it and they don't get the opportunity to use it very much because they stick together.

Frank was a businesslike young man, tall, slender, dark, neatly dressed. People noticed him and said, "Hello, Frank," when he walked on his way down the block. Some of his social work had been right on the street where he lived and he thought about people's problems off duty as well as on, especially about the addicts, who "stole from everyone else and spent their relief checks on dope." From the days when there were active gangs on the block, Frank recalled a skinny, nineteen-year-old gang leader named Indio, which seems to be a generic name for a gang leader. Indio's enemies caught him taking a fix in a bathroom and forced him to take an overdose that killed him. After Indio's body was removed from the building across the street from the Serranos, his gang, The Unknowns, disappeared. Indio was a gang man but he didn't bother anyone, Frank remembered. "If you needed any help he and his gang came around. They talked to you and said they would protect you. They'd sit around and keep their eye out on the block."

The Serranos worried about "them"—the others. "We just didn't go out at night," Frank used to say. You didn't get familiar. Once you took a step they would keep after you. The prostitutes weren't much trouble; the kids were generally okay. The men were the troublemakers. At the same time, Frank had a good word to say about the neighborhood. He thought the West Side was the place for him.

"You can get work, you can get a good education, you can go to day school, night school—people have a chance here. There are two ways, a good way and a bad way. I don't feel discriminated against because I am a Puerto Rican, and I have a lot of friends, professional people, many of them. Discrimination isn't why Puerto Ricans stay together in these crowded places. They're afraid to leave their friends. Many of them go back but others don't. The ones on welfare wish they could go back to the island but they can't. I'd say 50 percent of the Puerto Ricans around here would like to return."

The Serrano family attended Holy Name Catholic Church on Ninety-sixth Street, where the priests they knew best were Father Bradley and Father Otal, who is Spanish. One summer Frank worked for the West Side Area Services Department, a city agency in the neighborhood, and inspected houses, including 68 West Ninety-third where the baby Sonia Rivera was found one morning dead of either pneumonia or the rat bites on her body—there has been an argument between city authorities and local residents ever since about the real cause of death. The Rivera family left the area, disappearing into Brooklyn somewhere. Frank said that was the way it goes. Somebody dies here, somebody leaves and somebody stays.

The Serranos were among the thousand people displaced by urban renewal who by 1966 were relocated in new public housing.

In 1964, when they were on Ninety-fourth Street, Julio and Ramona Acosta and their children—Inez, sixteen; María, fifteen; Orlando, thirteen; and Edmundo, ten—inhabited two "rooms." One of the boys slept on the floor, one girl slept on the couch, and the other boy and girl shared a double-deck bunk. The landlord rented the apartment as "furnished," in return for which the Office of Rent and Rehabilitation allowed him to charge $120 a month. The "furniture" was a rickety table, two broken chairs, and a bed which had to be thrown out. The family bought all the rest of their furniture and an icebox as well. Randy Dupree, a young Negro social worker at the Goddard-Riverside Community Center, tried to help the Acostas when they had no heat or hot water for eight days one January and had to keep the gas stove on all the time to keep from freezing. He notified the West Side Area Services North office, filled out a complaint for Area Services to forward to the Department of Health, and was told to come back to the office in two days to check on the complaint. He returned in three days but the Area Services employee who had taken the complaint had quit and there was no record of Dupree's ever having talked to anybody at the office. Mrs. Acosta sent in two applications for public housing: No. 930245, dated November 4, 1957, and No. 1254784, November, 1961. No answer. In the six years she waited to hear, she never had a communication of any sort from the housing authority.

The Acostas' apartment, a combination kitchen-living-room-bedroom, had a six-by-ten-foot cubicle in back, which enabled the landlord to register the place as a two-room apartment. There were one window and two closets. Each time smoke from the downstairs boiler poured out of the closet, Mrs. Acosta had to scrub the walls. If painting needed to be done, the family had to do it. The apartment was bright and colorful, with many pictures hanging up, including a color print of "The Last Supper" and a framed marriage license on the walls. Other appurtenances were two parakeets, a small turtle, flowers, an American flag, and a flock of paper elephants, pigs, cows, and smaller animals set up on window sills and bureaus, and a very old television set which Mr. Acosta thought he could repair was standing near the window.

The Acostas lived in the apartment and attended Holy Name Church almost all of the eight years the whole family were in New York together. Mr. Acosta came to the city alone nearly twenty years ago and lived for a while with his sister on 110th Street in the El Barrio district of East Harlem. He liked El Barrio better than the West Side but when his wife and children came to the United States in 1957 the only place they could find was a rooming house in the West Side slums. Mr. Acosta had been ill since 1955, and had not been able to work in the merchant marine since. He went off occasionally to Manhattan Beach Marine Hospital for treatment. Mr. Acosta often spoke about the narcotics addicts: "We never finish with them around here. They come inside, break the door down, and they go upstairs in the halls. Sometimes you go into the bathroom and you see blood and a can opener. They are not the people who live in the house. In the summer you see more of the people with the drugs. In the winter we keep the doors closed. We do not have a robbery but other people do. We have a lock on the door and bars on the window, with iron door in back."

There were some good things, some good people on the block too, Mrs. Acosta said. Her son Edmundo always swam in the Columbia

Grammar School pool, which was open to the children during the summer, provided they were more than forty-eight inches tall. She mentioned two "very nice families" who took an interest in the children. One was a Negro architectural designer and his Oriental wife who had bought a small house nearby and renovated it and filled their windows with bright green plants. Another helpful couple were William Houlton, president of the Ninety-fourth Street block association, and his wife.

Sickness always plagued the Acostas, parents and children alike. Edmundo had tuberculosis as a baby, and there were other serious health problems. But Edmundo, who was large-eyed and could not contain himself very long when adults were talking, saw the world as a more pleasant place than his worn parents did. He talked about his friends, days in the park, swimming, what he liked to eat. When his father mentioned that he likes to cook, Edmundo offered the information that he ate pie, any kind of pie—cherry, apple, blueberry, lemon. He looked forward to going to the Markland Camp (run by the New York *Herald Tribune* Fresh Air Fund), where he went for two summers. His mother did not know exactly where the camp was, but she always saw Edmundo off at the railroad station. Her son brought in his Markland T-shirt with a green pine tree stenciled on the front. At camp, Edmundo would get up early and go to the kitchen and get a piece of pie. During a hike he fell into a hole up to his hips, and saw snakes, bats, and deer. Flying squirrels ate fruit out of his hand. He got into some poison ivy but did not get sick from it. After every swim in the lake the camp doctor would give him a checkup.

Mrs. Acosta wanted to have the boys join the Boy Scout troop at school but the uniforms cost $10 or $12. She also thought the boys should go to college. The older boy, Orlando, had already decided he would go, but Edmundo and María said no. The mother said the children prefer to go to Holy Name School, but the children interrupted her and said they would rather go to public school. Perhaps this was because at the parish school the teachers sometimes hit the children hard on the hands with a ruler. Mrs. Acosta was satisfied with the children's progress in spelling, history, arithmetic, and the catechism, but she was surprised they did not know where Peru or Guantánamo was. The children did their homework together at the kitchen table.

When Edmundo spoke, everyone laughed, but his enthusiasm did not keep his mother warm. She wanted to go back to the island. "You know, the winter is very cold to me. I miss my brother. My mother is alone in Puerto Rico. I like it better than New York. It's more friendly. You have your window open there. Here you're too crowded and close. You don't see anybody. You don't go out. In Puerto Rico, *Mi casa es su casa*." Her husband's town, Ponce, had a social club on the West Side, but he didn't go. "You gotta wear a tie, get dressed up," he said. "We are not living in any condition to go places like that. We like to but we can't."

At the mention of San Juan, Mrs. Acosta brought out her photograph album. "This is my brother," she began, and her cheeks flushed with pleasure as she turned the pages. "The beach . . . people with their hands over each other's shoulders. My husband, the first marriage . . . one of the kids on the beach . . . this is my friend, this is the house where I lived where we are sitting around having a drink at the table. This is the house I lived in two months . . . this is an American fellow in the merchant marines . . . this is the mother of my husband and my brother, sisters. They live in California. This is my sister with my brother and this is the brother of my husband who lives here in New York. . . . There is Julia. She died two years ago in Puerto Rico. . . . This is the wife of the brother of my husband . . . this picture is four years ago and my husband is very fat . . . this is my aunt. I don't know about her anything now . . . this is when I was a little girl, when I stayed with my aunt in June, 1929. . . . I have a feeling I will never come back to Puerto Rico."

When the Acostas were displaced by urban renewal, they had to move far away, to another "gray area"—somewhere in the Bronx, people said.

Children without fathers are everywhere, but the family of Emilio García was an exception. In 1964 he was raising four motherless children in an apartment on Seventy-seventh Street. He was a medium-sized man with two jobs, one in a jewelry shop, where he worked for sixteen years, and another at home, where he cooked the meals and took care of Alfredo, seventeen; Flora, fifteen; Luis, fourteen; and Fernando, thirteen. He would come home from the jewelry shop at 5:30 every afternoon.

"The school is the important thing," he said. "I never went to high school. I worked too hard all my life. It's a very hard life to grow up alone. I don't make enough money, you know, $80 a week—I pay $50 a month for two rooms, kitchen, private bathroom. The children stay in one room, one room is mine. We don't have any trouble with heat or hot water. The building is all right. Taken care of pretty well."

Mr. García came to the United States before he married, after his mother and father died. "You live better here, you know. We are looking for to live better. I came from Ponce and I am glad I came after eighteen years, half a life, you know. Almost seven years I was separated from my wife and then I got divorced and had custody of the children. She comes sometimes to see them from where she lives in the Bronx someplace."

Alfredo had lost a month of school a while before but he would never do that again, his father said, because he was now seventeen years old, and able to take care of himself. "I say, 'You want to continue in the school?' He say, 'Yes, I want to continue in the school. Get my diploma.' He lost about four weeks the first time in school. After that he never lost a day." Alfredo's ambition to be an engineer pleased his father, and at the same time made him uneasy because he knew the difficulties. Flora wanted to be a nurse. All the father could say to this was to tell them they could not miss a single day at school.

Mr. García liked the West Side: "The block had a couple of bad furnished rooming houses, you know, but this house is very good." The Garcías' block on Seventy-seventh Street looked about as rundown as any other side street yet it was better because it had many families which had been around for a long while. "We never had any trouble. Lots of friends, good neighbors on this block. I know all the people in this building. Mr. Torres, Mr. Ruiz, they been here a long time too." The afterschool program at Junior High School 44 helped the area a bit. Flora was on the acrobatic team and Alfredo played basketball and softball and was in a singing group. Mr. García used to go to the programs at the school community center when the children were in a show. Something else which promised to improve the area was two new public schools being built nearby.

The father had relatives in Manhattan on the East Side, where he lived for about eleven years and where all his children were born.

There was a sister on the East Side, a brother on Second Avenue with four children. Sometimes the other children went away in the summer but the García children did not because the family budget was too tight. "If one goes, the others are kicking, you know, they all want to go. The school would send maybe Luis and he would like to go but sometimes when he is getting ready to go to camp he says, 'No, I want to stay. I want to play baseball.' In the summer I take them to Orchard Beach and Rockaway Beach all day. The kids like it very much. Now they grow up they go swimming. Sometimes the teachers take them up to Bear Mountains, sometimes to the park, to the museum. I sent Alfredo to Puerto Rico for five months. He liked it very much, because he got a little lamb, horse, mules. He like cow. He like playing in a camp near a small river, not big river like the Hudson."

The father did not think about finding a new wife. His thoughts were always with his children. "I'm afraid if I brought somebody in it would be a bad woman. It's very tough to take care of children. A woman taking care of somebody else's children, I guess that would be bad. Her own son, that's all right, but when I took the children I got some girl because they were too little but now I take care of them myself because you know what happens to kids here if parents don't care. Children here, ten, eleven, fifteen years old, out all night in the street. I don't want that to happen to my children. I send them to the center, afterschool center, almost every night. Sometimes they have a friend, have a party. Make it to ten o'clock, no more, because after ten children are supposed to be home. I love them very much."

Rafael Tomás and José Pérez were twenty-year-olds who went to school together, married pretty girls and dropped out of high school to go to work. Sometimes the couples seemed more like two pairs of high school classmates than men and women in their first years of married life, already with children.

Rafael, his wife, Anna, and their baby lived with his parents in an old building on West Eightieth Street. Everybody in the Tomás ménage worked. Rafael was a messenger for a photostat company and his father was owner of a TV repair shop and also was superintendent of the building in which the family lived. Until her death Rafael's mother was a sewing-machine operator in a dress factory. After her mother-in-law died, Anna left her job at Woolworth's and took a typing course paid for by the Goddard-Riverside Community Center. This led to a better-paying office job, and a girl upstairs agreed to take care of the baby.

Rafael was doing all right financially but he was uncertain about what would come later. "I don't feel too bad about leaving school or anything like that, but someday I'll miss it. I liked my teachers. Some of them were like my mother. The teacher I had in the eighth and ninth grade, Miss Schwartz, heard about our getting married and having a baby and she still talks to us over the telephone and I see her once in a while. We had a lot of friends at school. My friends are still around here, almost all of them, and we still feel the same. About four of them got married. We still play basketball and do everything together so we're like brothers, and all the girls are like sisters, the girls who got married."

Rafael liked the West Side, where he knew everything by heart. "We never have any quarrels with anybody that would make us move or anything like that. My father is one of the best building superintendents on the block. The tenants here are mostly Spanish and my father knows everybody in the building for at least ten years, so they get along good. If a tenant wants something to be repaired, well, he fixes it up and he has no trouble with them because whenever he needs money for repairs he asks the landlord and the landlord gives it to him."

The rents in the building ran $80 to $95 for five-room apartments with their own bathrooms. The main annoyance was a building out back filled with addicts and winos. Each day Mr. Tomás had to clean up the broken bottles and garbage in the rear courtyard. The new super of the building in back tried to stop the airmail, but without much luck. Rafael reported that the Board of Health might try to get all of the people out of the building and close the bar on the ground floor.

Most of "the others" seemed to live in the bars around the corner on Amsterdam Avenue. "The people who live on this side of the block are mostly Spanish and colored people and they get along all right. The people on our end of the block near Columbus Avenue have families, the people work, they don't take welfare. But down toward the other end of the block the others get unemployment pay, you know, and they work six months and then they quit. Down the block is where the bad comes in."

Rafael's mother would get very tired from working. She always wanted to be home in Puerto Rico, where she could relax. It was not that she had to work, her son says; she worked so that she would not have to stay home in the house all the time. Rafael said his father learned a great deal in the city. "He was only a captain on a ship in Puerto Rico, in the bays over there. Since he came here he's been studying television and he feels here you can learn and make money. The way I feel about it is that I learned a great deal in school in America. Probably if I had stayed in Puerto Rico I wouldn't have learned any of the things I know now. I probably would have learned my math and all that because I was going to a good school there and they teach a lot there but they don't have the things you want to learn like art. They don't have too many sports. Over there you have to learn by yourself. Here you have coaches and track teams. In Puerto Rico you just don't grow. You stay at the same height all your life. See, mostly Spanish people are small.

"The most important thing to us is our health. Whenever we would get sick in any part of our body, that would be the worst of all. And next we want to have our own home. We won't have to worry about where we sleep because somebody else is staying over. We'd be free."

Rafael's seven sisters and his brother preferred the city, and all but one sister married and settled down in their own homes. One brother-in-law bought a small house next to Yankee Stadium and a sister who married a Scotsman recently moved out near them. Rafael said he wanted his son to grow up on the West Side. "I don't know how they grow up in New Jersey and those places far away. They don't have the same places like the park where kids could exercise their bodies and do anything they want, you know. Over here you can go to any playground you see twenty or thirty kids who always have something to do. If I went out of New York to New Jersey or Staten Island I'd be lonesome. I'd probably become a pot-belly, drinking a lot of beer, sitting in a garden all day long. Here I won't be lazy. I'll be doing something, playing basketball. I will always have the center at the school. Every night of the week I am over there. I walk in the gym every night at 7:30."

Rafael hoped to be an artist or draftsman someday and used to get some practice by making posters for the school dances. However, it cost money to go to art school and Rafael was not sure he could make it. He knew that artists make more money than any person that works in an office or a stockroom. One reason he worked as a messenger at the photostat company was so he could see how the artists did things, and ask them questions. He had hopes.

"We're still young, me and my wife, and even though we're married it doesn't make any difference, it doesn't make us any older. We'll still be happy having a lot of fun. We'll think just like we did when we were going to high school."

It is impossible to write about the Tomáses without mentioning José and Carmen Pérez, since the couples were inseparable. The Pérezes lived with their in-laws on West Seventy-eighth Street. They had three children, the first two being twins. José was a stock boy in an electronics plant, where his father worked as a mechanic. José planned to get his high school diploma someday. His factory was on Seventeenth Street near a high school on Nineteenth Street where he could go to class at night. He was anxious and a little overcome by the fact that he was the father of three children, but his wife liked being a housewife and had enough faith for both of them.

Carmen took care of the babies and also managed to be president of the evening social club run by Goddard-Riverside Community Center of Junior High School 44. She was planning on her children's going to her old elementary school at P.S. 87 and remembered all her teachers, especially Miss Schwartz, who seemed to have quite a following among her ex-pupils.

When she was small, Carmen said she promised her mother she would never get married. Her father left home when she was very young. "He went to New York and my mommy used to say, 'Men are no good. Don't get married,' so I used to believe and I used to make a promise every night that I would never get married, but then when I met José I couldn't help it. I used to ask him, 'José, are we going to get married tomorrow? I want to have twins.' It so happened we got married and we had twins, but I did worry before sometimes because all the girls used to like him and he used to like them. I bothered him and he used to get mad at me.

"Now I stay home. The most I go out is twice a month to a dance or to a club meeting. Sometimes José takes me bowling, but not very much because I don't like to go out and leave the babies to my mother-in-law because she has two of her own and there's too much trouble with three more and they like to bother you. I don't miss going out. When we first got married, I missed it a lot. You have to get used to it anyway, like I have to do a lot of housework. I have to iron his clothes, do the babies' washing, keep an eye on them. Sometimes they invite me someplace and I say no, because I have things to do of my own. I feel proud about my babies. Not everybody can have twin sons."

Black

> *"When you see the vast majority of your twenty million Negro brothers smothering in an airtight cage of poverty in the midst of an affluent society . . . then you will understand why we find it difficult to wait."*
>
> —MARTIN LUTHER KING,
> *Letter from Birmingham Jail*, April 16, 1963

I don't know of any statistics that will back up my impression that the housing conditions of the Negro poor are more uniformly hopeless than those of the Puerto Ricans. The difference becomes apparent only after a good deal of poking around. On the surface there isn't much to choose between, but on occasions I found the Spanish located in a good-sized apartment which is actually rent-controlled, whereas the Negroes almost never had such luck. A superintendent seems more inclined to mistreat the Negro tenant. This may be a peculiarity of the local situation, where the Negro is more inclined to be a transient "loner," but the Puerto Ricans' loose unity and their impulse to communicate gives them a certain formidability. Often they know someone, like the Spanish teachers at the schools, who will put in a good word for them with the right agency. The Puerto Ricans have made more of a burning issue out of housing conditions in meetings, through the Spanish-language newspapers, and through vocal if not always effective housing groups, like the Puerto Rican Committee for Urban Renewal and the Spanish American Cultural Association.

The Negro poor in the Area have no such resources. In addition, they are black, which the majority of Puerto Ricans are not. They are barren of organizational support and get little help from local civil rights leaders, who are more interested in integration than in housing—who in fact often oppose public housing in the slums on the grounds that it will "freeze" the pattern of racial segregation. They support racial quotas in public housing, for integration's sake, which actually discriminates against the Negroes. The Puerto Ricans, for the most part, have just the opposite priority. They are not deeply concerned over racial integration because they feel it doesn't apply to them (they are "white") and they talk about better housing instead. The Negroes' housing problems are intensified by the fact that so many Negro families lack a male parent who can defend the family's rights and give the superintendent second thoughts about behaving himself. Also, the fatherless family has almost no chance of getting into the more desirable housing projects—at least those located outside the black ghettoes. Occasionally Spanish families pick themselves up and move out of town, or to a better part of the city, but by and large the Negro poor do not move, they are moved—usually because an agency has ordered them to do so. They have less freedom of choice about where to go next. In some parts of the Bronx and Long Island, for instance, landlords accept Spanish tenants and exclude Negroes. I know of no situation where the reverse is true.

According to the Kraft survey, the Negro poor in the Area feel in general that the housing they have is better than what they had before they moved to the West Side from other parts of the city. This cannot be a compliment to what they have, which is appalling; it can only emphasize the rottenness of what they have escaped. When the Negro complains about his housing, there is the special tone to the complaint, as if he were commenting on an incurable, lifelong disease. The Puerto Ricans object with a violence that means they expect something to be done. Of course these are generalizations, and as such there are at least half as many holes in them as cloth.

What the Negro sees ahead of him is precisely what he sees in the rear-view mirror looking into the past. I was impressed, in talking to Negro families, at the manner in which history intruded itself into the conversation and unsettled the atmosphere. The Puerto Rican likes to talk about his life on the island, his family, his town—his old place, in other words. To the adult Negro the past is something that cannot be discussed without anguish, yet something he cannot avoid talking about. Usually the only Negroes who talk about the South with any happiness are the children, who might tell about a grandmother's farm they visited in the summer. If there is any hope in the Negroes' talk about the future, it has to do with these same optimistic young children—I say "young" because the optimism fades rapidly by the time they are in their late teens. The Negro's stubborn, almost irrational hope in his children often seems to be the only support he owns. It explains why, over and over, the parent talked of education, and, in this connection, it is interesting to note that parents spoke in generally approving fashion and the children almost always affectionately about their schools and their teachers.

My impulse in writing about people like the Serranos and the Acostas was to use the past tense because life seemed to change rather rapidly for the Puerto Ricans—there were more and bigger ups and downs—and I had the feeling that anything said about them one day would be badly out of date a year later. In writing about the Negroes, however, it often seemed more natural to use the present tense. They seemed to be frozen in their predicament—they might move to another place, but their prospects would remain just about what they had always been. I mention this subjective reaction not to justify it, but to explain why I refer to the Negroes who lived in the building in the Eighties near Riverside Drive as if I had seen them yesterday.

The apartment house is an all-Negro island in a line of comfortable greystone buildings populated mainly by middle-class families, a good number of them Jews. The outside of the Negroes' building resembles the others on the drive, but the similarity ends in the vestibule. The door is locked, the buzzers are out of order, and it is impossible to find anyone's name in the buzzer slots, one characteristic of a slum property. The only way to enter is to wait until somebody comes out and then slip in before the door closes. The building has about fifty apartments and a superintendent who is invisible except on days when he has to collect the rent. The elevator is a relic of an age when the building was occupied by a different clientele. However, it does work, which is more than can be said for the basic appliances in the apartment occupied by Arthur and Catherine Whitman, their daughter Emmaline, and two children of relatives from South Carolina.

When Mrs. Whitman opens the door a beam of electric light from the apartment illuminates the black hallways and reveals that the walls and ceiling are cracked and unpainted. The Whitmans' apartment is shaped like a dumbbell with two nine-by-twelve rooms connected by a "hall" the length of the bathroom door which opens into it. One room is a combination living room and bedroom with an old rug and a couple of small tables. When the Whitmans moved in two years ago, about three-fourths of this furniture was in the apartment, which means that the landlord could rent the place "furnished" for $26 a week with the permission of the Office of Rent and Rehabilitation. The other room, a kitchen-bedroom, contains what amount to facsimiles of kitchen appliances. The stove would be rejected if offered to the Salvation Army's secondhand furniture store. Next to it is an oyster-colored sink a foot wide and two feet long. The cold water that comes out of the hot-water faucet is an improvement over the bathroom faucets, which have produced no water at all for two years. The family inspects its food before eating to make sure it does not contain flecks of paint that continually drop off the ceiling into the cooking pots.

Two large holes in the kitchen floor have been there so long that the Whitmans step over them without looking. The bathroom is ventilated by a large cavity in the floor left by the plumbers when they grew tired of trying to repair the toilet. Occasionally the hole emits smoke and gas. Various members of the family have asked the superintendent to do something, but whenever the Whitmans are able to find him he is just leaving the building and will not be back until tomorrow, or he may say that the Whitmans' rent goes to the landlord so they should talk to the landlord. This is impossible because the landlord is not a man, it is a corporation. For each of the several hundred weeks they have been guests of the corporation, the Whitmans have paid their rent from what Mrs. Whitman earns as a chambermaid in West Side hotels and what Mr. Whitman makes in a Queens car-wash establishment. They are not on welfare.

There is a free-wheeling sociability in the Whitman apartment, the center of their whole life outside of school and work. Emmaline's friends come in and out incessantly. A three-month-old baby zipped up in a plaid sleeping bag is lying on one of the beds. He is the only son of an only parent, a pretty twenty-year-old girl who is watching to make sure he doesn't roll off onto the floor. The Whitmans have many friends in the building, but they will leave gladly if they can get into a public housing project. "Never mind where the project is," Mrs. Whitman says. "Brooklyn, the Bronx, Staten Island, Alaska— just a place to live." Among other things, a place with a new coat of paint. On the wallpaper behind the couch where she sits is the sort of horizontal stain that comes from people's resting their heads against the wall over the past ten or twelve years.

The day's events, which include Mrs. Whitman's being laid off from her job, have not dampened her spirits. The business agent of her union, Local 60, told her that she should have had a week's notice from the hotel, and that she should keep going in and punching the time clock. Mrs. Whitman says that this would be silly. She is a big woman with a resonant voice, born in Atlanta twenty-seven years ago. Her husband is ten years older. They have been in the city for five years. Their daughter, Emmaline, fourteen, is a healthy, animated girl, and when she begins to talk she becomes even more attractive. She wears a bright red shirt, gray skirt and the white socks and sneakers that are more or less a trademark of the girls who go to Junior High School 44. Emmaline adds a few notes now and then to her mother's comments about the apartment. She reports the building has never been sprayed for roaches and shows her arm—"This is where I got bitten by bugs. The superintendent blames the bugs on my dog." There are no shades or blinds in the apartment, she points out.

Emmaline has a 90 average in school. "I love my teachers," she says. "You can talk with them. They're all real nice and they really know how to teach." She knows children who have moved away from the area but still go to J.H.S. 44. One is now in Washington Heights but comes to school on the subway. Even when such a practice was illegal, it was commonly accepted by the teachers, especially if the student was a good one.* One of Emmaline's big worries is that if the family is accepted in a public housing project a long distance away she will have to give up J.H.S. 44.

After she gets her high school diploma she would like to go to business school. The teachers have been giving her advice and telling her to aim high. She has thought about being a doctor, but she says it takes too long. "You have to wait eight years before you can earn a living. I thought about being a nurse too. In the summertime I work with the Red Cross. I can be a hospital volunteer next year because I'll be over fourteen."

Arthur Whitman gets home from his job in a Queens car wash by around six. He is a tall man with a sensitive, handsome face. The weather decides how much money he makes. He may work three or he may work six days a week, depending on the rain—people do not

---

* School authorities now allow a child to remain in the same school even though his family has moved out of the school district, if the parents wish to exercise this option.

like to have their cars washed on rainy days. It does not even have to rain to take away a day's pay. In the winter the snow lays the men off. If Mr. Whitman works six days he earns $60, but this does not happen very often. If he has the chance he will work ten hours a day. His employer gives no paid vacations.

Mrs. Whitman tells her husband that she has just lost her job. He nods his head and begins to explain why his family prefers New York to Atlanta, and why Emmaline was willing to give up her own room in a nice, clean project to move north.

"There's a different way of living up here. You're more free; you can get into an argument and call each other names and you don't go to jail and get beat up or turn missing. Here you can set where you want to and eat what you want to eat. Down South you have to eat out of a window, standing up. There's a difference between schools and the police down there and up here. People care here about education and the police are better than in the South. When you're arrested here you go to jail. Down there they whop you. If they don't like the way you smell they give you ninety days. Down there you feel like you're more like a child than a grown man. The way you're treated here is something different. It's better living in New York. The wages are better. Here you get $15, $12, $10 a day. The kids' education is better.

"I never had a chance to learn down there. My father died when I was a little kid. I got to second grade. Then I left to help my mother on the farm. They didn't care. When Emmaline came up here she didn't know anything. She just read a little but not much. But she took hold here. The teachers she had in Atlanta were interested in her but there were too many kids. Down there if you didn't have lunch money the kids would go hungry. They'd walk to school. Here it's different. My daughter's changed a lot. She knows how to talk now. She knows how to act. She can speak freely. She's not scared."

When he left his mother's farm, Mr. Whitman worked at the Atlanta-Thomas station on the railroad, loading and unloading. He also worked as a sanitation man collecting garbage. In New York he was a plumber's helper for a while but the plumbers' unions see to it that Negroes never graduate out of the helper's category, no matter how long they've "helped." His past jobs and his employment prospects gall Mr. Whitman, but nothing erases his happiness in his daughter. He spoke about a paper she wrote on the Cuban crisis when

President Kennedy announced the blockade. Mr. Whitman doesn't think about war very much. "They tell us to fight, but we got no country."

"We've got *this* country," his wife says. "We were born here."

When James Meredith went to the University of Mississippi, the Whitmans prayed for him.

Barbara Jarvis, the mother of two and the wife of no one, has lived in the building since 1961 with the children and her blind sister. She pays more than the Whitmans, $32 a week, for which she gets an extra bedroom and hot water and, most of the time, steam heat, which qualifies her place as a luxury apartment. Such luxury apartments Mrs. Jarvis wouldn't wish on her worst enemy.

"There are things like the plaster in the bathroom hanging and coming off. The toilet broke for three months. You had to pour water in to flush it. When I had the apartment upstairs the ceiling fell and I had to move out and come down here because they took so long to fix it. After the sprinkler system broke it took them about a month to fix that and we stayed in one room for two weeks. A lady is on the fourth floor and you should go in there. It's like being in the street, it's so cold. She pays $35 a week and gets no heat."

The building inspector visited the house about two months ago, Mrs. Jarvis says, and "he didn't even go into my bathroom to look at it."

Mrs. Jarvis' five-year-old daughter goes to kindergarten at P.S. 9 on Eighty-third Street and West End Avenue. Mrs. Jarvis has had a few meetings with Dinah's teacher, Mrs. Felt, but she doesn't go to the parents association meetings. Dinah is getting along well, and is happy with her teacher.

"We paste, we draw pictures, we paint, we play doll house, we go over to the puzzles, then we build houses," she says, the words tumbling out. "I want to be a nurse because every time somebody gets sick they have to get a doctor. My doll's name is Shirley Temple. My grandmother gave it to me for Christmas. She lives in New York, my grandmother. We always go to the library when it's cleanup time. Teacher, she plays the piano. Then we go to the library and we play with doll houses and we play records. Then we go over to the girls' bathroom and the boys they go to the other one. After that we come out for lunch. I don't go back after lunch. I play. In the summer I go outside and play in front of the house because my mommy tells me to do that so she knows I'm near."

The superintendent comes up in everybody's conversation. Everyone spells his name differently; Socco, Socolo, Stocker, Solow, Socow. Mrs. Jarvis uses a different name every time she refers to him. Mr. Socco discourages his women tenants from complaining by disappearing and feigning deafness. If this does not work he terrifies them. "Who needs you?" he'll say. "I'll put you out in the street. You're lucky you're here at all with those kids." Although such evictions would be illegal this is of no help to the tenants.

Mr. Socco's threats are law because the tenants do not know their rights, and they do not have the time or the money to hire a lawyer and go to court.

Mr. Socco uses the children as hostages in his war against their parents. For instance, Mr. and Mrs. Robert Lester have children, three, five, and seven years old, and have tried for years to get into public housing. They recently asked the super to fix the light in the bathroom. Since they pay $128 a month to the landlord, this would seem to be a small request, but the super told Mrs. Lester that if she didn't like it she and her children could move out into the street.

"We sleep in this room and the kids in the bedroom. We have just two couches. Today, we don't have no steam. The kids, they stay full of colds all the time. You know what I did? Once I held on to my rent to see whether the super would fix the heat. So he sends a dispossess notice. I've never had a lawyer. I asked the rent control people to help me but they couldn't find out the name of my landlord so they didn't come back. They just sent us a letter saying they couldn't get no information on him." Mrs. Lester had once thought about going around to the other tenants to see if they would also refuse to pay the rent but nothing came of it.

Plumbing is the universal curse. Rosemary Wellin tells about how, in her $128-a-month apartment, a pipe burst and drenched her clothes and the wardrobe of a woman in the apartment below. The heat Mrs. Wellin was getting at the time could be measured by the fact that several icicles formed in her room, some of them six or seven inches long. The superintendent promised to give the ladies a discount to take care of cleaning their clothes, but no discount ever materialized, and the women's things are still at the cleaner's.

When the plumbers came to repair the broken pipe, they knocked holes in the walls searching for the leak. One of the holes, never patched up, was so large that Mrs. Wellin had to put a cardboard partition over it to keep from looking into the place next door. Most of the heat, what there is of it, seems to go into the apartments on the A side of the building, while the people on the B side get nothing (the people on the A side say that the reverse is true). When Mrs. Wellin calls the building inspector about a building violation, the inspector will ask her to call him back later. When she calls back she is told that there are no violations in the building.

In the midst of this, Mrs. Wellin feeds the family and sends the children off to school. For breakfast she gives them hot cereal one day and cold cereal the next. She tries not to repeat the menu. Her greatest difficulty is to get them to eat their vegetables. They like fruit and fruit juices and canned spaghetti, pork and beans, and frankfurters. The rest of the time Mrs. Wellin tries to find another place to live by looking through classified ads in the papers and calling. Sometimes she comes across a good apartment, but, when she says she has three children, it turns out that the apartment is not available after all.

The Negroes and Puerto Ricans living along West Ninety-fourth Street, in the urban renewal area, pay about half the rent the Whitmans pay, but their housing is even worse, if that is possible. Instead of a Mr. Socco they have to deal with the city's Department of Real Estate, which acquired the building and will demolish it. The city purchased a corpse. What little maintenance the private owner had given the building ceased completely when the city announced it was going to condemn. The landlord's decision is simply good business, since condemnation prices paid by the city do not compensate for anything but major repairs, and sometimes not even those. Rents are slightly over $60 for a room and a half with a hallway bath. When the city took over, the previous owner made off with all the furniture, leaving each tenant a bedstead and a flea-bitten mattress. Looking out her window one day, Sarah Leighton, a Negro mother, saw her landlady peddling the icebox she had hauled out of the Leighton apartment a few hours earlier.

Any hope by Mrs. Leighton that a new era would dawn when the city took charge was misplaced. She makes the following report on the state of affairs under municipal management: "Bathtub and sink don't work. Holes in floor under sink. Plumbers came around a month ago and tore up but didn't fix. I complain but nothing is done. They expect me to pay rent but I don't see why. They want to throw you out if you don't pay. It's worse now than before the city took over. Besides, we got the same super as before. Sometimes one week we don't have no cold water. I have to go across the street to get water to drink. Sometimes there's no hot water. Sometimes no steam on cold days. This has happened since the city took over too. There is some plumbers here to fix things but nothing's been fixed. The pipes is all on the floor. You can't take a bath. There is no handles on the faucets to turn so you can get water. It's terrible."

An informal autopsy on one of the broken kitchen pipes reveals a flaky outer layer of oxidized iron. Next is a thick inner wall of a stiff gray substance which, when probed with a pocket knife, has the texture of a cirrhotic liver. The hole in the center of the pipe is about the circumference of a lead pencil. The electrical wiring is 90 percent illegal, encased in broken tubing, with wires winding in through broken chunks of plaster and terminating in sprigs of frayed copper. Much of the wiring has given up any relationship with sockets or fixtures.

Mrs. Leighton sits on the bedstead, her shoulders sagging. She minds her own affairs and doesn't mingle with other people on the block. "Since I've been living here, nobody hasn't interfered with me and I'm friendly to people who treat me all right." She has the distinction of never having been robbed. If a thief did enter her apartment, one quick look around would tell him he was in the wrong place.*

While Mrs. Leighton is insured against theft by her poverty she is defenseless against other intrusions. "You find in a house that's open all the time the lock is broken on the door. The people come in and out. See my door how it falls open. For the last couple of weeks somebody's been pushing at the door and if I don't have a dog here to bark when I'm sleeping or something I wouldn't know what would happen. It's so dangerous. It's very poor for a woman to live by herself. There's police protection, they say, but if trouble comes they're standing on the corner somewhere else."

* Even their poverty does not spare prospective victims. In some cases, a burglar, finding nothing valuable to steal, has taken revenge by smashing windows or throwing eggs, milk, leftovers, and other contents of the icebox on the floor.

She is also one of the vast army of people who are hoping to get into public housing. She once filled out an application for a project and received notice that the city would put her application on a waiting list to be "processed downtown." To be "processed downtown" is the end of hope. Mrs. Leighton has never heard a thing about her application since April, 1961.

Across the street from Mrs. Leighton, Mrs. Isabel Thoman has been emancipated from faulty plumbing, freezing weather, and cockroaches because she has the good fortune to have a superintendent who keeps up these services and cleans the hallways. The $109 rent for her two rooms in a shabby brownstone is not as exorbitant as that paid by the Whitmans, although $55 a room is not far below what the well-to-do tenants of the new Park West Village pay with air conditioning and utilities thrown in. Mothers in Mrs. Thoman's position demonstrate that, with housing aches and pains out of the way, the main subject on their minds is their children's education and personal safety.

To Mrs. Thoman, education is the escape hatch from the sort of life in which she has been imprisoned since she was born in Virginia. As a little girl she walked to a one-room schoolhouse with the other Negro children while the white children rode the bus. "We only went to school six months, the colored children, and the white children went nine months. We used to have to stop, we colored, because we children had to go to work in the fields." The "great mistake" of her life was a lack of education which has "pulled me down" ever since. "I didn't have a chance as a child to know things and how to grow up and make a real life for myself. My life was just a bad dream of a life. Child work, then housework later on till my back gave out and so I lost my own chance and I even lost the chance to earn a living for my children."

Mrs. Thoman's hopes hinge on the success of her three children in school, and the children feel the pressure. The oldest and the youngest of the three boys are excited by school and are doing well. The youngest boy is in a class for intellectually gifted children at P.S. 75. The oldest child is doing well at Joan of Arc Junior High School, where he takes Spanish and French and plays the trombone in the school orchestra. Many of his friends speak Spanish, which gives him an opportunity to practice. He is planning to go to Charles Evans Hughes, an academic high school. He reads the front pages and the sports section of the *New York Times*.

"My boy understands how important education is," his mother declares. "Him and I discuss it all the time. Just get all the education you can get, I tell him. He says he wants to get a part-time job and he's going down to get his Social Security number, now that he's old enough. He is going to try and save money for college."

William, the second oldest of Mrs. Thoman's three sons, is having a troubled time. He was getting along well at a former school, then slipped badly after being transferred to his present school, where he began sniffing glue. His failures are magnified by the success of his brothers. The school staff, finding Mrs. Thoman cooperative, has approached the boy's problem carefully and he has not been consigned to a "600" school for problem children. The Board of Education's Bureau of Child Guidance has conferred several times on his case with a doctor at St. Luke's Hospital, where Mrs. Thoman takes him once a week. Her neighbors tell her that her son will outgrow his problem, and have tried to discourage her efforts to get medical help. The mother has made up her mind to quit talking to her neighbors about the whole affair; her son, she says, can be helped and the time to do it is now.

"You'd be surprised at my neighbors who come from the South," she says. "They just don't know and understand the world. They don't do things. I talk to people who are supposed to have gone through high school but they are ignorant. One of my friends came from the South and just fell into the slums. Now he just sits in his room and complains. He doesn't think you can get an opportunity, but you do have the privilege of it." Some of Mrs. Thoman's acquaintances say she is a "sucker" for talking like this.

She has found help from other sources, such as the Houltons, the leaders of the block association, also mentioned by the Acostas. Everyone—the Puerto Ricans and Negroes—likes them, she says, because they take a real interest in the people. She says she used to belong to the NAACP and go to meetings, but "they never did work for me. They didn't do much in this neighborhood." Her disillusionment goes back to a time when, in attempting to help a young Negro girl get an apartment, she sent her to the NAACP. The organization did nothing, she reports, and she has never asked them for assistance again. Mrs. Thoman feels that the parents association meetings might be worthwhile but she can't find a baby sitter, and if she takes the children to the meeting they are asleep before it is over.

William likes the after-school recreation center at P.S. 163 but

about a year ago a gang attacked him, so his mother does not let him
go any more. The police have been very cooperative—"They are very
nice. They always come when you call them, just like they came the
night William was attacked, but then when they got there the gang
was gone, so what can they do? They just stood around." She thinks
the police "have been very kind to people but there's just too many
people speaking different languages, and they don't understand each
other."

One thing pleases Mrs. Thoman very much: "So many children
going to school together from different countries, they growing up
together, love each other. They don't have the feeling we had when
we were small."

I owe my acquaintance with Mr. Jennings to a Puerto Rican in a
tweed suit named Frederico Zayas. While I was in the office of the
Hudson Neighborhood Conservation project (an agency financed
with public funds to rehabilitate housing just west of the urban
renewal area), Mr. Zayas came in to complain furiously about
stopped-up toilets. He implied that he got very little cooperation from
his building superintendent, Mr. Jennings, a Negro. I made an
appointment with Mr. Zayas, but when I went around to see him he
wasn't in. But I did find Mr. Jennings.

The building is an ancient tenement on a corner of Amsterdam
in the middle Nineties. Although there are some roaches running
about, the hallways and communal bathrooms had been washed
recently. Mr. Jennings has two stuffy rooms, a bedroom and a living
room, each about ten feet square, and a closet-sized kitchen. Without
an electric light burning all day the place would be dark regardless of
the light pink walls. Mr. Jennings is a heavy-set man about 45, one of
whose legs terminates in a steel peg attached to a stump just below
the knee. A two-year-old baby sleeping in a crib in the corner stirs
when it hears our voices.

Mr. Jennings takes care of two apartment buildings. The building
where he lives has thirty-two units, which are furnished rooms and
apartments; the other building has six units. Since the buildings are
not in the urban renewal area and therefore will not be taken over by
the city, the owner has plans to break through the walls of some of
the apartments to enlarge them and install bathrooms. Single rooms
rent for $11 to $13 a week and the doubles from $14 to $16 a week.
All have kitchens with refrigerators.

Besides the baby in the corner, Mr. Jennings has a twelve-year-old son. His wife, Suzy, works all day as a laundress. He was born in Macon, Georgia, has lived in New York eighteen years, uptown, downtown, and crosstown. Since the city opened up the Hudson Neighborhood Conservation office, Mr. Jennings says he has been pestered with building inspectors, plumbing inspectors, electrical inspectors wanting to see what is going on and make reports. It is hard enough for Mr. Jennings himself to keep track of his tenants, who move in and out a great deal. A woman upstairs named Josephine has been to Puerto Rico three or four times but always returns to Mr. Jennings' building, which he says is a testimonial to the management. He maintains that he keeps a nice clean place but that when some of his tenants have a complaint they go to the city right away instead of coming to him. The first time he hears about a broken pipe is when the Hudson people send somebody in to lecture him. To avoid this roundabout system of communication, Mr. Jennings called a meeting to tell his tenants to let him be the first to know when something breaks down so he can fix it. If they don't get satisfaction after complaining, he said, then they should call in the people from outside. He says the owner of the building has been quite willing to provide money for repairs.

Mr. Jennings runs up and down a lot of staircases for a man with one leg. While he was a boy he was a tap dancer and traveled all around. He learned to dance after he lost his leg at the age of nine, when he fell under a train while riding a bicycle. Mr. Jennings' father was a comedian in a traveling show and Mr. Jennings went with him. "I used to hang around out in back, stealing some ideas off the folks that did this dancing and acting, and the next thing I knew I was out there dancing myself. I done real good up until the time I got hurt again. I was making $150, sometimes $300 a week with the big bands." Fifteen years ago Mr. Jennings had to give up dancing for good. During a show at the Apollo Theater on 125th Street in Harlem he was performing on a table which broke and he crashed onto the stage. After a time in the hospital he danced again until water formed on his knee. "They kept draining it and baking it off. Then I'd start back to dancing and then I'd have to stop because it would get worse. Finally the doctor said that if I didn't quit dancing I'd lose that leg, too."

Now Mr. Jennings climbs stairs, sweeps and cleans and carries furniture. It seems as if he has always been hauling things on his back. "The only time I ever minded carrying and working hard was when I worked in a furniture store here in Manhattan. It was all right. I had a good boss but when the boss's daughter married a fellow, the son-in-law became the boss. He never wanted to see us sit down." Up to this point, Mr. Jennings had seemed rather phlegmatic, but now he was becoming highly agitated. "He'd tell us to carry something out and then he'd say you can carry it back in. We'd have a truck come along and then we'd take stuff out to wait for the truck. Then the truck wouldn't show up and he'd make us take it in. He knew we'd have to bring it out again. Once I said I'd get a Pepsi-Cola and I came in and sat down. Right away he said, 'Put that couch over here, will you?' I said, 'I'll take it back in but I'm not gonna take it back here again.' As soon as I got it in he wanted me to take it back out and I quit. The boss came to me and said, 'Won't you come back?' I said, 'No, as long as that boy is there. He just doesn't like to see people rest.' Why, we even had to eat lunch out of tin cans while we was carrying things on our backs."

As his memories of the past lead him back to the South, Mr. Jennings becomes more and more restless. Two years ago he had been in Macon. "There were cops all over the place. You'd go in and drink a can of beer in a bar, come out and stomp your foot and they'd lock you up for a drunk. You only have to drink half a can of beer. I saw all kinds of people locked up on Friday afternoon back there. I saw a boy playing in the street and he stumbled and almost fell and a cop came up and arrested him. Lots of colored folks down there have nice houses but you can't do nothing. You're scared to drive a car for fear you're going to do something wrong and they're going to arrest you. You can't make a turn except at exactly the right place and you've got to make it just right because somebody is going to arrest you."

Mr. Jennings says in spite of everything even Macon is going to change. It will take time but "people ain't seen the end of it down there. When I was a kid in Macon there was no colored police. Now they got colored police all over. You can go in different stores and people can buy houses where they couldn't before. It will just take a little time."

For several years Mr. Jennings has tried to persuade his mother to come North but she worries about losing her pension if she moves. She says she is thinking about coming but she has been saying this for a long time. Mr. Jennings wants his children to grow up in the North. His older son goes to P.S. 75, which he says is a nice school, close and everything. He has thought about moving to New Jersey. He was over there one time when he was sick and liked it. He once hoped he might be able to buy an old house someplace with a spot to park his car. "But then I got laid off at DuMont's where I was working so I guess I'll never get out there to New Jersey."

With the past out of his mind, Mr. Jennings fell silent. The baby on the bed let out a faint cry.

4

THE OTHERS

Illegal People

EDNA, WHO HAS LIVED, OFF AND ON, ALONG WEST Eighty-seventh Street for the past seven years, has never had any dealing with pimps or middlemen and still has a good figure after several years of hustling, at an age when, according to the superintendent of her building, most prostitutes are "over the hill." She has just gotten out of jail after doing time for soliciting and will have plastic surgery over her left eye, where the brow is puffy and scarred.

Now that she is back in circulation Edna is starting from scratch, having lost her old apartment and everything in it, including her clothes and a bag of heroin. On leaving prison she received enough money to pay for her room and board for a night. Leaving jail was not exactly a graduation, since she has been in and out several times before—"you might say I'm a frequent visitor"—and she will probably go back there soon. "You sign a lot of papers when you get out. Then you go back and take up your old ways."

Edna's admission that she'll be in jail again is somewhat of a contradiction to a packaged optimism which she carries about with her like a handbag and opens up to the prison psychologist. This time, she says, she is going to make a change. The first thing is to go back to Brooklyn where she grew up and got her high school diploma. Anything to get away from the West Side, where she paid $22.50 a week for two and a half rooms on Eighty-seventh Street and was known to everyone on the Vice Squad. To raise the rent she had to hustle the first night out of jail. She does not want to see Eighty-seventh Street again or any of the people she used to associate with there. As far as family is concerned, there is none. "I've only got me," she says.

Edna has been enrolled at a number of state-supported educational institutions, beginning with Westfield, a girls' correction home in New Jersey where she was installed as a wayward minor at the age of sixteen by her grandmother, who thought she was too wild at the time. Westfield seems to have made sure that Edna would live up to the grandmother's prediction that she was headed for hell. When Edna emerged she said she was "a postgraduate in anything you want to name." Additional postgraduate training began in 1951 during the first of many terms at the House of Detention for Women in Greenwich Village.

Prostitution is Edna's method of raising money to feed a narcotics habit she acquired ten years ago. When she is on dope she stays at home until ten in the evening. Then she goes out on the street "until God knows when, depending on my luck." She no longer works Broadway, a favorite spot for hustlers. She never had any trouble there and was never beaten up, but there are too many policemen on the street these days. She claims she generally "finds favor with my friends," who use her because they are lacking something at home. They are grateful to her and she is grateful to them but she dislikes the wives, who, she claims, are behind the movement to put hustlers in jail. "After all, we don't go to the men's houses and ring doorbells. A hustler shouldn't be put in jail unless she raises a disturbance."

Edna's very short blue dress shows nice legs and an unscarred skin. She is proud of two things: her body, and the fact that she has never been on welfare—"I've always been able to support myself." Her arms are smooth except for needle marks on the inside of her left forearm. Some girls look pretty good, she says. "But then I know one girl, in two or three years her whole body looked like nickels and dimes. The difference between me and her is like night and day."

She claims she went to jail last time because a police officer lied, an automatic remark with all hustlers. A moment later she will say, "After all, it was the officer's job, you can't get mad at them. They have to keep up the record." She claims the officer who arrested her propositioned her and then "went all the way with me and busted me after it was all over. The way it goes, you are supposed to proposition the officer and then he can make the arrest, but it doesn't matter, they always say you propositioned them and asked for the money. In court it's the officer's word against you."

Some policemen apologize and say they are sorry but they need the arrest, according to Edna, then in court they may testify in such a way that the girl is acquitted.

"Other cops are plain nasty—what they got in there for hearts is just plastic surgery. They really hunt you down."

The way for a girl to protect herself is to have an agreement with the John (client) that if they are caught the John will tell the policeman that the girl "gave it to him for free." Sometimes the judge will be a little sympathetic. In cases where a John is asked to testify and happens to be married, the judge may tell him he doesn't have to talk, in which case the girl is let go. Most of the police are "clean," Edna thinks, and, despite what some girls say, they don't shake down hustlers. However, some girls arrested for soliciting suddenly find bags of heroin in their pocketbooks as they are standing in a station house. How does a hustler identify a plainclothesman from the Vice Squad? These days they have a kind of "Ivy League" look, she says.

The hustler's account of her difficulties with the Vice Squad gives the impression she is pretty much at their mercy, but from the policeman's point of view she is a difficult bird to trap, at least in large quantities. Despite the constant complaints about prostitutes in the section one sergeant patrols, he reports it is very hard to get a "direct" on a prostitute (that is, arrest them for making a "direct" proposition to a policeman). "Prostitutes can smell a policeman and they can run like a deer. It's their business to know what a policeman looks like. They are tricky. You have no idea. Policemen have to be taller than five feet eight to get on the force but they can't be too tall either, so the girls proposition real tall guys or real short ones, or guys with thick glasses who look like they couldn't pass the physical." Consequently, plainclothesmen may wear mustaches, carry tool boxes, or pose as addicts and beatniks.

A good percentage of the West Side's prostitute population spends at least part of its time in the Women's House of Detention, a home away from home that looks like a badly designed public housing project in the center of Greenwich Village downtown. Occasionally, particularly around election times, there are rashes of newspaper stories charging that the House is filthy and that its homosexual inmates indulge in regular sex orgies. The city always denies these charges categorically after conducting its own investigation. Never-

theless, along with its grimness there is a certain irrepressible informality about the place that suggests some of the penal institutions
and boarding schools described by Charles Dickens. When the
weather is warm, boy friends or families with children dressed in their
starched best stand on the sidewalks and shout up conversations as
high as the fifth or sixth floors. There is something of the same
informality inside the building as well, if one makes allowances for
the stringent security regulations and the fact that this is, after all, an
outdated, overcrowded prison. Many of the girls are on work assignments throughout the jail, and some wait on table in the officials'
dining rooms, serving, among others, the prison superintendent.

With all its faults, the House offers accommodations and a menu
which are an improvement on what most of the girls are used to on
the outside. In addition each of the girls gets medical attention which,
however spotty, is better than that which most law-abiding welfare
mothers and their children can hope for. One might define the House
as a municipally owned hotel for minor offenders which is similar to
most of the city's correctional institutions.* The racial breakdown of
the House population is about 60 percent Negro, 20 percent Puerto
Rican, and about 20 percent Caucasian white. These figures contrast
with the New York State prison population, which is 50 percent
Negro, 10 percent Puerto Rican, and 40 percent Caucasian, and the
figures in federal and state penitentiaries throughout the United
States, where the white population rises to 50 percent and the Negro
percentage falls to less than 50 percent.

Anna Kross, the Commissioner of Corrections under Mayor Wagner, did not advertise the virtues of the House of Detention. A short
lady in her seventies who wears oddly designed hats, she was one of
the few city officials in that administration who criticized their own
departments. She said that the only thing that happened to people in
most of her jails was that they were kept there a while and then
released to go out and do the same things that got them into jail in the
first place. The worst thing that can happen to an inmate of a New
York City jail, she said, is for him not to escape.

Dr. Kross said she needed twice as many psychiatrists to do the
bare minimum job in the corrections program, but she never got

* In New York City, 42 percent serve ten days or less, and in 1961 only
1,800 people served terms of one to three years for felonies. Of 150,000 con-
victions in the same year, approximately 47,000 served one-day to three-year
sentences.

them. Prison psychiatrist Dr. Harvey Bluestone says the prison system has positions open and the money to pay psychiatrists fairly well but that there is no supervising psychiatrist who can plan an effective recruiting program. The majority of psychiatrists in New York City use about half their time with private patients. The prison system has tried to compete for the other half of their time, but it has been unsuccessful.

Toni, a West Sider with a ninety-day sentence for soliciting, is one of the star boarders at the House. She is a small, pale girl with curly dark hair and freckles, wears glasses, and has a thirteen-year-old daughter who is in Puerto Rico with her grandmother. Toni does not remember exactly how many times she has been a guest of the House. "Just say numerous occasions." Her husband, a musician, knows about her narcotics habit and her prostitution. He is a former addict who broke the habit before he met his wife. She says he has "a strong will which I don't have, and he has been trying to help me." Once he placed her in Manhattan General Hospital but in two days she checked out. "What would have been the use? I've been in and out so many years I don't know what it would be like to be any different. I'm tired of being in jail. I wish I could start all over again but I know what starting all over again will be." The last time she was discharged from the House she stayed off the habit for two weeks. After other discharges she went back to dope immediately. Generally, the longer the jail sentence, the longer she is able to stay away from dope when she gets out, but never long enough.

Toni grew up in Spanish Harlem on 118th Street, just around the corner from the city's main center of dope traffic. Every other young boy, many of them of school age, seemed to be on drugs. The young ones "start with the three-dollar bag but as the habit gets big the cost of the habit goes up." She began with reefers at the age of twelve, and came around to heroin at nineteen when she was visiting relatives in Puerto Rico. Back in New York, she talked a man who had previously sold her marijuana into getting her heroin. "First, you start with skinpops, then you snort it, then you mainline—put it right into the vein." In 1953 she became a prostitute in order to get money for dope and was arrested for soliciting. Because her mother spoke to the police and offered to help, Toni received a thirty-day suspended sentence. Later she began a regular series of sojourns in jail.

On the outside, Toni now takes heroin five times a day. "You have to take more and more. If you don't take enough you get really sick."

She puts out her arms. "They don't look so bad. I stopped going into the arm because the vein was too hard to hit, so I started putting it in here." She pulls down the collar of her dress. The right side of her neck is laced with dark red gouges. There is also a dark red scar on the inside of her elbow.

When Toni was on the West Side, she woke up every morning thinking about where to get the money for her next shot. If she had a bag left she got out the cooker, usually a spoon. If her supply was used up she went out immediately for more money, or if she had the money she lay around until it was time to take a shot again. She does not go to shows because shows cost money and money is only for dope. She made extra money "boosting," a booster being a shoplifter who carries stuff out of stores between her legs, under her skirt. She was not interested in dancing. "You jump around and use up the stuff awful fast that way. I just want to sit and nod."

When she was going to high school, Toni thought about becoming a dressmaker or designer. Her grades were good, she says, but she is rather vague and melancholy about her school experience. She had difficulty making friends and was in difficulty with her mother. "I could hardly speak any Spanish. We couldn't understand each other. We didn't have the same language. I always seemed to be on the street, just like most of the other kids I grew up with. They're all addicts now, mostly in institutions."

A surgeon at Montefiore Hospital will remove the scars from Toni's neck and arms if she wants it done. She doesn't. "Why bother? I'll just be putting them back again."

Some inmates of the House of Detention have not committed any crime. One of these is the baby born to Dorothy, of West Eighty-eighth Street, an addict and a prostitute. This is a customary procedure for Dorothy. Of her six previous children, the first, third, and fifth were delivered in penitentiaries of some sort or another. Dorothy's new baby began life as a narcotics addict, and had to be detoxified in jail.* Another of her babies underwent this experience in 1958 and is now living with her grandmother. The dope habit costs Dorothy $200 to $300 a week. She has never had venereal disease and goes to a doctor on 125th Street who "takes all the girls and sees

---

* Dr. Alonzo Yerby, Commissioner of Hospitals, reported that 800 addict-babies were born in New York City in 1965, a rise of 20 percent over the previous year. *The New York Times,* March 18, 1966.

that they're clean." Hustlers have less VD, she says, than girls who do it for free, one reason being that if a hustler has VD she gets a tougher jail sentence. It is a good idea for her to be carrying a health report if she is arrested.

Dorothy, now doing her ninth term at the House, is also a graduate of Westfield, where she served eighteen months of a three-year term. The charges are always the same: soliciting. All but one of the fathers of Dorothy's six children are drug addicts locked up in various institutions. She had her first child when she was twelve, the second at thirteen, the third at fifteen, the fourth at seventeen, the fifth at twenty-five, the sixth at twenty-six. Dorothy has been hustling since she was twenty-three and has boosted since she was thirty. Her clients "come and get what they want. Then they don't care about me and I don't care about them. My father was a hustler and a gambler and my mother was a hustler. She was real easy for everybody. I was born out of wedlock. That was the only thing I had on my mind. My mother was born out of wedlock and so was my father." Dorothy considers herself a man's property when he pays for her. She will use contraceptives if the man wishes it that way but will not if he doesn't.

Dorothy supplements her income by stealing. "I go into a man's pockets if I can. I get his money first; if I don't, I have to lay in bed with him." No man has ever been interested in her although she has thought at times that she has met someone who cared about her. Now that she is in prison and there is no more heroin or cocaine, no habit, no stealing, Dorothy has other preoccupations. "When girls come into the institutions, a lot of them start liking each other. It starts back on the outside. Along comes a man on the street and he'll want two girls to go together. The girls have a relationship with each other and after a while they do it for kicks." Dorothy gets attention by telling the prison psychiatrist that she has homosexual leanings or by threatening to cut her wrists.

Whereas Toni and Dorothy are from broken homes in the slums, Joan is from a middle-class white family. She and her husband, occasionally of West Eighty-seventh Street, are both in prison at the moment, her husband in an Ohio penitentiary for forgery and Joan in the House of Detention for soliciting. She is a small-town Midwest-erner who has hustled for a year and has been an addict for ten years, since she was nineteen. She and her husband supported their habit by signing other people's names to checks. She has given birth to two addict babies in prison. When the infants were being detoxified they vomited, had convulsions and diarrhea like their mother when she undergoes withdrawal from drugs. Joan's first addict baby had to stay in jail two weeks longer than his mother to be cured, but even after he was brought home he threw up and had diarrhea, although the convulsions had stopped. Memory of the experience apparently has been insufficient to create a will in the mother to spare another child the same torment, and apparently birth control has never occurred to her. When she is brought to the House, she has a choice of how to break her habit. She can go into "the tank," in which case "they put you in a cell, lock the door and that's it." Or she can sign herself into the prison hospital and get medication, a much less uncomfortable way to get over the drug pangs. Joan has tried both methods. The only problem about withdrawing in the hospital is that girls who do it may get a stiffer sentence if they go back on the habit and are arrested again.

"We call the tank No. 4A. It's noisy, women throwing up, and a lot of physical pain. The place isn't insulated from the rest of the building. At first in the withdrawal you're wide awake, you can't sleep, you vomit, have diarrhea, twitches, cramps in your legs and back and stomach. You want to die. If you could get hold of something to kill yourself you'd do it. That's why they don't have any sharp instruments around. Cigarettes are lit for you. You can't have matches. Too many girls try to set themselves on fire. A few girls tried to strangle themselves with the chains on the bed."

The hospital room where the girls undergo withdrawal has about two dozen beds in it and is presided over by a small Viennese woman doctor. On weekends the place is usually full because Friday and Saturday nights are when most of the prostitutes are rounded up. Most of them lie quietly in the beds with the sheets pulled up over their heads, asleep or in a daze. The doctor explains that they are given doses of barbiturates to bring them around. Occasionally a girl will call out and say she is going to need something. If she is not administered to quickly she becomes panicky. She may stand up naked on the bed and scream for help.

The hustlers are able to defend themselves better in prison than out of it. On West Eighty-eighth Street or Broadway they are as easy to spot as an illegally parked automobile, but when they arrive at the

House of Detention they bring along a whole wardrobe of psychological overcoats which enables them to adapt to the prison climate.

The repeaters know how to make the correction people respond in certain ways. When Dorothy makes a project out of herself by telling the prison psychiatrist that she will cut her wrists, she is playing checkers with the administration. The seasoned inmate can get satisfaction as long as her demands are fairly trivial. Lorraine Moran, the former prison superintendent, acknowledges that the administration has to engage in a certain number of war games with the tenants. She says a girl will "have her moment" when she gets dramatic and emotional, at which point everyone else, including the inmates, will then go to work on her, tell her, "Come on, Dolores, calm down, take it easy." Thus Dolores achieves a satisfying prominence in the local community. The next day, lunch will be better. The girls have won a round, yet at the same time management gains too, because it is looking for an orderly situation.

A correction official admits that this prison gamesmanship sometimes creates a natural tendency on the part of some of the staff to gravitate to the mentality of the inmates and, figuratively speaking, indulge in baby talk. The situation is not helped, he says, by the fact that "many people who go to work in the prison system do so because they have been washed out of more socially accepted professions. They move into the prisons because the qualifications are very low and the pay scale, while not high, is enough to provide a fairly decent living. There are also very many side benefits, some legitimate and some not. The custodians come from exactly the same segments of the population as most of the inmates, economically and racially, particularly in large metropolitan areas. The racial element of the prison personnel is roughly parallel to the racial element of the prison population."

The official adds hastily that there are people of intelligence and dedication working on the rehabilitation of criminals in the New York City corrections system but there aren't enough of them. "As presently organized, people sincerely interested in rehabilitation work quickly learn that there is no possibility of such work in the correction system." In all the conversations the official has had with men in prison systems in the United States and abroad, not one of them has said he is willing to admit publicly to being a correction officer or prison guard. Such an identification, they think, is an extreme social handicap. "Only people at the top management level—the wardens and assistant wardens—get any public respect. This public attitude toward prison personnel, plus the inability of prison systems to develop rehabilitative programs, explains why there are only about fifty trained psychologists employed full time by all the prisons in the United States."

The correction department's Director of Research, a West Ninety-third Street sociologist named Sol Chaneles, says that if rehabilitation means simply how to get along and stay out of jail, "we should simply instruct people on how to avoid being caught. To convince people that they should not commit crimes to advance their personal interest would simply upset the whole American tradition." Dr. Chaneles thinks the main difference between most convicts and the rest of society is that the rest of society is not in jail. He cites the Porterfield study, in which four hundred white Protestant students from middle-class Texas families were asked to check any of the eighty crimes listed that they had committed.* The listed crimes ran over the whole spectrum—grand larceny, petty theft, felonious assault, automobile theft, attempted rape, seduction, sodomy, incest, etc. When the Porterfield questions were put to people of comparable social and educational background who were serving time in penal institutions, the results indicated that the group outside prison was committing more serious crimes than the convicts.

Dr. Chaneles says that rehabilitation programs should at least enable a human being to find ways of breaking out of a criminal habit and achieving a normal working relationship to his environment. Rehabilitation must deal with causes and treat the victim as a sick person, not as an obstruction to normal social traffic or as a moral outcast. "I see no such indications of a program like this anywhere in New York City prisons, and we are way ahead of the rest of the country."

Being way ahead of the rest of the country in terms of rehabilitation means that at the House of Detention the girls kick cold turkey, get a good scrubbing, powder their armpits, go to the doctor, serve their term and then go back to the West Side to hustle again.

Hannah is a short woman in her forties who walks her dog along her block in the West Nineties every morning about 10:30 A.M. and sometimes gives dimes to children. This munificence puzzles them,

* Dr. Chaneles is referring to *Youth In Trouble,* by Austin L. Porterfield (Fort Worth, Leo Potisham Foundation, 1946).

since she does not resemble anybody in their world, but they accept the dimes and wait to see what she wants until she sends them off with a wave of her hand. She has a checking and savings account at the local branch bank and stops in every other morning for coffee at a place on Columbus Avenue. She was divorced some time ago from a man she refers to as a "rat," and has been looking for a real husband who will love her and provide for her as well as she now provides for herself. Providing for Hannah would be no mean task. She has an income of at least $15,000, probably closer to $25,000, most of it tax free. She lives in a middle-income apartment building, eats out quite often in the better hotels, and wears the best clothes. In addition to the prostitutes who work with her, Hannah has another source of income. She buys high-fashion dresses, suits, and lingerie at wholesale rates from a place in the garment center and sells them to the girls. If the girls pay with their own money, the prices are cut rate. If the girl's client pays, prices are higher but still reasonable.

Hannah gets busy on the telephone every afternoon around four o'clock, setting up dates and checking the whereabouts of the girls, who may be scattered all over town. In the evening she works on location in the hotel lobbies or off the sidewalks on Fifth Avenue and Central Park South. So far, neither she nor any of her small group of Asian, Negro, and white girls have been arrested. They do not buy or sell narcotics, they do business by appointment most of the time, and their clients are men of financial standing and external propriety. A plainclothesman would have to be very sure of himself to walk up to one of these splendid-looking creatures and try to elicit a "direct" proposition.

Each of the girls charges $100 to $150 per client. If they get a job on their own, they keep everything. If Hannah locates the client, she gets the finder's fee, which is half. The system operates like a private art gallery or a real-estate firm, except that the commissions are higher. The girls prefer to have Hannah handle arrangements. There is less risk, complicated communications problems can be taken care of more easily, and the customers feel more secure if they can deal with a single full-time executive working out of a central head-quarters. The girls, six or eight of them, gross around $3,000 weekly when things are going well, and not usually less than half this in slow periods. If business falls off badly, or a girl gets in trouble (if, for instance, Hannah suspects "the bulls" are after her), she may go to Miami and reappear later with a tan.

Hannah says she has never had to pay the police, which is probably true because she is very afraid of them. She answers the phone as if she were peering through the peephole of a speakeasy. Each girl has a place to live and a place to work. They lease "offices" (apartments) on the better East Side streets, or check in and out of hotels in the same neighborhood. The main overhead items besides rent are telephone bills, taxi fares, clothing, and permanents. If a girl goes steady with one or two customers, they may help buy clothes and pay the rent. Although Hannah is primarily an administrator, she is what in professional baseball would be called a playing manager. If a man prefers an older woman and her colorful style of conversation, Hannah is available.

The other people in Hannah's apartment house know about her activities, but she has never been ostracized or persecuted or criticized. Some of these neighbors have rather bizarre habits and interests themselves—one or two of her homosexual acquaintances, for instance, get a certain vicarious enjoyment out of Hannah's very successful system of exploiting male appetites. Everyone goes to each other's parties and borrows from each other. The atmosphere of the building would not be so cheerful and cooperative if Hannah used her home as a professional apartment. As a tenant like everyone else, she is regarded as a person who sends money to her mother every month. Except when her terrible suspicions are aroused, she looks and behaves in the daytime like a sleepy housewife, pale and slightly puffy around the eyes and with her hair in purple curlers.

Hannah and her girls are part of what she calls a "sporting community" of West Side gamblers, pimps, prostitutes, and musicians whom she considers the most interesting people in town. Once or twice a year, the sporting community holds a formal ball, starting after midnight, at one of the West Side hotels, where everyone has a good time even when they are talking business, because they enjoy their business. Even in her off-duty hours, if there is such a thing with her, she carries on her professional research, taking down phone numbers, asking about the competition and about their prices.

Hannah is proud of her clothes and her girls, but the clothes are the less troublesome merchandise. The girls behave like children, miss appointments, oversleep, call in late, or forget to call in at all. Since Hannah has two phones, and both of them begin ringing steadily by 5 P.M. she is hard put to handle them both. One of her problems is the girl who will call to say she has lost the name of the man she is supposed to call, or that she has not gotten around to fixing her hair yet. Hannah responds sharply in such situations. She will tell the girl that she has a date with a cultured gentleman and that nobody can afford to have her take a night off. The girl is ordered to put her hair in curlers and not to appear in the Hotel Pierre lobby looking like a scarecrow. Another of Hannah's problems is a young woman with several aliases, which make her difficult to locate. If Hannah calls at the hotel where that one is supposed to be registered, she may have to ask for her by six or seven different names, which always arouses a hotel clerk's suspicions.

After lunch Hannah drifts about her apartment in a housecoat or negligee looking over the clothes she has ordered. She claims that much of her merchandise is sold retail only by stores like Altman's and Saks Fifth Avenue. Whether or not this is true, the clothes are as handsome as her girls. For instance, she will sell an avocado-colored leather dress for $35 that retails at Saks for $129. With access to such clothes at such low prices, it might seem logical for her to expand the garment business and forget the prostitution, but Hannah is not interested in opening a store. Also, if she got out of prostitution, she would be losing most of her customers.

About half of her phone calls every day are from men. "You'd be impressed at who some of these people are," she says. "Prominent people. New York businessmen. Quite a few doctors." Occasionally her male callers are bellhops employed in Fifth Avenue hotels. Hannah could use another telephone and a full-time assistant, but she prefers to do everything herself. She has unusual organizational ability and verve. She is wardrobe mistress, set designer, social secretary, producer, and leader of the orchestra all rolled into one.

About 7 P.M., with the day's logistical problems out of the way, she zips herself into a tight dress and wraps a piece of white fur around her neck. In the summertime, in the evening, it is still light outside when she emerges onto the sidewalk. She will stand there for a half hour or so, chatting and getting a breath of air, and giving sailing instructions to one or two of the girls as they roll to the curb in a taxicab. Then she walks off toward Central Park West on her way downtown to supervise.

Hannah blends in with the landscape and is not regarded as a public nuisance by anyone, but the large, visible homosexual community which has grown up in the area is something else again. Central Park West and Riverside Drive parents make a constant effort to insulate their children from homosexuals, who congregate along Broadway in the Nineties. Negro and Puerto Rican mothers sensitive to the street dangers usually link the homosexual with the addict, the prostitute, and the alcoholic when they discuss their worries about their children.* One hears frequent stories about children being accosted in washrooms of movie theaters or in Central Park. Fear of the homosexual may have a doubtful scientific base, but it is widespread nonetheless.

At the same time, the homosexual has found a privacy and freedom from persecution on the West Side in contrast to his haunts in Greenwich Village, where even the local Democratic clubs have been trying to drive him out. There are too many other emergencies for West Side parents to spend much energy on bursts of moral indignation. Captain Block of the 24th Precinct used to say that the police would "rush out of this station house like there was a homicide" if there was a report of child molestation, but that homosexuals were let alone so long as they behaved themselves in public, an attitude similar to that of the British police and the Archbishop of Canterbury. For their part the homosexuals emphasize in their literature that the homosexual has the same right to privacy any other citizen.

Because he inhabits the West Side in large numbers the homosexual can congregate freely with people of like mind and habits. He can even rate himself as somewhat of a conformist, in that he is part of a "movement." At the top of the homosexual pyramid, economically and culturally speaking, are the prosperous, well-educated men and women whose outer life is quite in harmony with that of the rest of the population. Some of them regard themselves as in need of psychiatric treatment. Many others have developed the sort of group enthusiasm about homosexuality that one ordinarily associates with patriotic societies and minor religious movements. They subscribe to the Mattachine Society's monthly magazine and attend Society-

* Interviewers working in the Kraft survey of citizen attitudes in Stryckers Bay report that respondents almost always lumped homosexuals together with narcotics addicts, prostitutes, alcoholics, and muggers as undesirable and criminal elements.

sponsored lectures at Freedom House on such topics as "The Role of the Lesbian in the Great Society."

At the bottom of the homosexual pyramid are male and female prostitutes and other antisocial types that include addicts, muggers, transvestites and exhibitionists. It is difficult to ascertain which comes first, the homosexuality or the other deviations, but, whatever the pathology, these types get into trouble with the police. A considerable number of them are sent to Rikers Island prison on disorderly conduct charges: of the eight hundred or so inmates at any given time, about 20 percent are drug users. An even greater percentage of the prostitutes in the Women's House of Detention seem to be homosexuals and addicts, but they are usually less dangerous than their unemployed male equivalents, many of whom commit burglary and felonious assault. It is presumably this group to which the American Medical Association refers when it blames homosexuals for contributing generously to a 200 percent national increase of syphilis in people under twenty during the past five years. (In New York City the VD rate has jumped 400 percent since 1957.) The middle-class, socially "integrated" homosexual deeply resents the homosexual underworld, and also the identification of criminals by police and the press as homosexuals, as if the homosexuality explained the crime. Writing in the Mattachine Society newsletter, they have also expressed annoyance with the stereotype of the homosexual created by exhibitionists who seek homosexual contacts in public places.

Fred Johnson, the former chief social worker at Goddard-Riverside Community Center, declaring that homosexuality is not contagious, says that young people more often become active homosexuals because of unhealthy parental and family relationships, in which case parents should be worrying about themselves instead of the street corners. He reports that the wealthier homosexuals offer their apartments as a social center for restless teen-agers who have nowhere else to go and would like to listen to hi-fi and have a Coke. The teen-agers' relationship with the presiding homosexual is what they wish to make it. Everyone in the group knows who the "queens" are, and although gang members may "roll" a homosexual and beat him up, Johnson says, generally a homosexual gets along without causing trouble—in other words he integrates with the community, unless, of course, he is unemployable. Then he will react as any other human being reacts to poverty. He may struggle along in a half-functioning state, or he can become permanently welfarized and sick, probably ending up in a hospital or a jail or spending much of his time lying flat on the sidewalk.

Johnson knows of no cases where homosexuals have abducted or injured children, but he has seen many neglected pre-adolescent youngsters, who will accept affection from almost anyone, picked up by homosexuals. The pickup starts a whole process in which the youngsters gradually become covert or overt homosexuals. The homosexual capitalizes on the child's family pathology, not on his innocence.

One fact not generally recognized is the exploitation of homosexuals by adolescents who are not themselves homosexuals. Johnson and some other professional social workers in the area call this "adaptation to an existing situation," their way of saying there are local adolescents who know a good thing when they see it. Various side benefits—money as well as the Cokes and hi-fi—can be extracted from a liaison with the homosexual. Johnson is not so sure, in view of the personality of the youngster who "adapts," that acceptance of a homosexual relationship is the worst arrangement a neglected child can make. It may afford at some level a "functioning and at least partly satisfying social relationship." To those who disagree, Johnson suggests taking a look at some of the child's alternatives, such as psychotic behavior or drug addiction. Sometimes, of course, the youngster will adopt not only the homosexual relationship but also all the "alternatives" as well.

To some uneducated jobless teen-agers, homosexuality seems to be a normal habit to pick up along with all of their other disabilities. They may drift into the lower reaches of homosexual life without even being sure why they are there, except that, as Johnson points out, they can find associations not available anywhere else. Such people rarely apply to social agencies for help. They have cut themselves off, or have been amputated from family and any regular friendships, and the world they subsist in is so chaotic as to be almost fictional.

One example is an eighteen-year-old Puerto Rican, Roberto. He failed to establish any identity for himself, even as a homosexual. He is a pale, emaciated boy, the most important event of whose life, next to his birthday, was being hit by a taxicab at the age of four. He is still lame from the accident but the limp has not prevented him from traveling long distances. About four years ago he ran away from his father and hitchhiked to California, where he stayed for three years, and then returned to the West Side. He has been to California and back more than once since then. Roberto is a dropout from everything, school, his broken family, society—even the underworld of the male prostitute and the addict in which he now spends his time. Roberto's dropping out began when he was about ten years old, when his parents separated. He stayed with his father, and his older brother with the mother. As things turned out, the brother, José, seems to have had the better time of it, and is now a capable social worker with a family of his own. Sometimes Roberto thinks he is a homosexual, and at other times he doesn't know.

"I always hung around with the queens, mainly on Broadway and Forty-second, but I used to come back to sleep at my mother's. The only thing the queens wanted from me was to help them buy some groceries, buy this and that. They did not want no sex 'cause hardly no queens want sex with another queen; they want it with straight people. They see a sailor coming off a ship. They know a sailor hasn't had nothing in a long time and that's the guy they go for, and they go for older men too, because they claim the older men got more strength than the young kids. The queens have boys and girls. They have a girl friend but that's nothing but a lesbian. The girls play the boys' part. Then they have their boy friends, the ones they run around with who wear a diamond wedding ring, shiny rings. They have plenty of fights like married people.

"In my block on Eighty-fifth Street there's a whole building full of queens. If I go out with a queen and I stay with a queen for the night I got to pay the queen. I don't have to but the rules is you got to pay them 'cause if I don't pay them I get beat up and they take all the money. I can't go to the cops 'cause cops ask me what I was doing in that room with a queen. I'll go to jail. Some queens get gang boys lined up. Then they pick up a sailor, bring him to the apartment and the gang boys jump the sailor and take everything away from him. The queen divides the money with everybody."

Occasionally Roberto has worked as a bellhop, with procuring as his main source of income. His attitude toward the girls in his "group" was rather atypical for a pimp. "We used to be in love, kind of, with the girls," he says—and they are the only women he ever speaks of with any affection. Roberto got names of some girls from other bellhops—or, in Los Angeles, he would go down and pick them up on Hollywood and Vine. Most of them were "amateurs" under twenty— "girls who want somebody new every day more than they want the money."

Roberto says he has only one friend in New York City, a social worker he sees once in a while. His older brother cannot help him because he has his own family responsibilities trying to earn a living. His mother doesn't like him in the house, and Roberto doesn't like to go there anyway. There are nine people living in the same apartment, and his aunt calls him a queer in front of anyone who happens to be around at the time.

"I might be a queen,"* Roberto says, "I don't know, but I don't want the whole world to know and especially my little brother. He doesn't know what the word means so he tells other people his brother Roberto is a queen."

He is trying to get his own place to live. He has a job fixing pocketbooks right now, which pays $60 a week, and he picked up a stray dog at the pound which follows him wherever he goes. It is unlikely that Roberto's job or his dog will last very long. When he gets enough money, he thinks someday he'll go back to California. Now that he is eighteen the police can't send him back to his family the way they did before.

Pedro is an eighteen-year-old Puerto Rican like Roberto, but the resemblance ends there. Pedro is strong, handsome, well-dressed, and sounds like a conservative. He does not wander from city to city. He talks a great deal about his friends in the Eighties, where he lives, whereas Roberto is a loner. Pedro belongs to the Royal Ravens, a thirty-five-member gang which used to fight but has now turned "social," into what is called a "street club." In the gang "everybody thinks the same," Pedro says. "Like somebody gets hit, somebody gets slapped—we always hit back." It reacts like one person. The Ravens have not been in a rumble for more than two years and spend much of their time in a center provided by a social worker who has sponsored them. Pedro drops in every night or so to play ping-pong or lift weights. Saturday nights there is usually a dance. If anything is damaged the boys have to pay up, so they police their own social

* The homosexual may refer to himself as a "queen," but not as a "queer."

events rather efficiently. Girls are allowed to use the lounge, but are told to stay out when the boys are lifting weights or having athletic contests.

The Ravens don't miss the old fighting days. Defending their turf got to be too much trouble. "Everybody had to keep proving themselves. You beat the champs, and you were the champs, but then the new guys all went after you." Also, the police harassed them more and more, so when the social worker offered them the meeting place they accepted with relief. The police have not bothered the Ravens very much.

Pedro is indignant about the narcotics traffic in the neighborhood. He would like to see all the rooming houses torn down even though he says this won't solve the problem. "When they knocked down Eighty-fourth Street all they did was move the junkies away. They didn't move the junk. The junkies come back for visits." Though dope is very easy to get, not all youngsters know where to get it because junkies do not like to deal with them. Youngsters talk. The junkies are not the only outsiders who move in and make trouble, Pedro says. "Men come around, say something to your girl, there's a fight. You go walking with your sister and somebody comes down the street and bothers her. Another thing is people breaking into apartments. I don't like the idea, you know, that you can't leave your house without somebody busting in." He is something of a xenophobe about the world outside his gang's own neighborhood. "You read a lot about the girls getting pregnant but most of the girls who get that way are the ones who think they're really no good with guys, you know. They're the girls who get pregnant because they don't know what's going on. Most of the girls who have sex around here are girls from somewhere else, Italian girls. Nobody bothers the girls who live around here. The guys, mainly what they do on Friday and Saturday, they go to school dances. They come to each other's places. They have birthday parties in the houses or they go to the Palladium. All this about sex, what they say in the press, is not true. The only kind of girls I go with are girls in the neighborhood. I make sure my sisters keep good hours. Their friends keep good hours. There are some other girls who fool around late at night, Italian girls do that."

Until he "gets in the army or something" or is accepted by the police force (he has applied for the police academy), Pedro plans to stay around and keep his job in a photoengraving shop. If he gets married he would like to move to a quieter place than Eighty-fifth Street. Social workers haven't done much to improve things in the neighborhood. "Sure they can come around here and say, 'Okay, kids, let's be good and let's do this and that,' but then they get into their cars and go home to their wives that live in a big apartment, you know, while some of the kids just go back to a two-by-four room. They don't understand the problem. They just read it in books. It don't work like that. Our guys ain't ignorant. A lot of guys are insulted because social workers think everybody here is a gangster. People come in the summertime, different groups of college people, to make surveys and they are surprised and say, 'Oh you guys got such good manners.' Well, what are we supposed to behave like, animals or what?"

Pedro is loyal to his group. He resents the people who run down his neighborhood. He wants peace, he says, looking into a mirror, combing his hair, straightening his jacket by humping his shoulders and pulling on the lapels. Such views would be news to the police because the Pedro in the mirror is the most violent member of his gang, has been charged with possession of a gun, and has been indicted as an accomplice in a cold-blooded murder.

Pedro made life difficult for his gang because they were never sure what he was liable to do. They knew enough about him after a while not to trust him with leadership. Members like Pedro brought the police and the Youth Board workers down hard on their backs and were one reason the gang disintegrated. Another jolt to the gang's equilibrium was urban renewal. The bottom fell out of the neighborhood and the gangs were left with no turf to fight over, and fewer and fewer youngsters to recruit. A gang unable to count on certain troop strength was in no position to go into battle. Today, the Comanches, the Hellburners, Apaches, and the Unknowns are nothing but names painted on doorways and the walls of supermarkets, as much a thing of the past as the reputed Irish gangs that preceded them.*

The last of the virulent gangs, the Apaches, passed away with the

* There is some disagreement about the so-called Irish gangs. Shirley Bernstein, a local schoolteacher, says they were just as bad as their successors. Dennis Mahon, former Democratic leader, denied this: "There were some roughnecks, but no organization." Some residents recall battles between Irish parochial and Jewish private school boys on West End Avenue but say that there was nothing worse than bloody noses sustained in these fracases.

death of its leader, a young man from an affluent Spanish family in the West Seventies. One of the Area's countless "Indios," the leader had picked out Ninety-third Street as a place to foment rebellion and impress young boys from slum families with his money and recklessness. The Apaches were involved in at least a dozen West Side shootings. Although Indio was probably the most troublesome gang leader in the 24th Precinct, his dedication to violence was somewhat offset by the fact that he became a personal friend of a sergeant in the Youth Squad in the police department. Indio's desire for recognition, and his penchant for talking about himself, often gave the sergeant clues which, put together with other intelligence, enabled him to make some accurate guesses as to when the Apaches were about to create an incident. When Indio died from natural causes, the Apaches continued their war councils for a while, but the new leader, named "Little Man," did not have Indio's money or his car. Although he established a reputation, despite his size, of being the strongest weight lifter in the area and claimed to have had intercourse with several women every day of his life, his exploits were no substitute for Indio's organizational capacity, and the Apaches eventually dissolved.

The Hellburners, recalls Detective Al Jackson, who once served in the area with the Youth Squad, had several members who were "really good kids, who would not do anything wrong. Our troubles lay with a few in charge." Working on the hypothesis that the way to de-venom a gang was to wean away the "good kids," the Youth Squad cooperated with a branch of the Y.M.C.A. located in the Grace Methodist Church on 104th Street, and with the Youth Board, to provide other amusements for them. At that time, the police Youth Squad decided no gang should ever be allowed to "take over any area as its own turf." When this happened other gangs would contest the claim and the rumbles would increase in number. Police credit the Youth Board and local social agencies for their part in neutralizing the gangs, also individual citizens who would call the station house when a rumble was in the wind.

The police system was not to "lock up the kids if we could help it," Jackson says. "The answer was constant patrol of the area, knowing the kids, knowing when we saw two gangs beginning to mix. Knowing how to break up the situation and send the kids away." How much forbearance the police should exercise was always a problem since some gangs could and did commit murder.

Although organized gang warfare has disappeared, other problems have not. The evening community centers and youth workers like Joe Ramos, who is trying to recruit teen-agers for his gymnastic teams, cannot offer the attractions of a paying job or the "rep" that a teen-ager could build up for himself by getting elected president of the Hellburners. The boys still move around in loosely articulated impromptu packs and in place of the old military campaigns there is an occasional gang scuffle with passengers on a subway train or bus. At least one group of ex-gang members operating in the West 100's has taken up a new tactic—"japping"—in which two boys will waylay an enemy and knife him or beat him. Marijuana smoking, something which was taboo in the fighting gangs, seems to have taken hold of the youngsters.

"The value system has changed," a Youth Board worker says. "Today, marijuana isn't considered so bad. In the old days it was very wrong. Very few of the kids in the gangs don't experiment with it now. The area is flooded with it and it's cheap. When I took some of the kids to camp last summer I laid down the law about no alcohol; it never occurred to me to mention marijuana. The kids kept their word about the liquor, but then I discovered they were sneaking out and smoking pot."

Ted Halliday, Negro Youth Board worker assigned to Goddard-Riverside Community Center, says many of the fourteen-year-olds who congregate on Ninety-second Street sniff glue, jimmy parking meters, and break open pay telephones. Another group Halliday deals with is "all homosexual," and solicits around Ninety-sixth Street. Most of the older gang boys don't work more than two months of the year. They will rent a furnished room and three or four will camp together, and make a point of locating homosexuals to pick up $5 or $10. "It got to the stage where I'd meet the group and a couple of them would be missing. I'd ask about them and then get told, 'Well, we're broke so they had to go out and hustle and get us some dough.' I let it pass. One day I met one of the gang members coming out of a house near Ninety-sixth and Amsterdam. I asked if he had a girl friend in there. He says, 'No, I just made myself $10, I just screwed a faggot.' As far as we know, however, the gang rarely beats up the homosexuals. As far as becoming gay is concerned, the gang members do it for the money. I don't think they're actually becoming homosexuals themselves."

The history of the gangs after they have been "adopted," or tamed by social workers who have provided them with recreational facilities, shows that they have become pacific but there is not much evidence that the youngsters have any better prospects than they did before. A social worker who took two members into his home and helped them get jobs is convinced that most of the teen-agers in these gangs will never be able to get decent jobs no matter how well they learn to behave.

The experiences of two separate gangs, the Young Devils and the Blue Knights, are instructive. The Young Devils, composed entirely of Puerto Rican youngsters, lived away from home, moving from apartment to apartment; some spent much of their time on Broadway searching out "faggots," and stealing to pay the rent. Nobody gave any of the boys in this group much of a chance to avoid arrest at some time. The Blue Knights, on the other hand, seemed to offer possibilities for rehabilitation. They were a heterogeneous group—both mainland whites and Spanish—and most of them lived at home. The Knights were given a recreation center and counseling by professionals, and the police went out of their way to help. In the end, however, the fate of the Blue Knights was not a great deal different from that of the Young Devils. They lost their center because of fighting and some use of marijuana. The police were forced to crack down, and a man who had worked hard to help them lost his job because he had sponsored the group.

Why did it happen? The boys were getting older. Most of them were sixteen or eighteen. They were men now, graduating into the ranks of the permanently unemployed, and the traditional crutches offered by social agencies were simply not enough.

My Mother Is My Father

"They ask me why I keep on having kids out of wedlock. I guess it gives me a sense of security." Dolores, a young mother of five, is a very pretty Puerto Rican—"inviting" is the way a welfare worker describes her. "You say no, you do not do it any more, but you take up with another guy. You believe him and wind up, you have a kid . . . you believe him, you know. They are going to marry you, they love you. They are going to help you up. When it's done, they go on and take off. The welfare people ask me about getting birth control, but I don't believe in birth control. I don't believe in any operations—they have some new thing, a loop, at Mt. Sinai Hospital. The doctor puts it in you. You go back every three years and he takes it out and puts in a new one. I would use that. Suppose I go out. I come in tired. I'm so tired I don't have the patience to go and mess with birth control. I'll use it the next night, you know, and then I get caught. I want something steady I don't have to be worried about and bothered by putting on. Some girls come home too drunk so they forget about it and go to bed. Pregnant the next month. That's what happens." Often "what happens" takes place in a one- or two-room apartment with children present, if they have not been sent out on the street.

Dolores is one of a group of unmarried mothers and two dozen "O.W.'s" (the social worker's term for an out-of-wedlock child) who have a whole building to themselves on Ninety-third Street. All on welfare, they have their own intramural social system in which advice, gossip, food, cigarettes, occasionally men and children are passed around. A good percentage of the mothers and their mothers before them were born out of wedlock, and their children are frequently unaware of either their fathers or their grandfathers.

Dolores says unmarried mothers should be given preference for public housing instead of being barred from it. In the first place, it is easier for married people to look for apartments, since a single girl is stuck at home with the kids. Also, in view of the fact that almost all unwed mothers are on welfare, it would save money for the city to put them in a public housing project at $70 a month instead of paying a private landlord $125. If the city Housing Authority is unwilling to have unmarried mothers in its regular projects then it ought to have special housing projects for them. Dolores' proposal for still another kind of segregation would make a sociologist's hair stand on end, yet it has a certain logic.

If Dolores reasons like a child, it is because she is a child. She reads paperback sex and her children's comic books. She does not want to become pregnant again but she takes no precautions with the man she has on a morning or afternoon when the children are out. She says she doesn't believe in birth control, then in the next breath wishes she had a reliable and convenient contraceptive device. She has fits of temper and threatens to move out of the house, then makes up quickly with her friends and forgets the whole affair. She wants her children to do well in school and loves them, but she is erratic in her affections and attention. Her main hope in life seems to be to find a man, preferably someone lighter-skinned than she is. Her social worker doubts that the family will ever get out of the hole it is in—there are simply no ladders around. She describes one of Dolores' children, a four-year-old boy:

"He was the saddest, most neglected child I had ever seen. He had been placed by his mother in a foster home for a year; no one seems to know why she took him back. Dolores commented several times to me that the boy was 'spoiled—just like his father.' The other women sensed that Dolores was taking out her dislike of the father on his child. They should know, because they are doing the same thing to their own children. Whatever the reason, she left Raimundo naked on the bed, alone in the house with his baby sister, for hours at a time. At the beginning of the summer, we never even realized that he existed, she hid him so well. The first time we took him to the park he was filthy; his hair was long; he cried and whined constantly and was unable to walk by himself but had to be carried or pushed in a carriage. He stuffed himself with food. He sat down beneath swings and seesaws, hitting his head frequently but never seeming to care enough to watch out for flying objects; he seemed to get no satisfaction out of anything. If I gave him a piece of bread he would throw it on the ground, but if I attempted to pick up the bread and throw it away he would begin screaming; then if I tried to give the bread back to him he would reject it again, screaming. He paid no attention to the other children and very little attention to me except when he wished to be picked up. In the beginning, picking him up was the only way of soothing him. He really seemed to want the kind of physical contact a baby desires (often, by the way, he tried to grab a carton of milk himself). Gradually, Raimundo began to improve. I usually had to persuade Dolores each morning to send him with us. Several times when she was not in the apartment I dressed him and got him ready. However, one morning she took him to get a haircut and a new pair of shoes. Toward the end of the summer he would be waiting for us on the stoop, dressed, clean, and ready to go. He seemed to profit from the experience of going into the park more than many of the other children. He was able to walk to the park holding some adult's hand. He cried, but less frequently, and discovered ways to enjoy himself. He played in the dirt often; sometimes he imitated a monster, chasing after other children. He liked the swing and seesaw and playing in the sandbox. He learned to play ball with one other child and he seemed to stuff himself less at mealtimes. Toward the last week or so we were elated, seeing Raimundo laugh and smile and run around the park, really enjoying himself. While I have reservations as to how his new behavior will last, I have no doubt that we helped him, even if only for a short while."

The social worker went back to college at the end of the summer. For a couple of weeks after that Raimundo used to look for her every morning.

Some of the unwed mothers at the house on Ninety-third Street are considerably more mature than Dolores and can focus more realistically on their families. At the suggestion of a social worker three years ago, a group living in the house on West Ninety-third Street formed a "family circle" which met on Wednesday nights to talk about "what we want for ourselves and what we want for our kids." According to a Puerto Rican mother, the women in the building are learning how to sew and make clothes for their children. "We discuss everything, what a child feels, what he should and shouldn't do, how you should scold a child. We give parties, but most of the time we talk about the children. If a child tells a lie or takes something he's not supposed to take, you don't call it stealing. We just explain to the child that he should never take anything that doesn't belong to him. Always return the change. You should never give a child too much money for his allowance, not more than $1 every two weeks. Never promise a child something unless you are going to give it. Never lie to them. If you don't lie to them, they won't lie to you." Some of this sophistication was undoubtedly introduced by the social worker who attended the earlier meetings.

Encouraged by a field worker from the Goddard-Riverside Community Center, the family circle even got up its own softball team, and was also able to persuade several of the "fathers" and the current "boy friends" to come to family circle meetings and listen to a few words on birth control and parental responsibility from the social workers.

Sara, a Negro member of the family circle, has four children but she gets no financial help and very little support of any kind from any of the fathers. Meanwhile the children are learning some of the facts of life early, from seeing the winos and prostitutes who come and go in the hallway.

Interviews between a Negro mother on welfare and a white teacher rarely take place unless there has been some incident. Sara's visit with a teacher took place because Blanche, her oldest daughter, had come home crying that another girl had "up and slapped her." The mother decided to get the story from the teacher. The slapping incident had a good effect because the mother and the teacher see each other more often now. Recently when Blanche had a toothache and was going to have to stay out for a few days, her mother took the trouble of going in to see the teacher and explaining why her girl would be missing school.

Sara is pleased that Blanche's class is "all mixed up with colored and white." She herself went to school with white children, and as long as there is some racial integration in the classes she doesn't worry about the percentages. When her children bring up the matter of race, she talks to them in terms which, if not entirely clear, raise fascinating subjects to think about. "One day one of the children asked me, 'Mommy, why is my skin so dark and others so light?' " she reports. "I said, look you don't know what color God is, and I told her if someone asked her that to say, 'If I sneeze out of my nose, what do you sneeze out of?' "

The mother was born in North Carolina and lived there until she was fifteen and then came to New York City. She has eight sisters and three brothers. Three of her sisters are married. She moved into her present place when her sister moved out and went to Brooklyn. All of her sisters are on welfare. The husband of one of them left when she was pregnant with her last child and she never saw him again. Another sister's husband went back down South and he hasn't shown up around the West Side for some time.

Sara's relationship to men is approximately what her great-grandmother's was as a slave on a plantation. "They leave as soon as they get your belly pushed out." But sometimes it is the woman who flees. "My mother and father got married. She had five girls by my father. She found another man. She ran off and left my father and us but my father stayed with us. Me, I hope and pray to God that I don't have more children. I think four is enough. My boy friend and me have a relationship with each other, but by me being lazy and not getting up the next thing you know your belly is pushed out. The man say, 'Woman, that's your problem, it's not my fault.' Me, I wouldn't go for abortions or birth control. I don't believe in it. My religion don't call for me to have abortions and I'm proud to be a Baptist. They're opposed to birth control because my father say, if we get pregnant, to go ahead and have those children. Don't ever try to do away with them."

The fathers of her children were not casual acquaintances. Each man was someone she kept company with for several months to a few years, one at a time—a practice called "serial monogamy" by welfare workers. "They always were interested but when they discover I'm pregnant they just vamoose. My oldest daughter's father, I had been going with him for at least two years and he came out with that jive about we'd be married. After we had a baby, next thing I knew he was in Connecticut and he never sent money, didn't come to see the child. When Blanche was about three years old, one day he came in the house and told her, 'I'm your father.' She said, 'Oh no you're not.' He asked why not. She said, 'Oh no, my mother is my mother and my father. She's the one who fixed it for me to eat and sleep and sees that I have clothes. I don't need you. I got my mother.' "

All males are the same, Sara says, with one exception. "They don't come by, they don't give me nothing, but the last one's father, he does come by and gives me a couple of dollars to buy the baby something. He likes *all* the children. He takes them to the park, plays with them, takes them to the movies, on picnics, to Coney Island. He pays $21 a week for just a room and kitchenette and he don't make but $50 so I don't expect him to give me nothing. He ain't got nothing to give. As long as they come by and make me think they're still thinking about the child it wouldn't be so bad."

One family counselor whose pending visit causes ambivalent feelings is the case worker from the Welfare Department. Sara says she has had good investigators and bad investigators. "When they talk nasty to me, I talk nasty back to them." Departmental questions about financial data eventually get around to her sex life. "They ask things I don't think they should ask, especially when it's a man asking. When they get down to my personal life I would rather talk to a lady.* I had one Spanish investigator one time. She asked me why I

* One welfare investigator said that while she was single her women clients would not talk to her about birth control. After she was married, the subject was raised constantly. "After I had been married three months, they began patting my belly. When I didn't get pregnant they wanted to know if I was sterile or didn't like children."

was having all these kids. I said, 'Well, it wasn't my fault. When you go out on the street to look for a man you don't want them to think you're out there hustling, which they put you in jail for. You go out with the kind of man you like and you wind up with another baby and he'll go off and leave you again.' So she asked me, 'Why don't you go off and marry one of the fellows?' I said, 'When the right one comes along I will.' I'm intending to get married, the kind of a man a woman appreciates. As long as he comes in just looking for you to feed him, he has a relationship with you, fine—but then goodbye, you don't see that man no more."

Ironically, her one faithful suitor has been the only man who has gotten Sara into trouble. "The investigator last time said, 'I hear so-and-so is coming around to see you.' I said, 'Sure, he comes to see me. Is there any harm?' He said, 'Oh no, does he stay here?' I said, 'No, he has his own place.' He said, 'The way I hear it, he was living with you.' I said, 'Where did you get that from?' He said, 'I'm not gonna call no names but it came out of this building.' I don't like that."

What she liked even less was the next bit of gossip the investigator produced, that her man was also going around with some other girl in the building. "That word came from the top floor," she said, leaving no doubt she knew exactly who had started that tale.

"It's not one big happy feeling in this building. There's a lot of fighting going on. Third, fourth, and fifth floors get along with each other and the first and second floors stick together. People up there think they're better than the people living down here, but I don't know. All of us is on welfare. They're no better than me."

In late August Sara begins ironing every day. By the time P.S. 84 opens, the children's clothes are stacked up two feet high. It is important for the children to look right in school.

Retirement Living

The least appetizing of the so-called "transient" hotels scattered over the Area have the atmosphere of crowded and unsanitary bus depots. In the lobbies there are always several men resting or sleeping in the upright positions people assume when they expect to be disturbed at any moment. One of the grimmer transient hotels, which shall be known as the Hotel Babylon, is on a central avenue in the

Seventies. Its conglomeration of hundreds of rooms is in constant use, either by day-by-day customers, or by "regulars" who seem to have been there forever. The population of the Babylon can run as high as fifteen hundred, about twice the size of the town of Union, Connecticut. Rates depend: a sleeping room is $13 a week; a bedroom, bath, and kitchenette goes from $20 to $28 a week, and the largest unit, four rooms, costs $80.

Many of the tenants are single persons who do not want to be bothered, who simply want a place where they can sleep, and sit, and pass their troubles away, and feed themselves from the top of a hot plate. Several elderly white people have been living in the hotel for twenty or thirty years. When one of them achieves final dissolution, the event passes unnoticed except by the management or, perhaps, a local minister who is called in to arrange disposal of the remains.

The old people, and everyone else who behaves himself, have a protector in Ralph Attana, a man who weighs well over two hundred pounds and moves about like a Sherman tank. As house detective at the Babylon he has looked into most of the hundreds of rooms at one time or another. He says the hotel's young single people feel they cannot play any big part in society and just go along from day to day. "I mean he or she will be satisfied in having enough money for a cup of coffee and a pack of cigarettes a day. Their outlook on life isn't like myself. I'm always planning for tomorrow and would like to get ahead in a lot of ways. These are people who live their lives as it comes. Their amusements are something hard to describe, really— some drink, some gamble, then you have the sex fiends who do different and odd things for amusement. Some people like to fight, some people steal."

Attana had left a job at a suburban amusement park when the detective agency he worked for could not get anyone else to volunteer for the Babylon job. When he arrived at the hotel the addicts were wandering through the halls, and prostitutes were using the public bathrooms for their business. Every week, it seemed, Attana would find an addict who had taken an overdose, who had "what they call the old gorilla on their back." He worked twelve or sixteen hours a day to clean up the establishment. A little knowledge of psychology came in handy, Attana declares. He often had to face people with knives and bottles in their hands, "the types you would call undesirables. It was very easy to run across enemies, where they start watching you and planning how they can get even with what you've done to them." The house detective worked closely with the policemen from the local precinct.

The bad pennies that turn up over and over are Attana's most dangerous problems, because they build up grudges against him. One chap who had been thrown out a year ago came back and began riding the elevators. "He says to me, 'If you want to give me trouble, I'll give you trouble.' As I approached him he put his hand in his pocket, and he never did pull out the knife, but I knew he had one. I walked away from him. Later on he was in a corner restaurant. He didn't see me. I approached him when he couldn't get his hand in his pocket and asked him to turn his pockets inside out. A five-inch-blade knife fell out. I asked him what he was intending to do with it. I know for myself what he intended. If he ever got a chance he would cut me, so I brought him back into the hotel and took him into the back room. I told him, well, if he was intending to cut me, I was going to give him the chance to do it. I tried to make him take the knife. He wouldn't take it, so after giving him a light workover, I let him go and told him to stay out of here. That's one of the minor things."

Attana follows the example of the London bobby. He has not carried a gun since the third week he came to work at the Babylon, when he tried to break up a ruckus in one of the rooms. "Well, with the force of breaking down the door I fell in the room pretty far, right in the middle of ten men fighting. The first thing one of the lads did was to reach for my gun. I mean I really had to fight to keep him from getting it. That gave me the idea right then for this type of job it wouldn't be wise to carry a gun. Since that day the only thing I carry is my handcuffs and a night stick. You pray to God you can get them before they get you."

Not everyone in the Babylon is a bum, he says. The hotel has its decent people who would not give any trouble, but then there are others who, "after they get that one drink," try to tear the building down. Visitors are not allowed after midnight and Attana asks the people in the hotel to keep their music and their voices low. Anyone who wants to throw a party has to check with the management first. He doesn't like to run things this way because it makes the place seem more like a prison, but if regulations aren't enforced, "people would pick up the whole place and run away with it."

Spring and summer, when the outsiders try to move in, are the worst seasons of the year. Faces appear in April that the house detective hasn't seen since the previous summer—Attana calls them "the visitors." Their "visits" are to make "contacts" with customers. "The girls used to stand in the hallways and make it right in front of us—it was a matter of having four, five, six lockups a day and having to spend all my time in court."

Each floor of the hotel has several wings, one man covering each floor all day. Attana says a lot of people have come in lately who are steady workers but his worries begin to mount each month when the moon is full. "This full moon business—this is something we believe in. We figure for two weeks of the month it's going to be quiet, the third week things start brewing and around full-moon time you get your biggest troubles—fighting, dope, prostitution, homosexuals scratching each other's faces and pulling hair. A man in my position that goes up to a room has to be ready to be a priest, because some of these people, that's how you got to talk to them. You have to cheer them up. There are places where I think nothing can happen, then I'll go into a room and there's been a killing, you understand. It's very hard to say, but I believe around every full moon we are going to catch it.

"Last full moon we had, I was called up to one of the rooms along with my partner, and a man in there had cut his common-law wife so badly she had to have 125 stitches on her body, and that was just one incident. Then we had three or four people fall asleep with pots on the stove. Two men were running around looking for these fires. Then along with that we had the people who get down in the lobby and start punching and wrestling. Then you get those who go out and get drunk, knowing that when they get back you're going to meet them at the front door, escort them to their own door, put them inside and lock the door. They'll stagger in from wherever they are and if they can make the front door they know they are safe. I carry a pass key so I can let them in. If we find out about a person being an ex-mental patient—nine out of ten times they're on welfare—we try to get the welfare department to take them off our hands. We do have one or two living in the building but they are harmless and don't bother anyone."

With all this turmoil going on a place like the Babylon strikes Attana as an odd place for elderly women to be living out their last few years, but the practice is quite in keeping with prevailing custom.

Hotels like the Babylon are frequently used by middle-class families as deposit boxes for ancient relatives. As such they are a source of deep despair to ministers like Charles S. MacKenzie of the Broadway Presbyterian, whose congregation includes many of these old people. Most of the old people in the Babylon ought to be in decent rest homes, Attana says, where they can get at least as good care as they would in a prison hospital. Many of them are unable to come down to the street to get a meal more than once a day. If they are on public assistance and fall ill, Attana calls the welfare department. Only in serious emergencies does he take it on himself to phone the relatives or have the person taken off to a hospital. Attana says he has never turned his back on anybody.

Whether or not they have living relatives, the old people in the Babylon would be alone in the world without their lumbering house detective. Usually they are white people and have a faded, patrician look about them. Perhaps because the Puerto Ricans have a different attitude about their matriarchs, or because they can't afford separate housing at the hotels, the Spanish families keep their old people with them, under their own roof. Whatever old Negroes are in the Babylon are put there by the welfare department. Negro grandfathers and grandmothers are not very common in local Negro tenements: there are only women and fatherless children who are in no position to afford refuge to anyone. The luckiest of the outworn Negroes are still living in shanties or farmhouses in the fresh air of the Carolinas.

The old white people sometimes have grown children who live in suburbs fifty or sixty miles away and who send rent checks to the management. One ninety-year-old lady, who looked as if she were made of porcelain, never had any company until the day of her funeral. Then her son, who was the chief of police in a Connecticut town, and half a dozen relatives came to the Babylon, to pay their last respects.

The Area's two settlement houses, Goddard-Riverside Community Center and Grosvenor House, have programs for old people who, after they walk in the door, are briskly addressed as "senior citizens." Before Grosvenor moved to a new fawn-colored brick building on 105th Street it occupied a storefront on Columbus Avenue and carried on a lively schedule, which included, on Tuesday and Thursday mornings, a "friendship meeting" for these senior citizens, many of whom come over from the East Side. A lady with bright red cheeks played an upright piano, there were other people who played horns and harmonicas, and a man beat time on a kettle. The instruments varied from week to week but not the mood or the repertoire. The songs were "Tipperary," "I'm a Yankee Doodle Dandy," "Darling Nelly Grey," "The Old Gray Mare," "She'll Be Comin' Round the Mountains, "I Been Working on the Railroad," "My Bonnie Lies Over the Ocean," "Smiles," etc. On Mondays, Wednesdays, and Fridays, when there were no friendship meetings at Grosvenor, some of these same senior citizens went to friendship meetings at other settlement houses.

No census of the senior citizens who attend these affairs all over town has ever been taken, but settlement-house workers say that there are quite a few overlaps and that if all the people who went to meetings were lumped together they might conceivably fit in one or two rooms. Grosvenor's director, Jerry Janowitz, concedes it is difficult to get very many senior citizens involved in social or community programs and that those who do turn out for settlement-house activities are perhaps those who need the activities least, since they are the more extroverted ones. A man who makes up for lack of professional staff by doing as much as five people, Janowitz says a few have discovered ways of pulling the introverted and more home-bound senior citizens out of the past—for instance, the Katharine Engel Center at Ninety-sixth and Broadway. In general, Grosvenor and other settlement houses simply do not have enough full-time people to go into building after building and do the necessary pulling and persuading, so many of the old people in the area who do not have the financial resources, the family support, or the will to function in the present are recluses. One reason for people's failure to turn out for friendship meetings is the enormous effort necessary to work themselves up into a state of jollity on Tuesdays and Thursdays. Some old people do not relish being called senior citizens and talked to like children. They also admit they would rather talk about their ailments and the good old days than be whipped into a state of hollow optimism by program directors. Avoidance of the subject of old age, and particularly the practice of holding birthday parties at which they are congratulated on being "eighty-seven years young" emphasizes to such people how very old they are, while their salvation really depends on their ability to think about something else.

Goddard-Riverside Community Center's four-story brownstone on Eighty-seventh Street has a more varied program for senior citizens.

Around noon the air is scented with hot biscuits. Besides dancing, singing, and impromptu orchestras, there are a finger-painting class, bridge, pinochle, cribbage, and a lunch for twenty-five cents. The menu may include soup, salmon casserole, biscuits with butter, dessert, and coffee. In the afternoon there is a snack. Goddard-River-side has certain regulars at its friendship meetings who appear to like the programs and the chance to be with each other in pleasant surroundings. The attractiveness of the program is enhanced by a minimum of intervention by staff members and volunteers of the settlement house. Very few of the senior citizens who come to the house are grumblers. Many live as neighbors in the same hotel nearby. They appear to have a capacity to become almost totally absorbed in amusement: if there is a hunger to be useful as well as to be amused, it is not readily apparent in conversations with them. Their appearance of contentment may depend on their having ac-cepted the unspoken hypothesis that, being old, the only issue is whether the party was a good one.

The ability of old people in the Area to seem content with their situation, or at least impassive in the face of it, is apparent on the benches located along the narrow esplanade running down the center of Broadway. As soon as the weather is warm enough for people with poor circulation, they come to the benches and sit there until the leaves in the park blow away in November. They look at the pedestrians, identify the makes of cars, and look at license plates and faces. In spite of the number of old people who use these benches, it is rare that anyone is overtaken by his Creator in the middle of Broadway. As they become less able to move about, the old people make fewer and fewer trips from their rooms or apartments to the street, and when they die they are somewhere out of sight. There was one exceptional case, talked about for quite a while afterward, of an aged woman who rolled off a bench and fell to the ground in a coma. A West End doctor summoned to the scene took the old woman's hand and said she was dead; however, the caress must have stimu-lated some last inner reserve, because as an ambulance arrived to take her away the lady's lips stirred and a great murmur went through the crowd. Eventually she walked off. In other places the incident might have been regarded as a miracle, but on Broadway it ruined the doctor's reputation and he lost a great many of his patients.

A bourne into which many old people disappear for the last time is the nursing home where, depending on the quality of the establishment, the process of disintegration is slowed down or accelerated. The Commissioner of Hospitals speaks darkly of some of these places. I used to walk past one such establishment regularly, a smoke-blackened building on West 105th Street; it looks like the fortress of Chinon. If the season is right, some of the people there come out and sit on a dark porch and look across at the high wall of rock running along Central Park across the street. They can also watch pedestrians and people waiting at the bus stop, but this is more difficult because of a tall, iron fence they have to peer through. It is even harder for a pedestrian to observe the people on the porch because he has to see through an iron porch railing ornamented with curlicues and other fretwork. The effect is disconcerting, as if one were looking through a keyhole and discovered an eye or a mouth and a nose, framed in black iron. Seen this way, features seem abnormally large. It is better to look down into the porch from the top of the rock in the park, where no fences can intervene. At this distance the people seem like motionless bits of white paper.

The number of indigent elderly people in the Area has remained somewhat of a mystery. The Department of Relocation and officials of the Housing and Redevelopment Board say quite often they are trying to discover how many old people need better housing, but the answer to this question is not available yet. One problem about a census is that most of the old people are invisible, almost as if this is what the world expects of them. There are some excellent apartments for older people in the new Stephen Wise Towers (public housing) and in a middle-income cooperative on Ninety-fourth Street. A few old people do not need these accommodations. They are already in institutions such as the one run by the Little Sisters of the Poor, or, if they are able to afford the rates, the modern, attractive Jewish Home and Hospital on 106th Street. Many other old people sit at windows looking out at the street, and when the time comes to knock down the house where they have spent a good part of their lives they are moved somewhere else. Studies show that they do not last long in their new surroundings.

5

THE GREYSTONES

MOST OF THE MIDDLE-CLASS POPULATION IN THE Area is white and votes the Democratic ticket. Some, like the Irish, vote it a little less enthusiastically because of a dislike for the liberal reformers who now control the party on the West Side. Also, a small percentage of those well-to-do Jews who are in or past their sixties (an economic and age group that forms about half the local Jewish population) read conservative papers like the New York *Journal-American*, wish the Negroes and Puerto Ricans would move somewhere else, and look favorably on Barry Goldwater. In the main, however, the Area's middle-class whites have not taken Republican nominees very seriously recently except for Senator Jacob Javits and the 1965 mayoral candidate, Representative John Lindsay, whom they helped elect mayor. Both these men did well in spite of their party label because West Siders considered them far more liberal than their Democratic opponents.

The younger middle-class Jews dominate the organizational life of the Area, with the women making up most of the active membership and holding offices. Except in certain traditionally Protestant agencies, such as the settlement houses, the WASPs (white Anglo-Saxon Protestants) ordinarily occupy subsidiary positions. The situation prevails not only because the Protestant population is outnumbered. The younger Jews feel a far greater need to "participate" and to seek leadership, and behind them is a tradition of public service and philanthropy unequaled by that of any other group in the city. The tradition explains why the best-run social agencies in the Area, the leadership of most of its parents associations, the main source of its political activists, and an unusually high percentage of its public school teachers and welfare workers are Jewish.

The middle-class population is concentrated on Central Park West, Eighty-sixth Street, Riverside Drive, and West End Avenue. Some of it is also sprinkled around in comfortable apartment houses and brownstones, usually rent controlled, on the better-kept side streets. One large middle-class settlement which is somewhat of an island to itself is Park West Village, the huge housing complex facing Central Park and running from Ninety-seventh to 100th Street. Park West is unique in that a large percentage of its tenants are Negroes, whose average income is often as high as or higher than the whites'. The Park West tenants as a whole do not play a permanent role in the Area. They move in and out rather rapidly and fewer than seventy-five children from Park West are attending local public schools.

The most noticeable characteristic of the middle-class sections, besides the markedly superior housing, is the relative peace on the sidewalks. These sections are well patrolled by foot policemen, and the doormen and watchful superintendents in most of the buildings reduce the chances of burglary and assault. The tranquillity is not an easy one, however, real security being more a state of mind than an actual condition. The middle-class white tends to worry more about the physical safety of his family than do the people around the corner who spend their lives in the very crater of disorder and mayhem. An occasional shocking crime, such as the murder of a tenant in the Hotel Greystone, has kept apprehension at a high level, and created a wave of protest against the type of unsupervised self-service elevator in which the man was stabbed to death.*

While it is almost impossible to avoid the subject of housing when talking with a low-income Negro or Puerto Rican, the subject is not a top-priority one with the middle-class white. Even so, about one out of three complains about his housing troubles.† The difference is that he is usually objecting to "fringe" discomforts, such as noisy radi-

* Asked for specific complaints about the area, middle-class respondents replied: (1) lack of safety (80 percent of the upper-middle-income groups, and 62 percent of the lower-middle-income groups made this complaint); and (2) the "composition of the population of the area" (74 percent of the upper-middle-income groups and 45 percent of the lower-middle-income groups made this point). By "composition," most respondents were found to be referring to specific types—alcoholics, addicts, deviants, prostitutes, etc.—rather than to any ethnic or racial group (Kraft Survey).

† Ninety percent of middle-class families with school-age children told interviewers that they were concerned about physical and moral danger to their children. The second greatest problem for the children was lack of play facilities (several elementary schools have been without adequate playgrounds for years) (Kraft Survey). See footnote p. 6.

ators or a small rent increase, rather than a total breakdown of plumbing, heating, and sanitation services. And when the middle-class tenant does make a complaint, he is far more likely to get results. Local superintendents deal more cautiously with tenants who are organization-minded and know how to defend their rights. Alcoa, the proprietor of Park West Village, has been taken to court by its tenants' association, and the list of tenants of a Riverside Drive greystone regularly includes attorneys, public-relations men, and housewives who know how to make a landlord suffer. The owner of a side-street brownstone thinks nothing of turning off the heat and hot water for a week in January to cut down the fuel bill, but when a boiler has to be shut off for a few hours and be fixed on West End Avenue, the superintendent posts an apologetic note in the elevator several days in advance of the repair job.

The spaciousness of the apartments on Riverside Drive and West End Avenue and their reasonable rents (six rooms and two baths for $200 or $275 is not unusual if a tenant has been able to get into a rent-controlled building) attract young couples with large families. A major attraction is Riverside Park. The parents, or their live-in maids from Europe or the West Indies, wheel the infants across the drive and take up stations on the same park benches every day. Mothers with children old enough to walk may organize a baby-sitting pool, which allows them an afternoon or two off for an appointment at the hairdressers, or to get "downtown." The early childhood social experiences take much the same shape they do on the beach of a suburban community: parents impress the young with a certain rudimentary socialism centered around the principle of sharing with others, and at the same time expect them to learn the meaning of private property and how to defend it. Inevitably the mothers have occasional altercations over whose child has been overaggressive, but on the whole the "park benchers" get along better with each other than the parents at Stuyvesant Town, the gigantic lower East Side middle-income housing development, where the competition for limited play space is much more intense.

Sometimes an apartment building is a small suburb unto itself. The more intra-building social contacts the children have, the better for the parents, who otherwise have to ferry the children about in taxis to friends scattered all over town. Child rearing and education, along with politics, are the favorite topics of adult conversation, and the mothers' literary life revolves to a great extent around the writings of Drs. Spock, Bettelheim, and Gesell. Dr. Spock became more popular than ever when he led a demonstration at the UN against U.S. involvement in the Vietnamese war.

It would be a mistake to assume that, because so many middle-class families are child centered, children of middle-class backgrounds are safe from difficult or abusive parents. Teachers and social workers attest to the contrary. One private-school instructress reports that most of her elementary-school children seem to be attending the psychiatrist regularly, and that many parents are using the school as a baby-sitting establishment. In such situations, she says, birth control among the wealthy is as much to be desired as it is among the unwed poor. There are middle-class mothers who are well known to the Society for the Prevention of Cruelty to Children, and others who should be but are not.*

When the children are four years old, many are entered in a private nursery school. The mothers say that the lack of public nursery schools (a few have been started recently in the Area) is one reason the public schools lose children to the private schools. Once a child has begun at Calhoun's nursery school, for instance, teacher-parent contacts are established, a heavy investment in conferences and interviews is built up, and if the teacher and child get along well there is a temptation to continue the child at Calhoun in spite of the high tuition.

The private schools vary considerably in quality. Several girl students at one of the more free-wheeling "social" schools crowd into a local drugstore at noon for a cigarette and Coke, and others eat lunch at Stark's restaurant on their own charge account. At another school, the emphasis is on academic achievement and on getting into an Ivy League college. One school forbids the use of cosmetics, while at another, where there are few restrictions on dress or makeup, the girls "sew" themselves temporarily into tight, abbreviated flannel

* The case of the baby of a well-to-do college-educated couple on Central Park West is an example. The child was an "accident": both parents exhibited intense, unremitting hostility to her from birth. The mother refused to talk to her, or hold her, even while feeding. The mother expressed displeasure when visitors picked the baby up and tried to amuse her. She often said she had no intention of allowing the child, whom both parents referred to as "the monster," to interfere with her social life. At nine months the baby weighed less than twelve pounds, and appeared to be autistic, never smiling and giving no sign of emotion when played with or talked to.

skirts every morning, in the same style that is popular at nearby Joan of Arc Junior High. The private schools proselytize middle-class parents relentlessly, even advertising in the newsletters of the public-school parents' associations. The P.S. 75 parents association's news-letter runs a note urging readers to "patronize our advertisers." The advertisers are expensive. Kindergarten tuition at the Walden School, for instance, is $1,200 annually and a year in its elementary school costs as much as $1,750. Families with two or three children who find they cannot keep up the expense and who still will not use the public schools move to the suburbs.

Many Riverside and West End parents would bypass the public schools, nursery school or no nursery school. The same objections come up regularly: the schools are concentrating on the "special problem" or underprivileged children at the expense of the normal or gifted children, classes are too large, and there is too much confusion and uncertainty in the organization of the schools. White parents are not the only ones to be dissatisfied. More and more children from middle-class Negro families now go to private school, and large numbers of Puerto Rican parents prefer the parochial schools.

The private school parents usually say that they believe in the principle of public school education, but they are not willing to experiment with their children. Their negative attitude about the public schools as often as not is based on secondhand information. While the Area's public schools, with one or two possible exceptions, are of good quality, the fact that local average reading achievement levels are a year behind the citywide public school average is enough to frighten off many parents. Actually middle-class children in these schools do quite well in their reading despite the school averages, if they have parental support at home. Matters have not been helped by the intense attacks on local schools by integration groups anxious to change their racial balances, and by other groups that are so opposed to any integration proposals that they constantly threaten to withdraw their children if matters are not settled their way. The school boycotts of 1964 and the resulting bitterness and anxiety among parents have not eased matters.*

* Several local elementary school principals reported that after the February, 1964, school boycott by civil rights groups, they noticed a change in attitude of Negro and white children toward their teachers and each other. "Many children seemed to be more aware of their color differences, and they had less respect for their school," stated one local principal.

Ill feeling over the integration issue even breaks out among public school parents. Some of the leaders of the P.S. 84 parents association became incensed in 1962 when thirty white children scheduled to enter their school (about 70 percent Negro and Puerto Rican at the time) were transferred to P.S. 75 (40 percent Negro and Puerto Rican) by special permission of the Board of Education at the request of their parents. The P.S. 84 parents association officers felt that race bias was behind the transfers.

The mothers who transferred their children to P.S. 75 deeply resent the charge of bias. Marcia Pivnick says her children attend P.S. 75 because it is nearer and because they do not have to walk across three dangerous traffic arteries.* She also points out that her children had attended P.S. 93, the predecessor of P.S. 84, which was as heavily Negro and Puerto Rican as P.S. 84. "What is more," she said, "several of the parents who transferred their children to P.S. 75 were among the most active people in the P.S. 93 parents association."

"You can't lump people together with remarks about their being for or against racial integration," she says. "There are certain people who have axes to grind, even on integration. For example, one couple talk as if they want to save the country for democracy but underneath they have their own selfish motives. Actually they raised such a fuss about the transfer because they were afraid the loss of white children from P.S. 84 would jeopardize continuance of all-white IGC [for intellectually gifted children] classes in which their children were enrolled. Their children have never been in a class with more than one or two Negroes and the mother once admitted to me that as long as her children are in an IGC class at P.S. 84 she will keep them in the school, but if they are dropped from the class she will put the children in private school."

On the one hand the Area owes a great deal to its middle-class population. It forms the spine of the local organizations, raises money for good causes, and gives a lively intellectuality to the Area's social and political life. One of the great advantages of living in the Area is the excitability of its political spirit and the abundance of people who are "interested" or who "care," as the saying goes on the West Side.

* A year or so after this controversy a Chinese child, May Yee, was killed by a bus at the intersection of Ninety-second Street and Columbus Avenue on her way to P.S. 84.

At the same time, some of the most vocal middle-class liberals have distorted the direction and quality of public discussion, particularly on education and housing. Socially conscious but less assertive people are often displaced or drowned out by what Harry Ashmore has called the "emotional freeloader," whose excursions into the civil rights movement satisfy his own psychic needs better than they serve the minority groups he claims to represent. The "emotional freeloader" has a short attention span and exhibits a distaste for long-term active personal commitments to any particular cause, but he often rises to the top of organizations because of his intense desire for recognition.

Such leaders activate themselves most successfully at large public meetings, and have shown themselves least reliable when it comes to assuming a continuing individual responsibility for any local undertaking. Their tendency to substitute their own ideas on what should be done for the poor without considering the views of the poor on the matter are slightly reminiscent of the Lady Bountiful who used to deliver Christmas turkeys to the poor in the family Bentley. The persistence of this submerged condescension among some of the most militant liberals has helped to increase the estrangement of middle-class organizations from the poor. When such people are allowed to dominate programs set up under the federal government's so-called "war on poverty," they give the programs a paternalistic and erratic character.

It should not be surprising that organizations run by people who leave their middle-class world only in their imagination have been so unsuccessful in attracting the participation of low-income groups. The blame for this nonparticipation is usually placed on the apathy of the poor and their lack of education, but the unresponsiveness of the poor might better be attributed to a logical lack of interest in middle-class activity and talk which has so little bearing on their own immediate difficulties. The pervasive dilettantism of much of the vocal left explains its gravitation to secondary issues, and avoidance of any sustained effort to deal with the basic education, housing, and employment needs of low-income minority groups.

The dilettantism produces some rather contradictory behavior. The integrationist who vehemently attacks so-called "racial imbalances" in the schools—and who may even suggest that individual classes be made up with racial balances as the main consideration—may also live in one of the Area's segregated white islands. One officer of a local civil rights organization who is quick to denounce others for bigotry has lived for years in an apartment house that has barred Negroes and Puerto Ricans. She has called for the resignation of the local school board because it has not produced a plan to get rid of de facto segregation completely, but she does not attend school board meetings and has never offered a plan of her own. Next door to her apartment house one of the Area's worst slumlords has cruelly and illegally persecuted his Spanish and Negro tenants for years, but she has never offered the victims her services. Then there is the case of a former high official of the City Commission on Human Rights who lives on Riverside Drive in a building that has never rented to a nonwhite tenant. Such cases, which are not exceptional, do not necessarily prove the crusaders in question are hypocrites. In organizing other people's lives, some people are forced to neglect their own personal responsibilities.

While most of the politically minded people in the Area would call themselves liberals, the spirit of liberalism, defined as a belief in open discussions among open minds, is not easy to find. Despite its plenitude of controversy, the West Side is not a shining example of the democratic dialogue. Public meetings on controversial issues usually resemble loyalty investigations. The citizens arrive with fixed, angry positions and later depart exhausted from having abused each other for two or three hours.

A statement presented at a local school board meeting in March, 1965, by EQUAL, an organization of white parents interested in school integration, illustrates the extent to which some members of the liberal establishment are committed to suspension of the dialogue. The EQUAL statement declared that the board should hold no public discussions of educational policy matters until after the policies had already been decided upon.

One consequence of the abandonment of thought has been the proliferation of clichés and formulas that enable people to take positions on any matter of grave public importance without thinking about them. In education, for example, one is for or against "quality integrated education," "heterogeneous grouping," "educational complexes," "decentralization," etc. At one meeting of the Joan of Arc Junior High School parents association, when a father declared that "anybody who isn't for the Allen plan [a report issued by the State

Commissioner of Education concerning racial integration] is against racial integration," the audience of a dozen or so people applauded enthusiastically, although neither the parent who made the statement nor, with two exceptions, anybody in the audience had ever read the Allen report.

Middle-class families are not only uneasy about each other's social attitudes, but there are also divisions within families over social and political matters. Parents may want to live in a racially mixed community but they are also almost always apprehensive about the turbulence in an unstable neighborhood populated by large numbers of economically depressed people who feel little identification with anyone else—"the others." The worries of the adults can cause conflicts between father and son, mother and daughter. Children growing up in the Area may be less apprehensive than parents who grew up in traditional, middle-class neighborhoods.

One family in which there are lively differences is that of Dr. and Mrs. David Baum, who live in a six-room apartment on West End Avenue. Dr. Baum is a specialist on the staff of a city hospital; his wife, Kitty, worked in the City Emergency Relief Bureau before their marriage and has been a delegate to Stryckers Bay Neighborhood Council, representing the Calhoun School, where her daughter Irene went before entering college. Mrs. Baum, who is a vivacious, well-groomed woman, dresses less conservatively than her daughter Irene, who likes to wear black and uses no makeup, but she is more conservative in other ways. She is more critical of the neighborhood, for instance. In her turn, Irene is impatient with middle-class parents, including her own.

Mrs. Baum feels the city agencies should do much more for people on the "low end" of the ladder, yet at the same time she says that the middle class gets very little help in its efforts to improve the community and cut down violence and disorder. She hopes that a rebuilt West Side will include all racial and economic groups but she does not want to see it become heavily loaded with public housing. She is critical of many local parents for neglecting their children. At a clothing depot at a local school, for instance, she says "some mothers come in every couple of weeks for new clothes. When the children's clothes get dirty, they just take them off the child and throw them away." When she assisted in a summer camp program at P.S. 75, many of the mothers of the underprivileged children in the school who came in to place their children in the summer camp were intoxicated, she said, and others seemed to be interested "only in handouts and in getting rid of their children. I finally asked myself, 'Why am I doing this?' The answer, of course, was that I wanted to help get the kids away from this environment. I went away pretty disgusted."

Irene, who attended P.S. 93 and was always in mixed classes, resents the aspersions commonly directed at Puerto Ricans, and says that all of her friends are Puerto Ricans and that she knows what she is talking about.

"You mean many of your friends, Irene, not all," her mother remarked.

Irene put her feet up on a stool. "Lots of kids are misjudged. If they see you with a Puerto Rican or a Negro, they blame you. I think they're held back too. I know a Negro boy who was. He started at our school in the fourth grade. He was much older than I was and he had to work. His father committed suicide. He had been working since a boy on Broadway. This is why he was behind in his class, yet nobody seemed to understand this and they thought he was dumb. On Broadway I was talking to a Negro near the subway and somebody called my mother up and said I was flirting with a Negro. This happens lots of times. There is somebody here in this building that always phones my mother every time they see me talking to a Puerto Rican or a Negro. They blame me for the way I dress and fix my hair because it looks the way Puerto Ricans and Negroes do it. They take everything at face value. If there is a stabbing on Eighty-third Street everybody says automatically, 'It's a Puerto Rican.' "

"My daughter is always for the underdog," Mrs. Baum interjected.

Irene continued without drawing a breath. "They don't give the kids a chance to do anything so the kids end by being dirty and the houses they live in are smelly and dirty. If they had a chance, they could do a lot. I think the Jews here are the worst as far as being prejudiced and they are the last that ought to be. After all, they've been persecuted enough themselves."

Her mother bridled.

Irene went on, "When Puerto Rican families come to New York, they come because they've been told they'll get a place to live and a job but when they get here they are just jammed in these rotten holes."

"You haven't been going to school with Puerto Rican children since the sixth grade," Mrs. Baum remarked.

"That doesn't make any difference," Irene answered. "I grew up with them and they are still my best friends. How does all the trouble start? A bunch of Puerto Rican boys will go into the park and meet and play baseball. Sometimes the Spanish girls come out and cheer and there are certain older men who sort of befriend the team. There is one they call Pop who is very nice and interested. The kids finish and they are hot, sweaty, and standing around talking, trying to cool off. Along come a bunch of white girls, you know, from nice families, dressed up and giggling. Then they see these boys approaching them and the girls say to each other, 'How are we going to walk now?' Either they cross over, which is so obvious they're avoiding the boys or else they just walk by and give the boys a dirty look. Well, the Puerto Rican boys don't like to get dirty looks. That's how it starts. Maybe the boys will say something because they're mad. Then the girls will go home and tell their families a Puerto Rican tried to rape them."

Irene has worked at Presbyterian Hospital as a "candy-striper," a one-day-a-week volunteer aid, wearing a red-and-white-striped pinafore. Irene helps nurses in the baby section of the hospital, doing errands, making beds, helping with the linen, carrying samples from the laboratory, wheeling patients. There are many Negro and Puerto Rican patients there and Irene likes to practice her Spanish, which she speaks fluently, on them.

Irene was indignant about the attitudes of many people that the Puerto Ricans have loose morals. "The Spanish people have wonderful traditions. The girls in the neighborhood are taken care of very well by their families. They go to church, they're moral. They have a wonderful family feeling, and when you get to know one kid you get to know everybody in the family. The brothers protect their sisters."

"The people I am angry with in the area are the women with sixteen kids and sixteen different fathers, the bums and dope peddlers," Mrs. Baum said.

"It's the older people, especially the single ones, that make the problems, not the kids," Irene said.

She did not think the police were fair. "I was looking out the window a couple of weeks ago at a group of white kids on West End Avenue. I recognized some of them as being from the so-called good families. The kids had radios, and they were shouting and there was a real racket. No policeman stopped them or questioned them. After about thirty minutes they finally went away. Pretty soon, on the same corner, the same day, a bunch of Puerto Ricans and Negroes got together, young people singing. It wasn't long before the police drove up and sent them off. I don't say it's the fault of the police necessarily. It's simply that someone in the neighborhood was not alarmed when she saw white children congregating, but the Negro and Puerto Rican children were a sort of instant warning that she should phone the police."

However, Irene had a few good words for the police. When a narcotics addict fell down in Ninety-third Street in the midst of withdrawal, she stood by until a policeman came. "All the time the boy was suffering, he kept saying, 'Get Sergeant Jackson, get Sergeant Jackson.' The sergeant was from the Youth Division and had taken care of the boy before." Irene also recalled a policeman who used to buy peaches for all the children. "That was a long time ago."

Esta Kransdorf, a dark, slender mother of two girls, is the executive secretary of the local Stryckers Bay Neighborhood Council. Because of her job and where she lives, in a $110-a-month, three-room apartment on West Ninety-third Street across from several rooming houses, she sees the Area in a different light from a resident of West End Avenue or Central Park West. A Jew and a political liberal, she can be critical of Jews and liberals. She dislikes complacency but would like a more settled atmosphere in her community.

Before moving into the Area several years ago, Mrs. Kransdorf lived in California, which she remembers for the "lethargy in community life out there." With all its turbulence, the West Side is better. "People are forced by social conditions to wake up and change their attitudes. The only thing you can say about us is that we are not complacent or slow moving." In a "set" community such as Sherman Oaks, California, she says, there is absolutely no impulse to change. "At 8 P.M. everyone was home and the doors were locked. Most of the people were middle-class intellectuals who had made it financially and had crept into a comfortable shelter where they didn't have to worry about the outside world."

Mrs. Kransdorf has an unconscious inclination to balance an unfavorable remark about the West Side with a favorable one.

"There are changes for the better. You hear less bigoted talk about 'dirty Puerto Ricans.' People are less panicky. When things first began to deteriorate, people called the cops every minute. Either because they got no results or because things kept getting worse, they stopped. This doesn't mean that people are getting more tolerant. Living in the same neighborhood with Negroes and Puerto Ricans has not softened the hostilities of many whites and Puerto Ricans and Negroes. The Negro and Puerto Rican see the white living in better housing and sometimes paying less rent than they do for a broken-down single room, and this aggravates them. The whites are quick to blame the Negro and Puerto Rican for being prejudiced against whites, but they won't recognize their own racial prejudices.

"Some people are hostile to Negroes because of the way they think they treat their children. They object to the children being out in the streets, riding bikes and running around late at night. Some white people are making an effort to get along with their neighbors because their children all attend the public school, but other whites are just beyond reclaiming as far as their prejudices go—you just have to give up on them. They want no changes."

Anti-Semitism in some parts of the West Side occurs because "here the Jews tend to be on the upper side of the heap, which makes them resented. It is assumed that the landlords of most of the slum properties are Jews. Except for the banks, most of the business establishments on Broadway are run by Jews. In New York, the Negroes see only that Jews are the whites and the ones on top and they don't distinguish much between them. To the Negro, the landlord is a Jew. Some people—and I include many whites—are not sophisticated enough to know that the real-estate agent or the man who collects the rent is not necessarily the owner and they are not wise enough to know that New York is not being run by a Jewish conspiracy."

In the East Bronx, where Mrs. Kransdorf grew up, "the Italians had all kinds of stories about the Jews then; they were the Christ killers. The Jews were pretty well ridden with various fears of the Italians and other people. Now the circumstances are different. Instead you have a sort of Catholic-Protestant cold war, with the Catholics rather contemptuous of the Protestants and the Protestants suspicious of the Catholics. It seems that this area is full of anger. The fever comes and goes."

A "disinterest among many Jews in promoting Negro rights" bothers Mrs. Kransdorf. "It is unfortunate that we do not have a dynamic leadership in our synagogues. A few clergymen like Father Gusweller, Father Browne, and Rabbi Edward Klein who take on the job of representing the poor and the minority groups in our religious organizations are pretty scarce." She mentions the case of a Freedom Rider rally on the West Side in 1961 when the Reverend Edward White suggested that West End Avenue landlords desegregate their buildings. "This quietly fizzled out. It wasn't a large romantic issue like the Freedom Riders in Alabama. It was a local thing and it meant that the Jewish community, if Reverend White had been taken seriously, would have split wide open, with Jews fighting on West End Avenue among themselves over the question of segregated houses that some of them own or live in."

Mrs. Kransdorf says that she is apprehensive about herself or her children walking home at night after there has been a bad incident, but eventually she gets over it. Soon, she thinks, things may be getting better. "Then after a shooting on Ninety-fifth Street I worry for another week and will have a friend walk home with me. Then after a while you go on your easy way again." She used to wonder if she ought to pack up and go to the Bronx. "You weigh it and then you forget it," she says. "If I lived in a different area, my kids would be identified religiously. They aren't here. In other communities they would be part of a synagogue group. Here this condition is not a matter of importance. There is not an acceptance problem. Socially, there are other problems. My children have Negro and Puerto Rican friends, but on a limited level. They have been at camp with them yet they're not on a comfortable plane of social experience with them." Even though her daughters go to Joan of Arc Junior High School, where there are a majority of Negro and Puerto Rican children, there is not enough opportunity for social experience with the minority group children; the girls are in small classes for intellectually gifted children. She says the classes are segregated on an intellectual as well as on a racial basis, because the testing programs emphasize achievement rather than a child's intellectual potential, and therefore tend to work against the Negro and Puerto Rican child.

The Area seems to have been ignored pretty much by civil rights groups, she thinks. The Commonwealth of Puerto Rico office and Aspira, a Puerto Rican organization that tries to develop leadership in Puerto Rican youngsters, relate better to their people than the NAACP or the Urban League or CORE does to local Negroes. "The civil rights groups are never involved in local parents associations even though the schools in the district have a heavy Negro and Puerto

Rican registration." Mrs. Kransdorf has called the NAACP a number of times on various matters, but as a rule they have not responded with much cooperation. They seem to have concentrated their work in the Bedford-Stuyvesant and Harlem areas. "This is too bad because on the West Side the people are at least physically integrated and there is an opportunity here to develop a community that could be integrated in spirit as well."

Her presidency of the parents association of Joan of Arc Junior High School led to her concern about housing, now her major interest. She likes to work at things where she can accomplish something on a personal level. She calls this a matter of picking realistic goals. "When I yelled about the kids' needing more books at school, something happened. It took three years, but we got more money.

"I'm discouraged about political parties. The local Democratic club is liberal, but it isn't doing much for the local people. There is more of a chance for direct action elsewhere. People do not lean very heavily on the local level of politics. You can talk to a Puerto Rican about voting, and maybe he will, but it won't make much of a difference in his life even if he does. You know it and he knows it too. Even if you get laws passed after fighting for them a long time, they never seem to get enforced. But if a Puerto Rican learns his classroom is crowded and needs more teachers, and that his child's schooling is affected, you have something to work on and you get to know the parent this way. It is a process of personal education."

Part III: BY THE PEOPLE

6

XXXX

A PEOPLE'S STYLE OF POLITICS

ABOUT ELEVEN O'CLOCK ON A JULY MORNING, MRS. Kransdorf arrives at the northwest corner of Columbus Avenue and Eighty-ninth Street and unlocks the door to a storefront office. She can hear the phone ringing as she turns the key. Putting a wedge under the door to keep it open and let in the mid-morning air, she drops a large packet of mail on her desk, then goes over to turn on an old, very noisy air conditioner. Back at the desk, she picks up the phone.

"Stryckers Bay. Can I help you?" She squeezes the phone between her left ear and shoulder, freeing her hands, and begins opening letters and stacking them in a pile to her right. Outside, a man is peering through the plate-glass window, between some posters pasted on it with Scotch tape. She waves to him and points to a chair. In the back room another phone starts to ring. By the time Mrs. Kransdorf hangs up, two elderly women have also entered the office, and a six-year-old boy named Freddy Dominquez is sweeping the floor. This is the way business usually gets under way five times a week, fifty-two weeks a year, at the headquarters of the Stryckers Bay Neighborhood Council, and it continues until 5 P.M. or later.

The council—which takes the name Stryckers Bay from a historic name once applied to part of the area near the Hudson River—was

117

born about the same time as the FDR–Woodrow Wilson Democratic Club, and in a number of ways its activities resemble the community service function many of the early reform Democrats wanted their club to perform. Since 1959, however, as the club's committees on housing, rent, social referral, urban renewal, etc., have become inactive, the council's work in these and other fields has steadily increased. Some of its most active volunteers—Nancy Brigham, the chairman of the council's housing committee, for instance—have transferred their interests from the club to the council. Over the past six or seven years the council has established a close relationship with many hundreds of people, young and old, whose lives have been disorganized by urban decay and urban renewal.

On behalf of this heterogeneous community of displaced and inconvenienced people, the council has practiced a pragmatic type of nonpartisan politics which has influenced the shape and the execution of housing and redevelopment policies which affect the Area. In contrast to the local political club, the council has concentrated on giving people first aid with their immediate problems and has managed to avoid scattering its energies. It has a small membership but a good percentage of its members are active volunteers in some phase of the council's work. The council's activities seem to have held rather closely to two general purposes: to inform the people, particularly the poor, about their rights and opportunities in a period of intense social upheaval brought on by urban renewal, and to defend these rights and opportunities against abuse by the administrative agencies of city government.

Of the many organizations that exist on the West Side, the council seems to have become the most relevant even though its services have been restricted by a low budget and a small paid staff, which has never been more than one full-time and one half-time employee. In fact, it has even been able to give new life to the other local organizations which individually have been weak and generally inattentive to the Area's daily economic, social, and educational problems. On paper, the council is an association of about fifty such organizations—religious, ethnic, educational, civic, and political—each of which has two voting delegates in the council. But in reality the council's staff and the tendency of its voting delegates to act as individuals rather than as organizational representatives give the council a life of its own.

Despite its name, the council is something rather unusual in the life of the area. It is not typical of the traditional "neighborhood" organizations found all over New York City, in which local taxpayers combine to keep out the "new elements" and encourage the planting of trees. While it is true that various degrees of protectionism and Protestant nostalgia dominate the thinking of some of the organization's charter member organizations, the significant fact about the council is that it carries very little baggage from the past. It was invented to cooperate with change, not to resist it, and to make it work for the benefit of the people instead of their total discomfort. In a sense the council has brought together whatever remains of the vigor of many organizations which have outlived most of their usefulness, while keeping clear of the mortgages the past has put upon them.

The history of the council is also the history of the West Side urban renewal plan, the most important event that has befallen the Area since the in-migration of Puerto Ricans changed the entire character of the upper West Side. The story of urban renewal is inseparable from the story of the council; taken together they are a major chapter in the contemporary life of the city. It might even be said that the council was one of the most important results of the urban renewal plan because it has provided an example of a new type of politics in which the interests of the poor have been represented, if not always successfully, at least with energy and understanding.

The urban renewal–council chapter began with the release in 1958 of a two-year City Planning Commission study of the urban blight that had overtaken twenty blocks in the heart of the area bounded by Eighty-seventh and Ninety-seventh Streets (south to north), and by Central Park West and Amsterdam Avenue (east to west). The ninety-six-page report, costing the public $225,000, provided statistics which outlined the extent of the Area's misery.

Since the Great Depression there had been no new construction on the twenty blocks, yet from 1950 to 1956 the population had increased 25 percent, from 30,000 to 39,000 persons. As the housing came into the hands of slumlords it rotted and subdivided. By 1956, there were 10,400 people living in quarters suitable for 4,500. Of more than 15,000 quarters in the Area, 17 percent were one-room units occupied by one, two, or more persons—many of them children. The number of children inhabiting these decaying cells had doubled in the six years covered by the study.

While living spaces were shrinking and decomposing, their rents were jimmied up rapidly. The rents in brownstones and old-law tenements averaged $2.86 and $2.36 per square foot per annum, respectively, as compared with rents of $1.30 per square foot in good elevator apartment buildings. Although the city was paying more to maintain fire and police protection, sanitation and school facilities in the area, it got no additional taxes from the landlords, who were busy raising rents, crowding the housing, and creating the need for increased city services. While rental income from the Area increased 40 percent from 1950 to 1956, the Area's contribution to the city in taxes fell 11 percent.

As the Area burned up, figuratively speaking, the white population declined from 31,446 to 22,346, while the Puerto Rican population rose from 1,700 to nearly 13,000, and the Negro population from 426 to 3,530, with both groups sifting into the worst housing. The twenty blocks changed from a middle-class area to one in which 58 percent of the 17,990 families had incomes below $3,000, and 30 percent had incomes between $3,000 and $5,000. The Puerto Ricans were on the bottom of the heap, with incomes of families and unrelated individuals averaging $2,553, while the Negroes' average income was $2,850. The landlord took the biggest single bite out of these people, with more than half the low-income families paying over 20 percent of their income for rent.

What was to be done? The City Planning Commission study advanced a general plan to divide the twenty blocks into three sectors, or "phases," to be renewed in succession. It proposed construction of a mixture of public housing, middle-income cooperatives, and "fully-taxpaying" (luxury) apartments. It advised that structurally sound buildings in the Area should be rehabilitated wherever possible, so as to preserve some of the character of the original community. The need for a "humane" method of relocating families to be displaced was stressed. A bulldozer would as usual be the ultimate weapon but this time it would be guided by someone more sensitive than Robert Moses, who had been the city's previous slum clearance dictator. The core of the misery would be cauterized and scraped clean, then brick and glass towers would rise on the site. At the end, a wasteland of aggravation and shame and expense to the city would be replaced by an attractive, well-ordered community which, it was hoped, would increase the city's tax revenues and require fewer policemen.

In 1959, a year after the study of the Area had been completed, a preliminary urban renewal plan, reflecting the thinking of the planners, top-level city officials and the real-estate men—"the big operators in urban life today," as a local clergyman put it—was presented to the people of the West Side. The new construction would include 4,700 luxury apartments, renting at an average of $50 per room. Added to this would be another 3,000 luxury units to be created out of rehabilitated buildings. There would be 2,400 middle-income units, renting at $21 to $30 per room, while another 1,965 middle-income units would be developed out of rehabilitated buildings.

For the low-income families who represented the majority of people to be displaced, the plan provided just 400 units of public housing, renting at $14 to $18 per room. This was to become the plan's most controversial proposal because it meant that the new neighborhood would be populated by an almost entirely new group of people. The main effect of the preliminary plan would be to upgrade the real estate of the Area—increasing the city's tax take by nearly 400 percent—and convert the section into an eye-catching upper-and middle-income neighborhood, the pride of Manhattan Island and the apple of the tax collector's eye.

It then became the people's turn to respond to the city's proposal, and at this point the Stryckers Bay Neighborhood Council appeared on the scene.

A provision in the Federal Housing Act requires that any urban renewal program aided by federal funds must allow citizen groups in the community affected to participate in the development of the program. In accordance with this requirement, Mayor Wagner had appointed a Park-Hudson Committee of leading West Side citizens to consult with city officials on the plan. With the appearance of the 1958 study, the Park-Hudson Committee began to meet with urban renewal officials and to hold public meetings. Significantly, the Park-Hudson Committee did not attempt to evaluate the urban renewal plan at these meetings, or to sound out community sentiment. Its function was largely limited to "briefing sessions" on what the law provided and how it would affect the Area.

Had Park-Hudson remained the official voice of the community, it is likely that local citizen influence on the shape of renewal would have been just as limited as it has been in other American cities where "leading citizens" groups have been the only officially recognized spokesmen for the communities affected. Such was not to be the case on the West Side. In the spring of 1959, it became apparent that a variety of groups and individuals in the urban renewal area were dissatisfied at being represented by people who, although distinguished, would not personally be affected by urban renewal and would tend to take a rather detached view of the whole problem. As one of the dissidents described Park-Hudson: "These leading citizens sat in their Central Park towers and planned for the area. They drove around in cars making 'windshield surveys' and never went inside the houses."*

A stocky, forty-year-old Roman Catholic priest, Henry J. Browne, who had taken up lodgings in St. Gregory's Church to teach at Cathedral College, was to become one of the most active objectors to the Park-Hudson approach. Although he knew little about urban renewal or housing at the time, Father Browne had heard some worried remarks about the plan from his pastor, Monsignor Joseph Flanagan. If all the Puerto Rican people and the Irish people were to be moving out, Monsignor Flanagan would say, and there would be no apartments they could come back to, well, that would mean a considerable dent in the parish.

Since he came out of a tradition of agitators (he is a specialist in labor history and had just finished a Fulbright year in Italy studying labor and immigration problems), Father Browne decided to drop in to one of the meetings sponsored by the Park-Hudson Committee in St. Gregory's auditorium. It was here he heard the first verbal shots of the local Irish rebellion. He remembers a towering, angry longshoreman named Bill Doherty standing up in the audience and shouting at the planners on the platform, "You say 'we' are gonna do this and 'we' are gonna do that—just who is this 'we,' and who thought up this whole thing anyway?" The atmosphere of the meeting, resentful and suspicious at the outset, grew more so when another indignant resident, a bearded landlord named Roger Hanafin, rose to declare that it was a "shame" for the city to say the urban renewal plan would "preserve" the community.

"Is it preserving the community when only 5 percent of the people

* "Citizen Participation in Urban Renewal: The West Side Urban Renewal Area." Graduate studies paper by Betty Bollinger, Harvard University, January 8, 1964.

who are going to be kicked out of the area will be able to afford the rent when the place is rebuilt?" Hanafin wanted to know.

After the meeting, Father Browne went back to his room on the top floor of St. Gregory's and examined a copy of the 1958 study to see what Doherty and Hanafin were talking about. Their meaning was clear by the time he had finished. With only four hundred units of public housing provided for in the preliminary urban renewal plan in an area where 88 percent of the people were earning less than $5,000 a year, he concluded that this was not "renewal"; it was "removal."

Of more interest to Father Browne was the fact that the community affected by the plan did not seem to be getting sufficient opportunity to question some of its basic assumptions, and in May of 1959, at a public meeting sponsored by Park-Hudson, he demanded greater citizen involvement in the educational and planning phases of urban renewal. In August, Father Browne was innocently informed by Monsignor Flanagan that his name had been "put in" for a "committee." The "committee" was a provisional group of local organizations brought together by two professional organizers from the Community Council of New York, in response to growing dissatisfaction with the Park-Hudson Committee.

Because of the shortage of time, and the amount of manpower needed to recruit a "mass" membership organization and educate them about urban renewal, it was decided the committee should act as a coordinating body of already existing organizations. In December, 1959, the provisional committee adopted a constitution and the name of Stryckers Bay Neighborhood Council. Each of the forty charter member organizations was entitled to two delegate votes. (Individual nonvoting members were not allowed to join until 1961.) The first chairman of the council was Milton Akers, the headmaster of a private school (Walden). Father Browne was appointed chairman of the Housing Committee.*

The heterogeneity of the council's members indicated clearly that it was not going to be a tightly knit, single-minded organization with a

* Stryckers Bay's method of organizing itself was in contrast to that of the Chelsea Community Council, a neighborhood group organized lower down on the West Side (Twenty-third to Thirty-fourth streets). The Chelsea Council had a greater voting membership and it blew apart in a power struggle between groups led by those favoring construction of the huge Penn South ILGWU Housing Cooperative and the opponents of the Coöp, led by tenants, largely Irish, living on the proposed Penn South site.

unanimous policy on urban renewal or anything else. A preponderance of its white, middle-class organizational delegates wanted urban renewal to get under way as quickly as possible and were anxious to avoid quarrels over details which might delay the plan. These groups included the block associations, the parents associations, some Protestant churches and synagogues, whose dwindling membership was largely middle class, and private schools. On the other hand, the Puerto Rican delegates found themselves opposing all urban renewal plans because they meant the displacement of Puerto Rican families. Representatives of small commercial establishments fought to the bitter end renewal plans for Columbus Avenue, where their shops and stores were concentrated. Supporting urban renewal with deep reservations but favoring more low- and middle-income housing were the Catholic parishes whose communicants would be affected, liberal political organizations such as the ADA, and some Democratic reform leaders.

The divisions in the council remained subdued until June, 1962, a few months before the Board of Estimate's hearing on the final urban renewal plan. The warnings of city officials that major changes in the plan would delay it forever crystallized the opposition of several council members to increasing the plan's provision for public housing. On their part, a group led by Father Browne, several Democratic reform leaders, and other liberal groups demanded an increase in public housing from 400 to 2,500 units. When the council took a vote on the issue, Browne's group was defeated.

Browne's response was to organize an ad hoc Committee for Fair Urban Renewal to carry on the fight for more public housing outside the council. Two significant meetings took place the week before the Board of Estimate hearings, which seemed to decide the controversy. At one, the reform FDR–Woodrow Wilson Democratic Club narrowly voted for revision of the plan to allow for more public housing, and since the club was the official Democratic organization for the district, this was an important victory. The second meeting was a huge rally in the auditorium of Holy Name Church to proclaim a united front for more public housing. Among groups represented were the two Catholic parishes, half a dozen Puerto Rican organizations, the Irish Institute, the United Irish Societies, the Association of Catholic Trade Unionists, the West Side chapter of the American Jewish Congress, the West Side chapter of the Americans for Democratic Action, several leaders of the FDR–Woodrow Wilson Club, CORE, the Manhattan branch of the NAACP (the national NAACP opposed any revision of the plan), and the International Brotherhood of Teamsters. Street announcements were made over a PA system donated by the National Maritime Union and installed in a convertible owned by Mr. and Mrs. David Piel, prominent members of the FDR–Woodrow Wilson Democrats. Stencils for leaflets were typed in the office of a private school and run off by the Teamsters. One of the songs composed for the rally by Flavia Alaya, a Stryckers Bay member, ran:

> East Side, West Side,
> All around the Town,
> Urban Renewal's upon us,
> The buildings are coming down.
> The new ones are luxurious,
> So to hell with Mamie O'Rourke.
> She can be relocated
> To the outskirts of New York.

As it turned out, the mere threat of the meeting was enough to get action from City Hall. At 4 P.M. of the day the meeting was scheduled, the chairman of the Housing and Redevelopment Board telephoned Father Browne and representatives of the Puerto Rican organizations to tell them they would get their 2,500 units of low-income housing and additional units of middle-income housing as well. The council's minority had led a successful campaign to force fundamental changes in the city's design for a new community.

Even with the victory won, the rally still took place. Such an organizational masterpiece could not be canceled in a matter of minutes. Father Browne recalls that it "was the greatest meeting the West Side ever had," which was something in an area where public meetings are as much a way of life as walking in the park.

If the city fathers had expected the council to serve merely as a temporary voice of the community on urban renewal matters, they were mistaken. During the commotion over urban renewal the council expanded its membership and activities and began to look into all sorts of matters: civil rights, law enforcement, health, education, welfare, relocation, and youth activities. Like many useful temporary arrangements, the council became permanent. For all practical purposes, Father Browne became its permanent president.

The council's monthly plenary meetings have become a regular local forum at which debates are held, resolutions proposed, committee reports criticized, and council officers castigated. Attendance is normally between forty and fifty, usually consisting of the same people. Some delegates remain mostly silent, some speak incessantly, and others rarely speak but grumble a great deal. Some matters turn up on the agenda every month, while subjects brought up from the floor are unpredictable. The meetings provide information about municipal behavior that has become valuable ammunition for council representatives when they have met to argue with city commissioners.

The people who attend the meetings regularly become quite sophisticated about building codes, behavior of city officials, relocation programs, and the habits of foot patrolmen. Their discussions are often incomprehensible to an outsider. One newcomer complained that listening to a Stryckers Bay meeting for the first time was like coming into the middle of an Alfred Hitchcock movie, and suggested that Father Browne provide newcomers with a synopsis of previous meetings and a glossary of such terms as "Mitchell-Lama," "skewed rentals," "title-vesting dates," "inspectional coordination," "rehab," and so on.

However, the real heart of the council's operation is its storefront office, a place where people can check up on rumors that deluge the Area and ask for help. The people usually in the council's office-clinic besides Mrs. Kransdorf, the paid executive secretary, are Mrs. Sandra Thomas, chairman of the tenant relocation committee, and Barbara Jeffers, who stand by when Mrs. Kransdorf and Father Browne are at a meeting. Thomas Purcell, a young Irish lawyer who gives free legal advice on occasion, also drops in frequently. Father Browne appears around noon. Once in the back room he removes his jacket and collar, studies papers, and begins telephoning. In the front room the women listen to every known variation of the injustices to which an individual can be subjected at the hands of unsound government and irresponsible landlords. Mrs. Kransdorf may give the victim some badly needed information, or refer the plaintiff to an agency that can help him, telephone a city agency about the problem, or help her client fill out an application form for public housing. More often than not, the plaintiff's aggravation is incurable because the conditions of existence dictated by his economic state make it inevitable that he be aggravated: his torture at the hands of the city may be quite legal. Psychologically speaking, Mrs. Kransdorf's experiences with the System are somewhat like those of a dentist who spends most of his day looking at decayed teeth.

Mrs. Kransdorf calls discrepancies between official policies and operational facts to the attention of the proper authorities, and, although she is considered bad news, city officials respect her and she is able to get through to the right people in the city hierarchy—something as impossible for the average citizen as roller skating up a glass mountain. Her phone calls may very well be about situations that, if ignored, might erupt into something ugly, such as a fire in an abandoned building, a flurry of rat bites, or—what is worse by far—a nasty newspaper story inspired by Father Browne, who is somewhat of a genius at public relations.

The council staff initiates communications between agencies that are unknowingly neutralizing each other's efforts. In one such case, welfare clients in a city-owned building complained to the council that the welfare department was holding up their rent checks because the landlord was not taking care of their building.* Ordinarily such action by the welfare department might seem like a blow for social justice. In this case, however, the landlord was the city's Department of Real Estate. So Mrs. Kransdorf informed the welfare department that it was conducting a rent strike against another city agency, then called the Department of Real Estate maintenance people and told them to get busy.

A couple of years later, when Mrs. Kransdorf's complaints about poor maintenance were unavailing, the council encouraged the tenants in neglected city-owned buildings on Ninetieth Street to stage a rent strike. In this case, the tactic brought painters, plasterers, and plumbers on the double, but in other cases the city's behavior is incomprehensible. Its action is sometimes extraneous. On one occasion, when Mrs. Kransdorf told the city that the bathrooms in one of its houses wasn't working, the Department of Real Estate delivered twenty toilet seats to the building the next day.

* Such action can be taken under the Spiegel Act, which makes it illegal for the Department of Welfare to pay rent in cases where the building in question has hazardous violations. The act, for practical purposes, is a dead letter because it is rarely invoked.

The council's meager budget and heavy reliance on volunteers and the many responsibilities it has taken on make it difficult for it to do more than to keep pricking and probing. One of the most persistent riddles the council has tried to solve has to do with the whereabouts of the people who lived in buildings slated to come down for urban renewal. The Department of Relocation is supposed to keep an accurate record of the addresses of all these people, both those who have moved off site and those who have remained until the department has found a place for them. The council had evidence that the department had lost track of large numbers of these original site tenants. Some estimates of the missing persons ran as high as 15 percent of the total site tenants, although the department claimed it was no more than 3 or 4 percent. At a meeting with the department in October, 1964, Mrs. Kransdorf reported that after the council had mailed out eight hundred letters to people on urban renewal sites, using address labels typed at the Department of Relocation from its own records, two hundred letters had been returned marked "Address unknown" or "Building razed."

An illustration of the diversity of the council's work is the record of a single week's activities in September, 1964.

The council gave information on housing and redevelopment matters to an average of fifty persons a day who came to the office, and an average of twenty-five persons a day who telephoned.

The executive secretary had three two-hour discussions with housing authority officials on tenant relocation problems.

The council president conferred with local experts and a U.S. Senate subcommittee on housing about the council's own housing committee report.

The council staff completed joint discussions with the Housing and Redevelopment Board, the Board of Education, and the Departments of Real Estate and Relocation about relocation of families from the site of a new playground at P.S. 166.

The council's relocation committee met to plan its activities as an advisory group to relocatees, commercial tenants, and permanent tenants in the area.

The council's police liaison Committee met with the local precinct captain to discuss a new influx of problems arising from an outbreak of narcotics addiction in the area.

A council subcommittee planned a "brownstone workshop" to assist homeowners to rehabilitate their buildings.

A council recreation committee met to discuss existing facilities for teenagers in the area.

The council sent a mailing to 4,800 relocated and on-site tenants encouraging them to exercise their priority rights for low- and middle-income housing in the urban renewal area.

The executive secretary arranged a series of meetings between the council and city officials to discuss local health and hospital facilities.

The council has its detractors as well as loyal supporters. Perhaps the most frequent criticism of the council is that without Father Browne's brilliant leadership it would be just another well-meaning, bungling group of paper organizations whose representatives are quite unable to cope with city officials playing the urban renewal game on a full-time basis. Some of Father Browne's bitterest personal enemies, inside and outside the council, feel the council is too often used as a megaphone by an allegedly ambitious and combative president. Still other critics say Father Browne owes his effectiveness as council president to the assumption by city officials that he speaks for the Area's parishes and the archdiocese itself. "If Father Browne didn't have his collar, the city wouldn't give him the time of day," is the way more than one person has put it.

Others acknowledge that the council has made a valuable contribution to the Area but feel that it has been given more credit than it deserves, while local social agencies receive little or no public attention for their work. Occasionally members of the FDR–Woodrow Wilson Club have said the council has siphoned off some of their most active, socially oriented people and that the council has not been willing to cooperate with the club in its efforts to help the community. Of late, however, as the club's own committee work has disintegrated, less of this type of criticism is heard: there is a growing feeling among some reform Democratic leaders that the council is indispensable in such areas as housing, health, and code enforcement.

Charges that Father Browne has used his council position to advance the special interests of the Catholic parishes seem manifestly unfair on the record. As the years have gone by, his militant "labor priest" philosophy, his record of continuous service and his re-election as president by organizations that are heavily Jewish or nondenominational affirm his remarkable capacity for presiding over a wide, very mixed constituency. In this sense, Father Browne is an interesting contrast to Father Robert Dunn of the Chelsea Neighborhood Council on the lower West Side, who finally incurred so much enmity from the council's non-Catholic groups that the council was destroyed. However, Father Browne does not sidestep any conflicts, with or without sectarian overtones. His opposition to what he feels is excessive favoritism of the city housing authority toward Goddard-Riverside Community Center, a council member which is nondenominational but with a Protestant board, in allotting it space in public housing projects to the exclusion of the Police Athletic League (with an Irish Catholic tinge) is one conflict in point.

Father Browne can be just as blunt and sarcastic as he can be diplomatic and engaging, but he is always sophisticated. He shares his friend Saul Alinsky's undisguised contempt for tradition-bound social workers. In public debate he employs a certain karate style of polemics his opponents do not forget. City officials are impressed and sometimes intimidated by his technical grasp of their subject, and irritated with his constitutional impatience with bureaucracies. Up to a certain point the council will "work" with a city agency, then, if things do not begin to happen, there may be some strong public criticism. Unless he keeps in close touch, a city official never knows quite what tack the council will take, and Father Browne never offers any guarantee of good behavior.

The council has had its failures, which seems inevitable in a small organization that finds itself constantly overextended. But, whatever its failings, it has played a most significant role in representing the feelings of the people in the West Side urban renewal area. The council has no counterpart. It is there, it is alive, and it is run by people who are competent and compassionate. Its office is one place where a citizen is not insulted or sidetracked, and where he can get information and action.

The council's ability to inform the community and to mobilize and transmit local sentiment has tempered the behavior of disorganized and frequently mindless city bureaucracy. The council has also tried valiantly to serve unpropertied and unaffiliated people from whom it has received neither dues nor active participation, and in so doing the council has greatly enlarged the traditionally narrow role of middle-class citizen groups that usually spring up in the midst of urban renewal projects.

Despite its leaders' early hopes the council never succeeded in becoming a grassroots organization. It has a negligible Negro and Puerto Rican membership, although one Negro, Percy Ifill, an architect, has been a member of the council's executive board. Its lack of Negro participation is not surprising in view of the fact that effective Negro organizations of any kind—the NAACP, CORE, and the Urban League—play little part in the life of the impoverished Negro on the West Side, and the middle-class Negro seems to feel little interest in the fate of the Negro poor. The two men who were for a time the Puerto Rican delegates to the council were involved in so many organizations that they spent most of their time at meetings and did not seem to have a broad or regular contact with the local Spanish population; now they both have city jobs and only one of them remains active in council affairs.

A former director of the West Side Neighborhood Conservation project, Juliet Brudney, says the council should not have been built on existing groups. "The truth is that most people who live in urban communities do not belong to so-called neighborhood organizations, and the people who do are not always very active. The result is that the representative of an organization who goes to a general meeting of the council does not really know the interests of the people he is supposed to represent. He doesn't usually even bother to inform his organization about what goes on in these meetings."

Mrs. Brudney thinks the council should have tried to reach the "great masses of nonbelongers" by following the recruiting and organizing techniques used by the Office of Civil Defense in World War II when it chose its block captains. "The function of the local organizations should be to go to people on the block and ask them to suggest an individual to represent them—someone who knows the block will have the people's respect. It was a mistake for the council to solidify the establishment by basing its voting membership on established groups that are unrepresentative and out of contact with the people."

Mrs. Brudney concedes that Stryckers Bay is "better than most but Father Browne has not licked the problem." She says her Bloomingdale Neighborhood Conservation project just north of the urban renewal area was "lucky because there was no establishment there, just people. Out of these unaffiliated people we got marvelous support and assistance: people who are alive and vital, who may have needed patient guidance and professional support, but who turned out to be so much more productive than the usual organization types."

To all of this Father Browne retorts that the record speaks for itself: that with all its financial support from the city and private sources, Mrs. Brudney's conservation program has never come close to equaling the council's contribution to the people. And, despite the validity of much of what Mrs. Brudney says, most observers would be inclined to agree with him.

It is true that, in the conflict over the urban renewal plan revisions, the majority of the council membership voted as members of the establishment and against the interests, presumably, of the economically depressed people of the Area. It is also true, as Mrs. Brudney says, that some council organizations are inactive and that their delegates either do not attend Stryckers Bay meetings, or, if they do, they do not talk over the agenda with the groups they represent. The members of the council who are most effective, by and large, are those delegates and general members who have made an individual and personal commitment to the council's work as officers or members of special committees.

But it must also be said that while many of the council members are absorbed in middle-class goals, its leadership is not. Father Browne and his staff are spending more and more time encouraging the poor to organize and to participate in running the local anti-poverty program. The council members have acted as news gatherers who were vitally important to the council leadership and its organizations in reaching policy decisions in planning action programs. It can also be said that the council was consciously organized to serve as a policy and action group to press a community viewpoint upon city officials, as well as a service organization. As an action and policy group the council had to be politically strong and had to organize quickly. It was the very fact that the council was a coalition of established groups, each with its own system of internal communication and avenues of influence in the city government which at first impressed municipal officials. Later these officials were even more impressed by a council leadership that knew how to negotiate with administrators and was well-informed enough to discuss technical matters on a plane of equality with the administrators.

If the council had tried to base its original membership on so-called "unaffiliated" individuals, recruiting them block by block, perhaps it could have spoken more literally as the "voice of the people," but it might have failed in its mission. It is probable that no matter what it did the council could not have attracted many of the Negroes and Puerto Ricans of the side streets. The fate of such efforts can be seen by the experience of the political clubs, the schools' parents associations, and the churches. Stryckers Bay learned what the Reverend Ralph Roy learned when he had to supplement his block-by-block efforts to organize a Methodist congregation on 105th and 104th Streets by going to the more stable, ambitious people of the Douglass Houses public housing project for the nucleus of his congregation. The Reverend Roy's lesson was that people become active in a community because they have hope, a goal in view, and a sense of permanent status in a community. To the transient poor condemned to be moved about for a lifetime, discussions about community improvement such as one would hear at a council meeting would be taken simply as a warning that the time was approaching when they would have to be deported again to make way for other, more comfortably situated members of society. But at the same time the poor did come to the council office for assistance.

The council's difficulty in crossing the gap that separated it from the people at the bottom of the ladder—the down-and-out occupants of single rooms—was demonstrated rather clearly at one meeting of the Eighty-ninth Street Block Association, a member of the council. The block association members were surprised to discover a delegation of strangers who had arrived a half hour or so earlier for the meeting. The strangers lived in a junk pile of a house on Eighty-eighth Street owned by the city, had seen notices of the block association meeting, and had come to ask what was going to happen to them when they had to move. Most of them were single Negroes on welfare, not eligible for moving expenses or relocation to other apartments by the Department of Relocation.

Several minutes before the meeting began a large, pretty woman who introduced herself as Pinky Mae stood up and talked to the people around her in a soft voice. She said she had no job and wanted to work and that she had to work because there was no other way for her to live.

"Can't somebody help me find a job? I am good with babies and little children. I know how to hold a child close to me so that he is warm and won't cry no more. I know little children and they know that I love them and that they can depend on me. That's what I can do the best. I'll do anything though. I'll take any kind of job." Pinky Mae talked on until finally another stranger in the front row said, "Pinky Mae, be quiet; this meeting is not a place to ask about jobs."

When the meeting started all the strangers tried to speak at once. Robert Tisdale, the chairman of the block association, explained that each person would have to be recognized by the chair. Nevertheless the commotion grew and the strangers became more and more excited. One man seized an old felt hat off his head and waved it in circles.

"What are they going to do with us, are they just going to drive us out of the house? Why can't we stay, why don't they fix up the place, what is the city going to do about us, can't you do something to stop them?"

There were great volleys of questions like this. Neither the chairman of the meeting nor the representatives of Stryckers Bay present could tell the strangers the truth, that there was nothing to be done for them because they were single and their house was hopeless because it was dead and would be torn down, and they would be sent away. Someone asked desperately if a letter couldn't be sent somewhere to some city agency. Finally the chairman had to ask the strangers to stop talking so that the meeting could proceed with the agenda. As the talk about schools, housing, and neighborhood improvement got under way, the Negroes left the meeting quietly, one or two at a time. By the end of the meeting only Pinky Mae and the man in the front row who had admonished her were still there, and then they went out too, and never again were any of these people seen at another meeting anyplace.

7

THE NEW HURRAH

MEASURED BY THE SIZE OF THE PLURALITIES ITS
assembly district rolls up for Democratic candidates, the FDR–
Woodrow Wilson Democratic Club has been one of the most success-
ful of the reform political organizations that has grown up in New
York City since the 1950's. It is the official Democratic organization
for the Fifth Assembly District North, an area on Manhattan's West
Side running from Eighty-sixth Street to about 100th Street, and from
Central Park West to Riverside Drive.

The club headquarters, over some vacant stores on Ninety-sixth
Street, is not a place where people drop in to pass the time of day or
play checkers. The meeting hall has dirty yellow walls, a tin ceiling,
and a slate-colored floor covered with dust. Hanging about are the
shreds of some colored streamers left over from a dance, and on one
wall is a poster advertising a gala at the *Club Deportivo de la Frater-
nidad Sudamericana* which took place sometime long ago at the
Casino Monte Carlo. Alongside the speaker's platform, ninety feet
away at the other end of the hall, are stacks of record albums, and in
each corner of the ceiling is a loud-speaker. The light bulbs are bare.
Some folding chairs are leaning against the wall and others have been
set up for a meeting. On an oak desk are some ashtrays full of butts
and posters proclaiming the withered candidacy of Robert Morgen-
thau, who ran for governor in 1962 and was annihilated.

A small room off the meeting hall contains paper cartons, crates of
empty Coke bottles, a six-foot-high pile of coat hangers, a refrigerator, disconnected plumbing conduits, doors to the rest rooms, and an
upright piano with most of its teeth missing. In another small room

135

down the hallway where someone has been wiping paint brushes on the walls, there are boxes of paper and gummed labels and two mimeograph machines bleeding ink. Most of the reading material in the room consists of obsolete campaign biographies. A large photograph of three politicians commands the public to "Vote Row C for Nunez and Rosenberg." Nunez, candidate for Supreme Court Justice, is on the right and Robert Wagner, who was then mayor, is in the middle with his arms crossed in a political pose known as the double handshake; the word "Urgent" has been rubber-stamped across Mr. Wagner's forehead.

One of the first arrivals at the club if there is an important meeting may very well be a mild-looking man named Ira Stark who was born three hundred yards from the clubhouse a half-century ago and has lived in the Fifth A.D. North ever since. He says he comes early to be sure nobody is pulling any "fast ones" on the membership. Stark is one of the few members of the FDR–Woodrow Wilson Club who used to belong to the local Tammany Hall organization which the reformers put out of business in 1959. He recalls that the building went up in 1932, at which time the Dennis J. Mahon Association, the regular Democratic club, "held a sort of ceremonial and took possession of the premises." Some of the people attending wore tall hats, including Mr. Mahon himself. "It was a little different in those days," Stark says, looking around. "It didn't cost very much to decorate so you could afford to do something with the place. In addition, the type of people who were members seemed to take more of a local pride in their establishment, maybe because they didn't live in the best possible apartments and liked to spend more time in their clubhouse. It was a social sort of place. People didn't come here to argue and pick on each other."

Stark points around the room at imaginary objects of the past. "There were some card tables here. In the front room there were some glass partitions so a resident of the district could come in and address his district leader, or his congressman or assemblyman, and have the privacy of a closed door. Over in back there Mr. Mahon had his own personal office. There were card parties and dances every Saturday night. We didn't have a bar because of Prohibition, and then later, after Prohibition was repealed, we still didn't have a bar because Mr. Mahon was a teetotaler. He used to get very annoyed, walking along Columbus Avenue and seeing all the taverns. 'Look at those buckets of blood with good Irish names over them,' he would say."

Refreshments were always served at the association's parties, Stark remembers. "The club was very much a family affair, with an Irish flavor, but with a good sprinkling of Jews, including Judge Dan Fink and his wife, Barbara, who was the female district leader until the reformers came along." The main activities of the club were "community benefit types of things because the neighborhood was occupied by a large percentage of poor people. I don't mean that Christmas baskets were given out, but there were gifts of cash in cases of dire necessity, definitely on a handout basis—in return for what we shall hand out to you, you shall hand out petitions and so forth. The club was oriented along quite a different line from now. The older leadership was a rather tight hierarchy, although I never heard of anybody being refused membership. There were never any fights about any issues. Under the very able, guiding hand of Mr. Mahon unanimity could be achieved readily.

"After World War II, the neighborhood seemed to go from Irish to Jewish in one fell swoop," Stark says. "The changes didn't help Mahon much because the newcomers turned out to like reformers pretty well.

"When Mr. Mahon went under and lost the district leadership to the reformers, the clubhouse merely changed hands and a new sign went up, that was all. An orderly transition, you might say, and Mr. Mahon's association went out of business forever. Very few of the old members came into the new club. I tried to get one of Mahon's ablest men to join, but he told me that the idea of climbing those stairs and seeing so many new faces in a new club did not appeal to him any more. It appears they were just used to their old friends, and it was a particularly bitter campaign that saw their defeat. You know the old saying of Mr. Dooley, 'If you see two people calling each other anarchist and communist, why it's usually two Democrats trying to unite the party.' "

Actually, the fortunes of the Dennis Mahon Association took a turn for the worse in 1952 on the day Adlai Stevenson accepted the Democratic nomination for the Presidency. Mahon, in all his thirty-five years of running the party in the district, had never been able to work up much enthusiasm for presidential candidates generally, since they seemed to have very little time to minister to the needs of the local Tammany club, and he was especially unmoved by Stevenson's bald intellectualism. However, Mr. Stevenson's appearance in politics did excite—deeply and permanently—a band of writers, students teachers, housewives, professors, ministers, advertising men, lawyers, etc., who formed a local Volunteers for Stevenson club. This first campaign experience and their devotion to Stevenson convinced many of them that they wanted to stay in politics, and in 1956 these people formed the core of the West Side Volunteers for Stevenson and Kefauver. Leaders of the group were two young attorneys, Myron Cohen, the chairman, and Seymour Schwartz; and among the volunteers was an ex-*Collier's* magazine editor named Pierre Salinger, who described himself as a "student of politics" and gave street-corner speeches.

It was Mahon's indifference to Stevenson in the 1956 campaign that led to his undoing. A good percentage of the Volunteers' forty workers pounded the sidewalks in Mahon's district, introducing themselves to his constituents, and trudging up and down staircases that had not felt the tread of a Tammany canvasser in many years. Each Volunteer collected his own evidence about the Dennis Mahon Association's unwillingness to work for the Democratic presidential candidate.

One such reporter was Irving Wolfson, an insurance broker who had recently moved to the West Side. As Wolfson was about to set off for Stevenson headquarters downtown to get some leaflets and campaign buttons, he learned that as a matter of fact there was a regular Democratic club on West Ninety-sixth Street. A few days later he went to the club and told Mahon, a white-haired, blue-eyed gentleman seated behind a roll-top desk, that he would like to do work for Stevenson. The district leader gazed benevolently at the man who would someday replace him, and told Wolfson that there was no need to worry about Stevenson, but that he would appreciate anything the Wolfson people could do for Dan Fink, the Democratic candidate for Justice of the Municipal Court.

Not long after this meeting, Wolfson wandered into the Volunteers for Stevenson headquarters, where he told his story. Cohen, who had heard similar reports, said the Volunteers had something in mind for Mahon when the presidential campaign was over, and he kept his word. Minutes after the polls closed on Stevenson's last run for the

Presidency, he gathered his volunteers and asked them to remember how little help they had had from the Tammany regulars in general and from the Dennis Mahon Association in particular. He suggested that the Volunteers get together again after everybody had had a rest, to talk about the future.

A few weeks later, the get-togethers began, most of them in Wolfson's Central Park West apartment. The result of these meetings was that in 1957 approximately two dozen West Siders voted themselves into existence as the Woodrow Wilson Democrats and set up headquarters in a Ninety-sixth Street basement with their main purpose a primary fight to unseat Mahon as district leader in the 1959 primaries two years away.

At the very time the Woodrow Wilson Democrats were meeting in their basement another band of reformers was planning its own strategy to unseat Mahon. This second group, which was eventually to call itself the Franklin D. Roosevelt Democratic Club, was composed of dissident officers and members of the West Side Democratic Club in the Fifth Assembly District Middle.

After the two groups learned about each other, they met to discuss ways of cooperating. The first talks did nothing but kindle permanent animosities, but finally the two clubs merged as the FDR–Woodrow Wilson Democratic Club. In a bitter contest for designation as the reform candidate to oppose Mahon for the district leadership, Irving Wolfson, supported by the Woodrow Wilson group, defeated Theodore Weiss, representing the FDR contingent, 248 to 200. Thereupon Weiss and his friends, almost half the membership, seceded from the merged club and founded their own Reform Independent Democrats in the Fifth Assembly District South.

Having settled its own civil war, at least for the moment, the FDR–Woodrow Wilson Club had to organize itself to function as a community service organization at the same time it prepared to fight a primary campaign for the district leadership. The members wrote and approved a constitution and appointed committees to undertake various neighborhood projects. The social referral, rent, and housing committees never lost an opportunity to proselytize people who came to them for help. The Mahon Association had done little to stop the decline of the area or to get city agencies to enforce violations of the building, health, and sanitation codes. The chairman of the housing

[140] THE AIRTIGHT CAGE

committee developed plans for a club-sponsored, nonprofit, middle-income housing cooperative in the area. The committee badgered the city about welfare problems, pressured the commissioner of the Department of Water Supply, Gas and Electricity to put in more street lights, and asked the park department commissioner to repair broken equipment in the playgrounds. The President of the Borough of Manhattan was told to fill in potholes in the street and repair the sidewalks, and the committee complained repeatedly to the Department of Sanitation about inadequate garbage collection. Members of club committees testified at hearings before the City Planning Commission and the Board of Estimate and they arranged meetings with the precinct captain for some complaining constituents.

Meanwhile, the club, under its first president, Myron Cohen, put to work the practical political wisdom it had acquired during the Stevenson campaigns. It set up a campaign organization on a block-by-block basis to gather signatures to put Wolfson and his running mate for female district co-leader (Catherine Hemenway) on the primary ballot. Each weekday night the candidates attended kaffee klatches to talk to small groups of voters. Saturday-night parties raised $12,000 for campaign expenses.

The petition drive in early July, compressed into three days, raised more than the necessary three thousand signatures. Then the volunteers rested for six weeks. Late in August, when the insurgents began their final canvass for voters, the Mahon organization had become apprehensive. Many of its district captains discovered when they began their canvassing that the reformers had been there ahead of them. Reform leaflets by the thousands were being distributed door to door on the streets and turning up in subway stations, supermarkets, theaters and restaurants. Even enrolled Liberal party members, independents, and some Republicans joined the club, manned telephones, and helped get out mailings, even though they were not eligible to vote on Primary Day.

What alarmed Mahon even more was the fact that the state's two most respected Democrats, Mrs. Eleanor Roosevelt and former Governor Herbert Lehman, had entered the campaign. Their decision dated back to the New York State convention in Buffalo the preceding year, when Tammany leader Carmine De Sapio had ignored Governor Lehman's wishes and dictated the nomination of Manhattan District Attorney Frank Hogan for the Democratic nomination

for U.S. Senator. The result was that in the following January
Governor Lehman, Mrs. Roosevelt, and Thomas Finletter formed the
New York Committee for Democratic Voters, which contributed
$6,000 to the Wolfson campaign.

The governor and Mrs. Roosevelt gave more than their prestige to
the reformers. They campaigned vigorously. The high points of the
primary campaign were appearances by Governor Lehman at the
Carlton Terrace Hotel on Broadway, and by Mrs. Roosevelt at the
Yorktown Theater, both before capacity crowds. Thousands of letters
endorsing Wolfson and Hemenway were sent out over the Roosevelt
and Lehman signatures.

On primary day, the FDR Club left nothing to chance. It had a
poll watcher at every voting center to guard against irregularities, and
its runners shuttled between the polls and club headquarters with
names of Wolfson supporters who had not yet voted. When the polls
were closed and the machines opened, the watchers made sure there
was no tampering with the totals.

As the Tammany workers phoned in reports of a huge turnout,
saying that hundreds of voters were people they had never seen
before, Mahon turned to one of his lieutenants and predicted: "It's
two to one against us." A few hours later the polls closed and the
results were in. The vote was 4,300 for Wolfson and Hemenway,
2,300 for Mahon and Fink. For the first—and last—time in his
active political life, Mahon had been right about the reformers.

The dominating position of Governor Lehman was to prove a
problem to many West Side reformers, including officers of the
FDR–Woodrow Wilson Club, who saw their victory as only the first
step in the bigger campaign to get rid of the city "bosses" and
Tammany influence within the city government. In 1960, the reformers considered the possibility of running a reform slate for major
citywide offices in 1961. But Mayor Wagner agreed to break with
Carmine De Sapio and the other Tammany leaders, and thereby won
Governor Lehman's support for re-election as mayor. The entry of a
reform candidate for the Democratic nomination against Mayor
Wagner was made difficult by the fact that Tammany decided to
oppose Wagner's renomination and offered its own candidate for
mayor, State Controller Arthur Levitt. Governor Lehman, convinced
that the entry of a third candidate would split the anti-De Sapio vote

and result in Levitt's election, issued an ultimatum to the reformers to support Wagner "or else." There was little the anti-Wagner reformers could do but yield.

"It took all the starch out of the reform movement," said one of the ex-officers of the FDR–Woodrow Wilson Club. "Up until we supported Wagner, a lot of people believed we really meant what we said about cleaning up city politics. After that, many people deserted the reform movement, not just on the West Side, but all over the city." Another unhappy club leader described the Lehman-dictated reform support for Wagner as a "death blow" to the reform movement.

Frustrated in its efforts to elect a reform administration, the FDR–Woodrow Wilson Club turned inward. Its position as the official Democratic organization of the Fifth North and its success in re-electing district leaders gave it responsibilities which inhibited the club's original free-wheeling character, yet real power did not accompany these responsibilities. Since the Wolfson victory, there has been a great turnover in membership and leaders. Few of the original founders of the club are still active in its affairs. Membership has declined from sixteen hundred to below eight hundred. Meetings, once regularly attended by several hundred people, now rarely number even a quorum. The club presidency and the district leaderships, once fought over in historic meetings with several candidates in the running, now go almost by default. With one exception, there has not been a contest for either the club presidency or the district leadership in several years. Sometimes the positions have gone to people not considered highly qualified by the membership. "Several people were asked but nobody wanted the job," is the explanation a club official will offer to people who protest belatedly about the club's choices. The club presidency, highly prized at the beginning of the club's history, for a while changed almost as rapidly as captaincies in the 24th Police Precinct.

Much of the fervor of the early crusades against the Dennis Mahon Association, and later for the election of William F. Ryan, who won the district's congressional seat from Congressman Ludwig Teller, has vanished along with the crusaders. In one way, the club's loss of membership has been a paper loss, since, of the sixteen hundred members on its rolls at the highest point, many simply paid their dues to express support in a general way but never attended meetings or were active on committees or in campaigns. Others, known as "bodies," had joined the club to back a friend for some office and lost interest in the club. Still others joined the club solely to qualify for its low-price charter flights to Europe.

The loss of another type of member, however, did seem to have raised complications. Many people had originally joined because they saw the club as a means of involving themselves in community activities. After the club won its battle against Tammany and itself became the regular organization, many of these people became bored or irritated by the less-exciting operational problems of running a club and dropped out.

To some club officers, the loss of the "social service type" seemed unavoidable. Nancy LeBlanc, a former president, says: "Many people who came to the club originally were the type who might have been working in Hull House, except that social service organizations today are so professional there is no longer much of a place for volunteers. It's a social service worker's world now, you know; you can't even work with a teen-age girls' club unless you have professional training. A lot of the people who came to us had no interest in politics. When they understood what a political club was, they were shocked. These people were purists; political action was a compromise. They didn't see that a political club was primarily related to the process of government, not to the community service process."

Theodore Weiss, now a City Councilman, says his new Reform Independent Democratic Club has had a similar dropout of community service people. The RID had hoped to function as a community service as well as a political organization, but the dual personality never seemed to work out. "Community service at the outset was something all our people felt was a vital part of our function as a club. We thought it was a field in which a new political group could demonstrate its superiority over the established club. It is ironic because the old-line Tammany clubs had been very adept at this social service type of thing before the social welfare legislation in the thirties turned this function over to the government—they built themselves up by taking care of people.

"Then government welfare programs began taking over many of these functions. The old clubs didn't know how to react or what their function was, and their world came down around their ears. But as the social problems got bigger and the government agencies lost control of the situation, the community's need for community service returned. It was both an opportunity and a problem for the reformers. We did make an effort to help, but in the end the clubs could not become community service organizations. The important thing was that the political machinery of the city was rotten. This was a political problem that demanded a political cure. It meant we had to take over the political machinery and get to the point where we could put responsible people in at the head of city departments, and this was the way we could help with community problems. The community service people didn't understand that if a political club couldn't demonstrate power on a political level, it couldn't be much help in rebuilding a community."

The loss of the community-service-oriented membership has not disturbed Hedi Piel, a former Fifth A. D. district leader. "We had a real gung-ho membership but many of these people were never really political to start with—this was a bit of a fling they had, then the fling ended. Granted, we have fewer activists in the club today, but I think they are more representative of the community, and many of them are active in community service organizations outside the club."

However, Wolfson, the club's first district leader and the chief proponent of the community service approach, feels that the community-service-oriented people were the very ones who were the most effective in the club's political affairs as well. "During the FDR club's first primary campaign the bulk of the election district captains and other 'political' workers came from the community service group; and it was these people who produced over four hundred votes in our club for Austin Laber's City Council candidacy against a combined vote of three hundred for eight other candidates backed by the so-called 'political' people. As another example take the reform Riverside Democrats, just to the north of us, where community service activities have been more actively pursued. The Riverside Democrats have a larger membership and are more effective politically than any of the other reform clubs on the West Side."

It seems to be commonly agreed that the club has also been damaged by intense personal conflicts among the members. One former officer says, "I don't know what is behind the conflicts—I doubt that it is just neuroticism—but nobody listens to what the other person is saying." A former acting president of the club described the difficulty as a "spirit of chronic insurgency."

Club officials who disagree strongly with each other on many issues are almost unanimous in saying that the membership has been abnormally destructive of its leaders, which accounts partially for the rapid turnover of officers. Some members argue that it would have helped if the club had had some of the benevolent social atmosphere of the Dennis Mahon Association. Members of the association never became upset about ideologies or issues and got along fine as long as the patronage was handled properly. To the reformer, politics is a series of intense emotional conflicts that could make or break friendships, and it seems to gratify all sorts of psychological, even sexual, needs. One club leader asks, "Where else in town could you get a group therapy for six dollars in annual dues?"

A former club leader, Seymour Schwartz, now inactive, thinks that a good percentage of the club's members, especially the women, are so intolerant if not "mildly paranoid" that they are constitutionally unable to cooperate with anyone. "With all our elected officials and all the programs and successes we had early in the reform movement, the leaders—with the exception of Congressman Ryan—who have shown real promise and ability have somehow been ground down. There is something inherent in reform politics that makes this grinding-down inevitable. Why? Because one big reason middle-class types go into reform politics is to assuage their guilts. This means you are going to get unstable and aberrational conduct. You will get a different type of behavior than if you had people in the organization looking for economic gain.

"When you get too many neurotics in any organization, political or religious, they will quickly find reasons to dislike their fellows, be intolerant of them, feel they don't represent the same high principles, ability, dedication, etc. They consider themselves the true carriers of the message. They search out the evil people and form their cabals. Any leader knows that he will always have a militant and suspicious minority working against him, absolutely convinced he is a liar, a crook, a shifty conniver, and that his only objective is to feather his own nest.

"To our club members, everything and everyone quickly became either all black or all white. After enough of this grinding-down of the original leadership, the people who begin to come to the top are those who have never committed themselves too heavily, who can pass from one situation to another without much trouble. These are the gray people who take over leadership positions in the reform movement, and unfortunately they are third- or fourth-echelon people; they lack ability, intellect, and imagination."

This view is spoken by a man who was driven out by his enemies. One of his friends, another leader who has become inactive, expresses a different view. "We should have realized that many people came into our club intrigued and excited, but also sensing an opportunity to earn some social or psychic income. They wanted a feeling of closeness to the center of activity, that they were sharing in the gossip and small talk. We just didn't spend enough time with our own people, although I don't know where we could have found the time to do this along with everything else. Maybe we should have kept the kaffee klatches going even when the campaigns were over."

One of the early club group, Barbara Jeffers, expresses a rather common feeling of pessimism. "Our club has lasted as long as any I have seen, and that's something. But I've concluded that, if you are going to have a good-government organization that means anything, it has to be built out of intelligent, articulate, hard-working, emotionally involved people who completely control, completely run the organization. They sit in the driver's seat and drive the officers; the officers do not drive them. But when you get this driving type of membership you build an organization that in the long run will tend to destroy itself because it is undisciplined. It comes into being to fight an old authority, and it dies because it cannot trust the new authority it has erected for itself."

Latter-day FDR club leaders are always irritated at the dour reflections and criticism of those who have moved to the sidelines. Very often the newer generation is composed of people who were treated rather contemptuously by the earlier leadership. Instead of having been groomed for the succession, they were paid little attention, or regarded as "zombies" or "creeps." They usually obtained club office only as the incumbents quit in disgust, because they could no longer afford to spend the time, or they grew tired of phone calls at all hours of the night. The leadership of the moment will usually speak more hopefully about the club's future—in public. Privately they agree that personal conflicts and factionalism discourage old members and hurt the recruiting of new, active people.

Out of the club's total membership, it is doubtful if more than a dozen people are active enough to spend much time each week helping with the club operations. In the club's early days, the moment anyone suspected that a handful of members was taking too much power unto itself, there would be a protest that a "clique" was taking over and before long mutiny would break out in the ranks. Today, according to Nancy LeBlanc, the fourth of the club's many presidents, the membership refers most decisions to committees or the president.

"As soon as an organization starts leaving everything up to the officers, then they don't care, and if they don't care they don't volunteer, and then where are you?" she comments.

In the past three or four years, the various club committees have slowed down considerably or have gone out of existence. For a time, the club's small but articulate public affairs committee studied state and national issues and passed on suggested policy planks to the executive committee, covering such matters as condemnation of the McCarran Immigration Act, criticism of civil defense programs, and statements on foreign affairs. It also held a few successful forums. The auditorium was packed to the rafters in 1962 when the club debated and voted on a resolution supporting the inclusion of more low- and middle-income units in the West Side urban renewal plan. A public debate on the military budget held in 1963 drew over one hundred people—almost all of them in the middle-class, white professional group typical of the attendance at most club affairs. But, except for a meeting packed with "bodies" in April, 1965, to vote on a district leader contest, there have been no events at the clubhouse to compare with these meetings. At most FDR meetings, says Nancy LeBlanc, "you worry about whether the first three rows will fill up. You just sit there and die, especially if you are new to the reform movement."

In the spring of 1963, the club's executive committee, faced with a shrinkage of its activities, combined its community affairs and public affairs committees. At that time, the club still had a functioning housing committee, but a few months later even the housing committee was out of action, yet it had once been the most energetic in the club, and had been responsible for such projects as a middle-income housing coöp in the urban renewal area, a rat control program, a rent clinic, a program to harass slum landlords, a program to uncover fire hazards in substandard dwellings, a survey to chart attitudes of relocated families, a grading of housing accommodations in blocks adjacent to the urban renewal area, and a comprehensive study of the city's West Side Urban Renewal Plan with carefully thought-out criticisms and recommendations.

One explanation for the club's difficulty in focusing its energies has been the immense variety of demands made upon it. In addition to everything else, it has tried to serve as a forum of debate on what club members consider the basic governmental, social, and moral issues in American life. An old-style Democratic leader would not understand such a political organization.* A discussion of Medicare on the agenda of a district political club would strike him as irrelevant, yet the FDR Club members consider that the club should educate the public on such issues, and "take a position."

Preoccupation with the "big issues," characteristic of many reform clubs, put a heavy tax on the FDR Club's time and energy. The meeting agenda is defenseless against the intrusion, at particularly inappropriate moments, of a resolution calling for the end of the war in Vietnam, or abolition of civil defense drills. Debates on such matters not only sidetrack local issues, but they seem to fan personal animosities which always lie beneath the surface. The protagonists in these intense but transient commotions have very little patience with anything else the club is doing. Once their particular hurricane has blown itself out, they are not seen at meetings again. The extent to which some of the more ideologically canted members narrow their interests is illustrated by the experience of a candidate for district leader who had asked a young couple to vote for her. The husband phoned with one question: "Where do you stand on the recognition of Red China?" Assured that his candidate favored the idea, the man said, "Fine; you've got my vote," and hung up.

---

* The attitude is illustrated by a comment from John M. Bailey, chairman of the Democratic National Committee, to the author at the time the latter was chairman of the Democratic Town Committee of Westport, Connecticut. The committee, dominated by ex-Volunteers for Stevenson, met often and argued long about education, foreign aid, civil rights, local zoning, tax assessments, etc. "Why do you people hold so many meetings?" Bailey wanted to know. "What is there to talk about?" He then added that the best way to run a political organization was to hold as few meetings as possible, preferably once a year.

Club leaders have ambivalent feelings about the ideologues among them. One ex-president says, "I'm not sure they care anything at all about political reform. They speak the language of reform, but they seem to want to use the club for their own personal desires. They're againsters. They are infiltrators. They are energetic, but their energy doesn't help the club very much. Most of the time we can't get a dozen people to come in and run off a few stencils, but let the executive committee pass a resolution that has to do with, say, something the SANE nuclear policy people are for, and suddenly you get a whole army to run mimeograph machines, and send out nineteen stencils, and type letters to everybody in town telling them about the resolution. Okay, I don't object to people trying to propagandize, but if we passed a resolution tomorrow having to do with discrimination against Negroes not one of these would show up to do any work."

One reason for the frequency and bitterness of the club's internal conflicts may be, ironically, the thorough trouncing the reformers gave the Tammany regulars in 1959. Since that time, the club has had things pretty much its own way in its own district. There has been no threat to its power from any local party sources. In Greenwich Village, the reform Village Independent Democrats—where the internecine warfare is just as intense—have had to call off their civil wars from time to time to repel the efforts of ex-Tammany chieftain Carmine De Sapio to regain the district leadership. No such threats materialize in the Fifth North. The absence of local Republican party strength means no challenge from that source, either. Left with no other adversaries, and since conflict is vital to many amateur politicians, the FDR Democrats "fracture each other."

A certain kind of inbreeding also contributes to the conflict. The club's predominantly middle-class white membership suffers from the absence of people who speak a different social language and who have different priorities. One might say that the club is culturally deprived. The lack of fresh and contrasting viewpoints encourages repetitive, ingrown discussion, stained with all the guilts and complexes of introverted, middle-class professionals. The FDR club is not the only reform club to have this sort of trouble. Weiss's Reform Independent Democrats have not been able to attract a significant number of Spanish-speaking members, and, while the Riverside Democratic Club has done better in this regard, the situation is not satisfactory there either. The FDR Club has three dozen or so Negro dues payers, but there is little representation of low-income Negroes who could provide new avenues of information and ideas. The Negro members of the club are, by and large, like the white members, professional people, a good number of whom send their children to private schools and who are often afflicted with certain ambivalences of their own. A Negro taxidriver who is an election district captain is an exception.

The scarcity of minority group members in the club is not because the club has tried to discourage their participation, despite allegations to that effect which have been made on occasion by Alberto Gerena-Valentin, president of the Puerto Rican Federation of Home Towns.* FDR Club canvassers who have tried to register Negro and Puerto Rican voters in the district and interest them in the club have given up after almost total failure.

Many of the club's running arguments are never resolved. Although there have been no recent bouts over the club's position on patronage (especially since the election of a Republican mayor), the subject comes up continually in conversations with club members. Some of them want to go further than the official position that reform club officers and district leaders should not hold political jobs in government. They oppose all patronage, a reaction against the old organizational basis of Tammany politics in which patronage was the bait to attract and hold party workers.

Another group argues that the hard line against patronage is not only impractical but that there is a certain amount of hypocrisy among those who are against it. One rather outspoken partisan in behalf of patronage is the recently deposed female district leader, Hedi Piel, who thinks "it is impossible to demand of people that they give unstintingly of their time without any kind of compensation. I question whether the holier-than-thou attitude of many reformers on this matter is even genuine—many of the people who go around attacking the idea of patronage are applying for jobs like mad on the side. I also question whether a club's barring patronage actually benefits the community in the long run. Wouldn't it be better if someone had a patronage job that would give him the time to spend

* These allegations were made many months before the FDR Club endorsed Gerena-Valentin for the Democratic nomination for City Commissioner-at-Large.

the day at a Board of Estimate or a City Council hearing, where he could represent the community?"

At one full-dress debate on patronage, the classic points pro and con were stated by Jane Mills and Noel Gilmore. Mrs. Mills (who was later appointed to a city job) felt that the club had a responsibility to get people into city government who were responsive to the reform point of view. In response to Mrs. Mills, Miss Gilmore declared: "We are so preoccupied with patronage that we are not doing the things we should do in the community. This club is far more important than all of the patronage jobs we consider. We should be strengthening our club, getting more action out of it; we should not be tearing ourselves apart over patronage matters."

The flare-ups over patronage have subsided because the arguments never seem to get anyplace, also, because patronage is an academic issue as far as the majority of club members is concerned: their sources of financial and emotional support lie elsewhere. As people, generally in the professions, with nonpolitical careers, they have at times felt imposed upon by what they feel is a small group interested in personal political or financial advancement. It should also be said that the club was not overwhelmed by job offers from a Wagner administration quite aware of the club hostility.

The club's loss of vitality is so obvious that there would seem to be no point in denying it even if anyone wanted to—and nobody wants to, particularly a club member like Murray Richmond, a young attorney, who was talked into becoming president of the club in 1964 and then marooned by the people who had urged him to take the job. Although he was one of a group in the club which strongly opposed the early leadership of Wolfson and Cohen, Richmond at times sounds more bitter about the club than his old antagonists. After refusing the club presidency several times he finally agreed to take the job, on one condition.

"I told seven or eight people who wanted me to take the presidency that I would do it if I could count on them to give a lot of their time to the club. I had an objective. I hoped we could get our middle-class people in the club to take a much more active part in the civil rights movement. This meant I would have to have at least a small corps of people who would work very hard, who would be available. I told my friends that I didn't want to end up sweeping out the clubhouse and piling up chairs after meetings. The president was going to quit being a housemaid for the membership. I thought my friends, who had been active in the civil rights movement, would stick by me on this, even though my whole experience in the club argued against any such expectation.

"Well, what happened? I found myself fixing the lights, and climbing ladders. I had to repair the banister one day. I had to call up the secretary to get out the minutes, and so on. Where did all my supporters go? Most of them seemed to have other things keeping them busy—another campaign to work on. One of them even joined another club. So I resigned."

Richmond does not dwell on the usual complaints—the rivalries, the loss of the community-oriented people, the dissipation of the club's energies over too many areas. He agrees that these developments have damaged the club, but they are symptoms rather than causes of the club's decline.

"The fact is that the club had to fail. It was fated to lose power; it has been a narrow, parochial, middle-class organization. It never understood the Puerto Rican and the Negro. Most important, it lost its determination—if it ever had it—to make a complete break with traditional big-city Democratic politics. Reform could have succeeded only if it had been a truly revolutionary movement in city politics. Reform should have aimed at overthrowing the leadership of the Democratic party in New York. The movement was doomed the moment it abandoned this objective. Reform defeated itself by accommodating itself to tradition. The endorsement of Wagner for mayor in 1961 was a prime cause of disillusionment in the reform movement. But if it hadn't been the Wagner endorsement, something else would have happened to cause the disillusionment."

The early reform movement "was full of promise and idealism. Today it's a sad contrast. The club has no housing committee, no school committee, no rent and social referral committee, no committees at all outside a campaign committee." Richmond says that in the first few years the "contribution of the club was immense. The club was loaded with talent. Leadership played an important role. People strove for leadership. We had many members who worked five days a week until two or even six in the morning. They asked for nothing in return. There was an intense zeal in the club to do something in the community. Hopes and expectations pushed people forward. But people can't go along on that sort of dream forever. The disenchantment began, and the people know now the club will never do what it set out to do. The institutions in this city are too great, too strong. They won't give way and now the desire to make them give way is gone."

The trouble was, Richmond says, "we didn't keep the promises we made to ourselves."

A PLACE TO BEGIN

Bloom

WE ALL WATCHED VERY CLOSELY WHILE THE NEW school was being built. The dust in the air, and the yellow mud in the streets from the dump trucks made West Ninety-second seem even more like a road to the battlefront. But an exciting show took place. After the bulldozers, a monstrous power shovel arrived and scooped out a hole for the foundations, then a skyscraper crane picked up steel I-beams and lowered them into place like jackstraws. The concrete was poured, the plumbers, electricians, carpenters, brick-layers, glaziers, sanders came and went, and suddenly it was September, 1962, and Public School 84, a three-story brick and glass building costing two and a half million dollars, was ready.

Each weekday morning that first fall I could look over into a second-floor classroom just before nine o'clock and see a pretty, black-haired teacher writing on the blackboard and arranging flowers on her desk. Within two weeks she was out of sight behind a parade of paper giraffes, zebras, sunflowers, elephants, whales and Eskimos which her children had hung in the windows. Trees and bushes planted around the school added another fresh touch. But other things had not changed. The stoops of the rooming houses along Ninety-first Street, crowded with derelicts and prostitutes, worried many parents, who told their children to avoid that block and use the school's Ninety-second Street entrance.

Because P.S. 84 was a replacement for another school (P.S. 93), which closed the previous spring, it began with certain advantages.

154

Most of the teachers and a good percentage of the pupils had been transferred as a group from P.S. 93, so they knew each other and the area well. The school had another asset. It had been designated as a "special services" school, which meant that it had been given extra services and personnel to deal with the needs of the disadvantaged Puerto Rican and Negro children who would constitute the majority of the pupils.

In spite of the extra services, a corps of experienced teachers, and his new building, the new principal, Milton Forrest, had to face several unpleasant realities almost from the moment he opened the doors. For one thing, his substitute teachers were sent to him by the Central Placement Office of the Board of Education so that he had no choice in the matter. More depressing was the discovery that thirty or so middle-class white parents in the West End–Riverside Drive area in P.S. 84's attendance district had obtained permission from the Board of Education to transfer their kindergarten-to-second-grade children to P.S. 75, a predominantly white school, in an adjacent school zone, but nearer to the families involved. This transfer reduced the already small minority of white children registered in P.S. 84.

The principal regarded the transfers as a slight to his school and decided not to take this sort of thing lying down. He sent out newsletters and bulletins describing the school to parents, neighborhood groups, churches, and city officials. He asked social agencies in the area to cooperate with P.S. 84's six-day-a-week, afterschool program. He made a special effort to bring outside resources into the school, particularly those which would enrich the reading and arts program.

Forrest got some early results. A group of volunteers, trained and sponsored by the privately financed Public Education Association and supervised by the Board of Education, took over one room in the school to give instruction to slow readers. Under the program one volunteer would work for an hour at a time with one child on a regular weekly basis. The Advent Lutheran Church at Ninety-third and Broadway established an afternoon homework center where P.S. 84 children could receive remedial reading lessons and also play ping-pong and have refreshments. Another homework center was established by the Richmond Foundation, in which public school teachers were paid to tutor elementary school children in the daytime and junior high school children in the evenings.

The school also acquired some extracurricular cultural assets. The principal and the parents association wangled free tickets to Lincoln Center so that whole classes could watch rehearsals of the New York Philharmonic and the ballet. Young Audiences, a private group which sponsors professional brass, woodwind, and string concerts for public schools, put P.S. 84 on its schedule. The school staff arranged special events for children's assemblies, including puppet shows, recitals by Asian dancers, a ballet program by Melissa Hayden.

Children from other schools gave performances at P.S. 84 assemblies. One of the most memorable of these was a recital by children from P.S. 171 in Harlem. Dressed in home-made folk costumes, bright skirts and scarves, they danced, sang "Havah Nagilla" and other songs in Hebrew, also harvest songs from Nigeria, France, and Puerto Rico. Since P.S. 84 was named after Sol Bloom, the West Side leader who was a member of the House of Representatives at his death, the principal persuaded the Sol Bloom Foundation to give money for six annual scholarships for P.S. 84 children, three to the Art Students League and three to the David Mannes College of Music. On one of my first visits to P.S. 84, I ran into Stewart Ktonis, director of the Art Students League, looking over the children's paintings.

The school started out with a rather remarkable group of teachers and supervisors. One of the assistant principals was Dorothy Ziman, a fresh-faced blonde who had begun her teaching as a substitute in a Harlem school. She was one of P.S. 84's assistant principals until she went on maternity leave. Although she lived in New Jersey, she was a former West Sider and spoke Spanish, having taught a completely non-English-speaking class for more than two years.

"There were great rewards in working with children who came here without friends," she recalled. "Many of our children came to us distrusting all adults. I don't mean just the Puerto Rican children. You would be surprised the number of middle-class families represented in P.S. 84 that were broken or on the verge of breaking. Our job was to get the children to trust the teacher. Then it would be easier to trust others.

"The children often began by testing their teachers. They were very perceptive; they would try everything. You didn't have to say a word; they knew just how you felt about them." Mrs. Ziman was fairly well satisfied with her teachers even though several of them were taking their first classes. Most of them were "pretty dedicated, and where there was not enough understanding at first a lot had to do with the fact that these girls were from middle-class backgrounds, suddenly facing all kinds of children. It took a while to empathize."

From the very start the staff's main concern—and the children's most difficult problem—was reading. Technically, classes were grouped "homogeneously," according to Board of Education policy. Actually, however, there were children of many different reading speeds in almost every class. A teacher would form several reading groups and give each one different books. In some ways a P.S. 84 classroom resembled a one-room country schoolhouse, with one cluster of children sitting on the floor, around the teacher at the front of the room, with the other groups at their desks reading or taking a test. In most of the classes I observed each group seemed to concentrate rather well on its particular job.

Mrs. Ziman and Beatrice Trubin, who supervises teachers working primarily with language-handicapped children, were not satisfied to order reading materials just because they were commonly used in other schools. They checked all materials listed in the Board of Education brochure and consulted with specialists to be sure they were what their particular school needed. Mrs. Ziman also encouraged teachers to write their own books, something she had done as a fourth-grade teacher. Many of her fourth graders were reading at second-grade levels so that regular texts were not usable, so Mrs. Ziman "watered down" (the official word is "adapted") the fourth-grade material into sentences the children could understand. The subject matter of these home-baked texts, typed at home and run off on the office ditto machine, were built on the everyday experiences of her Puerto Rican and Negro and white children—in a sense the children contributed the research. "We would write about what had happened on the way to school or on a trip to an office, work up a vocabulary that applied to what we saw around us, and suddenly we would have a book, a good book."

One of the several new teachers who learned quickly how to "empathize," as Mrs. Ziman put it, was Patricia Smith. Her third-grade class included several emotionally disturbed children, and some other pupils were reading at first-grade level. The class had been difficult even for the experienced teacher who preceded her. Miss Smith was untested and "scared" (by her own admission) but her warmth and spontaneity enabled her to bring the class together, to keep it whole. She would keep each of her reading groups with her for a few minutes, then when all had had their turn she would unite the class and let things circulate. The faster children sat with the slower readers and I noticed that in their various tête-à-têtes the children pointed at words in each other's books and asked questions of each other. Except for a healthy buzzing, the room was quiet enough for the visitor to hear Miss Smith's heels clicking when she walked around. She always touched base every few minutes with a despondent-looking Puerto Rican girl, and a well-dressed white boy with a similarly anxious, sad expression. The girl would whisper in Miss Smith's ear or interrupt her with a quick movement. The boy would touch her arm or her hand briefly, silently.

A teaching supervisor watching the class gave me the background of both children. The girl's mother and another member of the family had died of cancer, and the father was unable to cope with the situation. If the teacher did not reassure the child constantly, she became unmanageable. The white boy was the son of a wealthy businessman. His mother had deserted the family and the boy had been sent to live with relatives. The father had not mentioned the boy's existence to the woman who became his second wife until after they were married.

"The father assumes that he has provided very well for the boy's material needs. He has the attitude that the boy will outgrow his difficulties," the supervisor said. "There is nothing our teachers can do to reassure the child. They can only keep the sense of rejection and apprehension far enough below the surface so that the boy will not break down."

The supervisor watched the teacher voyage around her class, and then returned to the two children again.

"I don't know which child is the more tragic. I do know that the white parent did the most damage."

One of the more mystifying entries in public education's glossary of terms is "non-English coordinator." The aforementioned Miss Trubin has this title at P.S. 84. She is a small, blue-eyed woman who explained that she was responsible for improving the instruction of non-English-speaking children. She counseled teachers, gave teaching demonstrations, and suggested classroom materials for new teachers and those assigned her by the principal. Where help was not asked, or the principal did not "guide" a teacher to her for help, Miss Trubin remained at a discreet distance and hoped for the best. She called herself a "fellow teacher," not a supervisor.

In her teaching demonstrations, Miss Trubin stressed the importance of having all the children working at the same time: "If half the class is reciting and the other half is just doing busy work, then half of the teacher is taking a vacation." Miss Trubin expected the teacher to work with one group while the other groups were engaged in independent activity in which they reinforced their skills in math, reading, or spelling. Three reading groups in a single class during a one-hour period are about the maximum a teacher can handle effectively, Miss Trubin said: a beginning teacher should not try to handle more than two. Even grouping doesn't work if achievement levels in a class run to too great extremes. Such extremes are found frequently in P.S. 84 because of the large percentage of children learning English as a second language. One reason the school has been given additional teachers is to keep the average class register to twenty-eight or twenty-nine, so that it can cope with the problem of the extremes.

The language handicaps of the children may not be their most serious difficulty, Miss Trubin said, although it is not easy to unravel all the causes for retardation. "They come to school with many strikes against them—broken homes, large families, in cramped quarters with no bed of their own, insufficient and improper food and a great deal of illness in the family." She spoke of children who have an "absent father." Miss Trubin also blamed inadequate and unrealistic teacher training programs for some of the difficulties disadvantaged children have had in school systems. Too many teachers have done a disproportionate amount of their student teaching in private schools, where the children, if no less difficult than those in public school, had very different problems and were getting more outside attention to their needs—psychoanalysis, cultural stimulation in the home, proper health care, etc. "The private schools are a dream world," Miss Trubin said. "As a graduate of Columbia Teachers College, I say students need far more knowledge about the New York City public school in low-income areas. Fortunately, the teacher-training institutions have begun to improve their approach in this respect."

Miss Trubin was preoccupied with the Puerto Rican children, whose families cannot be compared to other earlier foreign-language groups that came to the United States. "First of all, our own culture is the same European background from which the early waves of immigrants came. English in Europe was often the second language and immigrants from these countries, if they did not know English, were required to learn it in order to qualify for citizenship. Puerto Ricans have neither the Western European background nor, because they are already citizens, have they had to learn English. Many of the Puerto Ricans come here with the feeling that the onus is all on us mainlanders, that we have been unfair to them. They are resentful, they often have a chip on their shoulder—sometimes with good reason. We have to try constantly to prove our good faith and sincere interest in the welfare and development of the child. Parents are difficult to reach and this increases our problems."

Despite all this, the lot of the Puerto Rican child seemed to be improving in the schools Miss Trubin had known. When she came to the now defunct P.S. 93 a dozen years ago, the majority of Puerto Rican children were illiterate even in Spanish and did not know what to do in a classroom. Now only a very small minority of Puerto Rican children come to New York without schooling, and many can speak and read some English. The city has brought Puerto Rican study material into the school system, and ten years ago the Ford Foundation underwrote a language-teaching experiment with Puerto Rican children which helped improve teaching methods. Under the Ford project, three different types of classroom instruction were used. In one classroom the teacher used vocabulary, in the second the teacher taught language patterns, and in the third the teacher relied on "experiential learning." The discovery that the children in the experiential classes learned English much faster led to the development of Puerto Rican study bulletins that standardized teaching procedures for all children in predominantly Puerto Rican classes. There has been a steady record of progress in teaching Spanish children since that time.

Of course not all the progress comes out of bulletins on new teaching procedures. Patrick Brody, for instance, developed ways of his own to make school an exciting place for newcomers. Most of the children in his sixth-grade class were born outside the United States, and a majority of them came from broken homes. Brody had not had a great deal of teaching experience but he had something else which is helpful, a background. He has three children, is a musician, and has been a children's camp counselor. During two years when he was a case worker for the Department of Welfare, he learned something about the poverty in which so many of his children live. Before taking over his class, Brody assisted two guidance teachers with disturbed children who could not be assimilated into the activity of a normal classroom. He is a sandy-haired, square-faced man, who talks in a matter-of-fact way, sometimes with an index finger on his chin or his arms folded. There is something very contemporary about him: he is "with it" as the children might say. For exercise in penmanship he once told the children to write letters to movie stars.

Brody had three reading groups and two mathematics groups. For children who had just come from a foreign country and had no English, he had a "language emphasis" section, in which he used a tape recorder to check the children's language progress, playing the tapes of their voices back to them. On subjects other than reading, language, and math, the class worked together. Brody found that art and music are the best way to join together the class's temporarily severed parts. When he brought out the puppets, Spanish children lost their shyness. Their big eyes fixed on the dolls they were manipulating, they talked freely, clearly, excitedly, if not always in English, and no actors ever had better audiences.

During the last fifteen minutes of the period, Brody would hand out Xeroxed copies of the music and the words of "The Gaucho." The pupils opened their desks and took out pear- and cherry-wood recorders. Brody brought his banjo out of the corner and a Peruvian boy went to the closet for his accordion. At the teacher's signal there was a hush, then his twenty-four piece orchestra began to play quite precisely, with alto parts under the melody. At the end of the song, the room filled with a murmur of pleasure. Other songs were played and sung: "The Happy Wanderer," "The Marine's Hymn," "Long, Long Ago," and "Fifteen Days on the Panama Canal." George Polite, a small Negro child, came in with a special beat on a small xylophone he could hold in one hand. When the bell rang, the children put the recorders away and looked at each other appreciatively.

Brody was not sure what was in store for his children. He said they behaved beautifully, were sensitive. Music brought them together and they loved school. Until four months before almost none of them had ever seen a recorder or played a musical instrument of any sort. But only seven children read at sixth-grade level. Many were two years behind in reading at the point when they were preparing to enter junior high school.

"If we only had more time," Brody said, putting his banjo back in the case.

A new Puerto Rican child coming to P.S. 84 will be confronted by a big, burly mustached teacher named Federico Aquino. A Puerto Rican with a master's degree from Columbia, Aquino is the school's "auxiliary teacher," with a special responsibility for Spanish youngsters and the Spanish community in the school district. He interviews Puerto Rican parents to get an idea of the quantity and quality of their child's previous training. The placement of the child depends a good deal on what Aquino thinks, not on IQ test results, which are not considered very meaningful if the child is behind in English. "If the child doesn't know English, I ask him to read Spanish. This gives me an indication of how much he knows, how much he has been learning, something about what he can learn."

Aquino tells the parents the unpleasant facts of life about employment and housing in their adopted city. He cooperates closely with the school guidance counselor, whose job is to help children develop to their fullest potential. He interprets for her and the school psychologist when they confer with parents on behavior problems, and he introduces the Spanish parents to the teachers. He is also available for parent-teacher interviews—if the teacher asks him. If a parent does not feel he is being treated right, Aquino tries to find out what is bothering him. In cases where a child has a special difficulty, he recommends a social agency. He finds that the parents, by and large, meet him at least halfway. While he will offer help, he "will not be a crutch," he says. The parents will have to make decisions and follow through on them.

Aquino thinks that there are "always some Puerto Rican parents who think the schools are just another institution to keep the status quo. You have to be careful to accept their anger without becoming angry yourself. There are parents who think that because teachers are American they cannot do as much for us as if they were Puerto Rican. This is the attitude that only one from your own group can understand you fully, and of course it isn't true. Puerto Ricans have met many antagonisms on the part of authorities and many people here resent us. Sometimes we have a problem getting our people to trust in the schools. When the Americans themselves say the schools are not good, then those who are just coming in say, well, something really bad must be going on if the Americans say so and send their children to private schools. Many people simply do not know how to evaluate all they hear. But the majority of people in our Puerto Rican community feel that the school is a good and fine one."

Judith Ferrari is the type of teacher who makes Aquino's job a little easier. Most of her Puerto Rican and Negro first graders did not go to kindergarten but they like the routine of school now. They are absorbed in doing things they will want to talk to her about later, and in these conversations the teacher gives them many chances to feel pleased with themselves. In their turn, the children have conspired with her to get their parents to come to school—something Spanish and Negro mothers rarely do unless there is some kind of trouble.

Mrs. Ferrari runs an orderly class, which in first grade is not the same as a quiet class. Things move along. While she has a group of bright children up front for a reading lesson, the others make masks, wrist watches, dogs, elephants, and necklaces out of green, yellow, and blue Plasticene: they handle clay as if they were kneading dough. Some art teachers feel that children should use self-hardening clay, so that the results can be preserved and the children can look at them later. Mrs. Ferrari holds out for Plasticene: the children like the cool, rubbery feeling of something they can clench, squeeze, and pinch; and perhaps they will want to make something slightly different out of yesterday's masterpiece. Wrist watches can be made bigger. A horse can easily be transformed into an elephant by stretching its nose to make a trunk. Since the money for the Plasticene comes out of Mrs. Ferrari's own pocketbook, there isn't much the art teachers can do about it. The children bring their sculpture up for approval, and Mrs. Ferrari adjusts several necklaces.

The class got the parents to come to school by inviting them in for a breakfast. Preparations for the event took several days. The children were told to study what went into a good morning meal, then went out shopping for Post Toasties, milk, and fruit. When fifteen parents arrived on the appointed morning, the children served the breakfast and gave the adults a lecture on the importance of children's having a good breakfast every day in the week. They told their parents that coffee was all right for grownups but that children should drink milk. The party made a lasting impression. Some children who had been starting the day off with coffee and bread told Mrs. Ferrari that their mothers are now giving them "real" breakfasts.

The personality of the teacher is especially important to the Puerto Rican children. The stiff and pedantic teacher, although well meaning, will generally fail with them. But while the children's demands upon the teacher are great, they are also ready to give a great deal in return. A real teacher is a second parent to them (*los maestros son los segundos padres: hay que obedeceres*)—they will obey through love, not fear. A warm teacher can break through many of the psychological barriers the newly arrived Spanish child faces in trying to read and speak English. Much depends on relaxing him so that he is not afraid to make mistakes.

Puerto Rican children have often learned their English on the island from teachers who have never been to the mainland and speak with a thick accent that transforms words like "iron" into "ire-on," and "how are you" into "howard-dju." On the first day of school the child is so afraid he will do badly that he may say he speaks no English, and the screening staff at P.S. 84 is careful not to make quick judgments about the children's language capacity. This is a point at which Mr. Aquino's intervention may be crucial. The teachers also avoid giving the child the feeling that there is something "wrong" with Spanish—they don't say, for instance, "don't speak Spanish" when a child lapses into his own tongue. In fact the school has Spanish courses for Puerto Rican children to improve their use of their natural language.

The fourth-grade class of one of the Negro teachers, Vivian Anderson, is one in which the daily struggle to speak and read is less painful because she has the children's confidence, and because she herself is a relaxed person. The children also admire her because she is young and stylish. Although the class is the second fastest on grade, most of the twenty-two children read considerably below grade level. Only a handful of the children are mainland white or Chinese, the rest are Puerto Rican and Negro (the latter have their own serious language difficulties).

When a group of the children gives standing recitations Miss Anderson frequently has to tell a child to speak up three or four times before he can be heard. On the playground, of course, the same voice can be as loud as a steam whistle. Almost every child seems to be struggling against a lack of self-confidence. As each child finishes, the teacher makes a complimentary remark. Most of the recitations, good and bad, are applauded enthusiastically by the group, but when a tall girl speaks almost soundlessly, the children object and tell her to talk louder.

A Puerto Rican boy, Carmen, refers in his recitation to "Roosia." "That is the Spanish way," says the teacher, smiling. "In English we say Rushh-ia." The "shh" travels around the room. The children are testing the sound for themselves. In discussing sounds of New York City a Puerto Rican boy speaks a new word—"wonderful"—and feels his way around the word several times, grinning. Another Puerto Rican child forms sentences with his lips, blowing his cheeks in and out with exasperation, flipping his hands, twisting his fingers. The silent lip motion turns out to be a prelude to spoken sentences which he expels with considerable difficulty. He speaks with a very heavy accent and many of the children stare into space as he struggles along. The boy is quite literally in agony.

When the teacher has finished with each group, and the children are back in their regular seats, the better readers and talkers are mixed in with children in the slower groups, and a certain amount of mumbling and whispering begins—the sounds of cooperation. They work on their study books, draw lines connecting words on one page to pictures on another, and "practice" on words. Then, for the last few minutes, Miss Anderson reads to them, rounding out the day's experience with language.

Adele Lerner, the school's only guidance counselor, is supposed to know every one of the school's nearly nine hundred children. Also, about half her time has to be spent with "problem" children—the emotionally disturbed, mentally retarded (the school has a special CRMD Program for the latter). The other half of Mrs. Lerner's time is spent with parents whose children require special help and with community organizations which could support the guidance program. On the face of it, the assignment seems to be one of the impossible jobs which are common in an educational system permanently afflicted by acute personnel shortages. The city's guidance programs are so understaffed that they represent, in most cases, a token effort in an area of immense need. However, Mrs. Lerner is more than a token counselor because she has a great deal of energy and an ability to dovetail her work to that of the classroom teachers and supervisory personnel. The fact that the principal is flexible enough to allow experimentation is also helpful. Thus Mrs. Lerner manages to avoid being diluted to the point where she vanishes into thin air.

Her office is next to that of the Spanish auxiliary teacher, Mr. Aquino, a sensible arrangement since their work overlaps. Their waiting rooms are usually filled with children. More and more parents are also beginning to drop by, a sign that the school is closer to the Spanish community than its predecessor, P.S. 93. Mrs. Lerner would still like to see more Spanish mothers in the school's parents association, whose members are largely "mainland" whites. The parents association has been trying to do something about the matter, but in a rather spasmodic and sometimes self-defeating fashion.*

The strong hopes of many low-income Negro parents that their children will go on to college disturb Mrs. Lerner. The ambition, or the expectation, would seem to be a healthy one, but such hopes are unrealistic if the parents fail to recognize that their children may have special problems. Spanish parents also sometimes have unreasonably high expectations, since one of the main reasons they come to the States is to get a better education for their children.

"Expectations are all right but many parents offer little else but ambition, anxiety, or apathy to their children," Mrs. Lerner remarks. "There is a general misunderstanding about the purpose of an education and what is required of a parent if the child is to get the proper education. Negro mothers' tremendous ambition for their children to do well in school comes from the idea that school is the first step to college, and that college means success, a job, all the good things in life, happiness. The child is painfully aware of the parent's anxiety, which works great hardships both ways. As the child begins to fall behind, the parent becomes more and more anxious and

* The leadership of the parents association of P.S. 84 seems to have a rather split personality on the subject of the low-income family. On the one hand it has been trying to interest more low-income, minority-group parents in participating actively in the organization. On the other hand, in December, 1964, it sent a written protest to the Superintendent of Schools about the zoning of children from the newly opened Stephen Wise Towers public housing project into P.S. 84, even though the project was only two blocks away, on the grounds that the anticipated influx of these children would make it too heavily "low income." The superintendent acceded to the parents' request, and the Stephen Wise children were assigned to P.S. 75 unless their parents exercised an "option" to have them sent to P.S. 84.

friction develops. By the time the child is nine or ten and the parents see that, despite all their desire, the child is not going to make it, they feel a personal humiliation. They really take it out on the child, which only drives the child down deeper."

Mrs. Lerner tells a parent it is all very well for her to want the best for her child, "but such dreams have to be filled in," and too often the dreams are not filled in, so that by the time a child reaches fifth grade he may be retarded three years in reading. By ninth grade he cannot meet the requirements for vocational or academic high school. Ten or fifteen such children per class means mass retardation, with all the accompanying disciplinary and motivational problems.

Mrs. Lerner says that schools themselves tend to confuse different kinds of education. "If we are going to get a broad philosophy of education, it has to apply to different types of individuals. What we have in our own school is a diversity of goals. What we don't want is a situation where a 'fad' takes over, where one group of children is being pressured into the type of education that will lead them into the ultra-high ranks of scientific professions or, say, the Ivy League colleges. Because of faddism children who might do better in other fields go into science because their peer culture dictates it. What about the humanities and arts? Children who might do wonderfully in them are passing them by because of the tremendous pressure. Education has become contaminated with considerations of status. What is status, and what is education? While much of the competition in our school is positive in the sense that children have a tremendous sense of drive and need for success and feeling of achievement, we get into trouble with it. Children unable to stand the pressure end by feeling very badly about themselves."

Reading problems remain serious but not because of a lack of time spent on them by the teachers, Mrs. Lerner says. "The obvious answer would seem to be intensive reading instruction, but we cannot teach at a more intensified level because the children will not accept what we want to give. In some of our first- and second-grade classes we spend most of our time in reading readiness, yet by the fourth grade many children are not reading. It is a strange thing, but the more we push, the less successful we are. There are intensely devoted teachers who want these children to read more than they want them to do anything else, but this doesn't do the trick.

"The teacher says, 'Help me, tell me what to do, give me a

formula.' Our usual reaction is that it's not a question of doing, it's a question of being. Many of our teachers understand this and are responsive. It's not unusual for the children to line up at three o'clock and kiss the teacher on Friday before they go home. They are outgoing and affectionate and candid. They will kiss the teacher one minute and be naughty the next, but there is no relationship between the two. Every person dealing with children has to be aware that it's not merely being there in a room. It's being there 100 percent emotionally, physically, spiritually all the time, with everything you've got."

In the school's first year Mrs. Lerner ran a parents' workshop where she showed films and talked about child development. In her teacher-training workshop (dropped the following year because of "technical problems") Mrs. Lerner's teachers worked on case studies under the guidance of Dr. Florine Katz, a psychologist at City College who volunteered her services to the school. A teacher gave an evaluation of a child, Dr. Katz made her observations on the child, and Mrs. Lerner filled in the background of the child which she had obtained from parent interviews. When all of these people matched observations, they frequently discovered that a child at P.S. 84 who did not conform to standard behavior patterns was actually reacting in a way very positive and even healthy for him, considering his chaotic background. In that case unconventional behavior was a way of survival. A very bossy child, for instance, might come from a home where there was no reliable adult, and authority falls on him. "Many of these children have not had enough time to be children. They have been rushed into maturity without going through the normal stages of emotional growth."

"Children from all sorts of backgrounds are being pushed too hard," Mrs. Lerner feels. "They are pushed from being babies to replacing being mother when mother gets sick. They are pushed in other ways. The middle-class white parents, for instance, make terribly high demands on their kids—the wrong kind of demand. It is not enough for them to get the child into college. He must get into a rich prestige college. The children are almost forced to feel they don't rate unless they get an 800 on the college boards."

The "overly competitive" parent of a high-IQ child presents a special problem, according to Miss Trubin. These are the most vocal parents, and they bring a great deal of pressure on the school to assign the best and most-experienced teachers to the faster classes.

Other teachers agree with Miss Trubin that the middle-class parents are in the driver's seat because they know their children are badly needed to keep the school from becoming more and more racially and economically out of balance. To satisfy a parent sometimes a white child is placed in an IGC (intellectually gifted children) class although he is not qualified on the basis of traditional IQ and reading-achievement tests.

One of the most outspoken teachers on the subject of the high-IQ child and his parents—and also the most qualified by experience to talk about them—was Mildred Craig, who taught sixth-grade IGC classes. A tall, spare Negro in her sixties who retired recently, she was a regular teacher for forty years and was once chosen as the best public school teacher of the year by the Grand Street Boys Association. Although her pupils had high IQ's she said that "in some cases they had the Q without the I." She was referring in the main to children from white middle-class families. All but two of the pupils in her first class at P.S. 84, for instance, were white, a racial pattern somewhat typical of IGC classes, which has led some parents to charge that the classes are racially segregated.*

Mrs. Craig often wondered whether her children were presenting their own ideas in class, or just parroting their parents' opinions. "The overprivileged child," she thinks, "is difficult because his parents are difficult. Some of the children already think they have learned all there is to know. There is this constant rivalry and vying with each other. Not for love of knowledge for itself. Children criticize teachers, parents, and supervisors. Not all the children in our IGC classes are qualified to be in them but because of parental pressure the class is made up, and let's face it, we build a group of little snobs. There is constant difficulty between the IGC's and the other children, who will waylay them or pick on them. Every time one of the IGC children steps out of line, if the others are monitors, he is reported and they jump on him with a little special vindictive-

* As a means of giving IGC classes a more heterogeneous racial and ethnic character, West Side principals are using the Board of Education's Wrightstone tables, listing minimum reading and IQ scores for admission to IGC classes. By following these tables, it is possible for a principal to assign children to IGC classes who may score 25 to 30 percent below hitherto accepted IQ requirement, and who may be reading two years below the accepted reading level. The Wrightstone tables are intended to facilitate assignment of more Puerto Rican and Negro children to IGC classes. In addition, at P.S. 84 IQ tests have been officially abandoned and IGC class assignments are made on the basis of achievement and teacher judgment.

ness. There is even resentment toward him and his parents by other parents whose children are not in the IGC class." Mrs. Craig was not opposed to the IGC class *per se* but she wished it would not be labeled as such and that the class could be organized without the school being batted around by parent lobbyists.

"The first time it hit me was when the air-raid shelter drill was on. I said, 'Come on, let's get out of here.' 'We don't think we're going,' several children said, just like that. I said, 'Why not?' The whole thing mushroomed. Finally there were a half dozen who wouldn't go through the drills. Next they didn't want to salute the flag or recite the pledge of allegiance. One parent did a great deal of library research on the Supreme Court's decision about saluting the flag, yet there are many of these parents who would not send their children to school neat and clean."

Mrs. Craig seemed happier with her last IGC class, in 1965. She made some interesting comparisons between them and the children she had had the year before, whom she called the "againsters." Two-thirds of the "againsters" came from broken families and there were many more boys than girls in the class. In the 1965 class, all but two of the children were living with both parents, and there was an even split between boys and girls. "The children were more like children, affectionate and eager—perhaps not quite as bright on paper or informed as my earlier class, but alert and effervescent. They could take hold of a subject." She said that first they had to get over some bad habits left over from the year before—they fought a great deal and argued interminably for a while, and there were gaps in their learning. The previous year they had put on their own version of *Hello, Dolly!* Mrs. Craig did something about that. To let them do something that wasn't "imitation adult," she had them do the fence-painting scene from *Tom Sawyer,* and the raft scene with Huck Finn and Jim, the runaway slave.

Tessa Harvey, who taught a fifth-grade IGC class at P.S. 84 in the school's first year, is not as concerned as Mrs. Craig about the children's competitiveness. "If you ask a child a question and he has the information, he wants to give out with it. You can't prevent him from competing without frustrating him." Mrs. Harvey remarks that the teaching-machine method of programmed instruction is based on the need of children to respond and to be "reinforced" whenever they give a correct answer. "If they know the answer, you've got to hear it and say 'Good.' Then they learn it. Without the reinforcement, giving the answer is meaningless." While Mrs. Harvey agrees that many of the children in IGC classes are "spoiled and accustomed to being recognized at every moment, the situation has to be directed by discipline, good manners, and a little self-control, not by suppression."

Mrs. Harvey sees various weaknesses in the IGC program. "Some children in IGC classes don't belong in them but neither do they belong in the bright class right below mine, because there is a very great distance between the ability of the two classes." She would like to see schools doing much more for the bright child who is not IGC level and yet has no special place in the curriculum now. Part of the problem at P.S. 84 arises from the fact that many of the parents in the school attendance zone who have IGC-level children have sent them to private school. Had they not done this, P.S. 84 would have had enough children to have a good IGC class and also a good high average class on each grade level so that all the fast students would be getting the proper sort of education.

Whatever their disagreements and their frustrations, the teachers at P.S. 84 think highly of their school and want to stay there. Mrs. Lerner ought to feel discouraged if anyone is, yet she is convinced that the school is moving in the intellectual direction all the time. "The whole school is in a state of excitement," she says. "We keep telling people, 'Have patience, have patience, don't run away to the Bronx.' "

And Mrs. Ziman, the assistant principal who went on maternity leave, still keeps in touch. "My neighbors in New Jersey seem to think my school was a blackboard jungle," she reports. "Well, they couldn't be more wrong. The children are pretty happy there, and some of them enjoy it more than staying home, even when it's a home with six rooms and wall-to-wall carpets."

Finally there is Mr. Forrest's testimony. When school ends for the year, many children tell him they don't want to have a vacation.

"They ask me, 'What's to do in summer? Watch TV?' "

Dr. Gottlieb

One of the most interesting schools in the Area is P.S. 165. It is housed in an old five-story structure that looks like a Gothic warehouse. (The physical plant is quite a contrast to P.S. 84.) There is a perpetual rumor that P.S. 165—it has never been named for any-body—will be torn down and replaced, but the school opens every fall as usual. It is not an unlovely place, although the vaulted windows, impractical crannies, gargoyles, copper-covered towers and complicated staircases qualify it as a white elephant, architecturally speaking. It has a pleasant rambling quality that impressed me as the sort of school children remember affectionately long after they have grown up, full of echoes, the smell of chalk and wet raincoats and vegetable soup cooking in the cafeteria. After school scores of children come back to play basketball in the basement, dodging the pillars and holding impromptu track meets. Balanced against its intangible assets is the fact that the school was built to handle fourteen hundred children and has to accommodate almost seventeen hundred. Some of the youngsters have to climb four flights to classrooms under the sloping roof. Since the school has had almost no playground space in past years, the stair climbing has its advantages.

The zone served by P.S. 165 runs from 106th Street to 110th Street, just below Columbia University, and from Central Park to Riverside Drive. It is a complex school not only because of its huge population but also because of the varied ethnic, racial, and economic backgrounds of the children. About 800 are of Spanish origin, 360 are Negro, and the rest are white children, mainly from Jewish and Protestant families. Last year 90 children arrived at the school from the Dominican Republic. One of Mrs. Rebecca Blumstein's recent third-grade classes affords a cross-section. In addition to eleven Negro and twelve Puerto Rican children, she taught pupils from China, Cuba, Ireland, Surinam, Mexico, Russia, and Lebanon. Many of the pupils from Puerto Rico, Cuba, and Santo Domingo can speak no English when they register. Several Columbia professors, including a Nobel Prize winner, send their children to the school. The Negro children are, generally speaking, from low-income families in the nearby slums, but the number from middle-class Negro families is increasing. Approximately 700 children, close to half the total registration, take free lunch.

In recent years this socialized dining has been extended in an unconventional way. One of the assistant principals, an attractive young woman named Joan Abrams, started a "breakfast club" for about forty children who seemed to be suffering from malnutrition. In one year her breakfast club membership rose to one hundred. The children arrived at 8:30 and received a cup of juice, cereal, and a container of milk. Money for the club comes out of federal school lunch funds. A school aide supervises the breakfast and attendance is checked so that the authorities can judge the effect the breakfast has on the children's lunch consumption and general health.

The breakfast club is only one of the unorthodox activities that go on at P.S. 165. They are to be expected in a school whose principal is Edward Gottlieb. Dr. Gottlieb is a stocky, slightly rumpled man in his fifties whose gentle conversational tone is quite at odds with the rather revolutionary things he often finds himself saying. He is an old-line, professed Socialist who obviously does not really understand the workings of the bureaucratic mind as it functions in the Board of Education. Proof of this is the fact that he is chairman of the War Resisters League and has an office crammed with pamphlets and books by anarchists, land reformers, pacifists, and priests. Dr. Gottlieb's intellectual propensities would undoubtedly interfere with his progress up the educational ladder if he had chosen to make the achievement of a superintendency his lifelong ambition, but this seems not to have been his purpose. He regards P.S. 165 as worth the best he has in him. What struck me most about Dr. Gottlieb was the rapidity with which ideas radiate from him in all directions, very much like the hairs on his head. The fact that such a principal as Dr. Gottlieb exists says something for the community he serves.

Since reading is his ruling passion—something rather rare in school administrators—Dr. Gottlieb has more than the usual pedagogical interest in seeing his pupils read. This is fortunate in a school where reading is a permanent and serious problem. His ability to communicate his enthusiasm about literature is especially helpful when he works with individual sixth graders in an attempt to bring them up to reading level before the end of their school year. In the late winter and early spring months, Dr. Gottlieb, a guidance teacher, and a reading teacher give them a special afterschool test, and if the results show that the child has come up to grade level as a result of having taken special reading exercises and having used library facilities inside and outside the school, he will not have to be held back from junior high school. The decisive factor in these borderline cases is the extent to which the parent cooperates. The principal would like to break away from the more traditional teaching methods, and introduce the augmented Roman alphabet (a phonetic system) in the lower grades, having been impressed with the results in schools in other cities, but the Board of Education is opposed to the idea.* He has also, without board permission, grouped some first graders in heterogeneous classes without regard to IQ's or supposed reading readiness. He reports that at the end of the year the children almost without exception have been reading at or above level for their age. The parents who have allowed their children to participate in the program are happy even if the authorities are not.

Dr. Gottlieb had hopes that a temporary decrease in his school's population a year or two ago would let him get his class sizes down into the twenties and thereby make it possible for him to get a truly effective individualized reading program under way. However, as soon as it became apparent that the school enrollment was dropping, the Board of Education cut three teaching positions out of Gottlieb's staff allowance. When he protested about this at a public meeting of the local school board, he succeeded in annoying the district superintendent but didn't get his teachers back.

Dr. Gottlieb is restive about what he considers the continual failure of the public to wake up to the need for more money for the schools, and he would like to organize 100,000 people to march around the city to dramatize what he calls the "public guilt." He is curious about why New York City, which is supposed to be relatively sophisticated about education, should be less committed to good schools than Vandalia, Illinois, a town he has been reading about, which in spite of its economic difficulties has new buildings and high school class registers in the twenties. "In Vandalia the people have extended themselves. In New York we're putting up giant office buildings and luxury apartment houses. You would think the city was having a rebirth until you find the schools are lagging very far behind. New York City is the cultural center of the world, a place of ferment. Just being in this city is being twenty-five years in the future, so we ought

* The augmented Roman alphabet technique bears some similarity to the method used by the mainland Chinese to break mass illiteracy. *Han-yu p'in-yin,* a Latin alphabet for the phonetic writing of Chinese, gives the children a quick start in learning basic Chinese characters, then the system is generally dropped. In some cases, however, it becomes the basis of a written language for Chinese minority peoples. See *The Other Side of the River,* by Edgar Snow, p. 94. Random House, 1961.

to be taking a lead in a new national effort to put education in the place it belongs. This means someday we will have to spend money for schools the way we do for hard liquor. You can make a nice little book out of the Scotch ads in the *New York Times*. Every day that goes by we commit a tremendous wrong against children. The way things move today, even a great majority of kids who do well in school never reach the college level because there aren't the buildings for them and they can't afford the education. In my day, a 75 average gave you a high-school college-entrance diploma and you went to college, but now you get a Puerto Rican boy or a Negro boy who gets an 80 to 85 average on the Regents—and they're no easier now than they used to be when I went to school—and they may not get into a municipal college because there is no room. Usually their only hope for getting a college education is to pay through the nose, pay money they don't have. In spite of all we tell ourselves to the contrary, we're making it more and more difficult for the underprivileged to get ahead. Studies show that proportionately less people from working-class families get into college today than they did in 1900. The big explosion we face in this country is not necessarily on the racial question but on the question of our young people. Where are they to go? What are they going to do? We are building up an army. They are young, they are strong, they can move fast, they have no commitments, no ties, no jobs. Unaffiliated, unused, uneducated kids were the backbone of Nazism in Germany, and, just like in Germany, many of our unions are freezing the kids out with their seniority systems and their monopoly of jobs."

Dr. Gottlieb does not seem to see the trade union movement as a whole as being of much help to the poor—an attitude which is increasingly common among old-line Socialists and liberals. However, he does have hopes for the teachers' union.

He wishes the public understood that a teacher's self-respect depends on whether he has the tools and working conditions to do his job well. "When you serve the people, you serve yourself as a teacher. Doing good work depends on a human being's making a creative demand upon himself. He has to be true to his craft, whatever it is, whether he is a doctor, a carpenter, or a teacher."

He recalls watching a carpenter finish a job in a new store. "Just before quitting time he climbed down off the ladder. He only had a little more to do up there. When I inquired why he was coming down since he was almost finished, he said he needed a special nail. He had plenty of nails of all sizes at the top of the ladder, but this old gentleman put on his jacket, went to the hardware store, and got the exact nail he needed to finish the job right. He was honest in his craft. A teacher has to work under the same self-compulsions as the carpenter. The teacher's strikes were never understood by the public. The teachers struck because they wanted to be professionals and were struggling for a new image of themselves. Twice they have gone through a sort of catharsis with these strikes. They were wrenched professionally and personally by them. These were their trial periods, rituals in which the teachers were the victims of public misunderstanding. The public simply wanted no strike, wanted the teachers to obey, to conform. They talked about the 'dedicated teacher.' Well the 'dedicated teacher' the public talks about is the old stereotype of a pussyfooting, mouselike woman, something less than human. The teacher belongs to the human family, she is a citizen, not some foreign agent sent here to plague us."

Teachers in New York City, with their accumulation of experience with children and their technical knowledge, hold a wonderful opportunity in their hands. "If we could put their knowledge to use by good civic organizations, our city would become a cultural showplace." He does not see why David Dubinsky, head of the ILGWU, should be the symbol of social reform and liberalism in the city. He is a union leader who works with workers—"people with resources that simply don't compare to what the teachers can bring to a situation. Yet because no one else carries the ball, it is the Dubinskys, the Gus Tylers, and the Philip Randolphs and other union people in the Liberal party who represent the cause of social welfare and the human aspirations of this town. If we got forty thousand teachers and three thousand principals and assistant principals into a movement as big and with as many financial resources as the Liberal party, it could mean the rebirth of our city. We could throw our influence in all directions, developing our youth in art, literature, and science."

It often seems as if Dr. Gottlieb looks at the world through the eyes of a child; at least he is on the child's side against everybody else. "Our young people are going to go a long way ahead of us. I can't base this optimism on what I see in the school except that I can see kids 'pushing up from down under.' I find the American climate contributes to a kind of egalitarian freedom. Our kids won't accept any boundaries; they have an insistence inside about being treated fairly." Dr. Gottlieb recalls as an example a girl who was asked to do a special reading test before himself and a reading instructor. "She was nervous. When we asked the child to explain what she was reading, she came right back and said, 'Don't you think I have to read it to myself before I read it to you?' She was right. When you're taking a test, reading orally without preparation is not fair. I doubt whether many kids in the presence of teachers and an assistant principal and guidance counselor would have had the forthrightness to say so the way this girl did. The children have a different type of attitude toward grown-ups today and it's not bad at all. We do what we can to encourage a child in this school to stand on his own feet and realize he has equal rights. All people are born free and equal, including children.

"One of the handicaps many of our kids suffer from is authoritarianism in the home, where a child is never consulted or asked, but is just told what to do. Sometimes he is bribed when he gets ugly. One parent who registered her child did something I liked very much. When the child came in with her, she asked her to pull up a seat and sit down. That showed sensitivity. Usually when parents come in with a child, to talk to the principal, the child stands. One of the things that make so-called middle-class people successful with their children at school is because they create a rapport with a child like this. I think that Negro parents tend to be more authoritarian than the Puerto Rican or white middle-class parent. Often the Negro parents seem to be afraid to give their children a real sense of equality."

Occasionally the children, who understand their principal rather well, seem quite prepared to put his theories about equal rights for children to the test. One December, Dr. Gottlieb decided to redistribute some of his fifth-grade classes so as to equalize the class registers. To do this he had, among other things, to discontinue a fifth-grade "opportunity class" (for children who are severely retarded in reading and writing) and spread them around in other classes. Since the dozen children in the class had been together for several years, with the same teacher, Mrs. Edith Marcus, the principal realized they needed some preparation for the change. Accordingly, he took an entire period to explain to the class the reasons for the change. The attempt to explain was an uncomfortable experience.

"All the while I was talking to those kids, they looked at me as if they were members of the Board of Education," he says. "When I finished, they asked me two dozen questions. They wanted to know why other children couldn't be put in their class, instead of breaking up their class. They argued that their teacher had the most experience with them, so why give them another teacher? And so on. I got nowhere with them."

The next day, Dr. Gottlieb received a petition signed by each child in the class, protesting the change. When he went to the class to discuss it, he found them painting signs. He doesn't remember the exact wording on the signs, but he does recollect that "they were very legible for kids who weren't supposed to be able to write very well, and none of them was favorable to me." The children informed Dr. Gottlieb that they were going to picket in the schoolyard the following day, during their afternoon period when they would ordinarily have been making a trip to Central Park.

Dr. Gottlieb promised that he would be at his window at 2 P.M., the time for the demonstration. Matters went according to schedule, and the principal watched the children circling under his window for several minutes, then dispatched a student to the scene to act as a "reporter" and take down the children's complaints. Following this he invited the picketers into the office for a conference.

"I thought I'd soften them up with doughnuts and cocoa, but the kids were adamant," he says. However, a compromise was worked out eventually. The children agreed to disbanding of their class, on condition that two weeks after being assigned to their new classes they could "come back together" for an afternoon and give their teacher a going-away party. The party was a great success, and afterwards the children accepted their fate gracefully. Since then, Dr. Gottlieb has arranged that once a week a boy and a girl from the old opportunity class be "paired" for one period and assigned to help a small group of younger children in the school with their work. The experiment has delighted the children, and they still have a feeling of being together.

Once every several weeks I walk up to 109th Street to look in on the classes, and, if there isn't a crisis of some sort taking place, I can usually pin Dr. Gottlieb down for lunch. The experience always leaves me feeling much improved and with some new notes on the children. From a recent visit I remember a small, round-eyed boy, José Pena. His teacher, Rosalyn Gaissiner, was trying to keep his nose in books in the hope he would become as good a reader as he was a talker. José was doing all right socially, in spite of his various troubles, which included writing "seeds" as "seebs," and getting his "c's" backward. He did not seem to be disturbed about his work and was very anxious to know his teacher's reactions. He came to me several times to show me what he was doing. The classroom had a high ceiling and movable desks, spaced in what struck me as rather composed disorder. The children had started a garden, and there were already some sprouts poking their way up well ahead of the season, it being February at the time. The blackboards were inscribed with advice on how to prepare and plant seeds. Some play telephones were scattered about the room, and on the walls were flags, tinfoil decorations, painting, stained-glass windows of colored paper, the inevitable pictures of Eskimos and Hawaiians, drawings of dinosaurs and Japanese paper fish.

On one visit to the school I picked up a copy of a letter the children in a fourth-grade class taught by Mrs. Minna Gottesman wrote to Dr. Gottlieb when he was in the hospital. As a way of letting him know he was missed, each child contributed a phrase to the letter, promising that when he got back to school they would be as quiet as:

A pin dropping on a soft bed.
Touching a strand of hair.
A tissue falling.
An empty room.
A snowflake hitting the ground.
A feather floating.
A lady-bug landing on a leaf.
A picture hanging on the wall.
A butterfly flying by.
A lonely sphinx.
The sun setting.
Your eye-lids closing.
A spider spinning.
A star shining in the sky.
Glowing.
A cat walking on snow.
An angel landing on a cloud.
A flower opening.

On our way to lunch that day, as we were walking across the schoolyard, dozens of children ran over and every one of them said, over and over, "Hello, Dr. Gottlieb, hello, Dr. Gottlieb." No messages, just nice, smiling faces turned up.

The Child in Danger

Although P.S. 84 is new and temporarily underutilized, and P.S. 165 is old and overcrowded, they have a common problem. They are schools under increasing pressure not only to educate, but to compensate for the disintegration of family life which may be the single most ominous fact of life in the American city. Many of the children in both schools come from broken homes and semiliterate parents, and are already disadvantaged or traumatized by the time they enter the first grade. The problem is not confined to the low- or non-income minority group children, but the nonwhite child of the slum suffers the most. According to the 1960 census, for instance, 43.9 percent of Negro children from low-income backgrounds in the West Side urban renewal area came from homes where there was no father.*

Superficial administrative and organizational changes, such as redrawing attendance district lines and shifting school populations to get a better racial or economic "mix" does not promise to help the local situation very much. In addition, if the withdrawal of white and nonwhite middle-class families from the public education system continues, as is quite likely, many West Side schools will become even more the province of the poor after urban renewal is completed. Those middle-class parents who have been battling the secessionist movement by keeping their own children in the schools are not able to subdue a note of anxiety when they discuss the situation, and one is never sure how long even the most determined parents will stick to their guns.

The tragedy of the middle-class withdrawal from the public schools is that it is based at least partly on the false assumption that the public school short-changes the middle-class child in order to concentrate on the special needs of the impoverished, minority-group child. Then there is also the persistent stereotype of the blackboard jungle in the minds of parents who judge a school by what they see going on

* *Selected Population Characteristics of the West Side Urban Renewal Area* (Manhattan Census of 1960), Bureau of Community Statistical Services, Community Council of Greater New York, January, 1963.

in the neighborhood around it. Many of these assumptions would change considerably if the parents would visit their local schools, where, in most cases, they would find order, an air of excitement and constructive activity, teachers who for the most part are experienced and dedicated to their children, and average class sizes no larger than in most suburban schools. They would find the schools have a varied curriculum which will allow children to proceed at their own pace, and they would learn that—in the elementary schools at least—Latin, Negro, Oriental, and mainland white children are getting along rather well with each other without benefit of indoctrination in human relations from their parents.

Yet, with all their good qualities, it must be admitted that beneath the surface a disheartening pattern is developing in these local schools. Ironically, the trend concerns the low-income minority-group child, whose parents seem to be reasonably satisfied with the schools, rather than the middle-class child whose family tends to be so anxious and demanding about public education. For while the middle-class child has performed well, on the whole, and finds that there is always a "faster track" if he is ready for it, depressingly large percentages of the minority-group children are falling behind badly in their reading achievement.

Results of reading-achievement tests for sixth graders in the West Side elementary schools released in 1965 showed that children from impoverished backgrounds are sinking to the bottom, regardless of the extent to which the school has been racially integrated. Since most of these children are Negro or Spanish, the result is another type of segregation which neutralizes many of the social gains the children make by being in integrated schools. In P.S. 165, for instance, despite Dr. Gottlieb and a teaching staff that has made reading the first order of business, 125 out of 173 sixth graders scored below grade level in reading, with 79 children reading between third- and fourth-grade levels. Even in such schools as P.S. 84, where the average reading level is on or above grade, or P.S. 87, where the average for sixth graders is 7.5 years, there are huge groups of children from the low-income, minority-group families lumped at the very bottom of reading achievement, ranging from functional illiteracy to fourth- or fifth-grade levels. Yet both P.S. 84 and P.S. 87 are considered racially "balanced," well integrated as far as percentages go. Even if one acknowledges that reading-achievement tests have their weaknesses and are not of themselves reliable indicators of educational progress, it is impossible to avoid the conclusion that even in comparatively good special-service schools, where a degree of racial integration has been achieved, the slum child is in trouble.*

One fundamental barrier to dealing with the slum child's problem is the prevalent medieval assumption that poverty is a sign of low intelligence. Perhaps an even more serious obstacle is the confusion which some educators and writers have created by their own absurd generalizations—many of them contradictory. Witness, for example, the repeated assertion, now accepted as gospel in some civil rights circles, that inferior teachers are the cause of all the educational trouble of Harlem children. Or such remarks as that of John Hersey that "the most serious crippling single factor for the children of depressed or alienated groups is the conviction of their teachers or principals that they are educable to only a very limited degree."†

It is conceivable that Hersey may be right about some schools but his view does not apply to very many West Side teachers or principals. Some are indeed frustrated, some occasionally demoralized, but the frustration does not grow out of any attitude that the slum child is uneducable. It comes, rather, from a conviction that the disadvantaged child's chance for a normal educational achievement is constantly undermined by influences over which the teacher has very little control—influences encouraged by an indifferent society. A teacher who makes attempts to replace the mother and father as well as teach, and sees her children being eroded by ill health and a mind-sickening environment, is entitled to her own sick moments. If she doesn't have them she probably doesn't belong in teaching. In fact, her sense of frustration, if it impels her to protest publicly, can have the healthy effect of helping change public attitudes on education. (Whether the teachers' union will be a vehicle for such constructive protest, or simply another trade-union lobby, remains to be seen.)

Hersey's theory that new teaching systems based on "affirmative

---

* Reading and word-knowledge test results for the local school district released March, 1966 (covering the 1965 school year), indicate that the situation described by the above figures remains critical. In the fifth grade, for instance, 35 percent of the children scored below or slightly above third-year level in word knowledge, while 69 percent scored below fifth-grade level. In reading achievement, 37 percent of fifth graders scored below or slightly above third-year level, while 70 percent scored below fifth-grade level.

† The quotation and others by Mr. Hersey cited in this chapter are taken from his article "Education: An Antidote to Poverty," published in the *Journal of the American Association of University Women,* May, 1965.

cognitive styles" of slum children will solve their reading deficiencies is relevant if he is thinking of children who have some cultural and emotional support at home, and a degree of stability in their lives. Some West Side schools have worked very well with the affirmative cognitive styles of some Spanish and Negro children. But new pedagogical techniques of themselves offer little hope for children who are ill, who have nonfunctioning parents, and who are moved from school to school like gypsies. It is these children who are the hard core of the mass reading retardation in the West Side schools, and no amount of "positive thinking" by teachers is going to clean up the problem.

It does not help matters to picture the slum child as the repository of a whole set of special cultural resources, generated by his poverty, which only need to be tapped by an understanding teacher. Such resources, as listed by Hersey, include "the closeness and warmth of the extended family, humor, easiness, fluidity of feeling, freedom from parental overprotection and from inner guilt, the enjoyment of sports, games, music, acting, a physical mode of existence, a delight in doing." Freedom from parental overprotection indeed! To imply that children deafened, immobilized, and orphaned by poverty have acquired such assets in the process contributes to the sentimental impression that somehow life in the deep city ghetto can be character building, and can develop a healthy toughness lacking in middle-class children. This view of the very poor, whatever its relevance to people of the ethnic slums of the past, minimizes the murderous quality of modern poverty and all the diseases associated with it, and paves the way for easy assumptions that all any slum child needs is the right educational formula and a teacher who "cares." West Side parents who labor under such assumptions often talk about education as if it were a patent medicine.

It is time to stop putting all the blame on the teacher and de facto segregation and to direct far more attention to psychological problems of the child who is sinking to the bottom of the local schools, and to the disintegrating family situation that so often is at the root of his disorganization. While it is true that an emotionally disturbed child can perform quite satisfactorily, even brilliantly, in school, it is also true that reading retardation is one of the earliest and most common signs of psychiatric difficulty in children. Those who blame the white middle-class stereotype of a teacher for the underachiever usually refuse to admit the possible link between a child's psychiatric difficulties and his school performance, or, if they do admit the link, they dismiss it with a remark to the effect that the teacher is probably exaggerating the child's psychological difficulties to cover up her own deficiencies (although some teachers do). Civil rights groups have usually minimized the extent to which emotional disturbance and cultural deprivation have hampered the slum child, probably because they want to direct public attention to what to them seems the more immediate evil of de facto segregation. One sometimes gets the impression from these groups that the problem of the disturbed or deprived child will disappear once his school is racially "balanced."

In a similar way, a good part of the social work profession resists the idea that the slum child is often in need of psychiatric help. Dr. Viola Bernard has written perceptively about this particular blind spot of the profession. The fact is that racial integration, special educational services, and social workers will not eliminate mass underachievement. As long as the slum child lives in the middle of a sore, the temporary and often unrelated ministrations now provided by the schools and various public and private agencies are, with some notable exceptions, not likely to be of much help. While no teacher can be excused from making her best effort with every child, it is also true that our increasing use of the public schools as a palliative for poverty is only making the situation worse by further disrupting our educational system.

The number of emotionally disturbed children in the public schools —and they are by no means always delinquents or "acting-out" children—is not accurately known, but when the staff of one local junior high reports that approximately 250 of the children need diagnosis for possible psychological illness, the situation can be presumed to be serious. Although there have been improvements since 1962, when the Citizens Committee for Children issued its depressing report on the Board of Education's Bureau of Child Guidance and Bureau of Educational and Vocational Guidance,* the school program for diagnosis and referral and treatment of disturbed children is not much more than a token program. Because of the Board of Education's inability to find treatment for all children who

* *New York City Schools and Children Who Need Help,* by Alfred J. Kahn. Citizens Committee for Children of New York, Inc., 1962.

need it, many pupils receive tranquillizers to keep them under control in the classroom. Of a total of twenty-five thousand children enrolled in the local school district, local hospitals and agencies can add less than two dozen school children to their case loads each month. Schools of a thousand children have the services of a psychologist and social worker only half a day a week. The so-called "600" schools, which are supposed to take the worst behavioral problems, have long waiting lists. Some of the schools do surprisingly well, but in too many cases they are custodial rather than rehabilitative because of limited programs and personnel. Exceptions such as the "600" schools in Kings County and Bellevue hospitals show what can be accomplished with an excellent program, but they are certainly atypical.

A direct attack on those conditions which create a growing population of disturbed and dependent children cannot be postponed forever. Ideally, what is required, and there is no reason why it cannot be a practical possibility, is a drastic alteration of the physical environment of the slum child, and a sensible program of family rehabilitation where possible, or the provision of alternative care where it is not. It also requires that our economic system offer a real promise that these children will be able to live useful lives when they grow up. The projection of an abrupt revision in the living conditions of the people at the bottom of our society will be called revolutionary and therefore impossible, yet it does not seem unreasonable that a country which proposes to restructure the economic and social life of millions of Southeast Asians might also be able to initiate successfully a similar revolution at home.

If such a revolution occurs, it will have to be a "whole" program, national in scope with uniform standards, and financed by federal, state, and local agencies. A hopeful development in this direction is the proposed system of mental health centers for New York State, which will consolidate many services and help to maximize the efforts of private and public agencies, supplied by federal, state, and city funds. Other developments are Senator Abraham Ribicoff's amendments to the Medicare bill channeling Social Security money into a comprehensive child-care program.

A comprehensive child, health, and education welfare program will have to take another look at the responsibility of public agencies for humane treatment of children. Parenthood does not confer the right to abuse or neglect offspring to the point of severely damaging or destroying the child's health or his life. Yet intervention to protect the child except for the most extreme situations has been very limited and left, for the most part, to the Society for the Prevention of Cruelty to Children and to welfare authorities. The child is entitled to protection under law from criminal psychological and physical abuse by parents, just as he is from any other sick member of society, yet society's general reluctance to intervene in family relationships makes such protection largely theoretical. It does not seem unreasonable that parents be made accountable to the state for humane treatment of children without breaking down their protection against unwarranted intrusion into family affairs.

A step in the right direction was New York State's passage, in 1964, of new legislation which requires medical and other qualified personnel to report cases of child abuse and guaranteeing them immunity against legal harassment in case such reporting was done in "good faith." Until passage of this act, various individuals, notably doctors, who sought to protect a child from abuse were treated in the courts frequently as if they and not the parents, were the defendants; and they were always exposed to the possibility of lawsuits.

There is also an important nonlegal deterrent to protecting a child against excessive cruelty. In some cases private or public welfare investigators may allow a child to remain embedded in a highly undesirable home environment because adequate institutional or foster care facilities are not available. A comprehensive health, education, and welfare program for children whose home situation seriously endangers them might encourage the courts and agencies to act more decisively and more often. In some way the situation parallels that of the handling of youthful delinquents: the judge, faced with the knowledge that there is no satisfactory rehabilitative program for the youngster, may have to let him return to the streets.

A health and welfare program for children should relate itself sensibly to the educational program by assuming the burden of consultation, diagnosis, referral, and treatment. The school's present efforts to deal with the needs of disturbed children have been quite inadequate and have further complicated an already overcomplicated school program. The new community mental health centers being set up in New York might well take over this function in collaboration with other agencies.

Another desirable aspect of a family-centered education, health, and welfare program would be a new approach to involving low-income parents in school-related activities. At present such parents remain largely outside the traditional parents' associations. One aspect of Dr. Martin Deutsch's early-childhood school programs in Harlem and lower East Side schools has been a system of monthly meetings between a teacher and the parents of her classroom pupils. So far attendance has been good, and mutual exchange revolving around the child's classroom activity has educated both parents and the teacher. The public school's pre-kindergarten program also does this, setting aside one day a week for parent-teacher discussion.

In some cases a comprehensive child-care program might work best in relation to the so-called "residential school," which some educators feel may be the pattern of the future for those slum children whose home condition is hopeless. New York City's More Effective Schools and its All Day Neighborhood Schools have already extended the child's daily relationship to the educational system. The objective of the programs, and of the residential school, is not to encourage parents to shift their responsibilities to the educational system, but rather to build a more hopeful basis for educational achievement and to improve family relationships wherever possible. The "residential school" idea is not new: the lives of disturbed or homeless children housed in hospitals and in such institutions as Children's Village are to a great extent centered around special educational programs, some of them very successful.

The various types of American residential schools for children are not entirely unlike the communal schools of the Chinese and the boarding schools of the Russians. Whatever our ideological differences with the Communists, it might be well to look more closely at what they are doing with deprived and disturbed children. The growing distrust of the family in these countries may arise partly from a natural enmity between totalitarian governments and the family, but the distrust also exists for the very good reason that in these countries, as in America's slums, family life has disintegrated. We might also examine the experience of Yugoslavia, which lost a million of its seventeen million population in World War II and had to face the wants of the orphaned and starving children left in the wake of the German occupation. Anyone who had a firsthand view of postwar Yugoslavia could not help but be deeply impressed by the fact that this had become a country where the education and welfare of children had become a national obsession.

Robert Hutchins has made an interesting observation about the Russian experiments, the problem of our own slum children, and the fate of the American family: "The state is limited to improving the material conditions within which the family operates. The success of the family as an institution for moral and intellectual development must depend on adults. The American family of the future will either be a mere reproductive unit—and the family as we have known it is not really necessary for that purpose—or it will become a center of learning." He concludes that "the new leisure that automation seems sure to give may provide the chance to achieve this high ambition for the family."*

In his remarks, Hutchins assumes the existence of an operating family. He does not discuss the fate of the child who has only the semblance of a family or none at all. For this child society will have to provide more than improved material conditions of life and more than educational innovations. If help does not come early to children in such great danger, even love is not enough.

* "Value of Family," by Robert M. Hutchins, column, Los Angeles *Times* Syndicate, June 15, 1965.

Part IV: A QUESTION OF SPIRIT

9
XXXX

CHURCH WINDOWS

LOCAL PROTESTANT CLERGYMEN STRUGGLE AGAINST a tendency to look back to the prewar past when the area supported congregations that could fill all the pews on any given Sunday. In recent years, attendance at many churches has dwindled with the flight of the middle class which formed the backbone of their congregations. The pastors spend a great deal of energy figuring out what to do with grand-looking edifices built when hope and collections were more substantial, and for various reasons they seem to feel more down at the mouth than a Catholic dignitary like Monsignor Flanagan, who is in an expansionist mood. Yet the prospects are not unpromising. Despite some new public housing units it is hoped that urban renewal will bring back the middle class and rehabilitate the churches that managed to hang on during the difficult days.

Whether or not the pews are filled, the church must go on, and frugal housekeeping does not eliminate such monthly irritations as fuel and utility, maintenance and repair bills. The pastor has fewer people to minister to but he also has less help and the work itself has become more complicated, entailing social and community activities that might have seemed outlandish to a clergyman of the thirties. Also, the aging parishioners have more complaints and make more comparisons with the old days. The shadow of the past falls across the desk of every pastor.

One of the oldest parishes in the Area is St. Michael's Episcopal Church, housed in a gray, Victorian-Romanesque church at Amsterdam Avenue and Ninety-ninth Street. Founded in 1807, the church at one time had seventeen hundred communicants. Today it has less than four hundred, but for the first time in more than fifty years church membership has begun to increase. When the rector, William Corker, a tall, aristocratic man with a touch of North Ireland in his speech, arrived in 1948, his congregation was an all-white, lower-middle-income group of technicians, local tradespeople, and craftsmen. Fifteen years later the congregation had become 50 percent Negro, with a small percentage of people of Latin American and Asian background. The congregation has also undergone economic and cultural changes; it has many more middle- and upper-middle-income professionals (advertising, law, publishing, business) than before and at least seventy college or university graduates. All of the vestrymen are residents of the Central Park West, Riverside Drive, West End Avenue, and Columbia University areas.

The transformation of the congregation has not resulted in serious divisions between the old and new membership, and there have been no overt racial antagonisms or tensions. One event that helped integrate St. Michael's racially was a slum-clearance project. Until the site for Park West Village was cleared, St. Michael's had maintained the segregated Negro Chapel of St. Jude on Ninety-ninth Street. Afterward the chapel was demolished and the Negro members who remained in the area were invited to join St. Michael's. Now, two members of the old chapel are members of the St. Michael's vestry.

The recent history of St. Michael's demonstrates that a pastor must be a businessman if he is to have a church to lead spiritually. At Mr. Corker's arrival the church's budget of $49,000 was beginning to cut into its capital resources. To rectify this, he asked a large banking and trust company to give financial advice to the vestry committee, with the result that the church unloaded its mortgages, and went into the stock market at a time when the market entered its post–World War II boom. To reduce operating expenses Mr. Corker tended his parish without an assistant pastor, cut down his office staff, put in labor-saving devices, and started a reserve fund. In the last dozen years the fund has accumulated $830,000 through investments, endowments, and savings on operating costs. Interest-bearing securities alone account for $88,000 income annually. Thus, in spite of its smaller congregation, Mr. Corker has seen the church double its budget, so that he can have an assistant pastor, a secretary, a full-time bookkeeper, two sextons, a full-time kindergarten teacher, an organist, and a part-time house painter. The congregation has helped improve the financial picture. Although the average income of the church members is low, the total contributions from the congregation has been rising steadily to the point where the average offering is almost twice what it was in 1950.

Incessant improvements in the church's physical plant have enabled it to be host to a number of community-service groups. At various times the basement has housed a well-baby clinic staffed by five doctors; St. Michael's Montessori School, serving mainly Catholic children; and St. Michael's preschool play group, attended by children from Asian, Jewish, and mixed-marriage, as well as Christian families. Upstairs, the church is also a bustling proposition; until recently a group of Russian émigrés produced plays and held socials on the third floor. A choral group rehearses in the church auditorium, specialists in geriatrics direct a "friendship club" for nearly one hundred senior citizens of different faiths, and there is a used-clothing store close by.

The pastor says that the parish house has "moved away from the days when people came in for cooking, sewing lessons, or weight lifting so they could expand their chest muscles." Athletic programs sponsored by the YMCA, YWCA, and PAL, plus athletic activities in the school and community centers, lessened the need for the church to help in these fields. There have been other, more subtle transformations in the church program. Until Mr. Corker came to the parish it was a church tradition to put on formal dinners served by caterers and staged in the second-floor auditorium. "I realized such affairs might be gratifying to the egos of some of the church patrons," he says. Now the church puts on box suppers for fifteen to thirty, so that people have a better chance to get acquainted with each other.

The church's summer religious program for children, reduced from six to three weeks in recent years, offers craft work, religious instruction, athletic activity, and trips to the beach and to one swimming pool, at the Hotel Paris. The assistant pastor is occasionally helped out by half a dozen college students in residence at the parish house. From the point of view of providing a convenient baby-sitting service, the program was all right, but according to Mr. Corker it failed to involve enough parents or to "deepen the religious and moral training of the children," so the program was curtailed.

St. Michael's has undertaken a rather ambitious program to cut down the high cost of dying. It has formed a burial society that can provide all funeral services from the moment of death to interment for as low as $250—or about what the Department of Welfare allows for burial arrangements. The price includes funeral services in the church's own funeral chapel or in any other Protestant religious institution and a small square plot in the church's own cemetery. The cemetery itself is quite a business enterprise, with a budget of $200,000 a year and thirty workers on the payroll. Its seventy-five acres of tombstones are a landmark to drivers on the Grand Central Parkway, and church members are proud of the fact that the crematorium has won a Queens County award for artistic design.

Mr. Corker, despite a certain outward reserve, has been known to speak sharply at times on a variety of subjects, including the police, whom he has charged with taking money from local storekeepers in return for allowing them to violate Sunday blue laws. When health authorities invoked technicalities to prevent his opening a school in the church basement, he promised them they would live to regret any such obstructionism, and the school opened on schedule. A group of teen-aged gang members who said they would break a few church windows unless they received protection money were warned that although St. Michael's was a peace-loving congregation it had one or two members with underworld connections of their own who would not look lightly on such mischief. Thereupon the gang canceled its demands.

However, the pastor is more circumspect in dealing with backsliders in his congregation. "I was thinking as I looked out over my congregation recently that it wasn't something that would flatter a man's ego," he says. "The people hadn't streamed out in overwhelming numbers to hear their famous preacher. On the other hand, it was a good solid congregation, more than 110 people at a rough guess, about 30 percent of our membership. Well, suppose at announcement time I said to the people in my congregation that I had decided that those who didn't pay their dues or come to church regularly would be summarily removed from the list. It doesn't take much imagination to realize this sort of discipline is something a minister could exert in a small village where everyone would hear about it and it would make a big splash. If I were to treat my people this way I might end up by abolishing the whole congregation in a very short time."

Central Baptist Church at Ninety-second Street and Amsterdam Avenue is one of the older churches, which has maintained its numerical strength through the years in spite of changes in the area. During more than thirty years the parish has been in the spiritual custody of the Reverend W. Taylor, and membership has never been less than three hundred or more than four hundred. The pastor hopes for the day when his church will have six hundred members and he is on the lookout for newcomers. Although his annual budget is only $25,000, Mr. Taylor's administrative job is quite as complex as Mr. Corker's and he has only a paid secretary, a sexton, and a part-time youth worker to help him. The congregation at present is well integrated racially, although church membership is not. On a typical Sunday morning, out of a congregation of around 125 about 30 are Negroes, but only half a dozen have become church members. The church does better with Negro children in the Sunday school than it does with adults.

There are no Puerto Rican members in Mr. Taylor's church because it houses an independent Baptist congregation for Spanish-speaking people, established shortly after World War II. The pastor of Templa Bautista, Ismael Ramos, a regularly ordained minister, preaches in Spanish on Sunday afternoons to a congregation of more than 150, and oversees a program which includes activities for young people and a women's group. Some of his communicants are nominal Catholics.

"If you ask the average Puerto Rican in this area if he is a Catholic or a Protestant he will say he is a Catholic," Mr. Taylor explains. "This does not necessarily mean he attends the Catholic Church, or that he won't attend Protestant services." In recent years, because of Templa Bautista, the church has been caught in a space squeeze and has had to turn down the applications of some civic and community groups for meeting rooms and clinics.

The church's own extracurricular activities are on the decline. Its neighborhood summer vacation Bible school was discontinued because of a lack of teaching personnel, and it has no released-time program during public school hours, finding it more practical to have a Bible and recreation class once a week after school. One of the church's most interesting experiments was run by half-a-dozen Columbia students, who supervised Saturday-morning programs for thirty youngsters, most of them Negro, featuring craft work, readings from the Bible, and refreshments.

The pastor is not as enthusiastic as some other Protestant ministers about enlarging the social activities of the church. He feels that his church should meet community needs through "an individual approach to the individual life, encouraging people, strengthening them to come in touch with the Lord. Ours is a pretty simple faith. We believe a person's great need is to come into a saving relationship with Jesus Christ. That doesn't mean a human being doesn't need a lift, sometimes material help, along the way. But when he's right toward God then he's right to himself, his family, and community."

Mr. Taylor tries to visit as many of his congregation as he can, but even with a small church there are endless assignments—church conferences, visits to the sick in the hospital and home, conferences with families having a serious domestic crisis, folks with children in need of counseling. As far as any methodical visiting on a house-to-house basis is concerned, he says, "I fail pretty miserably and I think a good many of us pastors do. This is not because we don't want to succeed, but there is so little time and so many things happening to the home. The home has become a swing-shift sort of thing. Now, by and large, both parents work. It is hard for the pastor to find a family when it isn't getting ready to eat supper, or trying to relax in its pajamas after supper. We can get out two or three times a week to visit but this doesn't mean very much in terms of a congregation.

"There has to be a longer-term investment in people. When the Columbia University men reported to us on their work in the community they said they had a great deal of trouble getting any sort of initial acceptance in the home, but because they went back again and again they were finally received with interest and cooperation. The students were almost overwhelmed when, on some of their last visits, children rushed down the hall to announce Mr. So-and-So was coming in. The students could sit down with a parent, talk to him about letting his youngster go to summer camp. Very poor families were willing to contribute something out of their own budget for the children's activities. It wasn't as if they were receiving handouts."

Mr. Taylor recalls some excellent volunteers who came into the church on a part-time basis under the auspices of a Bible society.

"One of the women, dead now, had the approach that could win out in any situation. She was Miss Ruth Brownewell. She constantly followed all paths to people's homes. She always had something of interest to offer, and love and concern for them, until it broke down every barrier. Some of the families she knew have come along socially and economically and they say God has blessed them. They say it was her constant going to them."

Protestant ministers agree that they don't communicate or cooperate very well with each other and that Catholic clergymen are rather stand-offish, perhaps because the Irish still harbor prejudices carried over from the time when the Protestants dominated the neighborhood in the early part of the century and looked down on the Irish as uncultivated newcomers. Doctrinal differences, of course, have something to do with the desire of local clergymen to go it alone, but there is also the fact that each clergyman is just too busy with his own parish problems, that he is too busy for interfaith cooperation, as Mr. Taylor puts it. Another Protestant clergyman is not so charitable as Mr. Taylor and speaks bitterly of the time when he and several other ministers were unable to get the cooperation of local Catholic parishes in taking a census of the religious affiliations of the people in the Douglass Houses.

The Reverend William McAlpin, pastor of the West Park Presbyterian Church and president of the West Side Ministerial Association, is one of those who thinks ministers don't do much cooperating. His own association turned out to be "pretty obviously a social club, where the men got together for lunch, heard a speaker or listened to a paper, and that was about it." The unwillingness of Protestant clergymen to dip into civic matters strikes him as unfortunate. He recalls that most of his fellow clerics took no part in the great debate over the urban renewal plan.

The ministers' apathy is about what one might expect considering the apathy of most of the church members. Mr. McAlpin thinks some congregations have a defensive attitude. "The Protestants feel that they are not going to be effective because they are in such a minority, so many of them don't attempt anything. They feel overwhelmed by the size of the Roman Catholic and Jewish constituency." Mr. McAlpin has gone into combat against the spirit of defeat but the experience has only lowered his spirits. When three children living in a slum house on Eightieth Street died from meningitis in a single week, he told his congregation it should care about what went on around it and asked everyone to write a letter about the tragedy to the mayor, the Department of Health, and the Department of Buildings. On the following Sunday he discovered that the only person who had written a letter was the pastor.

Some time ago Mr. AcAlpin decided to have another go at getting the churches together. He was one of a group of clergy and lay people who met to work out plans for organizing a West Side Association of Churches which would cover the area from Thirty-second to 104th Street. In contrast to the West Side Ministerial Association, the new group had a specific action program: (1) to include the establishment of four housing clinics, (2) to arrange joint support for a Protestant chaplain in the city's Roosevelt Hospital, (3) to plan ways to improve the service of Protestant clergy and lay volunteers to the nursing homes in the area, which are now neglected by the church. What the future of the new alliance is is anybody's guess. Mr. Corker is interested; Mr. Taylor is not.

Mr. McAlpin's West Park Presbyterian Church is a large stone structure on the corner of Amsterdam Avenue and Eighty-sixth Street. The building is not exactly an eyesore, but its spatial irregularities are a misfortune in a day when churches are expected to provide a shelter for community groups who have no roof of their own. Mr. McAlpin is sensitive to the structural inconveniences. "The rooms in the church are nicely furnished but they are not practical for conferences or meetings, except for the auditorium. This building looks pretty big from the outside, and inside we have nice high ceilings and mahogany paneling, but we could put two floors in the place of the single floors we have now. A great deal of space is wasted underneath the tall gables and there are all sorts of useless mezzanines and balconies. A fire marshal told me that walking around inside under the roof of the church gave him the feeling of being underneath a turned-over wooden ship."

With the church congregation down to 550 from a high of 750, renovation will have to wait until the church figures out a way of building up its congregation. Financially, at least, the church is on an even keel. At present about half the current church budget of $55,000 a year is paid for by investments in stocks and bonds and the rest from membership contributions. The church also owns the

Good Shepherd Faith Church on West Sixty-sixth Street, which serves an almost completely Negro congregation, and it pays for that church's insurance and contributes $1,500 to its administrative costs.

In spite of its space problems, West Park services a large number of community organizations. In bad weather the pupils of the West End Collegiate School use the gymnasium, and the League of Women Voters, the Brownies, the Cub Scouts, and Girl Scouts meet in the church. On Monday afternoons there is a Boy Scout judo class sponsored by the parents of several Japanese boys. Mr. McAlpin enjoys seeing Negro, Japanese, Puerto Rican, Irish, and Italian youngsters slamming each other down on a mat and grunting like regular black belt holders. At one time Alcoholics Anonymous also used the church, but because their meetings lasted so late into the evening they moved to a Methodist church nearby which seems to keep later hours. The wives, sisters, and mothers of alcoholics—"Al Anon"—still meet to discuss problems caused by an alcoholic member of the family. When Mr. McAlpin first arrived there was some discussion of putting a well-baby clinic in the building but space was unavailable. "How many times I wish I could tear this place down and start all over again," the pastor says wistfully.

The congregation is considerably more cosmopolitan than it used to be, with Puerto Ricans, Cubans, Koreans, Hawaiians, Filipinos, Mexicans, and a sizable number of European immigrants, including the president of the Loyal Order of Orangemen. When Mr. McAlpin arrived the church had never had a Negro member, but since then it has received Negroes at almost every communion service. The Spanish-language group has separate services, conducted by a Presbyterian missionary, and a Spanish ladies' group that meets during the week. The pastor hopes that the Spanish members will eventually be brought into the regular church services, starting with joint communions, which could be given in Spanish and English. One difficulty in planning for the Spanish is that as they improve their economic position many of them move out of the city. When a mother comes to tell him the family has bought a home in Jamaica, Long Island, the pastor tells them he is happy for their good fortune, but he admits that he has never gotten used to bidding his parishioners goodbye, although he has done it often enough.

The congregation is not a rich one. Most of the younger men and women are clerical workers or teachers, while a substantial number of the older women live on pensions or are on welfare. The latter get a dollar or so a day for food and live in single rooms, often in the more rundown transient hotels in the area. They attend Sunday services faithfully, dressed in black, and tend to center their social life around church activities. Many belong to the sewing circle. The pastor has not been able to organize a Golden Age Club because of the shortage of elderly men. Some of the women drop by the pastor's office nearly every day to say hello. Local service agencies may or may not recognize the fact, Mr. McAlpin says, but nutrition is a very serious problem with many of these lonely old people, and he is constantly telling them to "be sure and have a little meat today, or at least tomorrow." When an old person becomes ill, there may be an endowed bed at Presbyterian Hospital for her. The pastor takes her there and he is listed on her chart as next of kin. When she is well he brings her home. If she dies, the pastor goes to claim the body and engages the funeral director, holds a service in the chapel, and provides a cemetery lot in Woodlawn. He will also close the apartment of the deceased and sort out the clothing that could be used by someone else, or sold. At the funeral some of the older women in the congregation will tell the pastor that they hope he will do the same for them someday. The pastor has thirty-five wills locked in his office to be executed when the time comes.

Sometimes the church will move a woman out of a transient hotel and put her in a home for the aged, such as the Association Home on 103rd Street or the Presbyterian Home for Aged Women, which houses seveny persons. There are a variety of places for old people, such as the Home for Old Men and Aged Couples on Amsterdam Avenue across the street from the Cathedral of St. John the Divine, and several private nursing homes and city institutions for the senile. Mr. McAlpin does not say what he thinks of the care the people get in the nursing homes, which have been severely criticized by city health authorities. Presbyterians do not have enough space for their own elderly women, but the church is building an addition to an old people's home in Syosset, Long Island.

The church assumes responsibilities for the young as well as the old. In cooperation with the Hudson River and the Long Island presbyteries, the New York Presbytery maintains its two camps outside New York City. Only a handful of children from West Park have been attending in the last year or two because of the shrinkage of the Sunday school, which has had difficulties in finding parishioners who have time to teach and who will encourage families to send their children. There has also been a shrinkage of adult educational groups. One eight-week discussion program on democracy was successful, but in the last few years the meetings were so badly attended that the people who planned them became discouraged, and Mr. McAlpin says he hasn't heard from them since.

While many Protestant churches wait passively for a better day and provide space for community organizations, some churches in the area recruit new members very aggressively. The most affluent of these is the Mormon Church, which concentrates on the middle-class white population. Then, above West 100th Street, Negro Jehovah's Witnesses canvass on Sunday and sell copies of *The Watch Tower* for five cents a copy. The Witnesses are courteous, well dressed, and most persistent. If they locate a good prospect for conversion, a whole family of Witnesses—father, mother, and two or three children—may come around for a visit. Young Black Muslims, also well dressed and friendly, cover only those blocks below Harlem where there is a heavy concentration of Negroes, and do not proselytize as intensively as the Witnesses. Two or three Muslims will walk down each side of the street, calling out their message and distributing copies of their newspaper.

The Pentecostal "storefront" churches have sprouted like dandelions all over the area east of Broadway, wherever there is a concentration of Puerto Ricans. These churches occupy what might have been a cleaning shop, a small grocery, a tavern, a beauty parlor, etc. Behind plate-glass fronts painted bright yellows, greens, and reds in imitation of stained glass, the congregation sits on folding chairs and is exhorted to read the Bible, abstain from drinking, smoking, and loose behavior. The services, filled with lively music and singing, have some of the quality of a revival meeting and the pastor's appeal for self-discipline is not unlike the message of the Black Muslims. To the Spanish the storefront churches are very warm and very near. They are not afraid to come in ordinary clothes.

Another type of church, which has no history to contend with and which literally "grew off the streets," is the racially integrated but predominantly Negro Methodist congregation organized by Dr. Ralph Roy, a white minister. As the congregation developed it did not have to worry about a building fund, since it found a home at the Grace Methodist Church on 104th Street, a few blocks from where Dr. Roy lived. When the minister, a short, mild-mannered man who has been arrested in Georgia and Florida civil rights demonstrations, moved into the area with his wife after three years in Harlem, he noticed a marked lack of contact between local churches of all faiths and the people of the community. He decided to found a congregation in his own neighborhood, the core of which was a turbulent slum on the 104th Street block between Central Park and Manhattan Avenue. Behind Dr. Roy's effort was the conviction that the real hope for the Protestant church on the West Side lies in the Negro and not in the return of the middle-class white.

Dr. Roy started with the children. He found the Negro youngsters energetic, responsive, albeit erratic, and curious. Sunday school would be a "new" place to go to, and it was a novelty to have an adult male who wanted to make a place for them. Through the child Dr. Roy got an introduction to the parent. He visited all types of buildings—the rooming houses on 105th Street filled with children who went to P.S. 145 and mothers who had outside jobs and washed and cooked for the family; and hives like the "Spanish Plaza," a blackened tenement on Central Park West between 103rd and 104th Streets which was packed with hundreds of Puerto Ricans. The minister estimated that between a third and a half of the children who eventually joined his Sunday school came from around these two blocks.

Dr. Roy was not very lucky with the adults in his door-to-door canvassing. Many were alcoholics and prostitutes. "My heart was probably clearer than my head and I spent most of my time in places that obviously showed the most need, in the rooming houses." To many isolated and sick people his visits appeared to be an offer to solve all their difficulties. Sometimes more people called at his apartment to ask for advice or money than came to his church on Sundays. On 105th Street, where he recruited fifty Negro children for the Sunday school, he was able to obtain only one adult member for his congregation. Dr. Roy found he was becoming a social worker and psychiatrist instead of a pastor building a congregation, so he abandoned the door-to-door approach, and went after the middle-class white, Negro, and Spanish families.

The new approach did not work out very well either. Some of the middle-class families, Dr. Roy says, were "extremely difficult because while they were Negro in their psychology they very much tended to look down on the Negro poor—two or three of the middle-class families would not allow their children to associate with the poorer ones and gave me the impression they thought their children would be contaminated by such contact. It was very difficult for church authorities to get near these middle-class children because the mothers were so protective. The handful of middle-class parents who did become active in the church were the most faithful and useful members, but since they were also the very people who had the ambition and resources to move out of the area into better housing many of them were eventually lost to the congregation.

Dr. Roy's third and perhaps the most important recruiting method was to single out the more stable families who lived in Douglass Houses, the nearby public housing project. These families, some of them on welfare, were to become the foundation for his church. In Douglass Houses the families were concentrated, were identifiable, were usually intact, and had a different attitude about attending church and sending their children to Sunday school. Dr. Roy's experience in some ways was similar to that of canvassers for local political clubs, who found they had to put less emphasis on canvassing in the rooming houses and more on apartment houses tenanted by people who were easy to reach and who were more "permanent."

Establishing communication with the people in Douglass Houses and bringing them into his church did not end Dr. Roy's difficulties. As parents began to come to his church and bring their children to youth meetings and Sunday school, some of them would look about and ask, "Are all these other children from the block?" To these parents the "block" meant immorality and danger, the sort of thing they had been trying to get away from. When they discovered that many of the children were from the "block," some Douglass Houses parents dropped out of the congregation.

The first few services of the new congregation were anything but encouraging, even though the establishment of the congregation had been preceded by considerable publicity. Only twenty-five people attended the first service (although the congregation was eventually to grow to two hundred). There were also problems with the Grace Methodist Church, which was somewhat of an International House, with two congregations, both of which were ethnically self-segregated.

One was Japanese with four hundred members, and the other was a Spanish congregation whose minister did not look favorably on Puerto Ricans' joining Dr. Roy's racially integrated group—in fact, he tried to persuade the first Spanish family in Dr. Roy's congregation to withdraw and join the Spanish group. A certain amount of anti-Negro feeling in the Spanish congregation was sharpened by resentment at the way Dr. Roy's Sunday-school children rushed about the hallways and corridors of the church while the Spanish services were going on inside. There was also friction between the liberal social attitudes of Dr. Roy's congregation and the conservative views of the Spanish parishioners.*

Although he had at first felt that the churches were not related closely enough to the neighborhood, Dr. Roy soon found evidence that in some respects the churches were very much intertwined with the community, notably with regard to released-time education. As the Protestant churches in the area gradually cut out their released time programs because of the unruliness of many of their children, the Catholic parishes would accept the same youngsters into their own released-time programs. Dr. Roy discovered that a number of his new Sunday-school children were taking religious instruction at Holy Name and Ascension parishes and carrying orange released-time cards with stamps of Ascension and Holy Name schools and were on the point of being baptized as Catholics. Nevertheless, Dr. Roy built up his own Sunday-school enrollment to six hundred children.

Through some gentle pressure, Dr. Roy convinced the uptown YMCA to relinquish the church's gym so the Sunday-school children could have an athletic program, which among other things produced four basketball teams. Supervision of the athletic program was carried out by the lay members without outside money to help. "I have always said we had three curious blessings which other churches don't have," Dr. Roy declares. "We began with no members, which was good because some of the churches around here have an old

---

* Dr. Roy did not dare to hold a dance in the church until two years after his congregation had been established. The dance and subsequent ones were successful, but were strongly disapproved of by the Spanish congregation. The Spanish congregation was also critical of the Japanese congregation for its more relaxed attitude on some matters of piety. The Japanese pastor was considered by some Spanish members not to be a real Christian because he smoked cigarettes.

guard which give the pastors a tough time if they want to work in the community. We began with no money, which was good because some churches have big endowments and do not have to get out in the community so they become too comfortable. We had no staff, no secretaries, no gym directors, which meant that we had to develop a congregation that relied on itself, and we made our people feel indispensable. We pressed everyone into service."

In the eyes of his West Side Sunday-school children Dr. Roy will never quite cease to be pastor of Grace Methodist, even though he has now moved and taken over two parishes in the Bushwick and Ridgewood areas of Brooklyn. However, he is not sure even today how his predominantly nonwhite constituency felt about a white minister trying to organize an integrated congregation. He realizes some Negroes stayed away because of his color, but he believes that most of the Negroes wanted an integrated sitaution, wanted to get away from the old-time Southern-type "Negro" church. This was true especially of the younger adults, and most of the members of the congregation were under forty years of age, with many under thirty. (The president of the Women's Society was twenty-eight, the head of the Methodist Men's Society thirty-one.)

The white members of the congregation were an excellent group, Dr. Roy recalls. "Of course, there were one or two exceptions who did not sense the objective of the church, but there was desire on everyone's part to have the leadership concentrated among the Negroes in the congregation. On their part, some Negroes came to the church because there was an opportunity to be more than just a member. Most of them could have gone on to other, bigger Negro churches but they wanted the chance of leadership. These members were diligent in preparing themselves for responsibility. Some achieved their goal in spite of tremendous educational and emotional handicaps. When one member began as head of a committee he was a semiliterate. Each time he had to present a report he would arrive early and read his report over and over again. Even then, when it was time to deliver the report, he would become so anxious that he would stumble over words or mispronounce. However, after two years of this agonizing self-training and embarrassed exposure to audiences, the man gained the ability to do a splendid job before the public. All he needed was a chance.

Dr. Roy thinks his old church will prosper in time, because it offers a chance to people. "It was their church and they grew with it."

The handsome building of the Society for the Advancement of Judaism and its location near Central Park West on Eighty-sixth, one of the most desirable residential streets on the West Side, tells something about the economic status of its congregation. The members of the synagogue are predominantly from the middle- and upper-income groups. Some have lived in the area for twenty to forty years; a large number of the rest are new arrivals. The SAJ has had a community affairs committee, and many of the synagogue's 450 members belong to various local organizations ostensibly devoted to civic betterment. Delegates from the SAJ, which is a member of the Stryckers Bay Neighborhood Council, attend irregularly the council's monthly meetings. "Our people are very sensitive to the requirements of democracy," said the synagogue's British-born rabbi, Alan Miller. A social worker who is a member of the congregation has a different view: "We have a lot of people who like to get involved for a lot of reasons," she says. "We're probably the most guilt-ridden congregation in the city, for one thing."

While many SAJ members feel they have a responsibility to participate in community affairs, at the same time they are reluctant to have their synagogue presume to speak for them. Rabbi Miller, a young, rapid-fire Oxonian who has had the congregation for five years, sees his congregation composed of rather individualistic people who prefer to do their own speaking out. "The people of the congregation subscribe to the same general ethical and moral principles," he says, "but highly ethical people seem to differ strongly with each other sometimes on specific application of these principles. Take, for example, their attitudes about capital punishment or how much middle-income housing we should have in the urban renewal area, as compared to public housing. If the synagogue is to commit itself on these and other issues, it must have a consensus." The rabbi leaves the impression that such a consensus is not easy to arrive at.

From the beginning the rabbi has said he would like to see the SAJ become more closely related to the controversies that have shaped the development of the new West Side. He has also felt that it was not his job as a rabbi to push his constituency into that relationship. Encourage an involvement, yes, but the method and timing of the involvement should come from the congregation. The membership should take the lead, perhaps even "drag" the rabbi along with it. Rabbis who have tried to prod their synagogues faster than the Board of Trustees wants them prodded sometimes get badly out of position. As a Britisher, Rabbi Miller has been more sensitive about pushing than a native New Yorker might be.

His walks about the area to visit his members have given Rabbi Miller more optimism about the West Side's future and increased his interest in having the congregation play a bigger role in community life. The development of Lincoln Center, the cultural complex in the Sixties, and the West Side urban renewal program mean the return of many middle-class families when the reconstruction is completed. He certainly has no desire to see his synagogue follow the lead of Temple Israel, which moved to the East Side, although his democratic instincts would not allow him to resign if his congregation voted in favor of such a move. "I think resigning is a cheap way out of moral problems, just as running away is always a cheap way out of a social problem." The rabbi feels that the synagogue ought not to be satisfied merely with sending delegates to the meetings of the Stryckers Bay Neighborhood Council, and paying its annual dues. A satisfactory involvement means holding meetings between the synagogue and local civic groups "where we could carry on a dialogue with each other."

The rabbi would employ a moderate approach. He recoils at the idea of having his synagogue "become an immense social service organization." "We certainly wouldn't want to have dinner every night with each other—you know it's hard enough to have dinner with one's wife sometimes. People are frightened of involvement, frightened that it might lead to more. At the same time the synagogue cannot hold itself up in that holier-than-thou attitude and resist involvement. I think a community should have the right to turn to the priest or the rabbi and ask him, 'What part are you going to play? If you haven't any views on what to do, why should we?' While a rabbi is not endowed with any larger measure of religion or spirituality than any other person, he is in his own congregation *primus inter pares* and should show the way. He must strive to lead a good life, a religious and spiritual life. He should try to emulate in his life what he says on spiritual matters."

As time has passed, after a few years of internal testing between leader and congregation, the rabbi has changed his views about "involvement." A year or so ago he said he could not envision his congregation "waving banners aloft, carrying scrubbing brushes and moving into the matter of social uplift. The synagogue is a cross-section of all people and obviously we're not going to turn into a sort of Salvation Army." Today, however, he is glad to see the congregation "waving banners." A group went to Washington, D.C., to participate in the 1964 Better Schools demonstration, and two hundred members of the congregation attended a symposium on city problems the same year.

The rabbi would like to see a common meeting ground established among the clergy in the area where rabbi, minister, and priest, Catholic, Protestant, and Jew might discuss their views. He does not favor a "mere socializing, which could be sickly and psychopathic and adds up to nothing," but perhaps there might be an interfaith center where a "rabbi could play ping-pong with a Puerto Rican boy, a priest talk to Jewish children, where we could rub off on each other and drink Coca-Cola and have socials for the children. Perhaps a dance is not such a good thing. It gives people ideas about inter-marriage and God knows what.* Ping-pong, that is a good thing, very innocuous. Also tennis and football."

The rabbi has a limited amount of time to participate in community affairs. The congregation now has its own high school across the street for seventeen pupils, and an elementary school with a staff of five teachers. Then there is the usual trouble in finding enough Sunday-school teachers. Some are always resigning because of other commitments. When he has to interview twenty or thirty people to get one substitute to take a class regularly, "the great issues begin to recede into the background."

In the next breath the rabbi says that Selma and Birmingham, Alabama, should directly concern his congregation. He admits that he would like to do "sixty things at once," also that there have been failures. For instance, he organized a group of a hundred or so young people in the synagogue, which he hoped would become a social-action group. He hoped the group would someday provide manpower for various local projects and "put feelers out to local institutions," but the social-action group never really came to life. However, the experiment was not a total failure. The rabbi thinks it planted a seed

* Rabbi Miller does not marry couples of different faiths.

that caused the congregation to hold a successful meeting to discuss urban renewal.

Some West Siders think organizing a meeting is no cause for rejoicing. The rabbi feels otherwise.

The physical location of a church affects the psychology of the pastor and his congregation. It also determines to some extent the relationship of the church to its neighborhood. The large churches at the intersections of avenues and streets have a more "open" view of the area since they command four corners. This has certain psychological advantages over a synagogue imprisoned in the shadows of a side-street tenement. The orthodox Congregation Ohab Zedek at 118–124 West Ninety-fifth Street is a case in point.

It is not possible to paint an attractive picture of the block on which the synagogue is located. It is reminiscent of West Eighty-fourth in the days when that street was known as the "worst" in the city. When the rabbi, Theodore Adams, came to the synagogue in 1953 it was losing members every week to such places as Washington Heights in northern Manhattan; Forest Hills, Long Island; and the New Jersey suburbs. As a result the congregation fell to an all-time low of less than 350 people. The rabbi, a heavy-set, unsmiling man in his late thirties, has been trying to reverse the trend ever since, with limited success. The regular membership of the congregation is up to 450, most of them from the Eighty-fifth to 110th Street area, and another 500 worshipers participate in the synagogue's activities.

One result of Rabbi Adams's tenure was the establishment of the Beth Hillel Foundation School adjacent to the synagogue, in which ninety children from nursery (three years old) school to the fourth grade are given religious and general instruction by a staff of eight full-time teachers. The school is accredited by the Board of Regents, an honor accorded very few sectarian schools. The rabbi hoped the school would attract new members to the congregation and hold the old. He had the same idea in mind when he founded a youth program for children.

For a while the school and youth groups helped reverse the decline in the size of the congregation. However, as the neighborhood continued to fall apart, it became more and more difficult for the synagogue to sustain itself. From the very beginning the rabbi assured his people that things would get better, emphasizing the fact that a large new middle-income apartment complex (Park West Village) would be going up nearby. But three years passed and the site of the promised apartment remained nothing but a parking lot. Then when Park West Village finally did appear, less than half a dozen of its hundreds of tenants came to the synagogue, and they were usually young couples or single people who were always moving somewhere else.

Rabbi Adams picked up the West Side urban renewal plan as his next message of hope. He carried copies of the plan around with him and discussed the promised middle-income apartments with his congregation. The people of Ohab Zedek foresaw the return of good, solid Jewish families with children who would come to the synagogue and contribute to its religious and social life. However, when the urban renewal plan was changed as the result of local controversy, and middle- and upper-income units were reduced to make way for a sixfold increase of public housing, prospects for a better day began to fade.

The rabbi favored the middle-income housing, not only because the congregation's growth seemed to depend on it, but also because he felt public housing would "stigmatize" or "ghettoize" the area. Right or wrong, people would hesitate to move into an area saturated with public housing, he felt. They would wait to see if the area was going to be safe, and this in itself would delay the possibility that it would be safe. After the years of delay, with almost no new construction except public housing, Rabbi Adams says, "We are holding on by the skin of our teeth." After the city took over most of the buildings, the situation worsened. Parents on the street say they fear for their children because of the fighting, dope, drunkenness, and prostitution. Demolition at the corner of Amsterdam Avenue has provided chunks of brick and concrete for toughs to throw at the congregation. The rabbi wrote the mayor about the matter but received no answer.

Despite the rock throwing, the rabbi will not put screens on the church windows. "If the day comes when I have to do that I'll move; it would be a symbol that we have cut ourselves off from the community."*

* Father James I. Gusweller, rector of the Eighty-fourth Street Episcopal Church of St. Matthew and St. Timothy (which was destroyed by fire in late 1965) also refused to protect his windows except to forbid ball playing in

The difference between the promises of city agencies and the facts of life impress the rabbi. On Ninety-fifth Street he says, "It takes five months to demolish a building. Empty, it is a menace. Rocks are thrown in the windows, no one is around to watch, no one sees, no one cares. But on the East Side I will drive down one day on First Avenue and see a sign, 'This building to be demolished'; I drive down the next week and this building is gone and they are already starting to build another."

For people who come to Ohab Zedek during the summer "it is almost a panic. Our people must be more than loyal even to come here because the hydrants are open, things are dropped from the roof, people are afraid to walk." Although the rabbi has called the police for help and sent them schedules of services on High Holidays so they would know when the largest concentration of people would be at the synagogue, "Somehow the police are conspicuous by their absence. They have many places to go, much to patrol, but at least I would expect on the High Holidays, when I have a thousand people coming in and out of the synagogue over a period of three days, there would be someone up and down the block. Once I had it out with the captain; in fact he came over one day. He was very upset and showed me the book where he assigned policemen. He may have assigned the policemen, and he may have signed in the book, I said, but the policemen weren't there."

The synagogue has never been the target for the sort of attacks that have occurred in the Williamsburg section of Brooklyn, where groups of Negroes have attacked children attending Jewish schools. The rabbi says that most of the children who live on the block—Negro, Puerto Rican, and white—are friendly to him and say, "Hello, Mr. Rabbi" when he walks up and down the street. The trouble comes mainly from people who don't belong on the block.

The possibility of violence is always in the back of the rabbi's mind. He has not forgotten his experience when he got the city to turn Ninety-fifth Street into a play street, a move which was opposed by most of the block residents. The rabbi did not foresee that the city would not supply adequate supervision or police protection, so hoodlum gangs from other parts of the city moved in and harassed

front of the church. He agreed with Rabbi Adams that screens symbolize a rejection of the community. St. Michael's Church protects its windows with aluminum screens. All of the clergy mention the high cost of broken windows.

everyone day and night. Three years of such a play street was enough, and the experiment is over.

The synagogue's expansion of its young people's social and religious center also increased the risks of trouble. Several of the two hundred youngsters attending the center's activities have been attacked and although nobody has been hurt seriously, the rabbi says it is "like you are sitting on a keg of powder." He tells the young people not to fight back or to answer when they are baited, but just to thank God they are not in the other people's shoes. In lieu of police protection, parents escort their children to and from all synagogue activities. (Parents of children attending the Jewish Manhattan Day School on 105th Street also do this.)

The synagogue's Beth Hillel Foundation School, the pride of the congregation, has helped raise the people's spirits. Tuition is $525 for the all-day elementary school and $375 for the half-day nursery school. Since it costs about $800 a year to educate each elementary school pupil, the synagogue supplies $34,000 additional out of its own $146,000 budget. After the children finish fourth grade they go on to do unusually well in other private or public schools. Its accredited teachers are paid $3,200 to $4,000, slightly more than half the salary they could earn in public schools. These are "loyal people who like the West Side, who still believe in it and feel it is a beautiful place in spite of everything," the rabbi says.

The rabbi believes deeply that the private, religious-centered school is one of the area's main hopes. He is as proud of the children that go to Catholic schools "as if they were our own. They have grown up; they have succeeded because of the discipline that a religious environment imposed on them. It is a self-discipline that evolves from the fact that we give importance to each individual. If one becomes religiously affiliated, he has an identity, he knows that he belongs to a Jewish group or a Catholic group or a Protestant group. This identity gives him status and recognition, something to look up to. The discipline of his religion and the ethics and morals it teaches make a better man out of him. The public schools cannot teach ethics and morality the way a religious school can. In public schools things are too loose, too permissive."

The looser the religious identification the more one tends to compromise, the rabbi says. Ideals and ethics are watered down gradually. "You invent easy goals and change them to fit your convenience. In other words, experience becomes the goal. The Catholic children who go to the religious schools have a strong goal. The goal is the top of the ladder. They go up one rung and two rungs and look even higher as they climb. This is why the Catholic Church is a great universal movement."

Rabbi Adams doesn't share Rabbi Miller's enthusiasm about public meetings. When the Board of Health decided to conduct a campaign of personal cleanliness and hygiene in the synagogue's auditorium, he circularized the neighborhood and invited everyone to come, but only a handful of his congregation attended, and the only outsider who showed up was a city employee. The rabbi considers people in the community apathetic in spite of all the organizations he hears about. As for clergymen's meetings and interfaith dialogues, they have a way of degenerating into political controversies.

"We ministers have to be honest with each other. We can pat each other on the back, we can talk nicely to each other, but the fact is that each clergyman has his goals and problems and has to face them in his own way. We are not going to change each other's minds on basic issues. What can Father Browne and I do if we sit around the table together? Am I going to convince Father Browne to favor more middle-income housing, which my congregation wants, or is he going to convince me to favor more public housing, which St. Gregory's parish wants?"

In the end, the rabbi thinks it is better to remain out of situations that are likely to become "political jockeying sessions." His distaste for politics is so strong that when a police chief called him at the suggestion of a politician to discuss the synagogue's problems, the rabbi told the officer to forget about it. "If the police will do what needs to be done on their own that is fine, but I do not want them doing it because a politician interceded."

In the past few years, the rabbi has been offered congregations in communities more settled and less complicated, where he could have a larger staff to help him. Although his patience grows thin as time goes by, and he is not getting any younger, he is not really interested. He feels like a horse pulling a wagon up a steep hill, and if he were to leave Ohab Zedek it would be like letting the wagon go when perhaps it was near the top. He says he has the fake illusion, common to all ministers, of being indispensable to his congregation.

Where does the synagogue go from here? "I don't know," the rabbi says. "I do know that I don't want to see us move this synagogue again. This is the fourth location of the synagogue since it was founded nearly one hundred years ago. We are part of these sidewalks on Ninety-fifth Street now."

PARISH AND SCHOOL

ABOUT EIGHT THOUSAND "NOMINAL" CATHOLICS live in the thirty blocks between Eighty-sixth and Ninety-second Streets, which form the Roman Catholic parish of St. Gregory's Church on West Ninetieth Street. For a decade or so a great majority of the parish's communicants were Irish; now they are predominantly Puerto Rican. Of the people in the parish who say they are Catholics, not more than two thousand attend Sunday masses. The great majority of nominal Catholics in the parish have little or no contact with the church. The problem is not peculiar to St. Gregory's. There is also a big discrepancy between the number of professed Jews and Protestants in the area and those who attend the churches and synagogues. Many Spanish who say they are Catholics attend the storefront Pentecostal churches or the older Protestant churches. Some who are "Catholic" when they are interviewed by social workers or census takers do not think very much about religion at all. The low-income single people in the area tend to be the most candid of the nonbelievers, a relatively high percentage saying they have no religion whatever.*

The task of bringing more Catholics to church is quite beyond the capacities of St. Gregory's Monsignor Joseph Flanagan and his three priests. The restless character of the Spanish population makes the job a little like chasing quicksilver with a thimble. The stable families who can be identified and may respond to the parish caller's knock are often preparing to move somewhere else in the neighborhood or out of it altogether. The urban renewal program hit especially hard at

---

* Kraft survey (see footnote p. 6).

St. Gregory's and its neighborhood parish, Holy Name, accelerating the forced departures and the moving around. In the past year or two some of the displaced families have moved into new public housing around St. Gregory's and things have begun to settle down.

The task of building a parish out of such a milling flock would seem to be discouraging, but the monsignor and his priests, most of whom are young and lively, have a feeling that the very changes that have been disorganizing the neighborhood will lead to new and better days—at least this is the view they state to the world. As the monsignor looks across the street at Stephen Wise Towers, a lofty public housing project completed in the fall of 1964, he hopes that a good majority of the tenants will be persuaded to attend mass regularly at St. Gregory's. At a point in life when he might well have begun thinking about an untroubled retirement, he is planning a new organization and new construction with all the fervor of a Baptist clergyman. The monsignor's optimism may be partly explained by the fact that he lives somewhat removed from the uproar of the side streets. His quarters and those of the priests are at the top of St. Gregory's Church, and the four floors below him serve as a sound-proof buffer against the nocturnal street commotions which St. Gregory's nuns in their little brownstone convent on West Eighty-seventh Street can block out only by using earplugs.

The monsignor's redoubt is impregnable from the ground. One has to ring at an iron gate on the floor below to gain admittance. The monsignor's assumption that he had nothing to worry about from above proved to be mistaken on at least one occasion, when some intruders climbed in through the skylight and made off with the assistant pastor's typewriter and hi-fi set. Since then, however, there have been no more such incursions. The monsignor has an ideal place in which to meditate and contemplate the economic riddles that confront the parish.

The rectory's eight one-room apartments have a common kitchen and a refectory delicately illuminated by large windows and the aforesaid skylight. There is an adulterated Florentine splendor about the straight-backed chairs, a ponderous dining table and heavy sideboard, silver plate, and thick rugs. This elegance does not carry over to the menu. The monsignor does not believe in overspending on food, with the result that his young priests often prefer to eat in Stark's Restaurant on Broadway, or to eat hot dogs at a nearby luncheonette.

Monsignor Flanagan's Irish personality is somewhat at odds with his Mediterranean lodgings but in any such cultural conflicts the monsignor always prevails. He has been in charge of St. Gregory's parish for more than six years, and at present he is thinking about blueprints for new buildings, scuttling off to public officials on parish matters, and exhorting his parishioners and priests to anticipate the new order. An unchanging, financially secure parish would be something new in the monsignor's experience. He recalls how things were in Scarsdale years ago when he assisted in establishment of a Catholic parish in the midst of Protestant folk who seemed to have a constitutional fear of papal invasions and who had "the wealth of the world" on their side to boot. From troubled beginnings, Scarsdale's Catholic community now supports three of the most flourishing parishes in the New York diocese. The opposite of the Scarsdale experience is taking place at St. Gregory's. Where once was a sound, predominantly Irish and Cuban parish that could look out on the world with confidence and even a modest complacency, St. Gregory's is now trying to hang on to what it has.

The trouble began several years ago, Monsignor Flanagan says, along the area where the Ninth Avenue Elevated once stood. "When the neighborhood began to break apart, it broke on Ninth Avenue at first, and a slum rose up, and the Irish began to flee." Those who stayed despite the slum fled later when urban renewal moved into the picture. Freckle-faced redheads at St. Gregory's school were displaced by olive-skinned youngsters speaking a language few people in the parish could understand. Fortunately, Monsignor Flanagan had worked in Puerto Rico for five years as a secretary to the Archbishop of San Juan and had learned Spanish, and he had a young Spanish-speaking priest to help him with the new situation. Although the Spanish-speaking priest is a man named Thomas Farrelly, he is now identified by Puerto Rican, Cuban, and Dominican parishioners as the "Spanish padre."

The great upheaval prevented the monsignor from thinking very much about the past. "With this urban renewal we have great faith. If many of the fine houses of the past are replaced by livable modern apartments, people will come back, not as many as have moved, but many will come back, and they're entitled to do so. We will then have an integrated congregation, Puerto Ricans in a goodly number, some Negroes, and a good number of Irish. What will be the future of the parish, that will be anyone's guess, but it will come back to its own, perhaps, probably in a different way. The strength of our church lies neither in wealth nor poverty but in the middle class. With what's coming in here, we will maintain our own very well. We've been at the bottom of the barrel and we're coming up now."

The situation is more hopeful, according to Monsignor Flanagan, because Puerto Ricans have advantages over other groups that have migrated to the United States. New Yorkers are making more of an effort to understand Puerto Ricans and their language—"Spanish has been almost our second tongue. There are many more people studying it than studied Italian or German when these groups came over." Spanish no-smoking signs, Spanish *graffiti,* and Spanish beer commercials on television, and now Channel 47, a Spanish TV station, attest to the monsignor's point. He thinks the Puerto Ricans will make their way up the ladder like other nationality groups before them to the point where, even if they do not earn big salaries, they will earn enough to maintain their families. "A great majority of Spanish people are willing to make sacrifices to give their children a good education. This is what was also true of the Italians and is why they occupy such a high place in our society today."

The pastor foresees the Puerto Ricans doing just as well as previous ethnic groups in fifty years' time. He is encouraged by the interest of the Spanish parents and the Mothers' Guild at the school. While many of the Irish parents do not seem to have time or interest, he says, Spanish mothers and fathers have given a splendid account of themselves in school-related activities. Their children are apparently doing well, too. One of St. Gregory's English prizes went to a Puerto Rican girl who had arrived two years earlier without any knowledge of English. "I think the future is safe in the children's hands around here. They are the real hope. The older people are set in their ways. They are not going to get the language quickly. They will continue to associate with their own, but the young will go with the others. They will be very much up in the structure when they are grown and they will be bilingual. There are no children more affectionate and more respectful to the priest than the Puerto Ricans. They are a pleasure.

"If you have a spirit of optimism at all—and that's the reason the Irish get along—you'll see a golden lining in this dark cloud of dust around here," the monsignor declares. "If we live long enough we'll see St. Gregory's come back. I must have that in mind or I would never go ahead with my plans. We are going to free St. Gregory's, free it from the Golden Past, so-called. What was the Golden Past, how far did it get us? Just as far as this one church building. We never progressed beyond it. It's been serving as church, school, and rectory since 1919."

St. Gregory's is going ahead with an ambitious building program, despite the financial squeeze resulting from a slump in parish enrollment. The monsignor is negotiating for a 65-by-100-foot lot on the west side of the church, where he will build a new convent and parish office. He is also purchasing a 100-by-100-foot lot to the east of the church for a playground. "I do know we don't want to be left too little too late," he says. "A swarm of children coming into this neighborhood means we have to enlarge the school. I'm ready. I'll move off this top floor and convert these eight apartments back to schoolrooms. Then I'll move to the hundred-foot lot and build a rectory." Land is not obtained in Manhattan by a mere offer to buy at a fair price. "In order to get these things you don't just dream about them. You have to work with the authorities downtown because there are plenty of people as interested in that hundred-foot lot as I am. It almost required an act of Congress to get the land we want freed from the urban renewal program. We had to send down to Washington for permission, and I'm pretty sure it will be granted. When the plans for the new urban renewal area come out, I think you'll see that these pieces of land are allotted to us, definitely." (They were.) "No money paid down or anything but the diocese will back me up on that."

It is expected that the school will draw many children from the new housing projects in the area, but the monsignor is not leaving this matter up to chance either. "I'm going to know every single family in the project across the street, whether they're Catholic or not. I'm going to visit them all and I daresay a good percentage of them will be Catholic." Visiting all the tenants in Stephen Wise Towers would seem to be a large order for a monsignor, and in fact it was. As things turned out one of the parish's older priests was delegated to do the job.

The priests can make only a superficial effort at a visiting program. The demands of the aged, sick, and needy take up most of their time. People with no special problems or who do not ask for help rarely, if ever, receive visits. An alternative is to increase lay parish activities.

The Holy Name Society for men and the Rosary Society for ladies have brought some new families into contact with the church. A few Puerto Rican and Irish wives who belong to the Rosary Society take summer excursions to Harrison, New York, and other suburbs, hold monthly meetings, arrange socials, card parties, attend lectures.

Until late 1963, the Police Athletic League ran a community activities center for children in the church basement. When the arrangement had to be discontinued because of space problems, there was great concern over PAL's relocation. Parishioners resented the fact that PAL lost out to the Goddard-Riverside Community Center in competition for space in the new public housing developments. "Politics" is behind the situation, according to some, who seem to feel that Goddard-Riverside has the "inside track" because a member of its board is related to a member of the City Housing Authority that decides on the allocation of recreation space in the public housing projects. While he expressed no opinion on this particular, it is obvious that Monsignor Flanagan feels there is not enough coopera-tion and too much working at cross purposes among community agencies.

To help close the communications gap with its own parishioners, St. Gregory's maintains an office with a priest on duty 10 A.M. to noon, 3:30 to 5 P.M. and 7 to 9 P.M. in the evening. At first the office was on the fifth floor but in view of the fact that "when you walk up five flights of stairs you're out of breath," Monsignor Flanagan ordered it moved to the first floor. Whereas arranging masses and other parish business was conducted previously on the telephone, now parishioners can come in and discuss anything they want directly with the priest. There are many types of matters discussed but most of the problems in the minds of the parishioners who have come to the office is the education of their children.

The 356 youngsters who attend grades one through eight of St. Gregory's school begin their academic exercise when they enter the church through a side door and climb a steep, dogleg iron staircase to their second- and third-floor classrooms. The principal's office is off the second-floor hallway. During the years Sister Bernadette was principal, a child coming up the stairs could hear the orange canary she kept in a cage on top of a filing cabinet. Through the window behind her desk the principal watched the crumbling of Ninetieth

Street, the exodus, the demolition of the rooming houses and tenements, and the construction of Stephen Wise Towers. While all these
changes were taking place, St. Gregory's lost a hundred pupils, but
the school was still overcrowded, measured by public school standards. Nevertheless, until the day she left, Sister Bernadette looked
forward to the time when registration would get back to what it had
been.

She was a tiny, fresh-faced woman who seemed to be fighting a
calm but losing war with a huge desk that had forced her into a
corner and was threatening to bury her under a pile of papers.
Although the job of running a school single-handedly meant that she
had to be an excellent administrator, Sister Bernadette always gave
the impression of being a teacher who has had a great deal of clerical
work dumped on her and has taken the whole business with good
humor. Her ability to keep from fossilizing into an educational
executive was a precious quality at St. Gregory's, where she had to
preside over a changing community of children. During her time, the
Irish children were rapidly replaced by Puerto Ricans and West
Indians; by 1964 more than half the children had Spanish names, and
nearly fifty Haitian youngsters were forcing the sisters to brush up on
their French. Meanwhile, less than a hundred of the pupils were
mainland white (mostly Irish), with about two dozen Negroes.

St. Gregory's is not exactly overloaded with faculty. The entire
teaching staff consists of eight sisters, each of whom takes an entire
grade as her home-room class and teaches them in nine curriculum
areas. Except for a music teacher there is no specialized teaching
personnel. If there has to be remedial work or extra tutoring, the
sisters provide this after school on a necessarily limited basis. Class
sizes run from thirty-five to fifty children.

The school accepts any child whose parents apply for his admission unless he is seriously retarded physically or mentally. In her years
as principal, Sister Bernadette did not have to refuse any child
admission or expel any for disciplinary reasons. However, if a child is
not accepted it is usually because there is a waiting list for admission
to the lower grades, in spite of the recent decline in total school
population.

Many of the children came to school not knowing a word of
English, and on their part the sisters arrived without any previous
contact with Spanish children. Most of the sisters were of Irish

descent and came from Staten Island, the headquarters of their teaching order of the Sisters of the Presentation. Their sequestered life in a relatively countrified atmosphere did not prevent them from coming to terms very quickly with children from a different environment and culture. As the sisters, most of whom have a faint Irish quirk to their speech, taught the children English, the children "Latinized" the sisters. Both sides seem to have been overcome by this culture collision. Today none of the sisters looks forward to the inevitable day when she will be transferred from St. Gregory's, since it will mean the end to what all of them say is the most rewarding educational experience of their lives.

The teachers are part of the area in which their pupils live, and yet apart from it. They have not tried to be social workers, but they have given help when called upon. They have also learned details about the family lives of many of the children, lives which leave a great deal to be desired, especially a responsible father, according to Sister Christina. The sisters' knowledge comes from the parish priests, from the children, and from their own life on a crowded side street where the truth unravels for anyone to see. They do not leave the area when school is over. Their convent on Eighty-seventh Street, its front entrance protected by a high iron cage, is not immune to intrusion and violence. The disasters to which the sisters have responded sensibly and quickly have been commonplace and frequently unnoticed by social agencies, which are closed after 5 P.M. and on weekends. Such emergencies also usually pass unnoticed at the rectory, where the monsignor wrestles with more cosmic problems. A woman giving birth in a freezing rooming house on Eighty-seventh Street is warm because the sisters gave blankets from the convent.

At certain times the sisters detach themselves from the life around them, to heal their own spirits and seek guidance. After the night Sister Assumpta saw a man stabbed to death on the sidewalk, the sisters withdrew into their convent at all times when they were not in school. Their way of shutting out the curses and sounds of street violence was to turn up their radios. In the early days of their stay, the convent was robbed four times, the thieves taking typewriters and anything else they could lay their hands on. The sisters had no illusions about any special immunities because of their calling. One of them discovered a thief in one of the bedrooms, but, when he was caught by the police later, she was afraid to identify the man because "he or his friends might do something to us later." The sisters share other memories, like the sight of a three-year-old child's body thrown into an alley beside the convent.

Sister Christina recalls the arrivals and departures during the days when the Area seemed more like a way station for refugees than a community. "The new children would be in class a year or less, perhaps until they began to learn some English, and then they would vanish. It was very hard to teach children who were always on the move and who were having a hard time keeping their wits about them with all the screaming and fighting in the streets, and the garbage and disorder and police sirens and fire engines."

As the Spanish mothers gained confidence in the school, they came to more and more of the events in which the children took part, and this stimulated more children to want to take part. The sisters were initiated into some new versions of traditional holidays. On the day of St. Patrick, the patron saint of the New York Archdiocese as well as of Ireland, the Spanish children danced Irish jigs and sang Irish songs in Latin accents; then on Teachers Recognition Day they treated the sisters to a Hail Mary in Spanish and a half-dozen Puerto Rican dances.

Although the Puerto Rican children participate in everything, Sister Christina says, there are many things that make their acceptance incomplete: one persistent obstacle is the idea that they are not as good as the next person, because the next person seems so often to have very different opportunities and a different expectation of what life is going to bring him. Sister Christina tells the children that they are going out into a world where they have to believe in themselves and not depend on anyone else to find out what they want.

Events at the school are designed to make the children feel and behave "grown-up." One of these is the graduation prom. In class the children all wear blue uniforms; at the prom they "dress to perfection, as if they were all bringing a movie star," Sister Christina reports. Another event is the bestowing of graduation rings. Monsignor Flanagan says mass in the church downstairs and each eighth-grade child goes to the altar to receive his class ring, and the ring is blessed. Afterward the seventh grade, which has spent many hours decorating the tables in the cafeteria, gives the graduating class a breakfast of rolls, fruit, and ginger ale. The event gives the two grades a feeling of unity, and emphasizes what a fine thing the eighth graders have accomplished.

Despite a teaching load which would be intolerable to a teachers' union and would cause an uproar among public school parents, the sisters rarely complain about overcrowded classes. Perhaps this is because there is no prospect of changing the situation, therefore it is a waste of time to talk about it. The class organization is much like that in a small Midwestern community, where a large class of children of similar background recite en masse. There are exceptions to the rule; for instance, Sister Mary Luke has divided her class into three reading groups.

If one asks if it isn't desirable to give children more individualized attention, the sister's answer is that if a child needs special help she will stay after school and give it to him. Classes of three or four dozen have been pretty much the rule at St. Gregory's for a long time. The teachers approach their task professionally, not as substitute mothers or drillmasters. Their moral and religious commitments seem to have stimulated and focused their energies as teachers. Measured by their academic attainments or the depth of their preoccupation with education, the sisters are clearly equal, if not occasionally superior, to their public school counterparts.

One advantage the sisters have in handling their large classes is that they do not have to spend a lot of time maintaining discipline. Over and over they remark how cooperative the children have been, although there are exceptions. But the main daily effort at St. Gregory's is to read, spell, listen, study, exercise, and think well of oneself. Physically the school is an old and unsatisfactory place, but not an austere one. Perhaps the most striking characteristic of the teachers is the warmth and sense of humor that lie just under the surface of their gravity. They avoid the sort of intensity which could upset children who are not sure of themselves and who are aware of demands put upon them. The children seem to sense that there are limits to humor and acceptance, and that there are certain uncompromising but reasonable expectations which they are supposed to fulfill.

It is, of course, impossible to tell from class observation how successfully the sisters can teach classes of forty or fifty children, particularly when the observer is accustomed to the minimal requirements that public schools have set for effective instruction. It is possible to see that most of the children participate actively in what is going on, even those who are having difficulty. Class recitations sometimes grow so excited that the teacher will ask everyone to pause and calm himself. When Sister Mary Luke asks questions, her second graders come to the surface like a school of minnows, waving their hands and calling "Sister, sister" until they drown out the sound of the air compressor in the street below the windows. At such times, the teacher lets them break through the boundaries of the discussion. The digressions lower the pressure without extinguishing the excitement. Even the classes in religious instruction seem to have this latitude, to the point where they often seem more like classes in comparative religion. Sister Regina, for instance, may devote the better part of a period to telling her fifth graders about Jewish attitudes toward the Bible, Jewish customs, and the history of the captivity and the flight from Egypt—all of this in connection with a lesson on the origin and meaning of baptism.

If one is to judge the facilities of the school by comparing them to what is available in the public schools in the Area, they are markedly insufficient. Although the school includes a seventh and eighth grade it does not have anything that could be called a science lab. Classroom demonstrations are all at the teacher's desk, and only basic necessities are available—the galvanometer, the Bunsen burner, the test tubes, the diagrams, and the books. The school has no shop or craft classes. Sister Bernadette put a library at the top of her priority list, but she never got one. Each classroom has a small supply of books, but there is no central collection of novels, texts, encyclopedias, etc., such as the public schools have, nor is there a librarian who can work with the children to broaden their reading interests. Such visual aids as its movie projector the school owes to the Mothers Guild.

Unlike the public schools, the children do not receive free tickets to such places as Lincoln Center and Carnegie Hall. However, St. Gregory's does have its own version of the public schools' "higher horizons" program. The children visit the Museum of Natural History and the Planetarium at Eighty-first Street, the Bronx Zoo, the Metropolitan Museum, and Central Park; take boat rides around Manhattan on the Circle Line; and see an occasional movie which may have some educational value. In most cases the children make a small payment for transportation, but no child is prevented from going because he doesn't have the money. The only tax-supported part of the school's activities is the federal free lunch program.

Because the school has no gymnasium or playground, the sisters escort the children across busy streets to a public recreation area. Exercises are held in the school auditorium or in the classroom. In Sister Luke's class, the gym teacher is a phonograph record which in a rather sugary voice tells the children to swim, fly, bend knees deep, clench and unclench fingers, and duck walk. The dose is made enjoyable by music and by the fact that the teacher is tall, beautiful, and enthusiastic; when the record says to spin like a top, she whirls until the crucifix and chain at her waist fly out parallel to the floor.

Whatever its difficulties, St. Gregory's gets most of its children into high schools, and once there very few of them drop out. To be accepted by a Catholic high school a child must pass a competitive examination supervised by the Catholic School Board. Each child is expected to apply for admission to four Catholic high schools. In a recent year graduating eighth graders were accepted in twelve high schools, some Catholic and some public, and this seems to represent the typical distribution. Youngsters who want vocational training must go to public high schools, since there is none in the Catholic system. Children also go to public high school because their parents cannot afford the $15–$30-a-month tuition at Catholic high schools —a considerable increase over St. Gregory's tuition of fifty cents a week.

St. Gregory's modest tuition and the limited incomes of a majority of the people who come to the church show the need for careful school financing. The job of budget director is ideally filled by Monsignor Flanagan, whose reputation as a thrifty man has spread well beyond the boundaries of his parish. The monsignor gives $100 a month to each of the teaching sisters, who pool allowances to run the convent, buy food and clothing, and pay the tuition costs of the sisters' study for advanced degrees (three of the sisters who have bachelor's degrees are taking graduate work for master's or doctorates in education). A percentage of the sisters' monthly allowance is sent to their mother home on Staten Island. As the Mother Superior of the Eighty-seventh Street convent, Sister Bernadette does the budgeting. "In the beginning it took some work to come out even," she says, "but since we don't need a great amount of clothing and we don't spend money on entertainment we make out all right."

The sisters' schedule begins when they rise at 5:30 A.M. and at 6 they chant a short form of the Breviary. "It doesn't sound so good, I can assure you," Sister Christina reports. A period of meditation on some event in the life of the Lord follows sometimes, at 6:50, the sisters walk to the church for mass; but usually Father Browne celebrates mass at the convent. Next, more chants and devotions, then breakfast in silence. Afterward the sisters walk to school with their group of boys who wait outside the gate. Sister Christina says the boys carry the sisters' books, "although there is nothing official about it," and talk about what they saw on television last night.

School begins at 8:40. Then at lunch one of the sisters takes over the "guard," which means that she supervises the corridors. Three sisters eat lunch with Sister Bernadette and two others stay with the children until lunch is finished and they are ready to go back to their classrooms. After this the sister on "guard" has lunch and two others come out to take over, one on each floor. The bell rings for the end of school at 3 P.M. Usually several sisters stay another hour for extra work. When they get home they have a recreation period for three-quarters of an hour and then chapel. One meal in the day is prepared by a cook, who comes in five times a week. After supper at 5:30 the sisters chant the office again for twenty minutes. There is free time in the evening and the sisters are able to get their lessons prepared. They may look at television. After 9:30 they observe silence.

In the summer, the sisters can go to a summer lodge in Putnam Valley run by the Catholic Youth Organization. There are swimming, plenty of ground to wander around on, fields, and a brook. For two weeks they are a long distance from the sounds of the street.

Holy Name parish is located just north of St. Gregory's parish, and takes in the section of the West Side between Ninety-second and 101st streets. Its large church, parish house, and school are the center of a religious, educational, and social community for approximately 3,500 adults who attend Sunday masses—or about a third of the estimated 11,000 nominal Catholics who live inside the parish boundaries. In addition, between 1,500 and 2,000 children go to the Holy Name Sunday school, and 1,000 adults who are prevented by age or illness from attending church regularly contribute to the support of the parish. This once-Irish parish has "gone Spanish" to an even greater degree than St. Gregory's, with about 80 percent of the church members of Latin-American origin. Also like St. Gregory's, Holy Name has not attracted very many Negroes; of those who do attend services, many are middle-class professional people who live in Park West Village, the middle-income housing complex which displaced so many of Holy Name's Irish church members.

There are many differences between the two parishes. With its large staff and diversified program, Holy Name is more the bustling, corporate community, while St. Gregory's has the atmosphere of a "village parish." Holy Name priests make regular calls on the sick, and a parish visitor conducts a continual parish census, recording information about baptisms, marriages, church attendance and family difficulties. The church is better than the local political clubs at making contact with new arrivals in the area. When a Catholic family moves in, it will probably receive a call from a Holy Name representative, who will encourage it to make the church the center of its social as well as its religious life. If there are domestic problems, the parents are invited to visit the pastor. If the family needs food the word is passed on to the laymen of St. Vincent de Paul, two of whom are on duty at the church every night.

The assistant pastor, directing the parish on a day-to-day basis, considers both the spiritual and the economic complaints of his parishioners. He takes no complaints at face value. If a family reports rent trouble, for instance, the church makes an on-the-spot investigation. Sometimes the solution is simple—the rent check has not arrived on time from welfare, in which case the family is tided over until the error is straightened out. Serious family crises requiring professional advice and assistance are turned over to Catholic Charities. In dire emergencies a visiting priest or sister will call up the assistant pastor regardless of the hour. The parish visitors' records are studied daily to discover people who may need assistance but have not asked for help. Other sources of information about troubled families are parochial and public school authorities and the public school children in the area who participate in Father Joseph O'Mara's released-time program. As is to be expected, the church's program works better on paper than it does in fact because there are too few people to do all the work, the population is shifting constantly, and a single low-income family may have enough problems to keep the church volunteer busy for weeks.

Where the Protestant churches leave a large part of the responsibility for neighborhood activities up to the settlement houses, private social-welfare agencies, afterschool community centers, and such enterprises as the New York *Herald Tribune* Fresh Air Fund, Holy Name parish maintains its own cluster of activities for children and adults. For the mothers there are the Rosary and Holy Name societies, for the girls the Sodality, for the boys the Catholic Youth Organization, with athletic events, dances, and skating parties and Tuesday-night education and religious classes that usually wind up with a social. Church groups sponsor activities for the Boy Scouts, Cub packs, and the Explorers.

The director of the parish youth program, Father William Bradley, keeps a file on young people which has been useful to the Youth Division of the police department. For two months each summer he runs a day camp for two hundred youngsters, five days a week. Most of the children in the program are Catholic, but when there are vacancies children of other religious backgrounds can participate. Father Bradley has the assistance of seven high school students who work as camp counselors for a few dollars a week. The summer camp is not the stay-away, out-of-town type. On Tuesdays and Thursdays the children board buses for trips to such places as Rockaway Beach, Long Island, or Sebago Beach at Bear Mountain. On the other three mornings during the week the "campers" go to Riverside Park and play baseball, then come back for free lunches at the school. In the afternoon the counselors take them to a museum or zoo. The only charge for the day camp is a $2 registration fee and a twenty-five cent charge for each bus and swimming ticket. Except for the transportation costs, the day camp budget is raised by the Rosary Society card parties.

Regular supervised activities are fine, says Monsignor Patrick Raftery, who until recently was Holy Name's assistant pastor, but the young people need something else very badly—a special place to socialize where they can "interact" without someone looking over their shoulders all the time and planning their activities for them. Of course there would have to be some authority, perhaps a policeman, stationed on the premises to see that a few rowdies did not spoil things for everyone else. But the main idea would be to let the youngsters run their own affairs. Father Raftery's idea is very similar to one advanced by Karl Bucholz, the former chief of a community psychiatric clinic at the Riverside Health Center. Bucholz thinks that the city might build a big structure near Broadway, perhaps with some glass on top like the Galleria Umberto in Naples. "It could have some of the casual feeling of a big European railway station, or an outdoor park like Inwood Hill, where you can go for a walk and not have anybody telling you to keep off the grass. People could sit at tables and drink coffee. The purpose would be to let people congregate, not seduce them into activities."

Although Monsignor Raftery is beginning to get a little gray, he does not think the younger generation is going to pot any faster than its predecessors; in fact the younger generation may be an improvement, although it is more bewildered. "In old New York there were plenty of roughnecks, the type we call juvenile delinquents now. We just covered it up better. If a boy or girl got into a scrape it didn't get so much publicity. The parents did more to get after the boy or girl and correct the situation. Maybe World War II hurt a bit. The children we call teen-age hoodlums were born then, and ran around when they were little, while their mothers went off to factories making money. By the time they got to be seventeen they were out of control.

"At school, many of the children are surrounded by discipline, respect, and people who expect something of them, and they do fairly well, but when the school and church influence is removed, there is nothing to take its place and the children are lost. It is an unusual child who can rise above a broken home," the monsignor says.

"The trouble with so many of the adults is that there is very little they can get from society even if they try, so they desert society. I am talking about the Negro and Puerto Rican without an education, with a job eliminated by automation. Society and the home must see to it that men get a fair chance to raise their families and earn a decent wage. Many of their personal problems could be overcome if they could be independent, but when a man is condemned to be sent to the bottom of society all we can do is try and prove to the young people that God loves them. This is a hard task in a society that gives children illusions, distractions, glamorous empty things. We live in a society that makes it difficult to make a sense of sacrifice appeal to a youngster—the sense that God is interested in him, that he will be rewarded if he remains faithful to his principles."

Holy Name has two schools, which are attempting to educate and encourage twelve hundred children. After attending first and second grade together, the children are separated by sex and are placed in separate schools which run through the eighth grade. The pupils of both the boys' and girls' school are predominantly Spanish in background. Only 10 percent of the pupils in the boys' school are "mainland white." Many children at Holy Name live in the Douglass Houses, the large public housing project across the street. School authorities agree with the teachers at P.S. 163, which also has a large number of Douglass children, that the project has stabilized the children's lives, and is good for their self-respect.

Classes in the girls' school average thirty-five to forty. Sister Francilda, a blue-eyed nun with a reserved manner, spends all her school time in administration, while the teaching burden is shared by fourteen sisters (ten Irish, three Italian, one Cuban) and six lay instructors. She transmits messages over a complicated public-address system near her desk, a piece of equipment which would seem quite out of place at St. Gregory's. Before her present assignment Sister Francilda had visited schools in Puerto Rico, Cuba, Haiti, and Jamaica, all of which have contributed children to Holy Name, and she supervised schools in Nassau, the Grand Bahamas, Bimini, and Andros. Her experience is put to the test at Holy Name, which has very few special services for a diverse school population drawn largely from underprivileged backgrounds. It has lay teachers for music and art, but no remedial reading, physical education, or home-economics teachers. The only formal "guidance" counseling is provided by the child's home-room teacher, who can do little more than advise the child on what high school to try for. Sister Francilda says that although there are large classes and a shortage of specialized help almost all of the girls graduate from high school (usually an academic Catholic high school with a commercial department).

Because of the teacher and space shortage and because Sister Francilda had a theory, the girls' school adopted a system of heterogeneous grouping. In previous years, the children had been grouped in fast or slow classes on the basis of language- and reading-achievement tests. After experimenting with heterogeneous groupings in the seventh and eighth grades, the school grouped all classes above the second grade heterogeneously. Since the two classes in each grade were made up on an alphabetical basis, Sister Francilda went over each class register with its teacher to make sure that in the alphabetical split not too many fast or too many slow children were together in one class.

The results of the experiment astonished the teachers, and exceeded the principal's hopes. At the end of the first two years there were only three children in each of the fourth-, fifth-, and sixth-grade classes who were more than one year below reading level. Previously under the fast and slow grouping, every one of the slow classes was more than a year below reading level. Under the new system every child in one sixth grade class was on or above sixth-grade reading level, while the reading spread in the eighth-grade classes never fell below seventh and ran as high as twelfth. These results came in spite of the fact that each class under the new program had only one reading period as compared to two reading periods for each of the slow classes in previous years.

Sister Francilda does point out that one factor in the success of heterogeneous grouping was that there was not too great a spread in ability among the children—probably not as great as that in some public schools. She also gives credit to use of individualized Science Research Associates reading kits and the McCall-Crabb three-minute reading tests. The school is not the only institution pleased by the experiment; since then Science Research Associates has donated ten more kits to the school, doubling a supply already larger than that of P.S. 163, the elementary public school across the street.

In contrast to the public junior high schools, Holy Name's seventh and eighth grades for girls are organized on a home-room basis with one teacher handling all curriculum areas. Sister Francilda favored departmentalization at one time but a questionnaire of her faculty indicated they wanted the home-room plan. "We deal with a child who is often extremely dependent upon the teacher because he comes from a broken home and needs the additional support from someone who seems to be his own personal teacher." While Sister Francilda would like to get a special teacher to work with television teaching and another to help with grading, she sees a danger in relying too heavily on specialized teaching programs. "When a teacher special-izes she ceases to be the sole teaching support for her children and, therefore, loses touch with them." Despite the unhappy family back-grounds of many of the children, Sister Francilda says she has had less trouble with pupils at Holy Name in her five years as principal than in all of her previous years of teaching, which included schools in Westchester County (New York), the Bronx, Staten Island. "My teachers really love the setup here because the children are so appreciative. When I first came I was fearful when I walked through this area, but when you get to know the children and the migrant families" (Sister Francilda never refers to them as Puerto Ricans) "you begin to see the things in their proper light. You come up against the broken home. As soon as we sense an emotional upset in a child we try to get hold of the parent. If an agency is needed, we suggest one where the child can go."

The principal's comments about parents associations sound like those of most public school teachers. She feels that they ought to be more directly interested in the children and worry less about raising money for the school. She does not like fund raising carried on inside the school building. The parents association should "establish communications between the parents and teachers on educational matters." The principal says she frankly doesn't care for all-day parent affairs at the school, although two open school days are held in May for parents and representatives of various local agencies. "The parents stack up in the different classrooms and move around and much time is lost. Evening meetings turned out badly because of the baby-sitter problem. The father would be tired so the meetings dwindled to maybe as little as twenty mothers. Then, of course, parent-teacher meetings get social—they'll talk about having a cake sale or a bridge party. The parents should be thinking about education, not these social events." After some false starts, Sister Francilda worked out a system whereby "the parents talk and the teacher listens." Parents with children in the same grade meet together. "They come at 3:15 P.M. and go at 4:30 P.M. They don't have to wait. Discussion takes place and that is it. They seem to be satisfied."

Most of the school's financial support comes from the parish, which runs a monthly lottery and turns over the proceeds to the school. Parish members buy tickets at a dollar apiece in the lottery, the "school club," as it is called. A parish member is expected to buy five tickets a month if he has a child in the church school. If he has two or more of his children in the school he buys three additional tickets. The parents are allowed to resell their tickets if they can find buyers, but most of them do not bother—they consider it a fair tuition to pay and besides there is a chance they may win some of the $1,000 in monthly prizes. Theoretically, the church does not require parents to buy the tickets if they are absolutely unable to afford them, but in fact the parents find the money even if they are living on welfare allowances.

The school serves 875 lunches, aided by the federal lunch program. Sister Francilda prefers to have the children go home for lunch if a parent is there. Public junior high schools which draw children from several different neighborhoods sometimes require the children to remain at school for lunch because they do not want them wandering about the streets. Holy Name does not have this system and there seems to be no problem about getting the children home or back. Very often the parents accompany the children to and from the school.

The classrooms at Holy Name Girls School are airy and well lighted, even though the school building is old-fashioned. Desks are fixed to the floor, old-fashioned style, but, in other ways the school keeps right up with the times. Around the middle of June, for instance, some of the Spanish children receive permission to leave school early and their parents put them on commercial airliners which provide special hostesses for the children. When a child arrives in Puerto Rico, Venezuela, or Bolivia he is met at the airport by a relative—perhaps a grandmother with whom he will spend the summer.

"Even the second graders make grand travelers. It is surprising how quickly the children get used to flying," Sister Francilda says, looking at a model of a 707 jet airliner which the children gave her when she returned from one of her own trips.

A peaceful coexistence of contrasting educational theories prevails at the Holy Name schools. Brother Raymond, the principal of the boys' branch of Holy Name School, groups his 365 boys homogeneously. He finds they tend to split into a "heavy bottom and a heavy top" and they are placed in fast or slow classes on the basis of reading classification tests given during the first week of school. Class sizes of thirty to thirty-five make the job of bringing along the slower achievers especially difficult. The teaching load is handled by four brothers, two lay men teachers, and four lay women teachers—all with teaching experience, and several holding advanced degrees or studying for them.

Until the urban renewal exodus caused a juggling and combining of some classes, from the first to the sixth year each grade customarily had one fast class and one slow class. In 1963 the principal combined the slow learners in the sixth and seventh grades in a single class and continued this arrangement the next year by combining them in a seventh- and eighth-grade class. The combined class received a double dose of math and English. The school has a remedial reading program with each child in the program getting one period a day. In addition to their regular report cards, every child has a reading record card all the way through school.

Brother Raymond thinks one of the advantages of homogeneous grouping is that it allows the faster readers to progress at their own pace. The school's faster readers (reading at sixth-grade level and above) are grouped together. Brother Raymond teaches one of these fast sixth-, seventh-, and eighth-grade combined classes. He gives these pupils reading on a twelfth-year level and a steady diet of novels and plays and poetry.

Whereas Sister Francilda uses the home-room system for all classes, Brother Raymond has departmentalized the seventh and eighth grades in the manner similar to the public junior high schools. In these grades the teacher takes a special curriculum area and moves from room to room. Brother Raymond feels it is an advantage for the boys to see different teachers throughout the day: they work harder and the transition to high school, where all classes are departmentalized, is not so difficult.

Brother Raymond says the upper-grade students are "not doing badly" except where there has been a language problem. The school's only Spanish-speaking brother teaches English to boys who are literate in Spanish. When the school has an intractable problem with a "nonlearner" he is recommended for transfer to a public school. When a child third grade or above comes without any English he is sent over to P.S. 163, which has an intensive language program. Within six months to a year the pupil is able to come back to Holy Name. Brother Raymond says the public school does "wonderful work" with these badly retarded boys. "They have the facilities and the special teachers. We are limited by a lack of money to do what the public schools do in this field."

The school's best efforts to build up the children's religious attitudes and their self-discipline are often undermined once they have left the elementary grades, particularly if the child goes on in public high school. Brother Raymond quickly adds that he doesn't blame the public high schools for this. The trouble lies in the fact that, once in their teens, away from the protected atmosphere of a religiously oriented elementary school, the children lessen their efforts or give up. "So much lack of interest and unhappiness in many of the homes cuts their chances way down. When you have a good home situation—and we have some very good ones among the Puerto Ricans—we get cooperation and the kids do well, but much of the time the parents create problems, not the children."

As in the girls' school, one gets an unmistakable impression that the teachers consider the parent groups more interfering than cooperative. One teacher says the parents' associations "can actually be burdensome in the extreme," and that "their meetings usually degenerate into fund raising, politics, and little cliques. They give us financial help, but then they want to know where it's going, who is being favored, and so on, so in the end it's much more trouble than it's worth. Parents can get too close to the school."

The Catholic and the public schools in the Area both concentrate much attention on the Spanish and Haitian children from low-income families. The two systems are both experimenting with new teaching methods, but there are fundamental differences in the magnitude of their problems. The shortage of teachers and the overcrowding in the public schools is nowhere near as critical as in the two parish schools. On the other hand, the American Negro child on the West Side, with his very special and pressing needs, is almost completely the responsibility of the public schools. Another difference in the two school systems is that while their school populations are predominantly low-income minority-group children, a significant number of "mainland-white" middle-class children remain in the public schools while the parochial schools have lost all but a small fraction of this group, probably for some time to come. Because of this development and because of their sectarian character, the parochial schools cannot give their children the same variety of cultural, social, and racial contacts available to children in the public schools. Whether this is a serious drawback to the child in the Catholic school is an unresolved question. Brother Raymond would say that his school offers more important compensations. He holds that a school program which seeks to build up moral and religious values as well as develop intelligence is the best preparation for an integrated life and that such a program is especially important to children exposed to the disintegrating pressures of slum society.

There is a pronounced difference between the attitude of the public school parent and teacher toward classes of more than thirty, the maximum allowed by Board of Education policy, and that of the Catholic sisters, who do not consider forty or fifty children in a class beyond their capacity. What accounts for this difference in attitudes? Sister Francilda provides one clue when, in explaining the success of her heterogeneous grouping, she says that the extremes between her children are not very great. The extremes in the local public schools are so great that there is always the danger they may cause a fragmenting of the curriculum, because of the competing demands of the parents of the children who make up the extremes. The fact that the Catholic sisters do not have a serious discipline problem also affects their attitude toward large classes. As religious as well as teaching figures the sisters are endowed with a double authority from the moment they step into their first classroom. The public school teacher, on the other hand, does not have the moral "rank" the church confers, nor is it easy for her to win respect for her status as a teacher from a society which has traditionally short-changed public education and looked on public educators with a mixture of condescension and contempt. Whatever concessions the teacher wins for herself depend on the force of her own personality and her ability to make some kind of a substitute mother of herself.

If the Catholic schools lead a less-troubled existence than the public schools, it is not merely because they solve their problems by turning them over to the public schools—as they often do because they lack the facilities to handle the problems themselves. The two educational systems have very different relationships to the communities they are supposed to serve. It is not part of the Catholic tradition for parents to be constitutionally distrustful of or hostile to their schools or to demand that the schools make up for the failures of the family, the church, or society at large. The public schools endure the fate of most tax-supported institutions, which is to be regarded as a service station for pressure groups, a target for every transient wave of popular hysteria, and a perpetual battleground for community conflicts.

One cannot help but notice the air of tranquillity in the Catholic schools and the manner in which the teaching brothers and sisters comment on their responsibility. Their analysis of the educational problem has a certain simplicity. There is a greater sense of confidence in their mission and a feeling of permanence in their calling, natural among people whose whole life is incorporated within the teaching and religious effort. Perhaps this is why they tend to be less frustrated and discouraged than many public school teachers, and to feel more satisfaction in what they do. Their discussion focuses more on the inner details of the children's lives and their personalities and their families, perhaps because the Catholic teachers, while they live apart, at the same time inhabit the neighborhood of the children they teach. The sisters do not seem to be as driven, confused, and divided about educational theory as the public school teacher, who undergoes a running inquisition on the subject from parent, school supervisors, even herself. Nor do the sisters face the dilemma of the public school teacher who is a member of a union and must weigh her responsibility to children against her new power to win economic concessions by the use of the strike.

The teaching sisters and brothers assume a fundamental task—the moral and spiritual guidance of the children—which the public school teacher is requested to avoid. In some ways the Catholic teacher's job is simplified by this assignment because she is left in no doubt as to her responsibility, whereas the public school teacher's instructions are ambivalent. On the one hand she is asked to be a part-time mother and guide as well as an instructor; on the other hand, classroom discussions of ethics or religious beliefs are often risky because there is no way of knowing how her remarks will be interpreted by the children or their parents. In addition, the teacher who emphasizes moral values exposes herself to the charge that she is trying to impose her own middle-class attitudes on children to whom they are alien or irrelevant. In such a dilemma, what is her responsibility? All that she can be sure of is that she cannot be neutral and still realize her potential as a teacher.

The parochial school is a household of authority and guidance, and since it *is* a household, the sisters talk more about children than about educational theory. Controversies between staff and parents and among teachers themselves over teaching methods, guidance, testing, rest periods, middle-class values, and air-raid drills are continually going on at P.S. 84 and P.S. 165. But if there are such storms at St. Gregory's or Holy Name they are well concealed. Parents may ask questions but they do not lecture Sister Bernadette on how to teach mathematics or Sister Francilda on the advantage of homogeneous grouping. There is something symbolic in the fact that in the public schools the middle-class parent makes the demands, interrogates the principals, and criticizes the teachers, while in the Catholic school it is the parents who are interrogated and told what is expected of them.

The Catholic schools have also remained out of the line of fire during the local controversy over racial integration. As sectarian and private institutions, they have not been criticized for their "racial imbalances": attacks on de facto segregation have been directed exclusively against the public schools. The Catholic schools function quite frankly as neighborhood institutions at a time when the neighborhood-school concept is under heavy criticism. The children who stand at the steps of the church are the children to be served, and that is all.

Part V: FOR THE PEOPLE

11

THE FIRST REQUIREMENT

ONCE A WEST SIDER VOLUNTEERS FOR SOME CIVIC duty, or goes to a conference and signs his name and address to the attendance sheet, his name will go on various lists and he will soon begin to receive mail from five, ten, perhaps a score of local organizations which hold irregular and usually badly attended meetings. The usual preoccupations of such gatherings are "community relations," civil rights, the public schools, "intergroup tensions," the need for more police protection, housing, urban renewal, and Democratic politics. The number of meetings held about any crisis depends on how vocal and determined the affected citizens are. A proposal to take over a part of Riverside Park for a children's playground caused a minor earthquake because many of the people on both sides of the struggle were in public relations and advertising.

In contrast, the local health crisis that afflicts the poor seems to have escaped the attention of most laymen except the victims, who are generally inarticulate. It is difficult to estimate the magnitude of the problem from statistical reports from the Riverside Health District, which covers the West Side from Seventy-fourth to 135th streets. A good percentage of the illness among adults, particularly noncommunicable diseases and varieties of mental illness, goes undetected, unreported, and, therefore, untreated. Also, the inclusion in the Riverside Health District of sectors of Harlem, where the incidence of illness is greater than in the rest of the city, complicates the picture on the upper West Side, where the population is economically and racially mixed. Public health authorities agree that very high numbers of children and adults in low-income families in the Riverside Health District suffer from cardio-respiratory diseases, mental illnesses, and parasitic infections. A good proportion, perhaps a majority, of the city's reported twenty-five thousand narcotics addicts (one-half of the nation's reported total) and an army of alcoholic derelicts have gravitated to the Area because of the abundance of slum housing, the last refuge for the socially and morally unacceptable.

It would seem on the surface that the children should be in a better position than the adults, since at least they are required to undergo periodic physical examinations in school. However, the children can be afflicted with a double burden. First, there is the physical and mental oppression of their own illnesses and malnutrition, often present among children dependent on public welfare, the "big daddy" of the slum household. Second, the child is exposed to the emotional shocks and physical hardships of living with debilitated or prostrated adults. Such considerations help explain the presence of so many disturbed children in the public schools, their institutionalization in mental hospitals, and the increase in child suicides which has alarmed city health officials.

Although statistics for communicable diseases in the Riverside Health District do not reflect the exact extent of illness, they give an idea of the relative incidence of diseases. Of the seven city health districts in Manhattan, Riverside (which with a population of 250,-000 ranks fourth among the districts), reported recently the highest number of cases of such parasitic diseases as amoebiasis, hepatitis, and schistosomiasis. It also has the highest number of cases of poisoning by drugs and chemicals (including heroin and barbiturates). The district is second highest in reported cases of venereal disease, with about one-fourth of the cases of gonorrhea reported in patients under twenty-one. There are as many cases of tuberculosis in the district as there are of measles, and seventy-two TB patients died in 1963. In the same year the lack of proper health care and health education (including birth control information) contributed to an infant mortality rate per 1,000 live births of 29.9 for Puerto Ricans and 41.1 for Negroes as compared to 18.4 for U.S.-born, or "mainland" whites.

Many parents poorly educated about health and from cultures where contact with public health facilities has been rare or nonexistent do not understand the meaning of preventive health care. They do not understand how in time apparently minor, or bearable, illness can develop into chronic disabilities or end in death. Families may not realize, for instance, that an abnormally quiet child is not necessarily a well-behaved child and that he may need attention more than a child with a lacerated face. Hundreds of cases of mental and physical illness pass unnoticed until there is some violent or shocking episode, at which point families may find themselves marooned, without advice, without knowledge of what help is available, and without the resources to do what has to be done.

The welfare worker without training in psychology or health care, as is usually the case, who visits these families every three or six months, can only refer them to a clinic which will in turn treat the family as unrelated parts. A referral to a social agency rather often leads the family to an agency that is already overloaded; hence there will be another referral. The referral system is a series of constantly dividing roads, and the sick person seldom gets to the end of the labyrinth.

The roads are doubly difficult for Puerto Ricans, who cannot read the signs or ask directions and who are handicapped by a number of exotic and primitive attitudes about illness. Their first need is a physician familiar with their background, who can speak their language. Few such doctors practice in the upper West Side and at times there has been only one doctor with a knowledge of Spanish and Spanish people in the Riverside Health Center. St. Luke's Hospital, one of the private "high social status" institutions, has begun to make an effort to improve its service to the West Side community, but it has been almost totally lacking in Spanish-language medical or nursing personnel.

Most of the low-income Puerto Ricans seem never to have had physical exams or proper health care on the island. As a consequence, they frequently have untreated parasitic infections—trichinosis, enterobius, ascaris, giardia, and schistosoma. Some of these may lead to severe anemia, causing agitation, restlessness, and an inability to sleep which is particularly hard on young children in school. Most of the children have not had eye examinations prior to school. Puerto Ricans seem to be susceptible to respiratory infections of all sorts, although the actual incidence of these infections is hard to establish. The susceptibility is partly attributed to the Puerto Rican way of living and dressing on the island. The Puerto Ricans have been accustomed to a warm climate and to wearing light clothes. When a Puerto Rican arrives in New York he does not often have a winter coat and very often he does not dress properly for cold weather. When he catches something, the Puerto Rican living in crowded, unsanitary conditions quickly spreads the illness.

Mental illness, especially for the transplanted Puerto Rican, is as pervasive as physical illness. Part of the difficulty is that a Latin family feels keenly that mental illness is a stigma. To be "loco" is a disaster: on the island there are no shadings—either a person is "crazy" or "not crazy." If he is mentally ill, he will often be kept under the family roof away from the hospital. The doctors have great difficulty even under the best of circumstances in persuading a Spanish mother to accept psychiatric treatment for herself or for anyone in her family. If the physician cannot speak to a Latin mother in her own tongue it becomes even more difficult to establish her faith in psychiatric treatment.

The gravity of the city's health crisis is magnified by the inadequacy of a hospital system which was quite unprepared to handle the demands put upon it as a result of the heavy postwar influx of low-income and unemployed Puerto Ricans and Negroes. Today the voluntary and city hospitals are overtaxed. Even to deal with a small portion of the crisis, the city has been forced to spend a quarter of a billion dollars a year on its twenty-one municipal hospitals (250,000 admissions and 435,000 ambulance trips, 31,000 babies delivered) and pay out another $65 million to private hospitals for free clinics— or a total of about 10 percent of the city's annual budget. Even when supplemented by the health department's large annual budget, this is far from enough. Although the number of hospital beds in the city is estimated to be ten times the need of the city's population—ten beds to a thousand persons, the highest per-capita rate in the world—many of these beds are not available to the local population because they are occupied by people who can afford the best treatment and who come from all over the world.

The most serious hospital problem is the shortage of facilities and staff for treatment of ambulatory patients. "Our biggest job is to handle the people who can walk," says Raymond Trussell, Commissioner of Hospitals under Mayor Wagner. Dr. Trussell acknowledges that there is not a single public or voluntary hospital which specifically serves the upper West Side between the eighties and 100's. At present, several hospitals play piecemeal roles in the Area and even these roles change from time to time as a clinic is discontinued or changed in location. West Side patients must go to clinics all over Manhattan. Only Metropolitan Hospital, located in East Harlem on the other side of town, or Knickerbocker Hospital, many blocks to the north, provide the Area with ambulance service. The situation threatens to become even more serious with the deterioration of Knickerbocker Hospital (voluntary), which provides the most service to the Area. The ghettoizing of the neighborhood in which Knickerbocker is located has meant that the hospital now serves a predominantly low-income and slum population. This has undermined its financial position and at the same time turned it into a racially segregated hospital that can attract neither white patients nor doctors. About 30 percent of Knickerbocker patients are brought in through its ambulance service. Sydenham, a municipal hospital which has also given some service to the West Side area, has had similar difficulties, losing most of its white patients although its staff remains racially integrated.

The shortage of psychiatric clinics and beds for psychiatric patients is great, and only a few hospitals have clinics for outpatient treatment. Some valiant efforts are being made to improve the situation, such as a program organized at Harlem Hospital for day-to-day treatment of discharged mental patients. But such effort, and the fact that the city has expanded its beds for psychiatric patients by only six hundred in recent years, leave the services quite inadequate. Dr. Trussell says that there must be a real planning effort in the mental health field, with state and federal governments cooperating.

The city's Commissioner of Health under Mayor Wagner, Dr. George James, criticizes both public and private health services, including those in the Riverside Health District. His main objective was to get more health centers affiliated with reputable hospitals so as to provide a comprehensive health-care program. Dr. James's programs as outlined in his departmental budgets and his theories about new programs were as advanced as those of any public health official in the country, but the health department was unable to fulfill its present commitments or to lay much basis for future hope. Perhaps it is a sign of the administrator's inability to prevail over his own bureaucracy that even those programs the commissioner was able to set up on paper had so little resemblance to the way they operated in fact. In addition, although he did not say so, much of what the commissioner would like to have done about comprehensive health care was impossible given the attitude of organized medicine that the city should not treat illnesses in its public health centers.

The attitude of the voluntary hospital is also a severe handicap, for these hospitals simply "did not see themselves as assuming responsibility for medical care in their area." Many of them, operated in conjunction with medical schools, do not want to build up their treatment programs quantitatively. These hospitals are preoccupied with "interesting" cases which would have some significance in terms of medical research and training of doctors. One West Side resident who has been continuously critical of hospital attitudes says that if an indigent patient wants to get into St. Luke's "he should paint purple spots all over himself and hope that he will be enough of a medical curiosity to be shipped up there for observation." Many voluntary hospitals, including St. Luke's, do not maintain an ambulance service. Failure to maintain this service is for some hospitals a way of slowing a heavy influx of uninteresting cases—knife wounds, tuberculosis, narcotics overdoses, fractures, etc.

One great shortcoming of the clinics is that they treat the "chief complaint" of the patient rather than the whole patient. For example, a woman may come in with a broken arm and it will be taken care of. At the same time she may be suffering from cancer of the cervix, but nothing is done about this because she is unaware of it and the doctor in attendance does not make a check. Four hundred women a year in New York City die of cancer of the cervix, and many of these deaths could have been prevented if the hospital took a Pap smear on all women coming into its treatment clinics.

As one way of attacking the problem of providing comprehensive health care, the Department of Health and the Department of Hospitals have collaborated in trying to erase the unnatural division between prevention and treatment of illness by bringing together all facilities under one roof and by getting more and more of the city health centers affiliated with hospitals with good staffs. The city's

Morrisania Hospital, for instance, now combines a city health center with hospital treatment facilities, and Lutheran Medical Center maintains its Sunset Park treatment center in the basement of the municipal Sunset Park Health Center. Bronx Hospital has an outpatient department in its local health center. In Gouverneur Hospital, which at one time was an inferior institution, there has been a rehabilitation of the facilities and staff and the Department of Health has a full district health center there with mental health and welfare offices.

It is Dr. James's feeling that such efforts will not be enough to solve the problem: government will eventually have to assume the cost of outpatient care. It is "ridiculous" for hospitals to try to pay for such care out of their receipts for inpatient care. There will have to be "quite a rearrangement of money" if hospitals are to meet the city's needs. If more money is available, perhaps more hospitals will open treatment centers. At any rate, there has to be some new thinking about health as well as some new money.

"Progress in health is achieved by redefining the unacceptable," the commissioner says, quoting Sir Geoffrey Vickers.

As seen from the outside by a patient waiting in hallways or standing for hours in long lines at public clinics, the hospital system is an incomprehensible maze populated by medical people who seem to have adopted the behavioral characteristics of employees in the Pentagon. Patients may stand by for an hour or more in one hospital while clinic doctors take prolonged coffee breaks, or they are sent around from place to place like interoffice memos. But it is an injustice to generalize about the professionals who inhabit the system. There are few people who come as close to the poor as those doctors, nurses, and hospital attendants who try to function compassionately and efficiently in spite of the system. For every medical person who has routinized himself to conform to the bureaucracy, there are others who give extra time, or, like some doctors in municipal hospitals, spend money out of their own pockets to improve their working conditions so that they can function better.

Unless he has gone through the system as a patient himself, the West Sider gets a very spotty visual picture of what is going on. He has seen the Knickerbocker and Metropolitan Hospital ambulances waiting outside a rooming house, and if he is curious enough he has watched the attendants bring out the patient—perhaps an old person in a state of starvation, who has been found in her room with a broken hip, or a female derelict who has been banging her head against iron railings He is also familiar with the green police wagon with its own emergency medical personnel, and he has at some time walked by the local Riverside Health Center, and assumed that here is a place where people can go for help.

Other work going on—that of the local team of public health nurses, for instance—is not so apparent. The daily activity of these nurses provides some interesting information about the health needs of young children and their families. One team member until recently was Helen Searchin, an attractive young woman with sturdy legs and a great supply of energy. To earn her Department of Health salary check she would give about 40 percent of her time to two elementary schools, P.S. 84 and P.S. 179, keeping the children's health records, trudging up and down tenement staircases in a ten-block area, and running back and forth to clinics in the Riverside Health Center and the Manhattan Health Center further downtown on Broadway. She and the other nurses on her team were also supposed to be available to anyone else in the district who had a health problem. In view of the quarter of a million people living in the health district, this assignment could only be theoretical.

Although public health nurses get higher pay than hospital nurses, most of them feel that their work load is "impossible," and eventually many of them, like Mrs. Searchin, leave for other jobs.* The situation is made worse by pressures from above. Supervisors will have a new program to be carried out, and the nurses are told to do it without regard to their current commitment, the result being that the nurses are forced to drop something else they have started.

The opening of school was the happiest event in Mrs. Searchin's year. During the first week of school registration at P.S. 84—"a wonderfully cooperative place"—she would get her first look at a whole crop of new arrivals, who would hang on to their mothers' hands and gaze back over their shoulders as much as they looked ahead. The children entering school usually met Mrs. Searchin in connection with a smallpox vaccination or a physical exam. She was a pleasant surprise for the newcomers, especially the Latin ones, who had never been in a New York school before. Being shepherded

---

* Mrs. Searchin recently took a job as a trainer of practical nurses under a federal program set by the Manpower Development Training Act.

about, examined, and admired let them know that here there were people who were quite serious about seeing that they didn't catch a cold or get a toothache.

Although immunization is not required by law, school authorites request that the child have certain inoculations if he is attending school. This is made easy because, first, the inoculations and the physicals can be performed by the school doctor without charge—as two-thirds of them are—unless the family prefers a private doctor. Secondly, teachers pass out forms to the kindergarten and first-grade parents which they are to fill out with the child's health history, including immunization record. At P.S. 84 Mrs. Searchin handled the distribution, collection, and examination of health forms for the second- to sixth-grade children. During registration week as many as a hundred parents would bring in their health forms to Mrs. Searchin. As soon as she got a look at the form, she had a fairly good idea of what her followup work will be. She might discover that a child was sleeping far too much, or "sitting six inches in front of the TV set" in which case she would explain to the parent that these might be symptoms of illness or eye trouble. A child with symptoms would be referred by Mrs. Searchin to a clinic at the Riverside Health Center, a local hospital clinic, or a private doctor.

A great deal of Mrs. Searchin's work was in educating parents about what they should do with a child who needed help. If she found that a child had a heart murmur, for instance, she saw that he was then referred to medical advice. The teachers cooperate, but Mrs. Searchin had a hard time with some parents, who did not understand that a child's whole routine must be watched and that it is just not enough to take him to the doctor. "They may dutifully take the child to a cardiac clinic for three years, but they will not realize the child shouldn't be running up and down long flights of stairs."

In the past, about 25 percent of the P.S. 84 children have had some visual difficulty. The school does not spend much time on dental care because there is a dental hygiene clinic in P.S. 66 on Eighty-ninth Street which handles all schools Mrs. Searchin served. The problem of nutrition, however, had to be gone into almost every time she visited a parent. If the child was thin or pale, Mrs. Searchin checked his health card, looked at the child's growth and weight gain and then went into his diet habits. Here there might be a "cultural" problem. In Puerto Rico the family's breakfast might be coffee, milk, and a roll, and the other meals might center around the bean and rice staples. Beans and rice in themselves are not a handicap if the parents add other nutritious food to them, but they are not solely sufficient. Mrs. Searchin liked to have the Puerto Rican families keep their old habits of eating because they would cooperate more quickly. However, she did have to work hard to impress upon the children and the parents the relationship between a child's getting dizzy or having a headache at 11:30 in the morning and the fact that he didn't have anything but coffee for breakfast.

The food at P.S. 84 is of good quality but at times the diet aides seem to concentrate on those children who bring back a full tray rather than the many others who do eat right. Mrs. Searchin felt the school rushed the children through their lunch; sitting down for ten or fifteen minutes and bolting one's food is not the way to have a meal, or to wean a child to new eating habits. A nutritionist in the health district works with the school in promoting a program to get the children to try new foods and then eat them at home too. The nurses keep an eye on this, although they do not themselves become involved in trying to change the children's food habits.

Newborn infants were another of Mrs. Searchin's responsibilities. She was supposed to keep track of babies living in the area who were born in the ward of Metropolitan Hospital. The hospital gives these babies' names to the well-baby clinic at the Riverside Health Center and Mrs. Searchin would chase down those parents who did not keep appointments at the center. The center's well-baby clinic works in collaboration with the Children's Health Center on Ninety-first Street and Columbus Avenue, a private agency which is part of what was formerly known as the New York Diet Kitchen. Mothers are asked to bring their babies to the well-baby clinic about four to six weeks after they are born. The child gets a complete physical, and the mother receives advice on how to feed the baby. During the first year, the mother brings the baby in every six weeks, and she is also given a physical exam herself, if the doctor thinks it is necessary. The nurse rather than the doctor may often be the first to recognize any problems because she has been the first to be in touch with the mother and is familiar with the family's social and emotional character.

When she first interviewed a new mother, Mrs. Searchin compiled a financial and social history of the family, which included such details as who worked in the family, how many people lived in the apartment, the number of rooms and the condition of the apartment, whether the baby had a crib, where it slept. "You open the door for the mother to say to you, 'I need help here,' or if she doesn't say it you begin to sense from the conversation where they need the help."

The center's well-baby clinic does not service anywhere near the number of babies who should be using it, because the center does not have the names of area babies born in voluntary hospitals, which do not participate in the well-baby clinic. Also, there are no health and hospital records of babies that have just arrived from Cuba or Puerto Rico, some of them only a month old. When Mrs. Searchin discovered one of these infants on her rounds, she would make a referral for the child, and if the parents didn't keep the first appointment she would set up another one for them. "We publicize the well-baby clinic as hard as we can, but some people from the Latin American countries never find out about it because they don't know people here who are using it." Most of the TB cases Mrs. Searchin and the center run across are adults. There are not many TB followups in school, although the Board of Education in March, 1964, announced a special program for wiping out the disease in children of school age.

Urban renewal makes life difficult. Houses are torn down, people are relocated and nurses are not kept informed by the Department of Relocation. Mrs. Searchin carefully selected the day's visits to TB and venereal-disease patients and mothers of newborn babies. After she decided on what calls to make first, she might make ten visits and find nobody; she might not even find the building. On the average, she was unable to locate about half the clients. The nurses have come to accept disappearing families in buildings and wrong addresses as part of the job. Efforts have been made by the Health Department to work out a plan with the Department of Relocation to locate "traces"—a trace being a family that has moved and has to be rediscovered.

The nurses have had no trouble being accepted by the families they visit. "Every door opens," says Aida Solomon, the health center's former head nurse. "Sometimes if a nurse is worried about a particular house, we send them in two at a time. It's been suggested that the girls carry whistles, but none of them have and it doesn't seem to have been necessary. The uniform and the nurse's bag are well enough known. We have felt all right even in the single-room-occupancy buildings. A man in one of these buildings climbed five flights to find someone for me. I don't think he was sober, but he said he would locate the people and he did."

The Riverside Health Center is the local outpost of the Department of Health, which serves as the home base of Mrs. Searchin and the other nurses on her team. The center is housed in an impressive yellow brick building next to a branch of the New York Public Library on 100th Street, and across the way from the 24th Precinct police station. The director of the health center is as reticent as the police chief about giving out information. He is a tall, reedy gentleman named Daniel O'Connell, who smokes thin cigars and gives the impression that any intimate details about the operations of his center and the health problems of the area it serves had better not be made public. A similar apprehension about interviews is also evident among some of his subordinates. One cannot interview anybody without "clearances" from a host of Dr. O'Connell's superiors in the city's health hierarchy. Even then there is usually an uninvited person present to chaperone the interview.

In view of all the clearances that have to be gotten, Dr. O'Connell's disclosures are something of a disappointment. He speaks enthusiastically about the opening of the health center in 1961 and says that the center is "busy" but provides neither data nor informed guesses as to the number of daily visits to the center's various clinics. For any statistics Dr. O'Connell suggests a consultation with the Department of Health headquarters downtown. If one begins the search for information downtown, however, the health commissioner's office will send the researcher to a Dr. Carl Erhard, who, placing the tips of his fingers against each other, says that the person who has the necessary information at his fingertips is Dr. O'Connell. If the researcher persists, he will eventually discover that the apex of the information triangle is back at Department of Health headquarters. Officials there will present history and statistics having to do with Dr. O'Connell's Riverside Health District with Dr. O'Connell listening.

Jointly planned by the city, St. Luke's (voluntary), and Sydenham (municipal) hospitals, the center opened in 1961. Several of its doctors were serving on the staffs of these hospitals. The center includes the well-baby station, an adult health maintenance clinic, which gives diagnostic services for patients twenty-one and over, a cardiac consultation clinic, a child health clinic, dental and eye-care clinics, a social hygiene clinic, and clinics for prenatal and post-partum care. The center also maintains various consulting services provided by other health agencies, and from time to time it has housed a community psychiatry clinic sponsored by St. Luke's hospital.

From the very beginning, Dr. O'Connell says, the center's lay public health advisory committee gave all these clinics "tremendous support" and did its best to acquaint the community with what the center offered. For instance, when the doctors at the center had difficulty finding parking space, Dr. O'Connell telephoned his committee, which made arrangements with the management of Park West Village, the nearby middle-income housing complex, for the doctors to use Park West's parking area. The center made a "strenuous effort" to become acquainted with the community. Local agencies were invited to have their representatives tour the center and hear panel discussions about services offered. As a result, it was hoped, the agencies would encourage their clients to use the center. Dr. O'Connell says the tours were one way of "reaching the unreachables."

To what extent the center has "reached the unreachables" is difficult to say in view of Dr. O'Connell's unwillingness to discuss specifics. Some of the center's staff contradict Dr. O'Connell and say the center is not used properly. Among the public health officials who agree with them is the Commissioner of Health himself. One thing that strikes the eye of the visitor is that the big new building seems rather empty much of the time, a strange situation in an area where there is so much sickness. The explanation for this seems to be that the center staff does not treat patients; its program is "preventive"; the result is that many of the poor people in the area, who go to a doctor only when they are already sick, don't come to the center.

The health center does offer one service which until recently was not provided elsewhere in the city's health districts: an adolescent health clinic.* The director of the clinic is a young woman who is somewhat more candid than Dr. O'Connell. She is Dr. Ruth Waldman de Camacho, the American-born wife of a Cuban lawyer, both of

* In early 1965 the Department of Health opened up a second adolescent health clinic in the same district. The decision has been questioned by some doctors, who feel it would have been more sensible to enlarge the already existing facilities at Riverside, or to found an adolescent clinic in another health district.

them refugees from Castro. Dr. Waldman is one of the few doctors in the area who speak Spanish (she also speaks four other languages). Her European training is an asset with Puerto Ricans in the area, who seem to be somewhat more impressed with European than American physicians.

Dr. Waldman's experience with Puerto Ricans as a staff member of Dr. Beatrice Berle's East Harlem project* has been useful to the West Side, and the fact that an adolescent health clinic exists at Riverside Health Center is in large part due to her personal interest in such a project. Mrs. Searchin talks about small children, Dr. Waldman talks about teen-agers. Although there is a great deal of civic exasperation about adolescents and their physical and emotional problems, New York City hospitals as a whole, and the city's Department of Health in particular, pay very little attention to them as a group—an attitude fairly typical of city health services in United States cities.† Besides Dr. Waldman's, the only other adolescent health clinics in New York City in 1964 were in private hospitals, and the programs were generally limited to middle-class white children.

The Riverside Health Center's adolescent clinic serves 425 children on an ongoing basis, with its care terminating only if a child dies, moves out of the area, goes into the service, or reaches twenty-one. Most of the children are from low socio-economic backgrounds. About 40 percent of them have severe mental problems requiring more than case counseling, and 60 percent have physical problems. Dr. Waldman, who is an attending physician in pediatrics at New York Hospital's Cornell Medical Center and is also affiliated with St. Luke's, spends two afternoons a week in the clinic. She outlines the plight of the teen-ager:

"When the children get to be twelve, pediatrics clinics don't want them, yet until they're eighteen or nineteen no other clinic has an adequate program for them. The youngsters who have a problem

---

* For a description of Dr. Berle's local clinic for a selected group of East Harlem patients, see *Eighty Puerto Rican Families,* by Beatrice Berle, Columbia University Press, 1955.

† An exception is Philadelphia, where Major James Tate has established a program for adolescents in the heart of the city's Negro area. The adolescent clinic provides general medical examinations, complete dental and psychiatric care. The program is conducted in cooperation with the Philadelphia Department of Welfare. Adolescent health programs have also been going on for several years in Boston, under Dr. Roswell Gallagher, and in Oakland under Dr. Arthur Roth.

usually go to an emergency room and ordinarily because they have acne, finger cuts, colds, or broken bones they get treatment, but nobody has the time to talk to them. This just doesn't do the trick. You cannot separate the physical, social, and emotional problems of an adolescent. If he has bad skin, or he is too short or too fat, these problems lead to other difficulties. They don't know where to go for health care and advice. In the hospital ward a child may be placed in a bed next to a seventy-year-old patient dying of cancer. The pediatric ward usually doesn't accept a girl after her first period at eleven or twelve, and then she is put in with women of all ages. The boys go into wards when they are thirteen or fourteen. The children in the pediatrics clinics get a great deal more care than the adolescents and the mother is more apt to bring a younger child in. The adolescent doesn't want to come and the mother cannot force him to come in the way she can a younger child.

"So many of our adolescents have no idea about anything as far as health goes, and this includes young married girls. How can a boy do well in school if he can't see, can't hear, has parasites, can't even sit still in his chair? How can we know if the child has parasites by just listening to his chest or looking down his throat in a routine physical such as they get at school? You have to have certain laboratory facilities."

Dr. Waldman feels that many of the illnesses and problems of adolescents could be cleared up if there was a comprehensive program for them. The program could handle adolescent ailments which become chronic in later life, such as hypertension and thyroid and endocrine troubles, also visual difficulties and parasitic infections. The adolescents need a much better program of preventive medicine in both physical and mental health. "The only kids who get treatment are the ones who are already screaming out loud, obviously in such need of help that they will disrupt the school or the community if they don't get it. I mean the addicts, the dropouts, the youngsters who have already committed crimes or have become acute disciplinary problems. We need to help children who haven't yet broken out with something, the kid who isn't using heroin yet but will if he isn't stopped. When a kid begins to feel he wants to die, we should be ready to head him off, not wait until after he's shot himself."

The Puerto Rican youngsters remain somewhat of a mystery emotionally, Dr. Waldman says, because "we have not developed adequate ways of learning about their intelligence or their emotional problems. The IQ tests we have used on Latins are misleading because they are culture-bound, as are the personality tests. Judged by these tests some Latins will appear to be schizophrenic when they are not so at all. The Minnesota Multiphasic Personality Inventory Test, once used at the center to screen adults and children, is full of questions which had no meaning at all to a Puerto Rican—even translated into Spanish they would be meaningless. What is the point of asking a Spanish child about *Alice in Wonderland?* If the test asked about 'Little Red Riding Hood' this might be different; the Spanish children have all heard the story of *'Capucita Roja.'* "

The family approach is the most effective way to deal with health problems, Dr. Waldman believes. To do this requires a neighborhood health center which will give treatments as well as provide examinations and health services.* The staff of the neighborhood center should include a pediatrician, gynecologist, obstetrician, internist, psychologist, psychiatrist, social workers, and some of these staff people would have to speak Spanish. Her suggestion is reminiscent of proposals her former colleague, Dr. Berle, made after her clinic experience in East Harlem.

"As things go now, Mama goes to Mount Sinai, Papa goes to Bellevue, Jimmy goes to St. Luke's, and nobody knows the health pattern of the whole family or what's going on," Dr. Waldman says. "A family treatment center would cut out the enormous waste of time spent on long trips to distant hospitals. The neighborhood center should be more candid with the patients about their health problems, tell them what's the matter. Everybody is so sensitive. In Cuba there isn't this mystery about illness. Most Cuban patients are told exactly

* One of the area's private experiments in community health facilities is the Metropolitan Health Center at 336 Central Park West, formed in 1961 by several psychiatrists, psychologists, therapists, and social workers who wanted to provide treatment for mentally ill people among lower-income groups. The group decided to locate on the West Side because they felt it was in a medical sense a "lost community" where there were many low-income people who were not poor enough to use city clinics but were too poor to afford regular private psychiatric care.

Cost of a treatment at the center runs from $1 to $9 depending on the financial status of the client, a fee scale possible because almost all of the fifty persons on the medical staff of the center work without pay. Financial support is contributed by private citizens. The center, licensed by the State Board of Mental Hygiene as a psychiatric clinic, is under the direction of the State Board of Welfare. It serves 125 patients and has made a special effort to reach Puerto Ricans: some of its staff do psychological work in Spanish.

what they've got, within limits. Cubans talk about their hypertension. The local treatment center will have to pay its staff if it's going to do the job. Good physicians won't give their time for a low salary, no matter what anyone says. The center should be affiliated with a hospital which could handle patients in an emergency, provide lab facilities, specialty care, and major medical or surgical care. The center should be run both for indigent patients and for some middle-income people—adolescents from different groups can learn something from each other."

If one is to judge from the difficulties Dr. Waldman has had in generating enthusiasm for her clinic among some high city health officials, it does not seem likely that many adolescent health clinics will be adopted as part of the city's regular health services in the near future. In part, it is probable that if she left the clinic the adolescent clinic would be abandoned or become a program on paper. Opposition within the department to her project seems to be one more example of what an official of the New York Community Council calls the "ghastly and oppressive atmosphere of public health bureaucracies in big cities all over America."

One cannot think very much about public health in the Area without being impressed rather forcibly by certain facts. One fact is the enormous burden placed on the "field" people like Mrs. Searchin. Another fact is the persistence of archaic public health procedures in many of the city's public and private health institutions. There is the state of isolation in which the inhabitant of the medical establishment works, and there is the lack of a plan for using even what health facilities are at hand, with the result that health care is either inaccessible to the indigent people of the Area, or is available in such an irregular way as to be relatively ineffective.

This lack of planning in the city's huge medical establishment—public and private—is at least as serious a problem as the money and personnel shortages with which it has been afflicted. On one hand, the Department of Health provides children with well-baby clinics and school programs, but it takes no responsibility for the sick child. On the other hand, the hospitals' primary interest is in the sick child. There is very little relationship between what is done for the well child and what is being done for the sick one, and the problem of getting information back and forth is insurmountable.

In addition to its failures with children, the Department of Health has also not coped effectively with the health needs of the elderly, although it has been tightening up on the dismal practices of private nursing homes and proprietary hospitals. Whether or not the passage of Medicare legislation will cause the department to reorganize itself is a question: it sometimes seems as if the bureaucracy is so paralyzed that it cannot respond even to fundamental changes in public policy and attitude. Even with Medicare, treatment of the ailments of the aged is not enough. Attention must also be given to those economic and social difficulties that affect the health. The health department's responsibility is limited mainly to diagnostic tests, and while screening for glaucoma or diabetes is, of course, necessary, the elderly need a total, comprehensive program of care where they can get the preventive program and treatment in one package.

Medicare, in other words, appears to be only the beginning of a program that may eventually lead to personal health services available to all regardless of income. These should cover the entire range of health needs: prevention, diagnosis, treatment, rehabilitation. In such a system every person would have a personal physician, with responsibility for insuring continuity of care, and all other medical people working with the patient would work in relation to this personal physician, so that the patient could have the full benefit of services of a high scientific quality and of sufficient quantity.

What are the blocks to providing personal health services to everyone? They are not simply a lack of adequate personnel, clinics, money, health insurance. The biggest obstacle may be poor organization and poor leadership. Health services should be planned on a community basis. The resistance against planning on a community basis comes from the medical profession itself, where the thinking reflects the attitudes of physicians in private practice whose concepts of private practice have not changed in half a century. Such concepts are a roadblock now, given the tremendous range and complexity of services which should be provided today.

Yet the blame for the present situation cannot be laid only on the doorsteps of the medical profession. Society has permitted the profession to be backward, accepting the views of medical people who have very human limitations, some of which grow out of their political conservatism and their loyalty to their colleagues. Society has deferred to the doctors' attitude that doctors are the only ones who know the answers because the problem of health care is a technical matter. But the creation of satisfactory health services is not primarily a technical problem; it is a question of how much communities will pay for such services, what type of health insurance is needed, how all the factors are put together. The answers to the social, political, and economic questions are far more important for the future of health services than the scientific and technical answers. And whether it wants to or not the public will have to make the basic decisions. If it does nothing, this in itself is a decision. There is some evidence in New York City that society can push the medical profession in the direction of social service. HIP (Health Insurance Plan) and the union projects run by the teamsters and the hotel workers in collaboration with Flower Fifth Avenue and Montefiore hospitals are examples. It is not enough to blame the bureaucrats. In fact, an informed citizenry would have received support at the top from able commissioners such as Dr. James and Dr. Trussell, but as things turned out much of the value of their ideas was lost or diluted because of the antiquated system in which they—and the Mrs. Searchins and Dr. Waldmans—were forced to operate. The communities themselves must do some experimenting and thinking on the neighborhood level.

None of these views are particularly new, and they are not confined to laymen on the West Side. Many doctors and people in the private agencies have been expressing similar sentiments for years. Only in contrast to established practices do their suggestions seem somewhat revolutionary. One of the most eloquent of these local people was Dr. Walter Lear, who was at one time chairman of the public health committee of the New York Community Council.

Lear always objected very much to what he called the "traditional approach of looking at the individual clinical problems in a neighborhood." He thought there was no reason why planning should be any more of a dirty word in dealing with community health problems that it has been in planning urban renewal and housing.

"Every time you suggest planning in the public health field, you get the reaction that this is 'socialized medicine, this is a monolithic health service,' " he said. "Well, planning and private enterprise are going to have to coexist someday in medicine. This doesn't mean the community should leave everything up to the government. Perhaps it ought to take some responsibility for filling in gaps in local medical services and for figuring out ways of cutting unnecessary expense. The government agencies don't understand what the neighborhood's problems are. The answer has to be developed jointly by community leadership in cooperation with official agencies. The community leadership and city agencies should exchange research and information. Tentative guesses would have to be made on the needs of the population for physicians, hospital beds, nurses, physical therapists, etc.

"The community should be treated as a whole," Lear said. "It is wrong to make distinctions on the basis of economic background from a health point of view. People made to feel that they are getting charity medicine are much more reluctant to take it and their health suffers, as does the community's. The independent practitioner must be made part of the team without completely revolutionizing his whole economics. You can leave the private practitioner in private practice and still do a lot around him. You wouldn't get very far if you tried to put the private practitioner on a team as it operates now in mental health clinics or rehabilitation clinics."

Dr. Lear never seemed to get very far with his recommendations while he was on the West Side, but somebody must have been listening, because recently he was appointed Deputy Commissioner of Public Health of Philadelphia. Perhaps he will have better luck in that city.

MONEY AND SYMPATHY

FOR THOSE WHO ARE CURIOUS TO KNOW ON WHAT level of opulence the average welfare family lives, it may be instructive to look at the budget on which Mrs. Clarissa Stack, a public-welfare client, supports herself and five children. For more than two years the family has occupied a one-room apartment on West 105th Street, an illegal accommodation a block away from Area Services North, a city office which is supposed to see that housing, occupancy, and health codes are enforced. The $110-a-month rent is paid by the Department of Welfare. For food and clothing and miscellaneous expenses Mrs. Stack receives $50 a week. Of this, $1.22 per day is for the mother's food, with slightly smaller amounts assigned for each child. The remainder of the weekly allowance is for the family's clothing and "incidentals," such as insecticides to kill cockroaches.

The past, present, and future of West Siders like Mrs. Stack and her children are locked up in the files of the Amsterdam Welfare Center, a large unlovely glass-and-aluminum building on Eighth Avenue and Thirtieth Street, just around the corner from a row of Turkish and Egyptian belly-dance night clubs. Under the direction of the Department of Welfare in New York City, the center's three hundred employees attempt to work out a limited version of salvation for approximately eighteen thousand clients who live between West Tenth and West Ninety-seventh Street. The clients are dependent children and their parents, elderly people who are indigent, single men who are unemployed, the blind and disabled, and former and prospective mental patients who cannot find work. The army that converges on the intake office to communicate its despair and ask for financial assistance includes several hundred drug addicts. The Amsterdam Center is one of twenty-two city welfare centers which together disburse approximately $300 million to nearly half a million people, more than half of them dependent children. Amsterdam itself, with an intake office staffed by fifteen interviewers interviewing claimants twenty-four hours a day, pays out around $10 million annually. And, like public assistance offices in cities and towns all over the United States, Amsterdam's clientele is growing rapidly by the month.*

Traffic in and out of the center is heavy, and moves slowly. Downstairs, welfare clients unable to reach their case worker by telephone may wait for one, two, or three hours for him to come down and see them, sometimes only to find out there is nothing the case worker can do for them in the first place. Two lethargic elevators, whose pace in a private office building would be catastrophic, add to the congestion. At the welfare center, where time seems to stand still, not a great deal is lost. Clients have little to do but wait.

The department case workers and their supervisors have their desks, eleven rows of them, on the fourth floor in an immense room that looks like the editorial office of a large but unsuccessful daily newspaper. On one desk facing the elevators are three telephones for the use of the entire staff, about fifty of whom will usually be at their desks at one time. Despite forty-five filing cabinets on the floor, each desk is stacked with dog-eared papers which, like the clients they represent, have been passed back and forth several dozen times. The administration of welfare is the administration of paper. It may take twenty-four separate sheets, typed and signed and countersigned, to process one application for assistance.

The history of the New York City welfare program and the center itself goes back to the days of the depression when President Franklin Roosevelt decided that the United States government was going to undertake a massive new program of assistance to families suffering

* From 1954 to 1964, while U.S. population increased 18 percent, from 162 to 192 million, the number of people on relief increased 42 percent, from 5.5 to 7.8 million. While welfare rolls increased almost 100 percent in such cities as San Francisco, Cleveland, and Chicago during this period, the rise was even greater in some suburban areas. The *Wall Street Journal* in January 8, 1965, reported that Nassau County, which embraces many of New York City's wealthiest suburbs, and a few of its slums, had 18,000 relief recipients as compared to 7,600 in 1960, even though the county's population had increased only 7 percent.

from unemployment. The program begun under Roosevelt took a second major leap in the administration of another Democratic President three decades later. Senator John F. Kennedy's trip to West Virginia during his primary campaign for the Presidency in 1960 gave him his first, shocking look at what unemployment had done to the men, women, and children of the area, most of whom had nowhere to turn for relief. When Senator Kennedy became President one of his most important objectives was to work out a new concept of welfare based on the rationale of the existing Federal Aid to Dependent Children program. He reasoned that if the government had a responsibility to take care of children abandoned by their parents, it also could not ignore children who, although not abandoned, were being crippled or destroyed by poverty. Congress's passage in 1962 of a temporary Aid to Dependent Children Act, enabling destitute families to receive federal aid, became the whole foundation of the practice of matching city and federal contributions for the support of the ADC program—in which category fall most of New York City's cases.

The administrator of the Amsterdam Welfare Center is Mrs. Lillian Zerwick, a substantial lady in her fifties with graying hair cut in bangs across a pleasant, responsive face. When she talks about welfare, it is quickly apparent that she is an especially confirmed New Dealer. The flavor of her philosophy and her manner of expression are reminiscent of such old New York "radicals," now grown gentler with time, as David Dubinsky of the International Ladies Garment Workers Union and Alex Rose of the Hatters' Union. Although she asks that any interview with her be approved first by the commissioner, Mrs. Zerwick does not have the constitutionally suspicious temperament which seems to be a personality requirement of welfare supervisors in such places as Newburgh, New York, or Sandusky, Ohio, where the main purpose of a welfare administration is to spot "fakers" and pare the welfare rolls to a minimum. In the Amsterdam Center, the welfare staff says it has a responsibility not only to give aid where needed but to rehabilitate the recipients wherever possible—at least this is the goal expressed.

The Amsterdam Center's role as a disbursing agency is hardly ever mentioned by welfare officials. They prefer to talk about objectives. Mrs. Zerwick says the relief program is "family centered"; that is, its aim is to foster the normal growth and development of the family.

Accordingly, the center has set itself four tasks: (1) to "prevent the tendency" to welfare, (2) to provide assistance when needed, (3) to rehabilitate the recipients, and (4) to contribute to the growth and development of the person as an individual. The new welfare concept, Mrs. Zerwick says, is a far cry from the justification for handouts which the "beer-drinking politicians of the twenties gave" when they talked about the terrible plight of widows and orphans.

What does the "family-centered approach" entail? "We look at a case diagnostically in terms of the strengths that lie in a situation and what we can encourage," Mrs. Zerwick declares. "We have totally abandoned moral judgments. Take for example a case of a family where you have one mother and anywhere from one to six fathers. A social, psychological, economic diagnosis of the family is required. We ask ourselves what is the alternative to refusing to support such a family—if we don't keep this family going what is available for the placement of the children elsewhere? If we can fortify and support the parent figure, the child should stay with the parent. We can keep the child out of an institution if we can maintain the parent figure. However, in some instances after interviews and observation we have to conclude that the mother of several children is an unfit person. Then, no matter how much we would like to keep the mother with her child, we have to take the final alternative and place the child somewhere else. In declaring a person unfit we utilize such information about her behavior as the fact that the children are not taken for their polio shots or sent to school or fed properly, alcoholism in the parent, cruelty, etc. We consider all the evidence of the parent's inability to accept responsibility for the education, health, and guidance of the children. In consultation with the school, we look out for indications that the children lack clothes despite welfare grants for clothes, milk, and nutrition. We look for medically-established rashes on bodies that have to do with unsanitation in the homes."

The department views sexual promiscuity in a "very individualized" way. "Obviously a mother with six children and six fathers is sleeping around. If we are impressed with the way she runs the home we try to help her understand her children and her right to claim legal maternity. We try to involve the father in paternal responsibility, and in some cases we have been able to bring the father out of hiding. We have a job to mend the family and we have done it in many cases, or helped it along the way." Recent federal legislation allowing the father to earn money in certain amounts without disqualifying the family for public assistance will help mothers.

In a recent case, when the department understood what was needed to bring the father back to his family, it moved quickly. The family had had an application in for public housing for three years. The department lifted it out of the files and got them an apartment in a new project. It also spent several hundred dollars for furniture, including bunk beds, and clothing. The department let the father know that it would help him make the effort. If one prefers to use the word, the department's action amounted to a "handout." The important question was, What was the effect of the "handout"? Did it weaken the man and increase his sense of dependency? Apparently not. The man has been with his family ever since and the department has been able to cut the family's welfare allowance because the man's income has entered the family budget and the family has become a stable part of the community. The man still must face the fact that automation will threaten him for the rest of his life, and that even if he keeps his factory job there is no prospect of his increasing his income or moving to a better job. What sort of an incentive can such a man have? In this case, the welfare department found just one—the passion to do what he can for his family.

When the department has the time to concentrate on an individual case, it does a thorough job and can put its theories into something like effective practice. Mrs. Zerwick will call in the client's investigator, her unit and case supervisors, and perhaps one or more representatives of private agencies which she would like to involve in the case. The investigator gives a detailed economic, social, and medical history of the client, and then there may be an hour or so of discussion to decide what steps have to be taken. However, the fact that preparation for such case conferences and the followup may take a hundred or so hours from six or seven people means that very few cases get this sort of attention. The great bulk of clients are simply "processed"; if their allowance is approved their status is checked every few months by their investigator.

One of the most noticeable characteristics about the bureaucracy which processes the welfare client is the amount of hostile activity that takes place among investigators, unit supervisors, and case supervisors. There is nothing personal about this pulling and hauling; it is a matter of conflicting priorities. The administrator, concerned with properly classifying cases in order to get the maximum reimbursement from the city and federal governments, runs head-on into the investigator who wants to cut the red tape and get his client help quickly. The federal categories, such as Aid to the Disabled, Aid to Dependent Children, and Aid to the Aged, receive a higher rate of reimbursement from the federal government than others, so the administration does everything it can to place cases in these categories whenever possible. The overburdened welfare investigator is not so interested in categories and he considers the flood of regulations and forms as a drag that reduces his efficiency by 50 to 100 percent.

Even those administrators who are strictest about compliance with the catalogue of regulations (the "book") admit that many of the regulations are superfluous and unenforceable but insist that there must be some show of complying with them because the general public assumes that welfare programs are more prone to fraud and mismanagement than any other activity in government. The department's complicated system of accounting is a device to assure the public that people on various administrative rungs of the federal welfare ladder can spy on their subordinates. The result of this elaborate system of internal security is that a dollar's worth of time is spent to prevent a nickel from being misspent. Even then nobody can really tell where the nickel went. The system does not make the employee more accountable; rather, it encourages evasions and falsification.

One might begin at the bottom of the departmental pyramid with the person who deals directly with the client, to get an idea of what some of these evasions are. An investigator with experience on the upper West Side declares:

"If the investigator tries to stick exactly to what the book (the regulations) says, he can spend one day on each case and cover five cases in a week when he has a case load of eighty, ninety, or a hundred. You start cutting corners after a while. Everybody does. The question is who's got the guts to cut what corners? People forge signatures. It happens all the time. My supervisor showed me how to forge them, by holding a signature up to the light and tracing it. Am I going to go out and make a field visit to get the client to sign a medical authorization? He won't even know what the hell he is signing anyway. If I happen to see him, I will ask him to sign it;

otherwise, getting him to sign it takes time away that I could be using to get food, clothing, and shelter for someone. So, okay, I forge the signature, I violate the book, I violate it in a hell of a lot of other ways, every time I need to do it. You do your job and fight your supervisor when you are supposed to and you are not going to get a bad reputation. You'll get a good reputation, and when it comes time to get referrals to other agencies for jobs and scholarships you will be getting them.

"There is a whole lingo you have to learn, a whole way of expressing things so that you can get something moving. For instance you don't say you made a telephone call when you write out a report. You say you held a 'telephone conference' because that is the way you deal with government. You always have to give your justification in the right government language. It can never be that you know something and the supervisor knows it, and your signature counts for something. There has always got to be the justification, so if anybody higher up asks the question you can stand up and say, 'Kill me, shoot me if you think I'm evil, but everything is in order right there on the papers, see.' The main thing is to justify, to get rid of your guilt feelings about breaking the rules."

Investigators feel that one of the department's main problems is that nobody in the department is willing to take responsibility for decisions. This would seem to be perfectly natural in an agency where the inordinate emphasis on procedure and paperwork diffuses authority or often prevents any one person from making a decision even if he is inclined to do so. In the end the paper blockade loses its effectiveness anyhow. A new case worker may try to follow to the letter every regulation and every order she gets from her unit supervisor. After a while she gets rid of some of these apprehensions, and eventually she learns she can get away with practically everything.

At the bottom of the department's pecking order is, obviously, the client. Above him is the investigator, then the investigator's unit supervisor. According to federal regulations the unit supervisor is supposed to have five investigators under her, though in practice the number is usually six. Since the unit supervisor has to sign every form filled out by her investigators, she spends most of her time pursuing the investigator to make sure he has done what he is supposed to do. Once she has gotten to know the investigator and make a judgment of his reliability, she may relax a little, even to the point of allowing him to sign her name to forms, but until then she spends most of her time worrying and hounding him. In her turn the unit supervisor is vulnerable to the case supervisor, who evaluates her work and, since the case supervisors have been in the agency for many years, they usually are quite capable of terrorizing the unit supervisor if they wish to do so—and often they wish to do so. Because the case supervisors are near the top of the ladder and have presumably perfected all the methods of detecting faulty procedures, the investigators consider them the "tough ones" in the department, the ones who seem to know exactly what they are doing and what questions to ask.

Yet there is no freedom from fear, even at the top. An experienced investigator says the case supervisor is tough because she is "usually frightened and on the defensive herself." One reason for this insecurity, she says, is that many of the case supervisors are old-timers who have survived and advanced by taking tests but who have not adjusted to the new philosophy of welfare and who look at things in moralistic terms even though they don't moralize when discussing a case. The attitude sets them apart from their colleagues and often produces a certain defensiveness.

The investigator is one reason the welfare establishment has a markedly different character from other city agencies. A majority of the investigators seem to have begun with a desire for social service even if they have not had very much training. Professional social workers are rarely found in welfare on the investigator level; the demand far exceeds the supply. While a majority of investigators have a college degree, they may never have taken a sociology course and their A. B. may have been earned in basket weaving. Nevertheless, they qualify so long as they have a degree from an accredited college. Only about a fifth of the department's investigating staff has had any training in psychology or sociology.

Many of the investigators are southern Negroes, some of them teachers who come North and into welfare work because they consider it a semiprofessional occupation where they can earn more money than they did in an Alabama or Georgia schoolhouse. These young Negroes provide a stable factor in the department because they show more tendency to stick it out in a situation where the total case worker turnover runs around 60 percent a year.

The salary levels of the department compare favorably with those in teaching, but they are not attractive enough to fill the department's need. After the two welfare workers' unions* ended a strike of several days early in 1965, the department raised a social service trainee's starting salary to $5,750 and a welfare investigator's to $6,050. In the department there is a common saying that there are four types of case workers: the type that wants to do something, the type that doesn't know what he wants to do, the type that can't do anything else, and the type that is putting in his time until he can get something better. Very often the most capable investigators will not stay in the so-called "line" function in welfare but will seek scholarships or accept work in other agencies where the job, at least from a distance, seems to be more productive. Some of the people who "stick" are invaluable because of their experience and the fact that they have survived the early disillusionment; others simply get used to the system and process cases like a piece of machinery. "We've automated welfare by using automatic people," an investigator observes.

The unpredictable impact that investigators of such different capacities and intentions have on their clients bothers quite a few people. As one investigator puts it, "The main question is, who do you have going out there talking to people—a guy or a girl who comes from the middle class with sets of values that way down deep in their guts they haven't worked out, or somebody who's thinking about the client and not himself?"

An investigator, in accordance with statute, manages to see a client with children on home relief only once every three months or so. Such visits ordinarily have the perfunctory quality of an annual automobile inspection, and how they can be expected to penetrate the truth about a family crisis is a question the department people would rather not talk about. Everyone knows the answers, or rather, knows that there are no answers. The sensible investigator will not try to make a family feel that its fate rests in the palm of his hand. He will give them his telephone number, perhaps, in case of emergency, but he has few illusions that he can help them improve their lives.

The investigator's limbo is sometimes as complete as that of his clients. He works the street and his buildings alone. Formal preparation and the department's directives give few answers to the indi-

---

* The Social Service Employees Union (independent) and Local 371, American Federation of State, County and Municipal Employees (AFL-CIO).

vidual questions with which he has to deal every day. The process of discovering how to operate is somewhat like tracking an animal in the forest or sniffing the wind. "You never have the opportunity to go out with anyone wise and watch him; all you really know is yourself," an investigator says. "You catch glimmers of what other people do, or your clients tell you, they comment on other people. You can catch a lot by reading the previous case records. If an investigator has been very hostile and uncaring to the client, that will show on the records. If he has been a sensitive person that will also show." There are clues around, he says, if you can read them and understand the strange language in which they are written.

Some knowledge of psychology, pathology, social science, counseling, investigative techniques, and the art of making referrals would all seem to be major requirements for a welfare investigator's preparation. Yet domestic emergencies, the breakdown of family arrangements, and paperwork take up so much of the case worker's time that even if he had the proper training, which he doesn't, it would be largely superfluous. Over and over, the client's basic problems are ones over which the Department of Welfare has very little control. He is abominably housed. He is unemployed, his family is broken, he is sick.* The shortage of low-income housing and widespread discrimination by landlords against welfare families, particularly if they are Negro or Puerto Rican (in the urban renewal area half the case loads are Spanish and a quarter are Negro) has forced the department into a position of being the single largest subsidizers of the city's slums.

Some case workers feel it is foolhardy to encourage their clients to look for better housing, on the theory that they will fail if they do and the failure will undermine the client's confidence in the investigator who gave them the false hopes. One investigator reports that in spite of having written scores of letters and having made hundreds of phone calls, he has managed to get only three families into public housing in three and a half years. Now he confines himself to dealing with smaller problems which he thinks he has some chance of solving. He feels most of his work is meaningless so long as his clients are forced to live in conditions that are breeding grounds for disease and discouragement.

* In one recent study, 67 percent of public welfare clients surveyed were suffering from known or suspected psychological disorders. *Survey of Mental Health Problems in Social Agency Caseloads*, by Violet G. Bemmels, American Journal of Psychiatry, pps. 136–147, Vol. 121, No. 2, August, 1964.

The enterprising client who does succeed in locating a decent apartment must have an experienced case worker who will stand on his head, if need be, to get the client into the apartment; otherwise the battle is lost. The case worker must figure out a way, either by subterfuge or by direct approach, of getting the landlord to accept the client. He must then thread his way through a labyrinth of regulations and forms which will satisfy all of his department superiors, especially the case supervisor.

"The safest thing to do is fail," an investigator says. "If you don't do anything, at least you can't make matters any worse." Take the case of "this woman sitting downstairs, with three children. She is living in a shabby furnished room, she's desperate, she's gone out and found a new place. Now she is depending on you to get her the rent, the security deposit, and the money for furniture. This is the biggest crisis of her life. She has done what you asked her to do, she has looked in the papers, she's asked her friends, she's walked up and down stairs and finally located a place. Now you have to get approval from the people above you in the department. The next thing you know, you just have to face that woman and tell her, sorry, I couldn't explain where the father of your children is, or something like that, which at the moment is pretty irrelevant. There is no way you can interpret this to that woman. It destroys her and it destroys a case worker's confidence in himself."

The investigator says he has learned how to "deliver" if he makes a commitment to help a client. "If my client finds a good apartment, I can get it for him. I can say that because I know how to twist and turn and put what is necessary in the records, whether it is true or not, to get that apartment." The investigator admits that both he and the client must be able to cheat if they are to prevail over red tape and prejudiced landlords.

The investigator compares the welfare client to the man who has been in jail and is looking for a job. Someone has to lie for him too. "It's understood among all the agencies that deal with these people that the agency should not say that the person has been in prison or in a mental hospital. The trouble is that on a lot of jobs the truth comes out and the person is fired. The ex-convict is in a terrible quandary. Should he tell the truth and trust that perhaps it will be understood and he won't be stigmatized for life? More likely he should not tell the truth because nobody will trust him if he does."

The gap between the department's official hopes and its activities was apparent in the West Side urban renewal area. The department made a special effort there. Instead of giving investigators cases scattered all over the welfare district, the usual practice, the center assigned a special six-man unit to deal with the urban renewal area, and set a limit of forty-five cases per investigator as against the seventy-five which seems to prevail in other parts of the city. The forty-five case load was never realized. One investigator had seventy of his own cases and several more uncovered ones originally assigned to other workers. The situation was rather typical. The urban renewal unit's problems were further complicated by the difficulty of predicting the size of the case loads from week to week. Sizes of case loads to some extent depended on the type of buildings assigned. An investigator dealing with a rooming house was responsible for everyone moving into it, which meant an abnormally high turnover of clients, since the people were constantly checking in and out of the rooming houses.

One way some investigators controlled the situation and cut down on their burden was to "close" cases, that is, to drop a client from the welfare rolls. One particular investigator in the urban renewal area kept his case load at fifty because he made life difficult for his clients and closed cases at a moment's notice. Another investigator who was reluctant to close out cases had his case load build up to sixty-eight in addition to uncovered cases of another worker. While a "closed-out" client can reapply for welfare within thirty days, he will usually go somewhere else in the city or move in with relatives and reapply in another area. Thus the case worker who closes out will be freed of the client. A client who has been closed out is not anxious to reassume a relationship with the unsympathetic investigator who first cut him off. The personality of the case worker can be a life-and-death matter for a welfare client.

One investigator in the urban renewal welfare unit was Harrison Blackwell, a young Negro graduate of South Carolina State University. With a case load of fifty-one he had just about enough time to make his statutory visits, see that his clients got their checks, and take care of special needs such as large clothing items and dental and eye appointments. He also had to study a number of "pending" cases to establish the eligibility of the applicant and classify the case as requiring changed living arrangements, special health care, or merely food, clothing, and shelter.

Many of Blackwell's families resisted him, although they often appeared to be friendly. He felt that even under the best of circumstances his visits were a strain on both parties.

"If I just happened to drop in on a client, consternation reigned supreme—this was out of context, I was not supposed to be there, I was not due for another month." Blackwell was willing to put up with a certain amount of such consternation in the interest of getting at the truth, and although the department has regular forms that could be sent out in advance of a visit he preferred to come unannounced even if he had to make two or three attempts to see the client. Another block in communicating with a client was that investigators changed so often that clients saw no point in being candid with any of them, especially if it had to do with a woman client's relationship to a man outside the family.

However, Blackwell did have some rewarding experiences. He used to spend one day a week in the office of the West Side Area Services South, an office charged with the attack on a West Eighty-third Street building in which Blackwell had twenty-five clients. Area Services set a whole fleet of inspectors loose on the building. After a cellar-to-roof inspection they found 185 violations. Area Services then got in touch with the owner, who had leased the house to a management firm which had totally neglected the building for over a year and a half. When the owner walked into the building he was shocked by what he saw and took the lessee to court and broke the lease, paying him several thousand dollars to vacate it. Then the landlord completely renovated the place and hired a couple to take good care of it. All the 185 violations were removed.

Thus the Eighty-third Street house was renovated. What about the rehabilitation of human beings the department talks about? "After you read the initial entry in a case study you might as well not have bothered to read reports on following visits," Blackwell says. "Subsequent reports were almost invariably the same; the resources would have changed, the status of the relatives would not have changed. You could put down a report on a new visit on six inches of paper." Nobody ever changed position in the family portraits of Blackwell's clients.

One does not have to be a detective to discover the shortcomings of the Department of Welfare. They are many and they are obvious.

The main point worth making is that the department's philosophy has little relationship to what it is doing. Welfare in New York City, despite a splendid rationale, is chiefly a disbursement of monies that enables the very poor to subsist in a state of total subjection which eventually becomes permanent. It is quite impossible to find an experienced investigator who feels that, except in isolated cases, the program is "preventing the tendency" to welfare or is able to "rehabilitate" the clients. The investigator's function is to establish the eligibility of the applicant for assistance.

To make such a charge is not to say that welfare administrators or investigators are hypocrites or that they have deceived themselves about the program. There is a consensus, stated obliquely by the commissioner himself that a welfare program is powerless to deal with the basic causes of dependency—illness, joblessness, poor housing, and broken families—and will be about as constructive as the soup kitchens of the thirties. What is different is that many of the people in the department at least have some vision of what is needed.*

Having better-qualified investigators and giving out more money will not change the situation until there is a very different public understanding of our welfare population and what needs to be done to stop its increase. As the welfare system exists today, it could be run just about as well and more cheaply by automatic check-mailing devices and a corps of census takers who would occasionally drop in on the client to see if he was still alive. The 1965 strike of welfare investigators proved this inadvertently. The program went on pretty much as always without the investigators: the only problem was in processing new relief applicants.

Superficially the welfare department bureaucracy appears to be cut

* It is interesting to note that the people of the urban renewal area, both those on welfare (22 percent of those interviewed) and those who were not, had a rather good opinion of the department. The Kraft attitude study of Stryckers Bay revealed that 47 percent of the people interviewed felt that the department and its investigators were treating the welfare clients fairly. Of the remainder, 38 percent had no opinion or were not sure. The Kraft figures also showed that people most in contact with the department, either as clients or as relatives of clients, were the most favorably impressed. For instance, 46 percent of the Spanish-speaking population interviewed were receiving welfare aid, and the Spanish respondents showed the greatest approval—55 percent. Of the Negroes interviewed, 47 percent approved. The lowest percentage of approval, 41 percent, came from the white respondents.

out of the same cloth as most other municipal agencies in that it is large, inefficient, and stuffed with paper. But there is a difference. The Department of Real Estate, for instance, is a complacent bureaucracy with what is essentially the antipublic philosophy of the commercial realtor. Its philosophy kills any possibility of a socially useful program. The Department of Welfare bureaucracy, on the other hand, at least has a social viewpoint. It is a victim of a program which has been constructed to suit a society with a medieval attitude on what needs to be done about the poor.

At the same time, the fact that the department is forced to preside over a program that is a naked monstrosity does not justify some of the deceptions it has practiced on itself. One important self-deception is the department's oft–stated policy that it abstains from "moral" judgments in dealing with clients. In one area at least this is not true. For a long time the Department of Welfare, as well as the Departments of Health and Hospitals, against its better judgment, yielded to Catholic pressures and refused to authorize a program to counsel clients on artificial methods of birth control.* The result of this surrender to pressures based on moral grounds has been that whatever birth control information was passed to clients was passed on furtively by investigators at their own risk. The department's blackout of birth control education has amounted to a moral judgment, even though the motive behind the blackout was a political, not a moral one. The department's action placed a moral stigma on the subject which was communicated to the welfare client. The department's policy has had tragic results on adults and children alike. It has led to self-induced abortions, to an increase in the already abnormally high rate of infant mortality among the poor. It has further disorganized family life, and it has brought more and more children into the world who will be neglected and mistreated the rest of their lives. The department's surrender on birth control was a costly hypocrisy that undermined what slender chances the department may have had to prevent the tendency and to rehabilitate. The governments of India and Puerto Rico have fully realized the link between the health and happiness of the family and enlightened attitudes on family planning,

---

* The above-mentioned "Catholic pressures," coming from certain levels of the New York hierarchy, do not appear to be representative of lay Catholic opinion: a Gallup poll in March, 1966, revealed that 63 percent of Catholics interviewed felt that the federal government should give birth control aid to cities and states if requested.

but in New York City the official policy has been to avoid the entire subject.

In some ways the immoral morality that has slowed birth control symbolizes the general primitivism of American attitudes toward the poor. The primitivism explains why Judith Mage, an investigator who is now president of the Social Service Employees Union, feels as she does. Given present attitudes and programs, she feels that there is little she can do as an investigator to make fundamental changes in any client's life. She is not shocked by the lies her clients tell her, but she is shocked at what she feels are the lies Americans tell themselves.

"I worry about my country," she says. "We are supposed to be wealthy, yet the living conditions of the people I work with are unbearable. When you see the money we spend on a single atom bomb, how can we justify not being able to get enough dollars together to make it possible for people to have jobs and decent housing and adequate medical care? It shouldn't be just a matter of luck or an accident of birth whether or not people have a chance in life. There was never anything mysterious or impossible about what we needed to do. We just never faced the facts."

PROTECTION

"We bring into the police service men from the same society in which a billion dollars a year is stolen from employers and then we expect that those officers will somehow be far above that society in their ethical behavior."
—WILLIAM H. PARKER,
*Chief of Police, Los Angeles**

The 24th Precinct

ONE PECULIARITY OF THE AREA IS THAT PEOPLE talk a great deal about policemen. It is rather uncommon to go through an evening with friends without hearing at least one comment about "the cops." Usually the remark is a reflection on their integrity or efficiency. The popular custom of discussing and observing the police is a measure of the extent to which people are worried about all sorts of threats to their personal safety, from an attacker waiting in a self-service elevator to the trucks careering down Columbus Avenue while children are crossing on their way to school. It is possible to get a rather good idea of the life and problems of the area simply by putting together everything the people say about the police, and everything the police say about the people.

Most of the so-called "neighborhood cops" have disappeared from the West Side. There are no neighborhoods for them to patrol any more, for one thing. The squad car has also helped do away with the personal touch—with some exceptions. Riverside Drive families are fond of a patrolman who keeps a close eye on their children in the park. Another police officer more or less adopted the pupils at

* *The Police: an interview.* Published by the Center for the Study of Democratic Institutions, Santa Barbara, California, 1962.

P.S. 84. A tall, mild-looking Irishman has done such an excellent job of coordinating police activities with the local schools that the principal at P.S. 165 says he would like to marry him off to one of his schoolteachers. But, by and large, the people of the Area don't know many of their policemen by face or name, and they are suspicious and critical of them.

The captains of the 24th Precinct appear and disappear as often as the people in the rooming houses. During the past six years or so, the precinct has had well over a dozen, and the local organizations find it a trying experience to have to get acquainted with a new police boss every six months, and brief him on what they think needs to be done in the area. The captains come and go rapidly because the police commissioner considers the 24th, which is regarded as one of the more crime-ridden precincts in the city, as a postgraduate training ground for future inspectors. If a captain handles this "make-or-break" precinct satisfactorily he is "promoted out" and another candidate for inspector takes his place.

The only captain I talked to at length was Monroe Block. He was rather typical, except that he stayed longer than the other captains, which led some people to think he must be flunking his inspector's test. In the end he made it like the rest. Captain Block had a sociological approach that went over well with the local agencies, and a good sense of public relations.

By the time he arrived, the precinct headquarters had been moved into a new yellow brick building on 100th Street near the Douglass Houses project and across the street from the Riverside Health Center and a branch of the public library. One bulletin board in the big room outside the captain's office was papered with "crime geography"— small index cards describing the location of the worst trouble spots in the area, and what was liable to be taking place at them. For instance, lewd acts were being committed in an abandoned building on West Ninety-sixth Street. And down on West Ninetieth Street was a hangout for bookmakers and gamblers. A public fountain was used by "teen-age roughnecks" as a wading pool, and so on.

Other information on display included photographs of a hundred or so known gamblers and bookmakers in the area, with short biographies and addresses attached. A chart hanging on the wall, usually kept rolled up, had some incomplete statistics that gave a not altogether reassuring picture of the way in which the local war against crime was proceeding.*

	Complaints	Arrests
Murder	8	7
Manslaughter	1	1
Rape	49	42
Burglaries	1,110	123
Grand larceny (autos)	678	61
Narcotics	115	93
False alarms	218	6
Felonious assault	577	390

The best time to see the captain was always early on a Sunday morning, when the usual Saturday night rise in the crime rate had subsided. Block dressed like a businessman, usually in a dark blue suit with a black tie which in the office was usually at half-mast. He wore horn-rimmed glasses when reading, and was often afflicted with hoarseness, which he tried to alleviate by chewing pastilles. Since he was always under pressure he would eat a hero sandwich in the office for lunch.

The captain blamed most of the crime in his precinct on the "lower strata"—"the people who live in the single-room-occupancy houses." He classified narcotics addiction as a major cause of crime and guessed that the precinct had a high percentage of all the addicts in the entire city.

The captain's familiarity with statistics on rising crime rates,

* The following ten months' tabulation gives a comparison of various crimes committed in the area in 1963 and 1964:

	1964	1963
Murder	17	13
Forcible rape	17	21
Robbery	165	165
Felonious assault	388	412
Burglary	925	1,103
Grand larceny	1,241	1,320
Grand larceny—motor vehicles	236	213
Other felonies	238	245
Total felonies	3,228	3,473
Total misdemeanors	3,950	3,924
Offenses (vagrancy, disorderly conduct, etc.)	1,722	2,132

arrests, categories of crimes, etc., was not surprising. Precinct head-quarters had a full-time statistician who made daily tabulation of every "occurrence" reported in from fifty-six precinct posts shown on a large colored map posted near the captain's desk. At the end of each month, the captain set a "hazard rating" for each post. Occur-rences were weighted according to seriousness. A mugging, for instance, counted more in setting a hazard rating than several petty thefts.

Precinct headquarters has several IBM machines into which the statistician feeds the name of every person arrested, the type of crime, the age of the offender, how long he has lived in the city, and the location of the crime. The computers break the data down and arrange it in columns. One IBM machine provides a running total of the crimes for the current month and the same month the previous year, the number of crimes for the year, and the types and percent-ages of crimes which have been "cleared" by an arrest. His various electronic assistants enable the captain to check precinct conditions as if he were reading the gauges on a boiler.

I got the impression at first that when the captain said a crime had been cleared the guilty man had been caught, but further questioning revealed this was not always the case. The department seemed to regard a case as closed even if the arrested man was not convicted. When I asked what happened if the court frees a defendant, he declared he didn't "keep too much of an eye on the conviction rate," which didn't mean very much because rules of evidence often allowed a man to be acquitted even when the police knew he was guilty.

A fair amount of the captain's time was taken up meeting with such civic groups as the Bloomingdale Conservation Project, the Youth Board, Grosvenor Neighborhood House, the Riverside Demo-cratic Club, the FDR–Woodrow Wilson Democratic Club, and the Stryckers Bay Neighborhood Council. Many of the same people show up at every one of these meetings, he reported, each time as a representative of a different organization. The captain preferred not to say what he thought of the effectiveness of these local groups.

"In this area we need them. My job is to weed out their com-plaints. The Stryckers Bay people want to talk more about personal problems, such as they want to make the streets better. The problem is to separate the objective from the subjective." By "subjective complaints," the captain meant small, personal gripes. He said his predecessor in the precinct, Captain William Brown, used to enjoy his meetings with civic groups—"he would even go out looking for them." I got the definite impression that Captain Block did not go out looking for them.

In his conferences with the police liaison committee of the Stryckers Bay Neighborhood Council, the captain handled himself as well as anyone on "Meet the Press." In fact, he often turned the tables on his inquisitors, keeping them slightly off balance and hurrying the discussion along in such a way that it was difficult to stick to any one point for more than a half minute or so. At the end of the meetings the local citizens would file out with the vague feeling they had not said all they wanted to say, and I always suspected that as soon as they were out the door the captain told the sergeant to chuck his notes in the wastebasket.

These community-relations meetings gave a good picture of the problems people expected the police to handle. At one session between the Stryckers Bay Neighborhood Council and a police captain in 1964, the committee began with a request for a special police detail to cover the Stephen Wise Housing Development to prevent derelicts from using the benches and getting into the building. But the derelict problem seemed to have discouraged the captain. He declared at one meeting that when the police had tried to harass the derelicts and addicts at Ninety-sixth and Broadway, making sixty-two arrests in twenty-two days, in three days the troublemakers were all back at the same place.*

The committee then objected to the lack of street lighting on Columbus Avenue between Ninety-sixth and Ninety-fifth streets, and the fact that exits and entrances to two garages being built in the urban renewal area opened on school streets, thereby endangering schoolchildren. These, and other complaints were very much the same as those voiced at dozens of previous meetings: they had to do

---

* At Stryckers Bay's last meeting with Captain Block, on May 24, 1963, the captain reported that the Department of Health had objected to police harassment of narcotics addicts who were coming to the department's rehabilitation center at Broadway and Ninety-sixth. The captain had answered that the center was supposed to be a clinic, not a gathering place for pushers, and that the department should keep the addicts off the sidewalks around the entrance to the center. The committee members at that time indicated they supported the captain's position.

with the "winos," indecent exposure, gambling, narcotics, violence, burglaries, obscene language, prostitution, noise, garbage in the streets, fire danger, illegal occupancy of empty buildings, and traffic hazards. The committee members seemed to be using the meeting mainly to express their feelings of frustration, without much hope that the police would get around to solving their problems.

Police watching is an easy and absorbing occupation for the inhabitants of any crime-ridden area, easy in the sense that a patrolman can be identified by the uniform, and interesting because police habits are mysterious. When police watchers talk about the police, their descriptions vary considerably. The people who live in the 24th Precinct have a great number of ideas as to what is wrong and what is right about the force.

The Kraft survey reported that about 50 percent of the people asked replied that the police were doing as good a job as could be expected. Given the amount of crime in the Area, they felt the situation was hopeless and that the main trouble with the police was that there weren't enough of them. About 30 percent who said they weren't satisfied with the police felt they were incompetent, lazy, had a habit of never being around when they were needed, and avoided the side streets where there was the most trouble. The charge of police brutality, stressed by civil rights leaders, was almost never raised. In fact, Puerto Rican and Negro respondents in the Kraft survey thought a bit better of the police than the middle-class whites, and wished they had more patrolmen around to protect them. Many people interviewed felt that the police were too timid and that they tried to avoid threatening situations.

In my interviews of several hundred people in the Area over a four-year period, I found the same general reactions, with one exception. While the Kraft survey brought forth very little mention of police corruption, I found considerable lack of confidence in the police on that score. Over and over the person interviewed said he had seen police taking bribes, on a street corner, in a store, through the window of a police car. Like the Kraft interviewers, I discovered that, by and large, the low-income Negro and the Puerto Rican was somewhat more tolerant of the police than the middle-class white.

The attitudes of so-called community "leaders" toward the police covered a wide spectrum. One of the Area's most prominent political leaders holds a view which, while not necessarily typical, is prevalent enough to be significant. "There is no relationship between the police and the community worth talking about," she declares. "I never recognize a policeman. I've noticed a policeman will never smile and say hello to you on the street. It's true I don't like them anyway, but I am prepared to make an effort. But I've never met a cop who made the initial move to be friendly. Why don't I like them? Because they're very anti–Puerto Rican, for one thing. There isn't a group that has more prejudices against the Puerto Ricans than the Irish. I don't know how many times I've stood on a street corner and chatted with a policeman and allowed him to expound. Then when I expressed my distaste for what he says—not completely, because he might arrest me for disorderly conduct or something—the cop would look at me as if I were crazy. Since I am white he doesn't understand how I can disagree with him. Maybe I am unduly sensitive to policemen, but I have a tendency to stop short and sort of watch whenever I see them doing anything except walking up the street."

Former Democratic leader Hedi Piel says, "A cop has a very lousy job around here. You have to be tough to be a cop. Some people expect them to behave like kindergarten teachers. I must confess I wouldn't like to pound a beat in the Nineties in the middle of the night. But it is a fact that the police seem to be popping up when nothing is happening and they don't pop up when something is happening. I find them in the coziest places sometimes. Around the entrance to our building on Central Park West, for one thing. You know, this is awfully sweet except that our doorman doesn't really need any protection. The other night I watched two patrol-car cops and two foot patrolmen talking to a fellow in a sports car for a good twenty minutes. Finally I went over and said, 'I am the district leader here and I get nothing but complaints about not enough police protection.' I said, 'It is damn nice of you four to protect that fellow in the sports car but he really doesn't look that helpless,' so off they huffed, probably to congregate to another corner."

Gilberto Gerena-Valentin, head of several Puerto Rican organizations and lately a candidate for the City Council, has regularly charged the police with brutality against the Spanish population, and with shakedowns of storekeepers. He has implied that the 24th Precinct police unnecessarily killed two robbery suspects (Maximino Solero and Victor Rodriguez) in a police car on March 8, 1964,* and that five Puerto Ricans found hanged in their prison cells may

* The police officers involved were cleared by a police investigation of the incident.

not have been suicides, or were able to kill themselves because of police negligence. These views are disputed, but they receive considerable currency in the press.

Officials of local municipal and private agencies seem to think better of the police than the rest of the population, which has some significance in view of the fact that the agencies deal with the police on a day-to-day basis and have a chance to know some of the background of police incidents that may puzzle the uninitiated bystander. The agencies have better luck than the individual citizen in getting quick police action.

Natalie Donahue, the administrator of the Douglass Houses public housing development which is near the precinct station, says the police have been "extremely cooperative." Bernard Veney, the young Negro director of the Hudson Conservation Project in the Stryckers Bay area, says the police have always responded effectively when he has called upon them. Both Miss Donahue and Veney had a special liking for Captain Valentine Pfaffman, a "regular type with a Bronx accent," and Captain William Brown, a "college type" who later resigned from the force and became a sociology professor. (Captain Brown once told a community leader that "what the citizens in this precinct need is a better understanding of the nature of Anglo-Saxon jurisprudence.")

Veney says the police and the city's Youth Board "do jobs I wouldn't take on a bet, running around with guys at two o'clock in the morning and trying to cool off a situation that is ready to explode. The police are understaffed and the total social situation is completely out of hand. People complain when they don't get action on an individual addict, but if the police were to spread a dragnet for individual addicts they'd be at it all day long and they would do nothing but haul them in and see the cases get thrown out of court because of *Mapp versus Ohio*."*

Veney says the police have a policy of containment. "If something occurs on Ninety-fourth Street, they say, 'Well, that's a very bad

* *Mapp versus Ohio,* 367 US 643. The U.S. Supreme Court reversed the judgment of the Ohio Supreme Court, which had reaffirmed conviction of a person for possession of obscene materials. Taking note of the fact that the police did not have a proper warrant for entering the defendant's apartment, during which raid the obscene materials were discovered, the U.S. Supreme Court ruled that as a matter of due process evidence obtained by a search and seizure in violation of the Fourth Amendment was inadmissible in state courts as well as in federal courts.

street. Let it happen as long as it doesn't spread to Riverside Drive, West End Avenue, Central Park West.' The police say, 'We know we have a problem on Ninety-fourth Street, we can't wipe it out but we will keep it penned up in that area.' I'm sure the narcotics division knows most of the addicts in the area; they have watched them. Undercover men have probably made sales to them, but they are just too small fry for them to be concerned about, unless some obvious thing has happened and an arrest has to be made because of pressure."*

One agency official, who does not go along with the Veney-Donahue view of the police, was for some time a top executive in one of the city's housing agencies. She is annoyed at the system of rotating policemen from post to post, and at the rapid turnover in captains. She is also dissatisfied at what she feels is the too-relaxed attitude of most policemen, some of whom "get so mellow one would think they were psychiatrists or clergymen."

She says that "the patrolmen don't go into the side streets enough. They are on Central Park West looking out at the traffic and the trees. The theory is that if you stand on the corner you can look down two different blocks, whereas if you stand in the middle of the block you can't. There was a time when there used to be four policemen at Eighty-fourth Street and Columbus Avenue, because at some point it had been written that that was a special trouble spot. When I once came out of a meeting near that corner, a woman was howling at the top of her lungs and the four cops were jawing away paying no attention. I finally walked up and said to the policeman, 'If you don't mind, there seems to be something going on around here.' He seemed amazed at my breaking in on his conversation."

A former agency official once interested several people on the block in forming an around-the-clock committee to check on how often a foot patrolman went into the side streets. "I took the diaries of these people in to the precinct captain and told him, 'Don't give us this guff about yes, a man is assigned at such and such a post,' because we know he isn't there. But the diary never seemed to have any effect; they never believed us."

"The Police Department was one place where the community

* One Puerto Rican policeman in training in 1964 related that a veteran patrolman told him that "if you see two guys fighting at night on a tough street, go into a hallway until the fight is over and then take the name of the winner."

wanted to have a full-dress revolution," this ex-official observed. "We wanted to go to headquarters and say, 'What about getting people assigned to the same beat for a while? How about some sergeants being given some knowledge about the neighborhood and let's have less of this cursory human-relations stuff and more of getting together with the people in the area on a regular basis, so that there will be an opportunity to learn from each other.' But nothing ever developed."

A local psychologist, Lloyd Thorne, says he is unable to rationalize police behavior, yet admits at the same time there may be perfectly logical explanations. Meanwhile, his antipathy to the police is fortified by such experiences as the one he had a few years ago at Broadway and 100th Street. On his way home, at night, he found a Negro crumpled on the sidewalk bleeding from deep gashes on his face. Since none of a group of two dozen people standing around the man had offered him any assistance—a typical local reaction—Thorne tried unsuccessfully to get some bandages at a nearby drugstore, and then called the police.

The policeman answering the call knew the victim and the fact that he was lying outside the building in which he lived. The policeman discovered in questioning that the man had assaulted a Puerto Rican woman and that some Puerto Ricans had knifed him in revenge. When the wounded man refused to go to the hospital, the officer considered his job finished and left the man, still bleeding. Perhaps this was, in fact, all the officer could do, Thorne says, but the sequel had no justification.

"The policeman's attitude was that it was just another case of a Negro being cut by a Puerto Rican," Thorne said. "Afterward he began to lecture me about how tough the neighborhood was and told me 'You know, I more or less run this place. You don't really understand this neighborhood.' He said he had to exert himself hard to keep things under control and to make sure people were scared of him. At this point, while he was talking, a Negro approached us arguing with a woman. The policeman said to me, 'Watch this.' He went to this Negro and told him to let go of the girl, which the man refused to do, so the policeman slugged the Negro, just beat hell out of him. The policeman was really doing this for me, just showing what he could do with impunity."

Despite this experience Thorne feels that indifference rather than brutality is the major police problem. "Perhaps the indifference is necessary. It would be pretty hard to get emotionally involved in every situation that came up. But I find the indifference hard to accept. Everything is routine to the police. The service they perform is something like the sanitation department. They clean up the messes, keep track of the accidents, and see that people finally get carted off to the hospital, if this is what they need."

One example of how a misunderstanding can develop between the police and bystanders is an episode that took place on January 16, 1963, on West Ninety-second Street. At about 9 P.M. a man began beating a woman savagely, propping her up against the wall of an apartment house. Despite the blowing of car horns and shouts from nearby windows, he finally knocked the woman down a flight of stone steps and stamped on her body. As the attacker stepped over the unconscious woman and disappeared into a basement apartment, at least one woman got a clear look at his face. When several police arrived a few minutes later, they made no attempt to go in and get the man. Meanwhile, the victim was shipped off in an ambulance. It was not until one bystander threatened to demand an investigation that the police brought the man out of the basement and drove him off in a police car. The next day the attacker, a merchant seaman, was back in the basement apartment, where he lived for two weeks until his ship was ready to sail.

The people in the block learned about the episode very quickly, and there was a wave of indignation over the release of the woman's assailant. What the people did not know was that the victim was his wife and had refused to press charges against him. There was nothing the police could do about it. Commenting on the incident, one sergeant told me that "we tread very lightly in these husband and wife situations. I learned a lesson very early as a cop. I once arrested somebody on a wife-beating charge. The woman went to the hospital and got patched up. When we got to court the next day, she walked up to her husband and kissed him. The DA couldn't make her sign a complaint and I certainly felt like a fool."

The usual West Sider's comments about the police reveal perhaps more about his own ethical attitudes than about those of the public. If he brings up the subject of police bribery he often does so in a matter-of-fact way. The feeling seems to be that the taking of small gratuities by police is part of a local arrangement which everyone hears about and accepts. To the local storekeeper who wanted to stay open

Sundays, or the tavern owner whose customers often behave very badly, the bribe is the price of doing business. The homeowner on Ninety-second Street, with several loads of refuse to be carted away, watches as the dump truck driver pays the driver of a police car to allow his truck to park illegally while it is loaded. Nobody complains because everybody has an interest that is being advanced.

Policemen are quite often open about asking for gratuities even with people they don't know. A Columbus Avenue shopkeeper reported that when he was about to get a ticket for illegal parking the policeman learned that he ran a store and told him to forget the ticket. On the following day he came to the store and asked for free merchandise. The policeman in question could be quite sure he would not be reported since there were no witnesses. However, this did not prevent the story of the bribe request from circulating quickly—one more anecdote to prove that the cops are venal.

The extent of small-time police corruption is of course impossible to estimate. A prominent Negro attorney in Manhattan and a leading official of the NAACP has said it is widespread, particularly in Harlem. "I can show you gambling places all over. Any twelve-year-old child can show them. I once asked a high police official who had a reputation for being pretty rough on policemen to take a walk with me. It is impossible for you not to see the evidence of lawbreaking and corruption, I told him. He didn't take the walk, of course.

"Men will get right out of the police car to take their two dollars. The kids see this. You can tell when a cop is testifying in a fix too, in court. You'll hear the policeman say he arrested a man in a hallway because he saw some numbers near his foot. Any lawyer knows that if he testifies he arrested a man in a hallway, but the man was not actually holding the numbers in his hands, then this is bound to result in the case being thrown out. The crook walks free, yet the policeman has made an arrest for the record. The judges wink at this. The police department knows about it. Until the situation gets embarrassing, the department doesn't do anything. Can I document what I say? Of course not. How do you prove corruption? You have to get witnesses and pay them. Are they going to take your money when they can get paid by the cops? The proof of the corruption and the fact that it exists can be seen, everybody sees it."

If a citizen knows of corruption he makes the logical assumption that the police authorities are also aware of it. The public theory that every policeman knows what every other policeman is doing is supported by a former high official of the police department, who declares that "obviously there has to be police complicity in all forms of vice that go on here and in other cities, or it would not go on. As a police officer, nothing could go on in my precinct that I would not know about."

What does the citizen see? From my own career as a police watcher, I recall many incidents. A typical one involved some street peddlers. Although it is illegal for peddlers to sell merchandise on the street without a permit, during the summer truckers sell fresh fish, watermelons, bananas, etc., at the corner of 103rd Street and Central Park West to people coming out of the Independent Subway exit. The truckers are not resented: they are a neighborhood convenience, since there are no stores nearby. Prices are cheap, and why shouldn't a man make a living? The police exploit this local support for the truckers. On an evening in June, in addition to a large watermelon truck, there was also a small two-wheeled pushcart operated by a Puerto Rican selling sausages and bread at the corner. I watched a police car turn onto 103rd and stop. The operator of the truck waved to the police. Then the police beckoned the pushcart peddler over. The driver spoke to him for several seconds, and jerked his thumb in the direction of Central Park West. The Puerto Rican pushed his cart off around the corner and the police car drove on, leaving the watermelon truck where it was.

I asked the pushcart peddler what had happened. The policeman had asked him for money, he said. He refused. The police had told him to leave.

"Why wasn't the watermelon truck sent away?"

"The watermelon truck pays," the Puerto Rican replied.

Or take the experience of a resident of Douglass Houses. She was shopping in a Columbus Avenue grocery story when a white man in civilian clothes walked in and nodded to the store owner. The two men went into a back room and in a few moments the proprietor returned and asked the person at the cash register to give him fifty dollars, saying, "It's for the man downtown." He took the money out back and later the white man emerged and left the store. After this the proprietor announced to everyone present that he had paid off the cops. In the summer of 1964, after press disclosures of police complicity in gambling, his store was raided, and a few weeks later it went out of business.

An interview with a policeman is an impossible interview. Like other municipal employees, he is suspicious of people who ask him about his work or his opinions. His usual response to an inquisitive citizen is to ask him to identify himself. In addition to his distrust of local civilians, the policeman is subject to disciplinary action if he discusses "police business" without the commissioner's permission. In the security-minded 24th Precinct, police business covers everything but the weather.

Under such conditions there are only two ways to get the policeman's opinions about his department and about the taxpayers he is supposed to serve. One is to talk to an authorized department spokesman. The other is to know a policeman well enough so that he will say what he thinks, knowing that he will not be reported to headquarters.

The man I found best qualified to give the department's official defense of its twenty-seven thousand policemen was Michael Murphy, a two-hundred-pound "professional cop" who was New York City police commissioner for four years. The campaign by civil rights organizations against alleged police brutality, the 1964 Harlem riots, and disclosures of police complicity in gambling made Murphy's last year particularly unpleasant and probably contributed to his decision to resign. "Of course we have wrong policemen," he observed. "Nobody knows this more than we do, but we do not feel that group libel of policemen is any more justified than any other type of group libel. Policemen in this city defend civil liberties with their lives, whereas some organizations only talk about civil liberties, or make it harder for the police to do their job."

The police department has a special program to train city policemen to deal intelligently with minority groups. For the four months' training period, the longest in the country, the police academy has asked for and received the cooperation of such groups as the NAACP, the American Civil Liberties Union and the American Jewish Congress. Their representatives have lectured at the academy. After the police candidates finish at the academy, the department encourages them to continue their education. Some take in-service courses or two-year courses in police science. More than fifteen hundred have gone on to college work, eight hundred are studying for their bachelor's degree and one hundred have their master's degrees. Murphy himself studied in his off-duty hours as a policeman, and earned a law degree.

In spite of the educational opportunities, recruiting is a problem. Not enough men apply, and of those who do the majority do not have the minimum qualifications. One reason is competition from industry and business. Another is the declining status of the policeman, helped along by constant attacks on the police from all directions. When the commissioner joined the force "the family thought that when a son became a policeman he was a success. This is not true any more. Today families that used to provide many of our police recruits are trying to put their sons into professional schools of medicine, law, and business."

Murphy took exception to the common criticism on the West Side that today's policeman doesn't know his area as intimately as he used to because he does not walk the old foot post as much. "He still knows the pulse of the community. The old system is impossible now. Handling the tough areas requires a certain mobility and it is economically impossible to put foot patrolmen everywhere. The police car is doing a lot of this work. To get the mobility, we had to sacrifice some of the old familiarity with the blocks. The city's army of police is not big enough to do all required of it. In 1964 it took one and a third policemen to do a job one policeman did in 1940, because of shorter hours and longer vacations today."

The commissioner was concerned about legal restrictions on evidence and arrest procedures which have seriously hampered the department's two-hundred-man narcotics division, 25 percent larger than any other division in the country.

"The rule in New York City used to be that whatever evidence was seized in a narcotics raid was admissible, but *Mapp versus Ohio** has changed this," he pointed out. "Let's take an instance. Some residents may say drugs are being sold in a certain apartment. This is not sufficient to allow us to act. We have to develop affirmative evidence that drugs are actually being peddled there, then go into court, prepare an affidavit and give a reason for a search warrant being granted. Then the police officers go down to the premises under suspicion, knock on the door and announce that they are police officers, state that they have a search warrant, and ask to be admitted. If admittance is refused then the police officer can kick in the door. But by this time the evidence can be thrown out the window or flushed down the toilet and there is nothing we can do. Some police

* See footnote p. 282.

officers have been killed shortly after knocking on the doors and announcing themselves."*

The commissioner felt that gambling was a prime cause of police corruption, an opinion he stated many times before the 1964 disclosure of police involvement with gamblers. But here too, he asserted, the department was operating at a disadvantage. "Nobody can prevent wholesale gambling or narcotics selling unless they can tap telephones, yet we have been denied by federal law the use of evidence obtained through wiretapping. Therefore, we have a situation where we have wiretap evidence that some police officers are engaged in illegal activity, but we are forced to keep them on the job because we can't use the evidence."

The greatest threat to police morale, in the commissioner's opinion, has been political interference. While he was commissioner he was grateful to Mayor Wagner for keeping his hands off the department, but he had no respite from other pressures, particularly from supporters of a civilian review board to investigate complaints about police behavior. Such a board, the commissioner was convinced, would put every policeman at the mercy of street-corner demagogues, local political machines, and the very civil rights groups which Murphy felt were out to "get" the department. It was at the height of the dispute over a civilian review board that the commissioner resigned.

A friend of mine, an Irish sergeant, speaking without any O.K. from the commissioner, has a patrolman's point of view, and he states it in patrolman's language. He has a good record and is proud of it, but in spite of his service he will never be a captain or an inspector. The sergeant is not the type of policeman to get the big jobs any more. He has a high school diploma and a wife and children. He has risked his life several scores of times as a foot patrolman and later in a squad car on the West Side, in Harlem and El Barrio. What is his policeman's view of the city?

"You ask me if the public has a fair attitude toward a policeman.

---

* In 1964 the New York State Legislature passed in March two laws urged by the police. One, the stop-and-frisk law, allows the police to search for weapons any persons suspected of carrying them. The second, the no-knock law, could eliminate the requirement that police with a search warrant must first announce the presence of an officer before entering. Both laws have been opposed by the ACLU, which questions their constitutionality and by many local political leaders on the West Side.

You can split your head open for the public and it means nothing in the end. A cop may have gotten four combat citations for shooting it out with burglars and holdup men, but if somebody comes along and complains about him, this guy is just like he is a brand-new cop or like he has been a crumb all his life.

"Harlem is supposed to be the toughest place in the city. But sometimes people there will listen to you and you can get across a point. In some parts of this city people do not want to know. We get all kinds of complaints from people in one area, about the dice games on the streets, men using foul language in front of women and children, and they block the sidewalks and entrances to buildings so people can't get in. Somebody calls the station house and the police get there. We grab three of ten men shooting dice and line them up against the wall. One of them hollers in Spanish, something like 'Help me' or 'Don't let them take me' and immediately the bottles start flying, the garbage comes out of the windows—anything they can get their hands on. They are throwing at the policeman who is trying to do a job for them, a policeman who came in to answer a complaint from a Puerto Rican family.

"Policemen can go by dice games all night long, it doesn't bother them one bit, but they have to do something when the public complains. So they try and they are pelted. I know a policeman who has a plate in his head today and he will never be the same again, a young man too. What did he do to anybody? Nothing except to try to do his job. A policeman is a nothing to hit in the head with a brick or a bottle from a roof.

"Okay, take the time we arrested three men and put them in a squad car with one policeman. The other policeman got after the people who were throwing garbage and bottles. The crowd surrounds the car and they open the car door and take one prisoner out. The policeman in the car is trying to hold the other two prisoners and he calls for help. The mob surrounds the three policemen outside and several men jump on their backs. The policemen are fighting off a mob. This is every-day-of-the-week stuff. The man who jumped on the policeman's back was knocked off three times before he was hit over the head with a stick and subdued and taken into the car. Only after a dozen cars from the area answered were we able to get him out of the block. One man on the block, an officer of a local Democratic club, gathered up a mob and marched on the police station and raised holy hell about the incident, yet he wasn't even there at the scene. He was in a house somewhere, he had heard the commotion, he looked out the window and came down and joined them. So immediately the police are wrong, he thinks. He has already formed his own opinion as to what happened and then he is leading the people on the station house. Such a man should have been arrested for incitement to riot but he is a politician and the powers-that-be won't let them be arrested.

"As soon as people see a radio car stop, they gather around. You always have your crumbs, they start it, the crowd picks it up, they know nothing about what's going on but they pick it up. Bottles, bricks, garbage, anything else that's handy. This is coming down at the policeman. What would you do if you were a policeman? Would you care to solve their problems or let them live with it? We can't say let them live with it, we are policemen, we are in uniform, we have to go there. So we do the best we can, but we don't go looking as far as I am concerned."

"Would you like another example? A mob formed around a police car after a woman had been arrested. In order to keep the prisoner a policeman and lieutenant got out. Finally, the policeman had to draw his gun. Somebody grabbed his arm, the gun went off and shot the lieutenant in the leg. They arrested the man who grabbed the policeman and brought him in and a mob marched on the station house. So the man who hit the gun walked out with a summons. There is a law on the books that says you should not interfere with a policeman in the performance of his duty; to do so is a misdemeanor. A misdemeanor is not an offense that can be handled by a summons, but because the powers-that-be are scared to death of a civilian they let him walk out with a summons—appeasement, appeasement, appeasement.

"I say there is too much civilian interference in the police department. The public thinks it knows more about police business than the police and in some ways it does, I guess. I can walk in my own neighborhood and go right into the corner store and the storekeeper will tell me exactly what's going on in the police department. Things I don't know, such as who's getting transferred, who's going to get promoted, who's here and who's there. Within the police department we don't know these things. It is not politically expedient to tell me. The higher-ups tell the civilian. This store owner is part of the neigh-

borhood council. These are the people who have contact with the
politicians, who can do something as far as getting you transferred to
a good assignment. The day will come when I hope the police
department will be disassociated with anybody on the outside. Let the
policeman know the law and let him enforce it."

"The policeman is all alone. The story is to do your job but if you
do you are holding that sack all by yourself. We want you to do it,
our superiors tell us, but if you do it and anything happens to create
trouble then you have had it. Don't expect our protection.

"A white policeman is crazy to get involved in a tough situation if
he is in a Negro or Puerto Rican slum area. The experienced cop will
tell the young cop to move on—you get no thanks from anybody. It's
not that a white man doesn't want to help a black man, but the people
the cops are trying to help turn them against them."

The sergeant says if he had his way he would take as many Negro
policemen on the force as possible and then let them work in the
Negro area. "This isn't because I want black precincts, but because
the Negro can do a job. If a white cop makes an arrest in a Negro
area, the people pick up the chant—you're locking up the man because he is black. They know nothing about the situation. If a colored
policeman were acting on a colored man nothing would be said.

"I don't know what type of neighborhood you grew up in but when
I was a kid if anybody on my block was brought home by a policeman, or picked up by him or taken to the station house, the rest of
the people would say, 'Stay away from that kid, he is bad.' Now when
a policeman brings somebody home, immediately everybody gathers
around to comfort him. They want to know, 'Did the policeman talk
bad to you, did he push you?' The policeman knows this and he has
no love for the people he is working with as the old policemen did.
The old policeman on the post knew everybody and everybody was
friendly to him. He was invited in for dinner. He was a part of the
block. If there were any bad kids in the block he knew them, he knew
their parents, and he knew when there was trouble, where to go. And
if there was a good kid in the block that started to go bad, all the
policeman had to do was to go up and knock on the family's door and
something was done about it."

Once in a while a white policeman will find support in an unfriendly crowd. The sergeant tells of such an experience in a Negro
area where a car had struck a woman and the police were standing by

waiting for an ambulance. "When they are hit by a car and are in critical shape, we are afraid to touch them. We are told not to as a matter of fact. Well, we had to wait for quite a while; I guess the ambulances were tied up, even though there are more ambulances at Harlem Hospital than any other in the city, and they give better service. They better give it. So people gathered on the corner and pretty soon some Black Muslims started yelling about Caucasians and other people took up the chant. I figured we were headed for trouble, when lo and behold from inside the crowd a man yelled, 'Leave them alone, they know what they are doing. They can't touch that woman and they are waiting for an ambulance.' I turned around and who is it? A Negro that we have chased a thousand times, a fellow that runs a crap game, a guy we have locked up over and over. Somebody we had really given a hard time to and there he was defending us. . . .'"

Police Powers and Police Values

My neighbors' usual response to the fact that the police are not able to provide anything like the necessary protection to the people of the side streets is that we need more police. Perhaps saturating the Area with bluecoats would bring matters more under control—a 52 percent increase in crime in the subways was reduced by addition of several hundred trained police in 1964, for instance—but in view of the inefficiency of the police we already have it seems as if saturation would simply be another extension of Parkinson's Law. Another widespread impression is that the police do not exert themselves very much except in the case of the most spectacular crimes (murder, rape, child molestation, and aggravated assault), or where matters can be disposed of neatly (parking violations). The in-between part of the crime spectrum (disorderly conduct, petty theft, obscenity, narcotics, gambling, prostitution, and "in-group" assault—Negro versus Negro, Puerto Rican against Puerto Rican, gets routine attention, if any at all, from police, who have a defeatist attitude about being able to control such activity. Yet it is this "in-between" type of crime that floods the Area and accounts for much of the insecurity and fear. Typically, the desk sergeant who takes the call about bottles or bricks thrown from a rooftop will ask, "Are they still throwing anything?" and if the answer is no, he says to call if the trouble starts up again and hangs up. Such incidents do not get on the police blotter. Calling the police about anything but a major crime is like dealing with any other branch of the city bureaucracy. The citizen is usually promised assistance that never comes or he is told nothing can be done about his complaint and that if he wants to be safe he should move somewhere else.

After a few experiences with an apathetic police, the citizen grows just as resigned as the policeman. If he doesn't move, he buys himself a police lock for the front door and assumes that whatever protection he gets he will have to provide for himself. One by-product of his sense of defeat and helplessness is a growing hostility and disrespect for the police, an attitude returned by the police, who say that it is the citizens who are apathetic about law enforcement and tend to side with the criminal against the police. Their attitude is supported by experience.

The prime victims of this mutual distrust and cynicism are the Negroes and Puerto Ricans who form the population core of the slum where criminal violence is part of the daily routine. They receive unequal protection of the laws because crimes in the slums are committed largely against the people who live in them, 95 percent of whom are as law-abiding and as terrorized as any part of the affluent white community. My own interviews and those of the Kraft Survey indicate that the Negro and the Puerto Rican are far more concerned about the breakdown of public order and the mob that supports the lawbreaker against the police than about alleged police brutality and racial prejudice: in fact—as I have indicated before—the subject of police brutality was almost never raised in these interviews.

It is not only the civilians who have noted the decline in police morale. A former deputy police commissioner, Robert J. Mangum, says the deterioration of morale is "total"; while he blames some of the decline on persistent attacks on the police by outside groups, he also blames the department itself.

"Fraternization between officers and patrolmen has had results similar to those produced in the armed forces by the so-called democratization, when officers fraternized with their subordinates to the point where you often couldn't tell a lieutenant from an admiral. Speeded-up promotion and the advancement of men with veterans' preference over older policemen have resulted in a cadre of relatively young officers who seem to be reluctant to deal strictly with their subordinates."

Mangum says infractions of the rules of police behavior are tolerated or pass unnoticed—smoking on duty, carelessness in dress, walking the beat in twos (citizens may be surprised to learn that patrolmen are supposed to walk their beats alone except in special emergency situations), and idle conversation while on duty.

At the same time, Mangum says, "the job of the police would be a great deal easier to handle if the community would change some of its own attitudes, toward gambling for instance. How can society justify a system in which gambling is allowed in churches, yet becomes a criminal offense when it takes place outside on the sidewalk or in a grocery store?"

What Mangum says about discipline is easily confirmed by day-to-day observation or interviews with West Side residents. On March 8, 1965, two police cars (666 and 1848) parked side by side on West 105th Street and the four occupants and a foot patrolman talked with each other for two hours. A patrolman in uniform makes sandwiches behind the counter of a Columbus Avenue luncheonette. On Election Day in 1964, police in one West Side polling place were smoking directly under a no-smoking sign. With an accident or emergency ambulance call, two or three policemen often will stand by for as much as an hour waiting for the ambulance to arrive. It is not surprising that some West Side police watchers feel that, if half the police force were fired, the remainder would work twice as hard and the citizens would be safer.

Police objections to political interference would be more convincing if they did not have their own system of internal politics. Their Patrolmen's Benevolent Association has all the characteristics of a veterans' lobby and has done little to raise standards of police efficiency. The PBA's behavior at public hearings, notably in opposing a civilian review board, has contributed to the unfortunate stereotype of the bigoted cop. The idea has been strengthened by Holy Name Society communion breakfasts for Catholic policemen* that frequently feature speakers of the extreme right. In April, 1965, for example, at the very time when the commissioner was defending his force against charges of race prejudice, five thousand policemen at one such communion breakfast gave William Buckley a standing ovation when he praised the police of Selma, Alabama, for their "restraint" in handling civil rights demonstrators.

* Of the city's 27,000 policemen, about half are of Irish descent, and 12,000 are members of the police department's Holy Name Society.

On his side the policeman has a strong case against the public. He is quite aware of the fact that almost every citizen disbelieves, in some degree, in the law as it applies to him, and will break it with or without the help of the authorities if he can do so safely. Automobile owners, liquor permittees, storekeepers, public and private officials, parents, inspectors, landlords are quite willing to pay the policeman for immunity from the inconveniences and restrictions imposed by law, and the policeman knows that such ethical attitudes are part of the general pattern of getting along in the city. The policeman sees the double standard at work in the courts, in business, in almost every aspect of the citizen's relationship to his society, sees that there is one standard for the Negro and another for the white, one for the poor and one for the affluent, one for the established and one for the disestablished, one for the property owner and one for the tenant, etc. Police officers who adopt these various double standards see themselves as operating realistically in a system where it is illegal to gamble on a sidewalk but a moral obligation to gamble in church. And, for a policeman, the next step after tolerance of the double standard is to profit from it personally, in return for which the policeman becomes a protector of what he judges to be technically illegal but morally harmless local interests.

The police are also sensitive to their loss of status among some segments of the middle class, who view a policeman as a head cracker who wouldn't be a policeman if his brains were as strong as his back, and among the poor who look upon him as a representative of somebody else's society. In fact many of the city's newer breed of policeman are neither. They have learned enough sociology to know that they have no power to deal with the sources of violence in the city, and that huge populations of sick and antisocial people will commit sick and antisocial acts, policemen or no policemen. Perhaps if the policeman were more like the stereotype of the dumb cop, he might be less defeated and less cynical.

As it is, if a policeman does what he is supposed to do in a blighted area, he spends his time trying to enforce laws, many of which are unenforceable (dealing with things like gambling, narcotics, and prostitution) or arresting offenders for whom there is no rehabilitation program and who will soon be back on the street. If he seeks the cooperation of the citizen in a specific situation, he finds the crowd is often against him, that witnesses will not come forth, and that if there is trouble he cannot even be sure his superiors will protect him.

Consequently, the policeman often begins to behave like the people he is supposed to protect. He returns distrust for distrust, and he avoids threatening situations, when, in his own judgment, his chances of handling them successfully are small.

The policeman resents those critics of the police who will never come to his defense even when he gives his best, particularly those civil rights leaders who have concentrated entirely on building up the stereotype of the police bigot and have never tried to explain the policeman to the public or speak out against the increasing number of attacks on officers performing their duty. An even-handed discussion of the police damage would be helpful to the Negro, Puerto Rican, and white inhabitants of the slums, who are most in need of intelligent and courageous police protection, but it is politically unlikely.

In any discussion of police behavior and attitudes, something has to be said about the clichés which have created a number of gross misapprehensions about the incidence of crime in our city and the identity of those who commit crime. Discussion of crime seems to oscillate between the alarms and sermons of J. Edgar Hoover and the opinions of sociologists like Richard Cloward of the Columbia School of Social Work, who feels that the situation is not so bad as it is painted by the press. "I think there is probably good reason to think that anxiety is being whipped up all out of proportion to the problem," Cloward declares. "While there may have been an increase in violence, I find it difficult to believe that the increase is as large as one would judge if you just read the newspapers and listened to radio and watched TV . . . it's just being exaggerated out of all proportion to reality."*

On the surface, Cloward seems to have a point, particularly in view of the fact that New York City annually ranks below several other major U.S. cities in its crime rate. The argument that the apparent increase in New York City crime—12.6 percent in 1964 over 1963— is partly attributable to better police reporting of crime also seems to buttress his view. But below the surface is the fact that the police department's "modernized" system of crime reporting is totally misleading. Any close investigation of conditions on West Side cross streets will reveal that an enormous amount of crime occurrences are not reported to the police by victims or witnesses. A West Sider will also

* Statement on *Terror in the Streets,* NBC-TV documentary, April 6, 1965.

learn, if he checks with precinct headquarters on crimes he has reported, that his calls are often not recorded and are frequently never investigated, also that reported crimes are sometimes improperly classified. Consequently there is good reason to suppose that New York City's crime rate vis-à-vis other cities is drastically understated.*

When decay and disorder in a slum area go above a certain level, the victims give up, accept the inevitability of crime, and cease to depend on the police except in the most dangerous situations. People whose apartments or rooms have been robbed two, three, four, or more times see no useful purpose in going through long explanations with the police unless they can put in an insurance claim—and since the poor cannot afford the enormously high insurance rates for the area, such cases are rare. One can interview a score of people on a block and learn of dozens of unreported crimes. A woman robbed of clothes, silverware, and a television set said, "Why call the police? They will not find the people who did it, they will not prevent it from happening again, they will not recover the stolen property."† Crimes which outrage the moral sensibilities of the entire neighborhood, such as the molestation of a child, will be reported, but many lesser crimes are tolerated without comment. In other parts of America a man cannot safely sell narcotics on a street corner, shout obscenities or hurl bricks into someone else's living room in the middle of the night. On Ninety-third Street one simply refuses to see or hear, and resolves to endure.

Perhaps, with the right sort of reporting, the cliché that crime is mainly a game for the poor and uneducated people may go out of style. Crime rates are based on statistics and statistics tell us mainly about the brazen crimes of the poor against person or property, but

* One indication of the unreliability of police reporting are figures released by the city's new Chief Inspector, Sanford Garelik. On March 10, 1966, Garelik ordered police to make their crime reports more accurate. The result was that for the twenty-day period after March 10, reported burglaries were up 96.4 percent over the same period in the previous year; robberies were up 88.9 percent; grand larcenies were up 54.2 percent; felonious assaults were up 44.6 percent; felonies were up 59.8 percent; and rapes were up 22.1 percent. The total number of complaints was up 24.6 percent.

In releasing the figures, Garelik said analysis indicated that there had been "no great increase in the actual incidence of crime" during the twenty-day period covered by the figures. *The New York Times,* April 5, 1966.

† In 1964, New York City police recovered only 3.6 percent of all stolen property except automobiles, down from 9.8 percent a decade ago.

very little about more civilized and invisible illegal behavior. The statistics lie to us about the incidence of crime just the way our jails, filled with minor offenders, lie to us about the criminal himself.

One can ask why, in a society where every economic group has its own accepted style of illegal behavior, where the slum itself is the product of an economic conspiracy, and where industry spends a billion dollars a year to protect itself against thieving employees, there are as many honest policemen as there are. Perhaps the cop hater is right after all, and a man must have a thick skull to be a policeman at the same salary as a sanitation worker. Especially if he ends up like Patrolman Henry A. Walburger, shot dead in a hallway protecting a Puerto Rican mother and daughter from a homicidal maniac, and leaving behind a wife who received no letter of appreciation from the professional lovers of the poor.

BUREAUCRACY

FATHER BROWNE, WHO OFTEN SPEAKS IN CARTOONS, says that New York City government is like the Empire State Building without elevators. Somewhere up on top is the administrative apparatus, the public is in the basement, and in between is a vast air space occupied by the civil service. The consequence of this three-tiered arrangement is that the unaffiliated citizen lives in nearly total bewilderment about his government and, on their side, the administrative officials work in general ignorance of what their own bureaucracies are doing to the citizen. Presumably it was a suspicion of this latter fact that impelled Mayor Wagner to rent himself a private mailbox (Box 100) to which he asked citizens to write and tell him the truth about his subordinates.

Although there was no reason to suppose that Box 100 was anything but another public-relations effort, some people took it seriously for a time. Peter Slevin, a member of the Irish junta of Stryckers Bay Neighborhood Council, used to send off communications to Box 100 regularly. "I wrote to Wagner, I wrote to the commissioner, I wrote to everybody," he says. "I have my own typewriting machine at home, and I send letters in complaining about the block, and also the whole neighborhood—how it is run ragged and all the different illegal things that are going on. I complain about the police department and the narcotics division.

"The only answer they will ever give you if you write to that Box 100 is a little made-up-in-advance letter of the mayor's. The last time I wrote him, I complained about the Housing and Redevelopment

301

Board and I put a note on the bottom of my card saying I didn't want the made-up letter, I wanted an answer from the mayor himself. Now, what do you think I got? I got the made-up letter. It told me that the mayor had turned my letter over to the Housing and Redevelopment Board, the same outfit I was complaining about."

A different style of frustration lies in wait for the citizen who thinks he can accomplish something by interrogating public officials at public meetings—by "putting them on the spot," as the saying goes. Ordinarily these inquisitions are an unmitigated fizzle. An individual who tangles with the head of a bureaucracy will find himself fighting way out of his class. Any commissioner worth his salt can dispose of any critic by telling him that "the situation you describe is certainly not typical," implying that a minor subordinate has goofed, or he will tell the citizen that he is "not in possession of all the facts." This latter rejoinder will almost always dispose of the case, because it is true; if the citizen had all the facts he would know a great deal more than the commissioner.

The cold gray truth about the futility of individual protest has been demonstrated over and over on the West Side. One of the many examples was the meeting called by the FDR–Woodrow Wilson Democratic Club to air objections to the way in which the urban renewal plan was being implemented. The platform groaned under the weight of several city commissioners and state and federal housing officials, and for a few moments at the outset it seemed as if, having flushed them out in the open, an aroused public would make short work of the bureaucrats. But every time a housewife, local politician, businessman, tenant, or organizational representative rose to shout his grievances, the appropriate official would suffocate him with an involved technical explanation of the city's program as it was supposed to work on paper. The more outraged the plaintiff the easier it was to strangle him with his own innocence. One of these was Elemer Vadasz, the owner of André's Pastry Shop, who said in apoplexy that the city was forcing him to vacate but had done nothing about its promises to relocate him properly. The Commissioner of Relocation patiently described the relocation program for commercial tenants and enumerated several forms that had to be filled out by businessmen to qualify. Then the commissioner elicited the fact that Vadasz had not filled out one of the forms, and with the exposure of this crime against the state the pastry shop owner was done for—at least for that night.*

Another speaker, Aramis Gomez, who at the time was still the neighborhood's official angry Puerto Rican (he was later to be appointed to a government job), attacked the Department of Real Estate for alleged failures to maintain properly buildings it had taken over in the urban renewal area. The Commissioner of Real Estate recalled irritably that he had once told Gomez that if he had any complaints he should report them to the commissioner, but that Gomez had never done so and, therefore, Gomez had no business bringing up his charges in a public meeting. This seemed to satisfy the audience, a good part of which was hostile to Gomez on general principles, and the scuffle ended without any further inquiry into whether Gomez's charges were, in fact, true.

The same commissioner handled Mrs. Marianne Jacobs, whose husband owns a local drugstore, with equal dispatch. Mrs. Jacobs stated she had talked to several tenants in city-owned buildings and had discovered they had not received rent reductions promised them by the city. The commissioner said this could not be so and explained the department's policy. Standing up for several minutes while a commissioner explains department policy will take the steam out of anybody and eventually Mrs. Jacobs sat down, never to regain the floor again. And so the meeting went, with the professionals taking the amateurs in stride, shriveling enormous personal crises to the status of petty complaints, responding to requests for information by offering the official philosophy. The common thread that stitched all the official responses together was their irrelevance to the questions. Such confrontations give the bystander the feeling of traveling through one of those amusement park concessions where iron bars turn out to be rubber and there are mirrors that make a man seem seven feet tall or seven inches short.

Of course there were roads besides Box 100 or public meetings

* Later Vadasz became so vocal that the Department of Relocation made a special project of him. News photographers were invited to take a picture of Vadasz as he received a check for $3,000 from the Commissioner of Relocation. Other displaced commercial tenants continued to have just as much difficulty as ever in relocating their businesses, and many of them found that private developers, approved by the city, were charging exorbitant rents for space in the urban renewal area.

open to the citizen seeking redress from his government. For instance, one could complain into a microphone attached to the mayor's "gripe-mobile," a contraption which rolled from borough to borough and gave citizens the illusion they were getting through to His Honor himself. Its value seemed to be largely therapeutic. The citizen might also try to call somebody up on the telephone or even barge into the bureaucratic establishment and demand an audience with the man in charge. These forays were easily sidetracked. People as well as letters always seemed to be addressing themselves to the wrong department, and on those rare occasions when the city answered a letter the signatures at the bottom were so illegible that it was impossible to tell with whom one was communicating. The corporation counsel's office had a standard signature that resembled a tightly coiled spring and could not have been deciphered by an archaeologist. A telephone call to a city agency was tantamount to wandering through a pitch-black cave, full of voices telling the citizen he had the wrong extension.

I used to keep a record of such phone calls. The following entry is rather typical: "Called WOrth 4–5656, asked for the Department of Real Estate, was given extension. Explained I wanted to find out about mortgages on my house, which had been taken over by the city. Switched to another extension. When I repeated reason for my call man said I should call Extension 462. He clicked for the switch-board, could not get it, then said, 'I guess it must be their coffee break,' and advised me to hang up and call WOrth 4–5656 again and ask for Extension 462. Did so, got 462, explained what I wanted, was transferred to Extension 415. Explained to information officer at 415 who said I had wrong extension and that Housing and Redevelopment Board had nothing to do with mortgages. He suggested I call the City Urban Renewal Maintenance Corporation. I said I had already called that office, which had referred me to the Department of Real Estate, which had referred me to the Housing and Redevelopment Board. The information officer replied, 'I can't help you; we shouldn't even be discussing this.' Repeated to information officer that I had been shuttled to him through several other extensions. 'Why did they misinform you?' he said. 'Tell me who referred you to me and I'll call him and tell him to stop.' I said I didn't know the names of the persons at Extensions 415 or 462. 'How do you expect help if you don't know people's names?' the information officer said. 'Could you tell me what department I should call to get the information I need?' I asked. 'Aren't you the information officer?' The information officer replied, 'Particularly no, in general yes.' He suggested I call a Mr. Pignato in the Department of Real Estate. 'You are wasting my time,' he said, and hung up."

I called WOrth 4–5656 again and asked for Mr. Pignato. Mr. Pignato's secretary answered and said it was the wrong place, that I should call the City Urban Renewal Maintenance Corporation. I said I had already talked to the City Urban Renewal Maintenance Corporation. Another man got on the line and said I should call the corporation counsel. Even better, he said, I should hire a lawyer. I called the corporation counsel's office. The man who answered told me to hire an attorney.

If anyone feels that this example exaggerates the norm, he is free to pick up a telephone and experiment for himself.

Although there is an infinite variety of bureaucrats and bureaucracies, in New York City they have certain common characteristics, one of which is an almost pathological fear of the inquisitive citizen. A request to a minor official for the type of information which is usually available in the mayor's annual report brings the response that the caller must first get "clearance" from the commissioner himself. I once called the office of the Commissioner of Welfare to ask about the salary scales of welfare investigators, and was told that information was "not to be given out." A Columbia Journalism School student produced a near panic at the West Side office of the Department of Relocation when she appeared with a notebook: a social worker who agreed to take her with him on his rounds was considered a fool by his colleagues for exposing himself to publicity. The "thou shalt not talk" rule is so firmly established that a school superintendent could once tell me before several associates, without a shade of embarrassment, that in interviewing school principals I should remember that "principals are not allowed to state opinions, they are only allowed to state the facts." Apprehensiveness about the public is widespread in every city department.

Another trait of most commissioners is their emphasis on "positive accomplishments." While such emphasis, as Dr. Norman Vincent Peale has often said, may be necessary for one's self-esteem and reputation as a go-getter, it results in the propagation of totally bloodless and unrealistic pictures of the social and economic disasters which have overtaken the people. Even when a commissioner will talk frankly, the comments about his departmental program have an academic quality about them and they grossly understate the crises. Former Commissioner of Hospitals Ray Trussell was one of the most intelligent and candid, but after listening to him one is simply not prepared for the shock of inspecting actual conditions in a city hospital. Representative John Lindsay's election campaign description of conditions in Harlem Hospital, based on what the hospital staff itself had to say, captured far more of the desperateness of the situation.

The reason commissioners talk as they do is mainly because they neglect their first responsibility to themselves, which is to do their own reporting. Inevitably the commissioner comes to see the picture through the eyes of subordinates who long ago became professional expediters. He succumbs to the built-in rationalizations of the administrator. He becomes the victim of his own public relations department, and after he has given the same speech over and over he believes it.

It might be instructive to select one city commissioner and get some idea of how he operated, and then look at the experience of one of the families who became entangled in his department. Perhaps the most interesting example of a bureaucrat was Milton Mollen, chairman of Housing and Redevelopment during most of the Wagner administration. His agency was one which had a persistent and determining influence on the life of the people in the area. Chairman Mollen himself was the most plausible and politically successful of the city's commissioners and at the same time one of the most resistant to public criticism. No other commissioner had as large a public relations apparatus, nor did any other receive such recognition and rewards. The mayor eventually promoted Mollen to the post of city Housing Coordinator, and later, in a political switch, Mollen sought and received the nomination for comptroller on the Republican-Liberal ticket of John Lindsay in the mayoralty campaign of 1965.

In contrast to Boston's Edward Logue and Pittsburgh's Bernard Loshbough, two of the country's most effective redevelopment experts, Mollen brought little special experience to the city's Housing and Redevelopment Board. He had previously been with the corporation counsel's office, was admittedly a political appointment, and his function as chairman of the Housing and Redevelopment

Board was to act as the mayor's political agent. This in turn explains why the personnel policies of the Housing and Redevelopment Board were so different from those of Loshbough and Logue. Whereas the latter insisted on keeping their agencies free of political appointments, technical experts in New York found themselves very much subordinated to the political wing of the agency.

A basic part of Mollen's announced policy as commissioner was what he called an "open-door policy" at housing and redevelopment headquarters. In his many speeches to West Side organizations, he would declare that "we ask you, the people of the community, if you have any problems, do not hesitate to bring them to us." But the ordinary citizen who took Chairman Mollen up on his invitation invariably found that the chairman and his chief subordinates were prepared to repel all boarders. If a citizen managed to see anyone in the department, it was one of the many members of HRB's huge public relations staff. Most likely he would be referred to a "community relations" specialist, a kind and patient listener named Elizabeth Kempton, who had no authority to deal with anyone's problems and who was able to give only routine information—the type the citizen usually already had himself. In other words, without a personal introduction to the chairman from a local Democratic leader, the citizen might as well spend his time hollering up a stovepipe.

Those who did manage to breach the walls of the chairman's office ordinarily found a third party present at all discussions—a self-assured, youngish man in a gray flannel suit who was the chairman's chief public relations adviser. This gentleman, Robert Seaver, seemed to operate on the assumption that a citizen who came to him for help thereby placed himself in a position of inferiority and therefore could be treated with as much rudeness as the occasion seemed to demand. Information on department policy was proffered as if it were classified material, with Seaver even going so far as to tell me once that he was "not to be quoted" on anything he had to say—a rather remarkable statement for a public relations man. Seaver displayed another common characteristic of city officials, a mild paranoia about the press. In my first meeting with him he complained about the activities of one Woody Klein, a *World-Telegram and Sun* reporter (later appointed press officer to Mayor Lindsay), who would call up the office for information without giving his name, keep track of the number of times he was shunted around to different extensions, and then write a story about the run-around for his paper. Such behavior, Seaver felt, was dirty pool.

The chairman himself was an affable, preoccupied man, slow to passion except when his department was criticized. His private interviews were exact replicas of his public speeches. One got the theoretical picture of urban renewal presented as an actual fact, in attractively worded generalities, accompanied by interpolations from the omnipresent Seaver. One always had the impression, in listening to Chairman Mollen, that the real Chairman Mollen had already left the office for another appointment. Unlike other commissioners, the chairman never admitted that there were serious shortcomings in his department's operation. At a meeting of the Park West Village tenants' association, for instance, he rejected criticism of his Area Services North office, declaring that the tenants of the urban renewal area were grateful for its work—a statement that could not have been made by anyone with the slightest firsthand knowledge of the tenants' real feelings. However, the discrepancies between official policy and operational fact were no problem for Chairman Mollen, since he was addressing himself mainly to the sophisticated middle-class types who came to meetings,—the people who had "weight" in the community. Such hearers, with little or no personal involvement in the urban renewal program, were quite willing to accept Mr. Mollen's advertisements at their face value.

One of those who learned not to take Chairman Mollen at face value was a man we shall here call José Rodriguez. Rodriguez is one of those uninfluential citizens whose fate helps illustrate the nature of man's relationship to his government in the twentieth century. The Rodriguez family's personal education about the democratic system began in earnest when José, his wife Christine, and their two young children moved into a rooming house in the West Nineties and acquired a notoriously callous landlord. The Rodriguezes liked their new location because it was just across the street from a new elementary school, and only a couple of blocks from a junior high school. Local authorities also had reason to be pleased with the advent of the Rodriguezes. Although both parents were employed, they took an interest in local affairs. On several occasions Rodriguez helped out with special events at public schools and hospitals, and both children quickly made an excellent impression on their teachers.

Rodriguez's income and that of his wife, who worked in a laundry, enabled them to pay on time each month their $110 rent for the new place, which consisted of two and a half rooms on the basement floor. It became apparent soon after they moved in that they were not getting anywhere near their money's worth. The apartment, no better and no worse than hundreds of decomposed compounds which flourish under the city's so-called rent control program, was badly in need of painting and plastering. Holes in the floor were covered by carpet or cardboard, and a large opening under the kitchen sink produced frequent visits from rats in the basement. Rodriguez also found that the toilet bowl was coming loose and water ran over the bathroom floor. The apartment was also overrun with cockroaches. Rodriguez asked for exterminator service, to which he was entitled. The landlord refused it. Nor did the landlord pay for a stove and kitchen sink which Rodriguez had bought for the kitchen, although the original equipment had been so decayed as to be unusable.

When Rodriguez found that he could not get his landlord to clean the filthy hallways or get rid of the vermin, he phoned the Department of Health until a department official told him curtly to buy himself a can of insecticide and stop bothering the department. Next he complained to the office of Area Services North, a local agency of the Housing and Redevelopment Board, which was charged with seeing that private landlords in the urban renewal area maintained their buildings properly and kept them free of code violations. Rodriguez's experience with Area Services North was typical; nothing happened.

So he wrote to Chairman Mollen himself. When the chairman also refused to do anything about the complaint, Rodriguez decided to write to the then candidate for the U.S. Senate, Robert Kennedy. The letter described the family's living conditions and declared that city agencies entrusted with the enforcement of health and building codes had failed to cooperate with the tenants.

"How much can a human being take?" Rodriguez concluded. "Please, Mr. Kennedy, help us."

A week or so later, he received an answer.

"I was shocked to hear of your plight," wrote Kennedy, "and I am certainly going to do everything I can to help you and your fellow tenants." What Kennedy meant by "help" was that he had referred Rodriguez's letter to Chairman Mollen, "who has assured me that he will have your situation thoroughly investigated."

Five weeks later, Rodriguez received a letter from Mollen describing the results of the "thorough investigation" the chairman had promised Mr. Kennedy.

"A check, both at our office and with the Department of Buildings, revealed that certain violations existed on said premises," Mollen also wrote that the attorney for the landlord had stated that several violations had been removed and that other violations existed because of Rodriguez's continued refusal to allow repairmen to enter his apartment.

Chairman Mollen then proceeded to give the back of his hand to the family Rodriguez. "In your complaint to Senator-elect Kennedy you stated that various city agencies involved in code enforcement had neglected to cooperate with the tenants. I am certain that if you cooperate the city will do all it can to see that conditions are improved."

At no time during Mollen's "investigation" did any representative of the Housing and Redevelopment Board or of any code-enforcement agency take the trouble to talk to Rodriguez or to look at his apartment to see if, in fact, any violations had been removed. Nor was Rodriguez ever given an opportunity to respond to the charges—which were untrue—that he had refused entry to any workman hired by the landlord. By his own admission Chairman Mollen's sole source of information was the landlord's attorney. Apparently no city official had the time to make an on-the-spot investigation. However, shortly before he wrote to Rodriguez, Chairman Mollen attended a tree-planting ceremony a few blocks from the apartment, at which occasion his photograph was taken for the Spanish newspaper *El Diario*.

Such rebuffs as Mollen's letter dealt the Rodriguez family a double blow. Not only did it mean they could expect little help from the authorities, but it also was the signal to the landlord that he could harass them with impunity. This landlord was not accustomed to having his tenants complain, and he decided to get rid of the trouble-makers as quickly as possible. Until their arrival he had operated the building and another even more decrepit one on the same street in defiance of all manner of fire, occupancy, building, and health regulations without any protest from his tenants. Most of them were Puerto Ricans desperate for a place to live, who were jammed into these buildings in violation of occupancy regulations; any complaints about their treatment would have meant their immediate eviction. A measure of the landlord's control over the tenants was the fact that he even distributed their mail. There were no regulation mailboxes in the Rodriguezes' house: the postman dropped the mail into the slot of a padlocked box to which the landlord had the only key. Rodriguez protested to the U.S. Post Office, but the postal authorities did nothing about it.

For nearly a year the landlord carried out a campaign of harassment to drive the Rodriguez family out of the house. He served several eviction notices, and on more than six different occasions he appeared at the door of their apartment with summonses charging Rodriguez with assault, theft, disorderly behavior, nonpayment of rent, or threats of violence. On most of these occasions, he was accompanied by a policeman who had been told by the landlord that Rodriguez was dangerous. To answer each summons or notice of eviction, Rodriguez had to take the better part of a day to find a lawyer, prepare a defense, call witnesses, and travel downtown to criminal court or the agency where a hearing was to be held. The summonses forced him to absent himself from his union hiring hall, thereby losing a chance at any employment opportunity which might turn up that day.

The truth of the landlord's charges can be judged by the fact that in some cases he did not even appear to press his complaint, and in all cases the charges against Rodriguez were dismissed. But, although he lost each time, the landlord succeeded in irritating and worrying the family, keeping it in a constant state of insecurity, using up Rodriguez's time, causing him expense, and interfering with his employment.

In the opinion of this observer, Rodriguez won his rounds in court in spite of the judicial procedure because he could speak English (although with a heavy accent), because he kept his temper both in and out of court, in spite of considerable provocation in both places, and because he kept a complete file of documents bearing on his case. Finally, he had some friends who were occasionally able to get him a lawyer without charge. Had he lacked any of these assets, it is difficult to say whether he would be a free man today. The proceedings in court had very little resemblance to the administration of justice as it is discussed in bar association meetings. Rodriguez was merely one of

a long line of people—largely Negroes and Puerto Ricans—who were
handled on an assembly-line basis by an overworked, harried judge
who sometimes did not appear to understand the charges. There
would be a "Now what's this all about?," then, after a few moments
of confused argument, the magistrate would berate both plaintiff and
defendant, tell them to stop picking on each other, and threaten them
both with jail if they ever appeared before him again. Or he might
just postpone things by granting the landlord an adjournment, thereby
prolonging Rodriguez's discomfort a little longer.

On one occasion when Rodriguez took the offensive and filed
charges against the landlord for failing to render services and correct
violations, the head of a city agency appeared as a witness for the
landlord himself, appealing to the judge to postpone a decision on
the case until her agency had had time to make an inspection of the
Rodriguez apartment—a plea which came months after Rodriguez
had vainly appealed to her agency and to her boss, Chairman Mollen,
for just such an inspection. When the inspection was finally held, the
two inspectors became angry at Rodriguez for having invited one of
his friends to be present as a witness, and Rodriguez was never
allowed to see the report of the inspection.

The conclusion to the harassment of Rodriguez could have been
predicted. For one thing, Rodriguez began to run out of lawyers.
Friendly attorneys were willing to help on a one-shot basis, but when
the next summons was served they were always too busy. Rodriguez
appealed to local civil rights groups, to Puerto Rican organizations,
to the FDR–Woodrow Wilson Democratic Club, and got promises of
help, but the help never materialized.

One night Rodriguez was arrested and arraigned in the 24th
Precinct police station, charged by the landlord with assault. This
case was also thrown out of court, but it was Rodriguez's last victory.
During a summer rainstorm a few weeks later, a marshal knocked at
the Rodriguez door with a court order evicting the family for nonpayment of rent. The order had been signed without Rodriguez's ever
having had a hearing on the charges, which were false. So the
Rodriguez family and all its belongings were moved out onto the
sidewalk, and all a handful of friendly neighbors could do was to
cover the furniture with plastic to keep it dry. Then the Rodriguezes

were transported to a fifth-floor walkup apartment in a frightful city-owned building a block or so away.

The unaffiliated poor are not the only ones whose nonviolent protests fail consistently. The experiences of many West Side homeowners who are pushed against the cutting edge of the urban renewal apparatus also illustrate the futility of resistance, even by those who—unlike the poor—know some of their rights and are in a position to put up a defense. The fundamental weakness of the homeowners' position is that they are an infinitesimal and unorganized minority and, therefore, are not taken seriously by public officials. Another handicap of the homeowner is that, despite official proclamations to the contrary, private homeownership is not compatible with the theory behind the city's real-estate policies. The earth of Manhattan is seen by the Commissioner of Real Estate as a source of tax revenue to be cultivated as intensively as possible. That is to say, the ideal use of land is that which provides the greatest dollar return per square foot. One might say that the city's preferred crop is the "money bush." It is obvious that a four-story, eighteen-foot-wide house is not a money bush, but a pestiferous weed to be plowed under to make way for apartment houses, parking lots, office buildings, and other money bushes.

A third handicap for the homeowner trying to defend himself is that local politicians, if they concern themselves at all about the area's tenants, logically concentrate their efforts on protecting large numbers of people in far worse shape than the private homeowner, who is supposed—sometimes incorrectly—to be able to take care of himself financially no matter what the city decides to do to him. In a sense, it is his very insignificance that makes the homeowner historically important. His fate is another example of how the bureaucracy disposes of the type of citizen it deems irrelevant.

My own campaign to prevent the city from taking over my home at 33 West Ninety-second Street is an interesting case history of what happens to the individual who attempts to do battle with his government. The house, as mentioned at the beginning of this book, was a twenty-foot brownstone that had been rehabilitated and converted into apartments at a cost of approximately $35,000 in addition to the purchase price. The rehabilitation had been carried out by a private builder in 1959 and 1960, with a permit from the Department of Buildings. On completion of the renovation, the private builder had received a certificate of occupancy from the department. I assumed that, in line with the announced policy of the Housing and Redevelopment Board of conserving "sound structures," my house would not be eventually condemned by the urban renewal authorities. I did not realize at the time that the preliminary urban renewal plan had marked it for condemnation under the mistaken assumption that the house was a one-family dwelling in a state of disrepair—something I discovered in my first conversation with a city appraiser. Since the house was located next to a modern apartment building and was on the edge, not in the middle, of an urban renewal site to the east, it was not an obstruction to new construction on that site. In addition to the foregoing reasons for preserving the house, it provided modern housing at middle-income rents and it was one of the few good brownstones in the area that were open to Negro tenants.

On my first attempt to talk to the Housing and Redevelopment Board, and after I had informed it of its mistake in classifying the house as a single-family dwelling, I found it was not going to change its decision to condemn. What the Housing and Redevelopment Board had presented to the community as a "preliminary plan" was as far as my case was concerned "a final and unalterable" plan. I was never able to get an appointment with any Housing and Redevelopment Board official who had the power to change the decision. Each time I sought an interview, I was referred to a community relations person who would tell me that she was "sorry" and that "nothing could be done" about my case. She did arrange one meeting for me with several officials, but even as I talked I realized that this was not a discussion but simply a *pro forma* occasion at which I was to be administered the last rites. My listeners wore the solemn, polite expressions of politicians at the wake of a constituent they knew but slightly.

Nevertheless, I persisted in trying to find out the board's reasons for condemning my home. With the board's arguments before me, I would have some basis for deciding on whether to give up or prepare a rebuttal. But I was never able to learn why the board had decided on condemnation; I was told over and over simply that "the plan cannot be changed." When I asked to see an architect's plan for the construction which included my site, I was told I could not see any such plan. I did not even find out if there was a plan. Finally I was told sympathetically that I would be happier if I stopped fighting.

Since patients do not ordinarily agree to an amputation without some sort of an explanation from the doctor, I tried to get the information I wanted from other sources. Eventually I managed to learn, by talking to tenants and owners of nearby condemned properties, that my house site was part of a package. My land would be part of a T-shaped plot on which a private developer would erect a luxury apartment house with an entrance on Central Park West, with apartments renting at around four hundred dollars a month. I also learned that the land on which my house stood would be part of the garden area for the apartment house. In other words the city of New York was using its condemnation powers to displace me and my family and tear down a valuable brownstone to plant bushes.

I discussed my situation with Mrs. Robert Landy, a resident of 325 Central Park West. Her building and my house were part of the same parcel. Mrs. Landy and her fellow tenants were as indignant as I about the plan for our part of the block, since their building was attractive, roomy, and excellently maintained. A typical apartment of five rooms—which I inspected—rented for $140 a month and could not have been duplicated for twice that rent in any new construction.

Mrs. Landy said she had had the same difficulties I had had in getting information from the Housing and Redevelopment Board. All that the tenants of 325 Central Park West could find out was that their building was supposed to be "structurally unsound," and that it was supposed to have "wooden beam supports." The tenants had argued in vain that the house was in perfectly satisfactory condition and that it did not have the alleged "wooden beam supports." However, the board told the tenants that the plan could not be changed and that they would not discuss it further. Later, HRB public relations man Seaver repeated to me what I had heard from Mrs. Landy, that 325 was "structurally unsound," that it had "wooden beam supports," and that it must go.

Although we were presumably in the same boat—part of the same "unalterable plan"—my fate and that of the people in 325 Central Park West were quite different. The tenants of 325 organized, hired a lawyer to fight their case, and generated political pressure on their own behalf. They invited Chairman Mollen and other HRB officials to a progressive dinner party in the house at 325. Subsequently it happened that one day without fanfare the Housing and Redevelopment Board removed 325 Central Park West from the condemned list, acknowledging in so doing the fact that 325 was structurally sound and did not have, as was originally supposed, "wooden beam supports." Today the tenants of 325 are turning the building into a cooperative.

Once the plan for 325 had been changed it seemed to me more logical than ever that my house could be saved since the "unalterable plan" would have to be redrawn entirely. I was wrong again. The HRB continued to refuse to discuss the case of my house, and at this point I gave up. But any expectation that my unconditional surrender would end my troubles with the city was unfounded. Now began a new series of difficulties, this time with the Department of Real Estate, the Department of Relocation, the City Urban Renewal Maintenance Co. (CURMCO), and the office of the corporation counsel. I shall only attempt to report on a few of these difficulties.

To begin with, the city of New York does not do business with a property owner it is about to dispossess. It ignores him. From the time the first city appraiser looked at my house until the day three years later when the city took title to it, I did not receive one signed communication from any city agency informing me that the government wished to take my home, what its procedure would be, or when it proposed to take action. During this period, the city made no attempt to negotiate the sale of the house, to tell me what it proposed to pay for it, or what steps I would be expected to take in handling my part of the transaction. I tried many times to discover what the city proposed to do with me—information to which I felt I had a special right since I was not giving my property up of my own free will. In all this time I received just one piece of "correspondence"; an almost illegible mimeographed sheet, with no explanatory letter or any identification of the sender, telling me that legal steps had been taken to condemn my property.

On February 1, 1963, a man rang my doorbell, identified himself as a city employee, and proceeded to nail up a yellow sign on the wall which stated that the premises now belonged to the city of New York and all tenants thenceforth should pay their rent to the City Urban Renewal Corporation office at 203 West Ninety-third Street. In this manner I was notified that I had ceased to own my own home and that I was now a tenant of the city (rent unspecified). Not until three months later did a city representative telephone me with an offer for my house of several thousand dollars less than the purchase price. When I refused the offer I discovered that the city was haggling; a few days later it increased its offer several thousand dollars to approximately what I had paid for my home. Even then the offer represented a substantial loss to me because I had put additional money into the house since purchasing it and I was losing a source of income as well. The city's second and final offer was accompanied by the common persuader used on recalcitrants, an ultimatum that if I did not accept the offer and chose to fight the case in court, it would take me two years to get my money.

While such a threat usually worked in situations where the recalcitrant had to have money immediately to move elsewhere, I was in a position where I could go to court, and the court's final award to me was $6,000 more than the city's first offer. After paying the lawyer's fees I cleared just about what I had paid for my house. I did not receive the final bulk payment for my property for twenty-two months after the city had seized it, during which time the city paid me 4 percent interest on the money it owed me while I was borrowing money at 6 percent in order to purchase another place to live.

My experience with the house also gave me a chance to learn something about the Department of Relocation. One of the city's alleged reasons for putting me out of my house three or four years before it planned to tear it down was that it wanted to use the apartments to relocate some of the people being evicted from condemned buildings in other parts of the urban renewal area. However, most of the apartments in my house remained vacant after the city took it over, despite the shortage of good housing in the area. After a few months, the city abandoned any pretense of maintaining the premises, with the result that the boiler of a new furnace blew up, and the two or three people still living in the building were without heat or hot water. Meanwhile city employees systematically pillaged the house. A maintenance man appropriated the furnace's expensive electronic control system, the front doors were smashed in by raiders, broken glass was strewn about the house, and policemen in uniform entered vacant apartments and made off with the refrigerators.

Today the house is still standing, an empty piece of wreckage which once housed six families. I never walk on Ninety-second Street now because I don't want to see it again.

CONCLUSION: THE AIRTIGHT CAGE

The Cage

            OCCASIONALLY ON A WINTER WEEKEND THE WIND blows the smoke and sulphur dioxide over into New Jersey and presents the people of 105th Street with a gift of clear blue sky. If the weather is cold enough to drive the prostitutes and addicts under cover, we hear the birds in Central Park instead of the usual street obscenities. On a Sunday morning, with the schools closed, the street is quiet and almost deserted, and at the end of the day we may have a crimson sunset at the end of the street, somewhere out beyond the Hudson River.

    On one of our rare good days one might get the impression, from seeing our block on the southern edge of Harlem that we are one of those small communities in the city where the so-called "urban villager" is supposed to flourish. In fact we do have a number of these villagers—people with a very local, civic way of looking at things. One of them is Pastor Mullen, who has weekly suppers in his brownstone Jordan River Baptist Church. Another is my next-door neighbor, George Zukof. He has shoveled the snow off my sidewalk when I have been slow in getting to it, and every two weeks he cashes everybody's welfare checks in his drugstore on Columbus Avenue. Another village-minded man, Leonard Keepnews, spends his spare time making arrangements for local children to go to free summer camps.

    It is the crowds of children most of all who contribute to the neighborhood atmosphere. According to my census there are about three dozen of them, mostly Negroes. Some belong to the Methodist Church Sunday school and sell Girl Scout cookies. All of them spend the summer racing up and down the block looking for something to

318

do. Since they do not have any equipment for the usual games, they invent their own, which is a misfortune for the city because the major emphasis—in spite of Sunday school—is on breaking bottles, setting fire to trash, opening hydrants, and sending in false alarms. But with all their rushing about and daredeviling, the children regard the four corners of the block as the outermost limits of the universe. Whatever travels they take are imaginary ones in the hulk of an abandoned car that periodically turns up along the curb. Very few of the children leave the block even to climb the big rocks that loom up on the edge of Central Park a few hundred feet to the east.

Actually the children prove the opposite of what they seem to prove. Looked at more closely, they reveal that there is not much of a community here and that what we are living in is more of a temporary encampment. We know most of the children by name after seeing them out in front all summer, but at the beginning of the following summer many of the faces we know are gone and we are looking at a new set of children. It is hard to find out what happens to them although occasionally we hear something definite. One mother of five was taken off recently to an institution after trying for two years to raise her family in one room, and the children were scattered about in foster homes.

Whatever the reasons, there comes a time when the families, or the remnants of them, move to a similar street somewhere else where the children help to fill up another ancient tenement and another school. This is the way childhood ordinarily proceeds for most of the Negro boys and girls who come and go on 105th Street, and it is probably the way things will develop in turn for their children. Communities and urban villages are not built on such life patterns as these.

Nevertheless, the upper West Side has several dozen "community" organizations, ranging from the St. Gregory's Mothers Guild to the Young Assassins. Most of them do not function as if they were on the same planet, let alone the same part of town. Some of these groups— the block associations, for example—have their handful of urban villagers and are more benign than others, but in general the villagers do not set the style of organizational life. In fact, officers of the more up-and-coming organizations consider the villager, with his preoccupation about sprucing up the local scene and doing apolitical good works, as a sentimental anachronism.

The officers may have a point. At the same time it can also be said that a good proportion of the local civic and political organizations are also becoming archaic, debilitated to the point where they have difficulty in getting together a proper quorum at meetings. The groups which do have a respectable amount of energy and financial support often burn themselves out in the most destructive competition with each other, as if there were not enough problems to go around for everybody. Many organizations have no active membership other than the people who elect each other as officers and send off resolutions to the *West Side News*. A large number of these press releases, coming at any one time, gives the impression that giant waves of public opinion are sweeping over the entire area.

On rare occasions when enough organizations are gathered into a bundle, and there is leadership, a Stryckers Bay Neighborhood Council results and can be a force for limited improvement, mainly because it has an energetic and talented leader as its president, Father Henry J. Browne. The individual organizations which make up the council membership are as anemic as the rest: without vitality or any real constituency. If at any time they were an active force for community, they are now largely neurotic reactions to the social disintegration which has overtaken the area, devices through which the people can complain about their environment. The best that can be said of many of them is that they offer their members an opportunity for self-expression.

The Area's service-directed institutions have made a more creditable response to the social situation, insofar as they have programs to do something. In some cases they have constructed an "interior community" floating in the general disorder. Perhaps the best examples of such interior communities are the public and parochial schools. A P.S. 84, a P.S. 165, or a St. Gregory's school is a place in which there is some agreed-upon direction to the proceedings, where a daily effort is under way, and where there are ideas, purposes, compassion, diversity—all essential to community. In spite of all the criticism that has been concentrated on them, the schools have an atmosphere of hope that flows over and softens the sharp edges of a good many unhappy particulars. Even in those many classes where children cling precariously to the outer edges and struggle unsuccessfully to speak and hear, something is being demanded of them and something is being given.

With a few exceptions a whole host of other service-directed enterprises in the area are isolated from each other, and the range of their effect is extremely limited. The settlement houses have acquired the knack of fund raising, but other free community-minded service enterprises are small, undermanned, and in a precarious financial state. They include an excellent day-care program run by the Children's Aid Society, the Police Athletic League recreation program, the Bloomingdale nursery school, several early-childhood education projects, a privately run mental health clinic, a college career guidance program for Negro and Puerto Rican youngsters, the many social-service and education activities housed in local churches, and a training course for unskilled teen-agers run by a Negro businessman. At the other end of this spectrum of microscopic communities is the rooming house where ex-mental patients have banded together to form their own society in exile.

In a true community, moving toward a common goal of social justice, such cooperative efforts would be running with the current, operating as part of a constructive program for the general health and welfare. In such noncommunities as the upper West Side, these enterprises have to fight the current; in fact, they are created to oppose it, antibodies in an unhealthy system, in perpetual jeopardy from the system. However, some people criticize these social-service groups because of their manifest inadequacy or because they are seen as the sort of local anesthetic an unjust society applies to its victims, and which makes the injustice bearable.

Unconsciously or consciously the people convey the feeling that they have no community worth talking about. The attitude survey conducted by the John Kraft public opinion research organization reported that West Siders then had only the vaguest idea of where they would turn in case of need. They almost never mentioned political organizations, government agencies, or elected officials, and no single institution was mentioned more than a handful of times. The despair among the poor also permeates a middle class that distrusts its public officials and is bored with its institutions. The only people who talk about community as if they believe in it are the people who are paid to be community organizers.

The one popular consensus is that there is no community. The group that cuts across all class lines is the army of noninterferers who remain passive while violence is committed on another human being, and who will tolerate the destruction of a neighborhood itself because they are resigned to its destruction. As a consequence of such a situation we have the Negro maid who puts a straight razor in her purse for protection, and the unanimous civilian boycott of Central Park after dark. These are the reflexes of people who understand that they live in a wilderness.

There are innumerable little airtight cages and bomb shelters which the citizen can build for himself as a defense against such an oppressive environment. If he is poor he can buy a police lock for his door. If he is a middle-class conservative with a suspicion of social cooperation he has no problem. It becomes almost a matter of principle to amputate himself from an immoral society and the undeserving poor who are at the bottom of the demoralization. The middle-class liberal has more difficulty in justifying his retreat into private life because his official philosophy requires him to believe in the democratic process. Nevertheless, he has plenty of plausible rationalizations at hand—the manifest futility of becoming involved, the corruption of politics, the demands of his domestic and professional life, the complexity of the problem, etc. The liberal belief in the welfare state can also ease any crisis of conscience. If there are social and economic needs to be satisfied, departments of health, education, and welfare have been created to take care of just such matters. If the old methods are inadequate, the answer is new legislation and more money. The liberal may also avoid a connection by making a connection, that is to say, instead of personally involving himself with a cause or a community, he can join an organization in which he makes a nominal commitment to the public interest on terms that allow him to be as inactive and remote as he likes.

If the political conservative never had a heart, the liberal has lost heart in the midst of the city's crisis. In most cases, he has come to accept, at least subconsciously, the idea that a trial of power is taking place in which the ultimate interests of his middle class are threatened by an invasion of the poor. His uneasy conviction that the poor—any poor (he lumps them all together in spite of himself)—constitute a public danger appears in many ways. One symptom is the congenital middle-class fear of public housing. Another is the apprehension over the influx of more and more poor children into the public schools, coupled with the conviction that only the middle class can save the city's public education system. Such apprehensions and beliefs are reinforced constantly by superstition, by rumor, and by an overwhelming array of social scientists and psychologists who maintain that a lower-class school will always be an inferior school. The soundness or unsoundness of these attitudes is beside the point. The fact that they exist is another contribution to the social disorder. Such attitudes are inevitable when the economy and politics of the city are busily promoting a class war over money and living space and services.

There are some liberals who punish themselves rather hard for this situation as if they bore the whole moral responsibility for what has happened. It is difficult to know what difference they could have made. On their side, the poor resist the sporadic and often patronizing attempts to draw them into a community for the very good reason that their style of life makes it impossible for them to become part of the customary social apparatus. The prerequisites for sharing in middle-class organizational life are jobs, baby sitters, and freedom from the health and housing problems that continually put the poor out of commission. A community institution requires stability and permanence for its people. For the poor who are temporary, such creations are designed for other people in other worlds.

The poor do not even have a unity of their own. Those who manage to escape the condition of poverty rarely look back, and those at the bottom of the heap live in almost total isolation from each other. This is particularly true of the single, unemployable Negro male, who is transient in every aspect of his life—economic, statistical, and sexual. He is side-stepped even by the Puerto Ricans, who understand that to be classified as one of the black poor is a sure road to destruction. In the worst extremes of poverty the only associations men have with each other are based on their addictions and illnesses, and in their time of greatest need they lose even these connections. Death itself does not give them any sort of personal identity: it is always a problem for the police to find someone who knows the name of the body and who can explain what has happened to the belongings of the deceased. The "culture of poverty" and the alleged community of the poor notwithstanding, there is less community in the lower depths than there was among the inmates of Auschwitz, who could not help assisting in their own destruction.

The Spanish poor would appear to be in a somewhat better

position. They share a common and positive culture and, having been treated as citizens on the island, they have developed the reactions of first-class citizens. Thus, while he may be more shocked than the Negro upon colliding with color discrimination, the Puerto Rican often seems to be more vocal and less despairing. The Spanish also have local organizations to complain regularly for them, which the Negro does not. However, the very plenitude of Puerto Rican organizations obstructs their effectiveness. They have a tendency to drown one another out, and show no conspicuous ability to cooperate with one another. The aims of the Spanish organizations have been primarily social rather than political, and they do not reach out effectively to the less educated, the darker skinned, and the more recently arrived Puerto Ricans, who have a rather insecure status in the Spanish universe of the city. In fact, the local Puerto Rican aristocracy feels rather defensive toward the black island minority that arrives in the area, goes on welfare, and becomes a "social problem."

A few "leaders" of the "Spanish community" are audible and visible at public meetings, the proving ground where they build up their credentials as spokesmen. They follow the traditional pattern of generations of other politicians who have based their career on ethnic or "skin" politics. By and large, the more successful these spokesmen become, the more remote they become from their alleged constituents, until at the peak of success they may get a job with the city and disappear altogether. This process can be called assimilation in the good old American tradition, or it can be called betrayal, depending on who is making the judgment. Anyone who attends a session of a politically-minded Puerto Rican organization will hear all sorts of angry complaints about former members who, once they have "made it" politically, no longer bother to consult with their old associates.

The physical breakdown of the area, the nervous movements of the population, the forced competition among economic and social classes, and the decline of politics have all played a part in killing off the democratic dialogue that is a basic requirement of the free community. The disintegration of communication is so obvious that it is even noticed by noncontroversial generalists like Rabbi Edward Klein, of the Stephen Wise Free Synagogue, in his remark that, "we live side by side but we never learn to live together."

The difficulties of local Democrats, and the shortcomings of the city's past Democratic administrations, should not obscure the damage the city's political and economic conservatives have done to the dialogue. The *New York Herald Tribune* in an otherwise excellent series entitled "City in Crisis" left the impression before the 1965 mayoralty election that the collapse of the city has been mainly the fault of the mayor and Democratic politicians. It remained for an outsider, Edward Logue, the Redevelopment Commissioner of Boston, to point out that New York City's business community had provided neither leadership nor constructive criticism in the crisis. The conviction that the Republican party has had no interest in the thoughts or the condition of the poor is well fixed in the minds of a great majority of West Siders interviewed in the Kraft survey. It is significant that in his successful campaign for the mayoralty Congressman John Lindsay won a large West Side Democratic vote on the grounds that he was running as a liberal man who had not the heart of a real Republican.

Another factor that has prevented the construction of a community has been the fitful role of the city's major educational institutions in urban affairs. An example is Columbia University, whose expansion program is the core of a new urban renewal project on the upper West Side. It would seem that in such a situation, Columbia might have seized the chance to educate itself systematically about the political, social, and economic dislocations that always accompany urban renewal. Yet, despite its proximity to the West Side urban renewal program, Columbia made no sustained effort to get into this laboratory. Its graduate schools of education, medicine, law, and urban affairs could have invented and participated in all sorts of experimental programs, but did very little. Only a few Columbia students, far ahead of their university, saw the opportunities and volunteered to work in the area and associate themselves with local work projects. Now, Columbia, the opportunity lost and facing rising resistance among the poor to its own plans for expansion, has hired a public relations counsel to tell it what to do.

What are the immediate prospects for restoration of some semblance of community? Other than expansion in the budgets of private and public social agencies—such as piecemeal improvements in the city's educational facilities—the prospects are very few. The response will not be constructive or even corrective; it will be essentially reactive. The one significant new hope for reversing the disintegration of the city may lie in the antipoverty program, which is pumping federal aid into local rehabilitation and education projects. But, while money is in long supply, ideas and carefully thought-out programs are not, and the excessive "crash" psychology of the war on poverty has damaged its effectiveness. The power struggle over how the program shall be administered—and who shall be in charge—has also delayed its implementation and could very well destroy it in the end.

As the Office of Economic Opportunity has stated its goals, the antipoverty program would not only try to cope with unemployment and improve the health, housing, and education of the city's slum population, but it would also try to draw the poor into participation in the life of the city by asking them to elect representatives to serve in "neighborhood" poverty councils. There is considerable doubt whether this ideal can be achieved, even if the opposition of the city's political organizations can be overcome. For one thing, the poor have not responded very enthusiastically, so far, to the chance to play an active role. In addition, as has been said before, the poor have a habit of being betrayed by their own protectors. Many of the organizations most loudly demanding the participation of the poor in the antipoverty operations have themselves demonstrated neither the ability nor the desire to involve the poor in their own activities. Some nonpolitical organizations quick to criticize "the politicians" for using the antipoverty program as a patronage device have themselves used it merely to bolster their competitive position vis-à-vis other agencies. Other organizational spokesmen for the poor have spent disproportionate amounts of federal poverty money on administration and in pushing highly publicized but superficial programs.

If the antipoverty program survives its early difficulties, and is not undercut by the demands of a rising defense budget, it could reconstitute the basis of community life in America. Not only could it begin to break down the walls separating class and race, but, just as important, it could provide the opportunity for creative social experiences very similar in spirit to the communal efforts in our pre-industrial past when rural families built each other's houses and harvested each other's crops. It is an irony that the communal act has almost totally vanished from our underdeveloped inner city slums at the very time when the Peace Corps is encouraging the people of underdeveloped nations to adopt this neglected American tradition in dealing with their own problems.*

Americans have been "liberated" from physical participation in community projects because of technology and the enormous pro- liferation of public and private services which can be bought as substitutes for personal endeavor. The availability of these substitutes allows us to disassociate ourselves from people who are unlike us and whose condition annoys us. It has also set us apart from every country which is fostering vigorous social cooperation as a means of building a healthy society. While the Chinese villagers combine to build a school and the people of India construct their own commu- nities, we join organizations, give to the United Fund, and wash our cars on Sundays.

Progress, of course, is what makes this all inevitable. Since we are not a primitive civilization, technologically speaking, push-button methods are available to discharge our public responsibilities, thereby conserving labor, gaining leisure, and losing our personal identifica- tion with the public interest. We have even lost the ability to comprehend the significance of the communal act. The general public reaction to the civil rights march on Washington in 1963 was illustrative: over and over the question asked was—what good did it do, and how many votes did it change? The fact that this was not a political rally but an act of communion seems to have been missed by nearly everyone except the marchers themselves.

Our physical and emotional distance from each other, combined with a national reverence for competition, helps explain why we respond so much more energetically to controversy than we do to cooperation. It is natural for the isolated man to be "against" rather than "for" something, so we are against anything that threatens our equilibrium, but it is difficult for us to be actively for a positive ideal—and the only meetings we attend in very great numbers are those where a decisive and bitter argument is in the wind. Yet a civic

* "In the United States, citizens are accustomed to working together in com- munity organizations to make known their needs and solve their own prob- lems. But in Brazil, as in many other developing nations, this tradition is almost totally lacking. The absence of local initiative and cooperative efforts in self-help is a great obstacle to economic and social development. Too often the people wait for the government to do something about their problems." *Brazil: Urban Community Development* leaflet. Peace Corps, Washington, D.C., 1965.

competitiveness, and a general predilection for fake controversies do not seem to have altogether obliterated the natural human instinct for cooperation. At least the instinct is very much alive among young people, who insist on taking seriously all the homilies on justice and equality inflicted on them when they were children, and who refuse to be "realistic" now that they are growing up. A stubborn insistence that America act in accordance with its constitutional and religious proclamations may be why young people march in civil rights and peace demonstrations. The proof that young people will respond to a chance to act together for a constructive purpose lies in the Northern Students Movement, a Harlem Educational Project, in the community center, and in the Peace Corps.

If the war on poverty can win anything but very limited success it will have to try to move us toward the type of community which has been eloquently defined by philosopher Richard Lichtman. In his words:

An authentic community commits itself to health as an end of social existence, as a primary value upon which the institutions of public life are based. Since such a community is serious in its concern it organizes itself affirmatively for the sake of human well-being. It is not simply content to correct the errors which are continually promoted in some non-communal sphere of social existence. In short, *a community is not a corrective but a constructive system of human existence.* Health is not to be cut and shaped to an ill-formed society . . . it is rather society that must be constituted to embody health, insofar as that is humanly possible. Everything communal men make of themselves and their world in their public life is infused with a concern for the vital functioning it promotes or hinders.

Since one of the root concerns of a community is the equality of its participants, their equal right to well-being is one of its fundamental imperatives. But as the health of men is rooted in their whole being, and in the particular mode of their social existence, it is their "life styles" too which must bear the equalitarian imprint. It is not sufficient that those officially charged with the health of their fellows act to undo the consequences of unequal privilege and maldistributed wealth. Equality must inform the community from its inception. For what men are entitled to by right is not the partial amelioration of their inequalities, but the full equal realization of their capacities.*

* *Toward Community*, by Richard Lichtman, p. 45. Center for the Study of Democratic Institutions, 1966.

If our frontier society, in which men could exist in relative isolation, found the communal life a necessity for survival, our specialized society needs even more to guard against the individual's disassociation from the whole. There is no security in our cities because there is no community in them. A society in which a fifth of the people live in poverty condemns every man to private oppression—an oppression which can be physical or a matter of conscience, or both.

The question in our cities is not whether the oppression can be avoided. The question is whether there will be a constructive outcome to the American ordeal or whether we will simply build higher walls and tighter cages to protect ourselves from the hard realities of our environment. Ideas and people who can cope with these realities will be immobilized until we get rid of the notion that we can escape into an illusory self-sufficiency, and until we understand that man's individual prosperity is not achieved by victories at the expense of others. It is a fundamental premise of a free society that the health of the community and the health of the family are inseparable, that community and family are woven together, and draw love from each other. We have, quite literally, a need to touch other human beings, and be touched by them.

The Squeeze

The government of the city has taken on many of the basic characteristics of the large, private aggregations of money and power, and has thereby become more and more the enemy of community. If the two circles of power, public and private, once functioned as countervailing forces against each other, they are now in important respects each other's agents. The corporation on one hand has become to a greater and greater degree a producer for government, and as part of the arrangement it professes a new sense of responsibility for the public welfare. On the other hand, the government agency has adopted the organization and technical innovations of the private sector and tailors its welfare programs and regulatory activities to conform to the accumulating pressures of a vast array of private interests. The resulting situation is exactly the opposite of the socialization which state power is supposed to be bringing about. Far from cutting away the base of the private sector, the governmental bureacracy has become a means through which private power—from banks to labor unions—has strengthened its grip on the development of the city, and has subordinated the general welfare to the private interest.

One can pick at random any one of thousands of case histories of the West Side poor to find an individual illustration of what happens to the unaffiliated citizen at the hands of government agencies infiltrated with the private interest and paralyzed by the weight of their own anatomy. And examples of the private invasion of the public sphere can be found in every phase of municipal government:* Bernard Weissbourd's remark that the self-defeating nature of public housing policies is determined by the private developers who are its enemies can be paraphrased to fit almost any other area of municipal governmental policy; land use, taxation, city planning, urban renewal, assessments, health and welfare programs, housing, the courts and law enforcement. The very size of government, once seen as a threat to the private sector, has made it more susceptible to private pressure. In Lincoln Steffens' day the pressure was erratic and personal, today the science of applying pressure and yielding to it has been automated along with everything else, to the point where the private interest controls not merely individual people but the whole climate in which the governmental apparatus functions.

The division of executive government power into impersonal and nearly autonomous agencies and "authorities" has put them as far out of the range of public protest as a private monopoly like the New York Telephone Company. The New York Port Authority is one example of enormous governmental power which has accumulated out of nowhere and operates primarily as a promoter of private business interests. The experience of confronting a public agency and a private monopoly like Consolidated Edison is practically identical—in both cases one is dealing with organizations preoccupied with internal security and populated in the lower reaches by a professional class fearful of innovation and responsibility and unresponsive to any outside stimulus except organized pressure. When such government agencies are allowed to dominate the life of the poor to the minutest detail, they isolate them from participation in community life.

* The situation in the city parallels that in the federal government, where agencies such as the Federal Communications Commission, Food and Drug Administration, and others are dominated by the industries they were created to regulate.

When even a middle-class citizen with financial and political resources has difficulty in defending himself against arbitrary government action, the position of the poor becomes hopeless. The commitments an agency makes to one of its impoverished wards are not written down, and they can be changed, lied about, or abrogated at will. The low-income Negro or Puerto Rican learns that the administrative agency is indefatigable in calling him to account for the smallest infractions, but when he seeks protection from that agency he finds that his rights are ephemeral and that his case disintegrates in a mass of technicalities. He learns that a code-enforcement agency takes little initiative on his behalf and has no will to protect him. Rather, on rare occasions when he insists on his rights vigorously, at some time or another agency officials may conspire against him, because they consider the complainant a troublemaker, or because they have been corrupted by the person who has violated the rights of the complainant.

Like the public agency, the law and the judicial process also seem to work most effectively when it is the poor who are being prosecuted. The fact is no secret. Some state bar associations openly acknowledge this to be the case, and when he was attorney general, Robert Kennedy paid a great deal of attention to the problem. Patricia Wald's report to the 1965 National Conference on Law and Poverty catalogues dozens of ways in which the judicial system is rigged against the indigent, and although she draws her illustrations from many cities, she could have found all the examples she needed in the life of the West Side poor. Given this situation, it is no surprise that the minority groups' hatred and fear of legal authority has occasionally fanned an isolated act of rebellion into a sustained outbreak of mass violence.

Perhaps because they are temporary political appointees and therefore in a more exposed and precarious position, the top administrative officials in the New York City government have been more sensitive to criticism than the eternal civil service employees beneath them. But when a commissioner admits his agency operates inefficiently or unjustly "at times," he almost always concludes by a remark that there are a few rotten apples in every barrel. The condition of the barrel is never questioned. One also hears from commissioners that the city is too big and the budget too small: the manner in which a department has used its resources is never discussed. Underlying all the apologies is the assumption, which the public shares, that the city is doomed. In the face of such an attitude, of course, it becomes impossible to reduce waste, reorganize departments, or create an atmosphere that would encourage innovation. The defeatism partly explains why, even when a costly budget increase is approved, the money is channeled into expansion of the administrative apparatus rather than into improvement of direct public services.

One impressive characteristic of the civil service and political appointees in the lower levels of the bureaucracy is their peculiar attitude toward the citizen they are supposed to serve—especially if he is poor and raises a fuss. Regardless of the employee's racial or ethnic background, he very often reacts in a negative way to any situation which jiggles his procedure-centered world. Life in a municipal office building creates its own rigid habit patterns and psychological attitudes, and outsiders had better beware of them. The civil service worker in some ways resembles a member of one of the more ingrown trade unions. If he has a social attitude he lays it away when he goes on the job.

The huge mass of administrative regulations is a boon to certain agency officials, protecting the mind that avoids responsibility and shies away from the special case. It provides dozens of legal pretexts for inaction. Worst of all, the almost unlimited power which administrative rules confer on the official often results in a subconscious attitude that he personally owns the services his department is supposed to provide the public. To understand fully the results of this proprietary attitude, one must have undergone some of the insulting interrogations to which applicants for public housing are often subjected. The applicant is frequently treated as a suppliant who, if he happens to rub the official the wrong way, can be groundlessly accused of everything from immorality to cheating on his income-tax returns. Since such comments are always informal and made without witnesses present, the applicant has no recourse—he might as well be arguing with a policeman.

A bureaucratic system riddled with such attitudes will respond only if it is badly frightened. But systems don't frighten easily. Even though individual employees may be constitutionally apprehensive, the system in which they work has dispersed responsibility so widely that it is almost impossible to call anybody to account: therefore inefficiency is pursued without interruption almost as a matter of policy.

Some elements of new life have managed to take root in fissures of the bureaucratic rock. For instance, in two of the city's most absurdly organized and top-heavy agencies—the Department of Welfare and the Board of Education—case workers and teachers with a social direction to their thinking have bucked the system and forced policy and organizational changes. The pressure of the teachers, made possible by their new union (the United Federation of Teachers, AFL–CIO) has given them a small voice in influencing the educational program, while the case workers' strike against the Department of Welfare has emphasized the unworkability of traditional approaches to welfare problems. It is unlikely, however, that such low-level pressures can ever force the administrative organization to be more responsive to the poor. For one thing, the pressures are too isolated. Also, as reformers achieve substantial successes, they lose their revolutionary impulses and tend to become accretions to the system. This tendency is already noticeable among the teachers, whose union is becoming more preoccupied with teachers' prerogatives and less and less interested in general improvements in the educational system which might interfere with these prerogatives. The union's drive to prevent school principals from observing teachers in class once the teacher's probationary period is over is an indication of this trend.

Some Steps Forward

One way of forcing the bureaucracy to be more accountable to the people would be a new branch of city government—a public advocate analogous to the *ombudsman* who represents the claims of the citizen against the bureaucracy in the Scandinavian countries and in New Zealand. He has inquisitorial power, and is independent of the executive branch of government. An effective public advocate would be one way of restoring the faith of the poor in their government. The *ombudsman's* criticism, his use of communications media, and his legal intervention could improve the efficiency of the agencies under inquiry, and his presence would also encourage those people within an agency who were trying to buck the system. The public advocate would be a useful means by which modern government could subsidize independent criticism of its internal administrative procedures and afford the citizen protection against an entrenched civil service which is out of the control of the top administrator. The idea of the *ombudsman* has already been broached on the West Side. A local city councilman, Paul O'Dwyer, has proposed an Office of Civilian Redress, and as borough president of Manhattan Constance Baker Motley stated somewhat plaintively that she would like to function as an *ombudsman*.

Father Henry J. Browne, whose work as chairman of the Stryckers Bay Neighborhood Council has been mentioned, has actually operated as a type of unofficial *ombudsman* or local public advocate. He has the ideal equipment—expert technical knowledge, an understanding of the law and the administrative process, and a familiarity with the political relationships within city government. On behalf of the council, Browne frequently has represented the individual citizen in his complaints against administrative actions or administrative neglect. He uses all the techniques for seeking redress of grievances: meetings with agency heads, informal hearings, resort to the courts for restraining orders against city agencies, and consultation with agencies on modification of program. He has also used the press as a means of circulating information and criticism.

The results of the council's work have not always satisfied its chairman or the community, but, given the size of the council budget and the immense demands made on it, the organization has been surprisingly successful in affecting the course of the urban renewal program, and in changing attitudes and practices in such city departments as Relocation, the Housing Authority, and the Housing and Redevelopment Board. Recently the council has taken another step in its effort to make the government more responsive, by applying for a federal grant to encourage the poor to participate in the planning and operation of the local antipoverty program.

The *ombudsman* would in some ways reinforce the work of the type of civilian review board proposed for the New York City police force, and of the public member board set up by the United Auto Workers (AFL–CIO) to review grievances of union members against their own officers.* However, the *ombudsman* would not be a substitute for the civilian review board. For one thing, he could not give any single agency the close attention required, which means he could not be properly held responsible for it. The civilian review board

* See *Democracy and Public Review: An Analysis of the UAW Public Review Board,* by Jack Stieber, Walter E. Oberer and Michael Harrington. Center for the Study of Democratic Institutions, 1960.

CONCLUSION: THE AIRTIGHT CAGE [335]

could be a valuable supplement to the *ombudsman,* and at the same time it would not be exempt from investigation by the *ombudsman.*

Any discussion of how to render governmental bodies more accountable to the public should not overlook the civilian review board's potential. The long-standing debate over the desirability of civilian review boards for the police departments has obscured the fact that public review boards might be useful in other areas. Outside the government apparatus there are powerful, well-financed social agencies that solicit public financial support and thereby have a responsibility to give an accounting of themselves. But in most cases these agencies do not provide anything like a detailed and objective account of their activities. Their annual reports are usually staff-written advertisements designed to impress their own board members and serve as fund-raising documents, and the press usually accepts them at their face value. Now that many of these social agencies are receiving sizable government grants to finance antipoverty programs, there is a good argument for public review boards that could question agency officials and give their own evaluations of the agencies' programs. The boards might investigate as a matter of course the financial and administrative practices of all private agencies which use public money. United Fund officials require such an accounting from agencies that share in its fund-raising drives, but for political and public relations reasons such a system leaves something to be desired. Furthermore, a great many agencies, almost all of them receiving antipoverty money, are not included in the United Fund.

A third force on the side of justice and community would be the neighborhood law firm. Prototypes of such law groups have already been functioning in some areas of the city. The Riverside Democratic Club on the upper West Side has offered some free legal consultation to the indigent, and the Hotel Workers' Union—in spite of outcries from bar groups—has set up a legal counseling service for its members, and encourages them to use it. Gradual improvement and expansion of legal aid societies and public defender systems have also been of great help to the poor in their daily collisions with the courts, but most of the free legal assistance has been cursory and the types of cases handled have been severely restricted. The result is a legal first-aid system which may keep a defendant out of jail, but which rarely follows through to the point where it can resolve many of the defendant's most persistent legal difficulties. The tenant harassed by an administrative agency or a landlord has a chronic malady which is not cured by pill-sized doses of legal assistance, each time administered by a different lawyer.

While it is too early to tell what will become of the antipoverty program's plans for neighborhood legal service, the Community Progress antipoverty program in New Haven, Connecticut, has been in operation successfully for some time.* A privately organized Legal Assistance Association offers a strengthened legal and defender program, a neighborhood legal program, and a legal research and evaluation program which have become a key part of Community Progress. Another example of a legal aid system supported by foundation and federal money is in operation on the lower East Side of New York under the supervision of Mobilization for Youth. The effectiveness of MFY's legal team in helping tenants is one of the reasons why the agency has been so bitterly attacked as "communistic" by local real estate and political interests.

Where the neighborhood legal aid program has begun to function successfully—as in New Haven and Oakland, California—it has tended to follow the lines that have also been suggested for a neighborhood public health program. The services should be comprehensive, near at hand, available at all times, and the client should as much as possible have the same practitioner throughout his difficulties. Ideally such a neighborhood legal aid system would require a regular team of adequately paid lawyers, but in fact it would probably have to rely on law students or part-time attorneys subsidized in part by public funds. The use of tax money to provide such services is quite as justifiable in principle as the use of public money to provide health, education, and welfare services. It is no more just that poverty should deprive a man of his legal rights than that it should deny him an equal chance for health and a decent education. In cases where society has placed an individual under the control of administrative agencies, it has a special responsibility to afford that individual some guarantee that his rights will be respected by those agencies. Legal counsel for the poor can be a positive public good if it enables society to police its own institutions. Perhaps in the future legal assistance to the poor might be partially financed by group insurance programs covering the less-costly types of litigation.

* Mitchell Sviridoff, Executive Director of Community Progress, has been appointed by Mayor Lindsay to plan New York City's new poverty program.

In discussing proposals for *ombudsmen,* neighborhood law firms, and civilian review boards, it has to be emphasized that, taken by themselves, new techniques—better ways of "making the system work"—will not reconstruct the city. One of the basic weaknesses of the "reform" approach has been its reliance on innovations that are not sufficient to alter conditions that have been mainly responsible for deforming the character of urban life. One such influence is the rapidly accumulating density of population. A second is the urban concentration of the jobless, the dependent, and the unwell. A third is the enormous, expanding complex of racial ghettoes in which overpopulation, sickness, and unemployment are centered. Proposals for a new society have little meaning in the shadow of these ghettoes.

The heart of the ghetto remains untouched. So far, urban renewal has too often been a process in which governmental power is invoked in the interest of private development; it has renewed racially mixed fringe areas which could be transformed into predominantly middle- and upper-income neighborhoods. Urban renewal has actually intensified the blackness and density of the ghetto and planted new ones. As the fringe slums are bulldozed, the thousands of displaced poor move to neighboring slums or to tubercular areas—the only type of area which will receive the poor—in other boroughs. As the D.P.'s arrive, and crowd into substandard housing, these "gray" areas turn black, and new fires burn away the economic substance and morale of the city. Thus the ghetto revenges itself on society by making fundamental improvements in the design of the city impossible.

Our automatic and unemotional acceptance of the ghetto as one of the permanent fixtures of the "free society" is an unmistakable indication of the futility of relying on the system to reform itself. This is hardly surprising in a society where almost all decisions, including moral ones, are the outcome of strenuous, competing pressures. The acceptance of the ghetto, which implies a general public disbelief in democracy itself, is responsible for the fact that even those inadequate urban renewal programs which have been undertaken have been deformed by the very influences that have a vested interest in perpetuation of the slum. The essential fact is that the slum is seen only as an inconvenience to be controlled.

It seems more than likely that effective action against the slum will have to be forced out of society by a series of explosions powerful enough to crack the surface of what Kenneth Galbraith calls the "conventional wisdom," explosions generated by the economic and political impasses that are inevitable when a fifth of the nation's population is living on or below the level of human subsistence, and much of it impacting in the urban areas. If the explosions are to be simply bigger, more destructive versions of the Harlem and Watts riots, violence or the threat of violence will be the commonly accepted way of getting attention from society. If the explosions are to be nonviolent, disciplined, protracted rebellions against irresponsible authority, of the type Martin Luther King has led in the South, they can be constructive. There has always been a place for peaceful civic insurrection in America at times when the public mind has become so insensitive to injustice that it will respond to nothing but a shocking experience.

One can argue interminably about whether the leadership for the rebellion will originate among the poor themselves, the middle class, or a coalition of both. The leadership will not have to be of the sophisticated type considered necessary to organize traditional political action; it will need only to be popular and durable. As Saul Alinsky's back-yards movement in Chicago has indicated, the leadership of the new rebellions may frankly assert that its purpose is to inflict painful discomfort on society at large exactly in the same fashion as labor unions and steel companies when they advance their claims for economic justice. The leadership will have the original character of labor unionism and will use its weapons. It will maintain a primary identification with jobs, economic independence, and housing; it will employ the strike, the boycott, the sitdown, and the street protest. The appeal will be to the law, not against it, an appeal that society enforce the law and improve the law where it insufficiently protects the citizen against private or governmental power.

It seems logical to assume that such rebellions would be directed initially against the slum, and that they would declare war against existing authority at the outset. Such movements would also function quite apart from politically controlled antipoverty programs and often in direct opposition to them. A significant by-product of an organized war against the slum could be new local political groupings that would supplant to some degree traditional party structures that are now quite irrelevant as far as the poor are concerned.

In New York a rebellion against the slum would require a citywide organization which, as it developed, would project itself into many other aspects of city life besides housing. Not only would the organization concern itself with racial discrimination, urban redevelopment, relocation and resettlement, code enforcement, the schools, and the police, but it might determine the prospects of the war on poverty at home. Again, the slum war organization would follow the patterns of the labor unions, which diversified their interests as they grew stronger—but, unlike the unions, which have become less and less interested in the unemployed and in many cases discriminate against the Negro (an exception is that wing of the labor movement dominated by Walter Reuther), the slum war organization could become a vital force in the life of the poor.

The organization might eventually become the basis for establishing "corporations of the poor," which could organize the political and economic power of people living in depression areas so that they could affect the direction of the poverty program and bring changes in the local environment. From the slum war could come the structural, educational, and financial groundwork for corporations that could establish credit unions, fight price discrimination in racially segregated housing areas, break down trade union barriers to Negro and Puerto Rican apprentices, and mobilize pressure on federal agencies so that they give greater support to expansion of businesses run by Negroes and other minority groups.

The tenant union movement has had its prototypes in New York City, most of them fitful and unsuccessful. One notable exception was the Harlem rent strike organized by a Negro, Jesse Gray, which tied up several dozen buildings over a protracted period and resulted in at least one court decision and in legislation that has broadened the basis on which a tenant may withhold rent. There is the example of a mass tenants' strike organized by the Stryckers Bay Neighborhood Council. The Metropolitan Committee on Housing has tried to educate organized tenants' groups and encourages rent strikes, but its effect has been mainly educational and propagandistic. The organization of a successful slum war would require much more—establishment of active committees on a district or neighborhood basis, for instance, with each committee including a legal staff. The committees would raise money, arrange for witnesses in court, recruit and plan demonstrations, circulate materials to the press and the public, publicly identify slumlords in their areas, and stimulate local institutions—churches, civic groups, parent associations, etc.—to support the campaign.

The main thrust of the rent strike would have to be directed at the core of the ghettoes, rather than its fringes. Strategy should focus a maximum of power against a sequence of selected targets. The breadth of its base and its persistence would determine what the slum war organization could do. In short-term engagements, the slumlord has always had certain advantages: he could remain anonymous behind the façade of a real-estate corporation, he could count on inefficient or corrupt housing inspectors, and he had the weapon of court delays and technicalities. But in a long-term battle, these advantages would begin to disintegrate, particularly if the opposition was supplied with lawyers and witnesses.

A slum war organization could also function as a citizens' planning board. As the slum war continued, the organization would have to think beyond code enforcement and extension of traditional public housing programs. What would happen, for instance, if a rent strike forced the city to take over large numbers of slum properties from owners who could not afford to correct widespread violations? What would be the character of the urban renewal, rehabilitation, and relocation programs? Special thought would have to be given to the problem of resettling slum tenants, the majority of whom under present relocation programs are simply moved out of one slum into another.

The growth of tenant unionism and the use of the rent strike would provoke sharp hostilities and tensions, but would also develop a new sense of community among the thousands of Negro, Spanish, and white citizens cooperating in the effort. Even the tensions would have a certain value, in that they would give the white populations of northern cities a taste of what southern whites have felt at the hands of the civil rights movement. It would not harm the northern white, who has coasted along on attitudes inherited from the Civil War, to be moved just as the southerner has been moved in spite of himself.

The whole hypothesis on which the city is built needs to be restated. We need to think more about the resources available for encouraging the growth of an entirely new type of city, different in physical structure and purpose. We need to think more about planning and the coordination of plans. We need to become dissatisfied with the fact that we are still an accidental civilization at a time when even the newest African nations have recognized the foolishness of relying on evolution by accident.

There are broad questions to be asked and answered. Why, for instance, must huge concentrations of unemployed and untrained human beings continue to pile up in financially unstable cities that no longer have the jobs, the housing, the educational opportunities, or any of the other prerequisites for a healthy and productive life? Why do we treat the consequences and ignore the causes of massive and purposeless migration to the city? Why are we not developing new uses for those rural areas that are rapidly becoming depopulated? Why do we still instinctively deal with urban and rural America as if they were separate, conflicting interests when in fact neither interest can be served independently of the other? Why have we not done more to unify federal, state, and city planning and policy so that sensible attacks on urban ailments will not be frustrated by fragmentation, delay, and bureaucratic confusion?

Although we substitute moralization for science in thinking about national policy, the responsibility for policy will more and more require a working coalition of all three levels of government—state, federal, and local—that will assume real authority for planning. The war on poverty will have to go far beyond the present concatenation of government services.

The airtight cage of poverty, frustration, and fear in which the people of the city are imprisoned can be broken open and new towns founded which could serve the purposes of the old urban center. New York City, which shortsightedly sold off precious tracts in Staten Island, could develop a land policy that would include acquisition of "rural reserves" on which it could build and incorporate subsidiary towns and cities, some of them at great distances from the old urban core. The traditional basis on which population centers have been established should be re-examined. Technology has been rapidly divorcing human beings from dependence on urban "centers" of production, of politics, of culture. In many ways the "center" has become an obsolete concept because our new technology makes it possible to diversify and disperse production and population. The President recognized this fact in his January, 1966, message to Congress asking for $3.6 billion to establish new "demonstration cities." But the magnitude of the task is still misunderstood: the President's proposal for all U.S. cities is only slightly more than what the Venezuelan government is mobilizing for construction of one new city, Ciudad Guyana.

Unless new communities are established, it is difficult to see how the poor, especially the Negro, can ever become truly integrated into American life. Efforts at so-called "desegregation" in the hostile environment of large cities have had great moral value, but in practical terms they are a mirage. Small numbers of Negro children are shifted from one school to another, and a trickle of adults manages to find its way into decent housing in middle-class neighborhoods, but that is all. Since the suburban ring about New York City has locked the Negro into the slum, new settlements would have to leap over this constricting belt. Townships could be located in areas with adequate natural resources, in every state of the Union. Migration to them would be open to everyone, regardless of economic status, perhaps under terms of a contract clearly stating the responsibilities of both parties. The citizens who signed such a "lease" would do so as volunteers in a flagship community, sponsored by government, which would set the pace for a racially integrated, heterogeneous new society.

The new communities would have to be planned architecturally, socially, administratively, and economically. They would include complexes of health and welfare services available on both a private and a public basis, and educational parks for the training of teachers as well as children. One function of the new community would be to provide housing for people relocated from urban renewal areas. The housing could be temporary or permanent, depending on the needs and resources of the individual family, and rental housing should be available for purchase by the tenant at his option. The new communities would have their defects and special problems, but they must be part of any sustained attack upon the city ghetto and on the dying towns in which the rural poor are concentrated. The redevelopment of land by these new communities would link rural America more closely to the cities.

There are the usual arguments against the new town idea: that it would be expensive, it would become economically and racially segregated, that communities cannot be created out of whole cloth without an economic base—i. e., an adequate demand for labor. However, expensive as the new towns would be, they would not begin to approach the costliness of the slum, and they could be the start toward a solution to the problems arising from high-density, badly housed city populations. Even if some new towns might become segregated or set in any number of various ways, segregation under such conditions would not necessarily be undesirable. The voluntary coming together of people with similar needs and a common purpose has always been the basis of new settlement. What is most important for the poor as a whole and for minority groups in particular is that they be provided with the resources to help themselves.

But the old arguments are disintegrating in the face of technological change and new economic and social perspectives. At the same time the traditional basis of the city as a center of industrially and commercially based employment is undergoing drastic alteration, new potentials for resettlement of our rural frontier are becoming apparent. For instance, if proposals to guarantee an annual income for people earning less than $3,000 are adopted—as suggested by the President's commission on technology, automation, and employment—they can revolutionize the future of urban and rural areas alike, by breaking the tie between jobs and income. A guaranteed income could give the poor a new mobility and choice of place to live that will affect the entire map of the United States, that could bring about a general expansion and upgrading of low-income housing, and it could help break down the walls that have kept the Negro penned up in the crowded core cities. Just as government policies have regulated the flow of credit, affected land development, agricultural production, and the dispersion of industry, they can influence distribution of the population and the opportunities of that population for self-expression.

It is not that the problems of the city are insoluble, or that the people lack the ingenuity or the resources to confront the causes of their discomfort. The difficulty lies in the failure to recognize the fearful consequences of what is being allowed to happen, to use sensibly all that we have, and to plan our national future as a whole community of individuals whose welfare is forever indivisible. The old superstition that planning will cost us our freedom has led Americans to entrust their lives to continual series of accidental developments conditioned only by the competing pressures of organized special interest. The result of this refusal to control history has cost us progress, economic security, and even our personal safety. The West Side of the city of New York is only one example of the manner in which human beings have been overwhelmed by the "monstrosities" which Arnold Toynbee says are the signs of a civilization in peril of its life—monstrosities that include the bureaucratization of life, the enormous waste of human potentiality, and the misuse of national wealth.

If the city is to be saved, it will be because the people adopt revolutionary means to save it. If it is to grow more diseased and die, it will not be the fault of the accidents that deal the final blows. If we come to the point when, as Harvey Wheeler predicts, we cannot move from one place to another without a permit from the regulators, it will be our own paralysis that will be responsible. As Toynbee contends, civilizations are never murdered; they die by their own hands.

The Process

The most important facts about the city are what I call tidal facts. These tidal facts illuminate the invisible, involuntary processes that are part of the character and the physical body of the city, processes analogous to breathing or the beating of the heart. When I say tidal facts give the essential truth, I am comparing them to facts about institutions like churches or the Department of Real Estate or what officials say about themselves. I gathered a lot of data about such institutions and people and the best that I can say about the information is that it provides a few helpful clues. The trouble is that one of the functions of a political or social institution—and of some people—is the manufacture of lies about itself and its environment. Although tidal facts cannot be counted or heard and have no color or particular shape, there is no mistaking one of them when you come across it. Tidal facts appear or they reveal themselves; they are not collected. The discovery of a tidal fact is inadvertent, sometimes, and at other times it appears in a very indistinct, bloblike shape after a great deal of lying awake and worrying about where the truth is. A bundle of data or a repetition of sights and experiences may point to where a tidal fact is buried. The main point is that the tidal fact is there and is incontrovertible. You find a rip or a hole in the surface of life and suddenly you are looking into things, not at them.

One of the tidal facts that impressed me most is the continual waste and loss of human life that is taking place in our city. I am not talking about the murders or assaults that have terrified most of the people that I know—poor people, middle-class people, well-to-do people. I am talking about the destruction of children. Of the enormous number of crimes that take place in the city, the largest number and the most terrible are committed against children. The ones who suffer the most are the children of the poor. Only a small portion of these crimes have to do with beating or physical abuse. From the time tens of thousands of newly-born infants are removed from the hospital they become subjected to what I call "the process." That is, they are introduced to a style of existence that eventually cripples or destroys huge numbers of them and occasionally other people with whom they have come in contact. I have not been able to discover any good reason why this should be taking place, even an economic reason. It is said over and over that the United States and the city of New York together do not have the public or private money to prevent the destruction of children and see that they are fed and cared for properly, that their illnesses are treated, and their minds and spirits nourished. It is said that the responsibility for such care lies with the parents, which is a non sequitur because there are no parents to speak of in this situation. Later on, when children born clean, ready and expectant begin to malfunction and cause trouble, hundreds of millions of dollars are appropriated to hire special teachers and policemen and youth workers and build special class-rooms and prisons and mental institutions and hospitals to keep these children under control. The children who do survive this tempering process become adults, but in my neighborhood an adult is a dead child. In the end the justification for such procedures is that this is the way things have to be done in a system of free enterprise, but in view of the fact that all the money is wasted as well as the children, this seems to be hard to believe. Wasting money is not part of the capitalistic system.

I have thought a great deal about the reasons for the destruction of children. Obviously it tells us something about the people that we are and the character of our civilization, but what? Trying to answer the question leads to a second tidal fact. We are, practically speaking, unconscious of what is going on. We seem to have pushed whatever knowledge we have about "the process" into a part of our minds that is not directly connected with our emotions or our motor mecha-nisms. The knowledge is there but it is lodged in such a fashion that it does not affect our behavior, and when we are presented evidence of what is going on, we respond to it the way we do to an act of violence on television or the movies. We have the so-called vicarious experience, in which a crime is relayed to us stripped of all its meaning because it is presented as an image of crime, not as a crime itself.

The ability to respond this way, or rather not to respond, is said by some people to indicate immaturity or lack of education. This perhaps is related to what Bertrand Russell says of the proper aim of education—that is, education is supposed to develop minds sensitive enough to perceive, to feel the shock of tragedies taking place thousands of miles away and somehow communicate a feeling to the heart. In my city the sensitivity to pick up the tragedy does not extend to the corner, or even across the street.

I don't think the problem is just a plain lack of sensitivity or of education. The ability to live with "the process" has something to do with a self-induced psychic disorder. I know of no name for this state of mind, so I will invent a name: auto-anesthesia. The first step in auto-anesthesia is to turn one's eyes away from the object or the act of cruelty itself. It is not necessary to ignore the object or act completely, but it is necessary to consider it only in the abstract—in photographs, television, books, speeches, conversations, etc.; then the mind, which is naturally intolerant of pain, can erase a great deal of the shock and guilt. I have found the procedure works. I have found myself laughing when I was describing something that thoroughly frightened or nauseated me when it took place.

If we go beyond the abstract image and force ourselves to look at the object itself, moving and wriggling and making noises, or if we see the event itself—an automobile accident or someone in the process of being beaten severely (these are the more spectacular examples)— we will discover that the problem lies not in being undereducated. I recommend that we try over a period of time looking directly into the faces of autistic children or the types of babies that can be found lying on beds in our slums. I don't think it is necessary sometimes even to see the children themselves. It is enough to see the shell in which the process takes place. I can remember the experience of going to the children's ward of a mental hospital. The children were not there, and all I could see were the cots and the cells, five cots to a room, and this was enough. After we have looked at enough of such objects we can have unpredictable mental reactions, certain types of dreams, for instance, which are revealing. One may be looking into a kaleidoscope, where each piece of color can become a child's face or a characteristic sound from these children—red being a cry, blue another failure, yellow the long unbroken periods of silence—these are the conversation of the children who are being subjected to "the process." I know it is possible for such dreams to take place because I have had them.

When I thought about "the process" and the way we adjust to it, I think I discovered what a good World War II German was all about—the German who knew and disapproved and who had his own way of living with "the process." As a matter of fact, I think I discovered I was one of those "good Germans." I think perhaps most Americans are "good Germans," some of them better than others, and I understand something that always mystified me before, which is how a "good German" felt when he was led through Dachau for the first time and had a look at the objects, not the victims but the objects. He learned how the process worked and he saw the testimony. He cried and said he did not know. I think that he was being honest and that he did not know. He had the tidal fact in the back of his mind someplace. He knew about places like Dachau but he had somehow disconnected this from the rest of his system. He had looked at images and reports and had listened to rationalizations until nothing was real, and the railroad cars were just taking the Jews off to a work camp someplace. Then I think he perhaps talked about his worries and this helped him control himself, which meant that he saved his life. I don't know what our excuse is.

I say I am a "good German" because when I was forced to look over a long period of time at too many objects and acts in my city I felt the German reaction, which was to justify myself by saying I have been put into a system, that nobody asked me permission for the system, that I hadn't wanted it. I will defend Hannah Arendt when she says that evil is common and that most people who commit evil are asleep. She has got hold of a tidal fact.

We are "good Germans" when we try to explain ourselves. We explain by looking for the criminal who involved us in all this. In New York City when we look for a culprit we usually point to the mayor or some other highly visible politician. He is somehow responsible for all this and there are people who would like to hang him for all of the things that are going wrong in the city, including the destruction of children. Hanging the mayor is another part of the auto-anesthesia, because if we can dispose of him in some way, preferably spectacular, we can feel that something has been done. This attitude means we are still seeing images of the truth. I think that if we stop looking at the images we will find that executing the mayor would be unsatisfactory and we might not even bother to do anything about him. We would be looking for causes and we would find them everywhere, just as the "good Germans" turned out to be everywhere.

All of this leads to another tidal fact which explains all the others. What has happened is that we are in the middle of a system which makes "the process" inevitable; which requires more and more human beings in various parts of our country—Appalachia, Selma, Chicago—to grow up to be dead children, or, as some people put it, welfare babies. The system I am talking about is turning more and more of our resources away from the nurture of human life and into the destruction of it. The system has just about been perfected and is now at the point where we have automated the process of conspicuous waste and destruction. I don't mean the waste of material and money alone. I mean the neglect or destruction of other people's lives, in Vietnam for instance, or in the last World War. I mean the piling up of children in the dark parts of our cities and leaving them to rot, the way we used to pile up boxes of 20mm guns and compasses and sextants in the jungle and leave them until sun and rain rotted the boxes and they broke apart. Over the past two or three years I have looked at many scores of children who do not look back at me because they cannot. If they could speak, I doubt that we could hear them, anyway. By some great bit of psychological magic we have surrounded ourselves with a transparent material that admits no sound or even a breath of air from the world in which they live.

The fact is that there is less and less room for all the children trying to get into the world we "good Germans" are fixing for ourselves. Sometimes, if you watch "the process," you may see the exact moment when a child gives up the struggle. I remember a plump, amiable Negro boy about thirteen named Larry who lived in a rooming house across the street. One morning the police went into the building and brought his mother out and put her in the police wagon. With all the neighborhood gathered around watching, a plainclothesman told Larry to get into the wagon with his mother. With the tears rolling down his cheeks the boy refused to move. "All right, son, you can ride with us," the plainclothesman said, and he opened the door to a black sedan. Then with a great, silent cracking of the heart the child was carried away like a seed on the wind.

INDEX

About the Author

Joseph P. Lyford, 48, grew up in a small Illinois town, graduated from Harvard, and served with the Navy in the Pacific in World War II. After some years as a reporter and editor, he entered politics, serving on the staffs of Governor Chester Bowles and of Senator William Benton of Connecticut, and running twice for the U.S. Congress from that state.

In 1954 Mr. Lyford was staff director of the Public Education Association of New York City when it undertook its historic study, *The Status of Public Education of Negro and Puerto Rican Children,* which exposed the inferiority of education in ghetto schools— a project financed by the Fund for the Republic. During the past eleven years he has been a staff member of the Fund and its principal activity, the Center for the Study of Democratic Institutions. Recently, as a Regents Professor at the University of California, Berkeley, he has been studying two Negro communities in the San Francisco Bay area.

With his wife, Jean, an ex-school teacher, and their young children, Amy and Joseph, Mr. Lyford makes his permanent home on Manhattan's West Side, where he is a member of Local School Board District 5.